D0264813

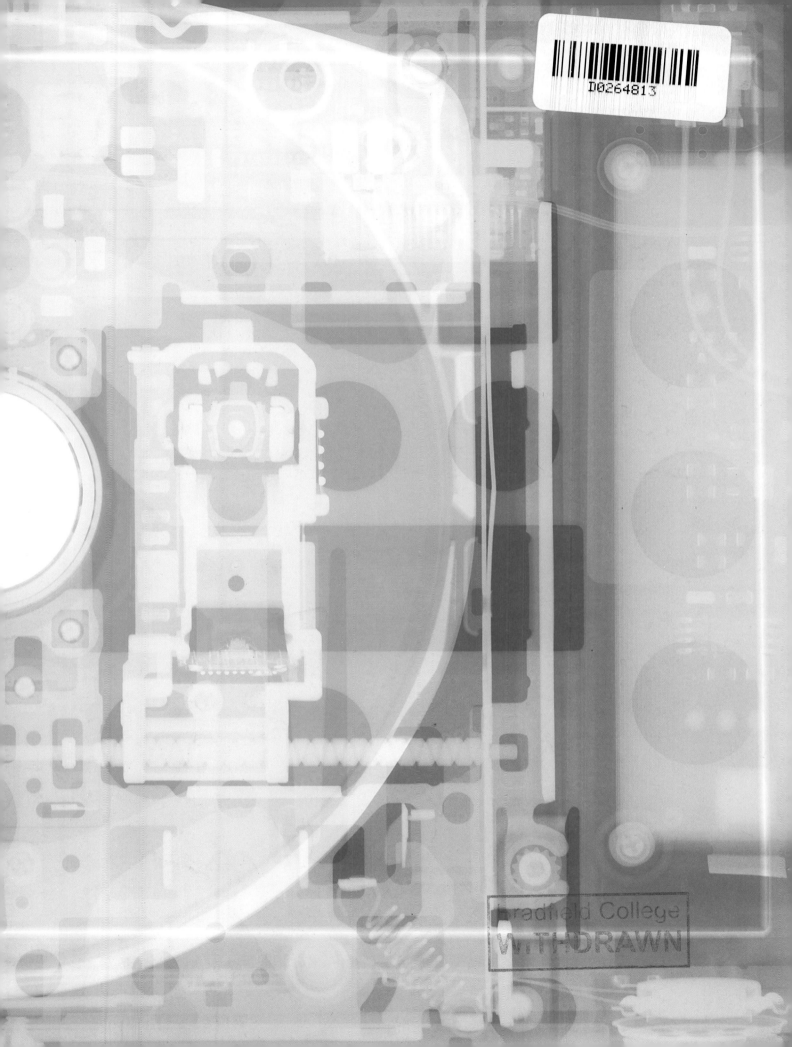

THE GADGET BOOK

AND HOW REALLY COOL STUFF WORKS

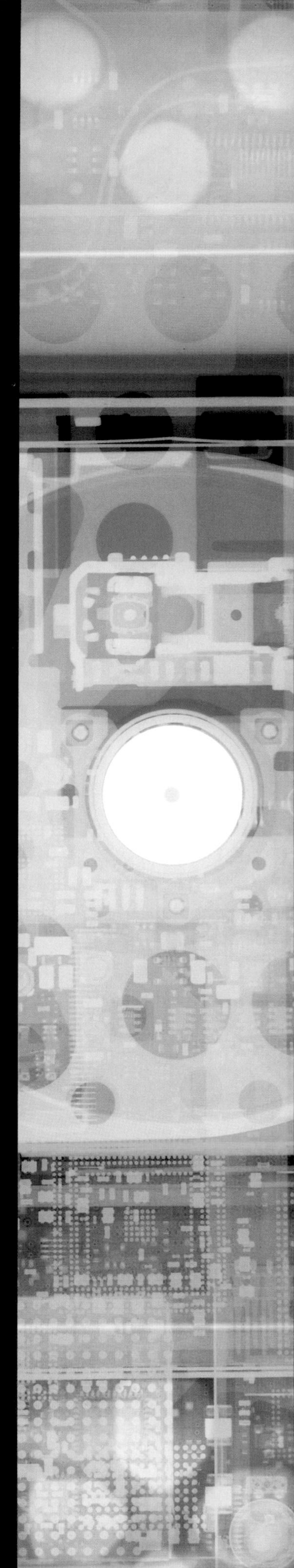

LONDON, NEW YORK,
MELBOURNE, MUNICH, AND DELHI

Project Editors Francesca Baines, Jenny Finch, Miranda Smith

Art Editors Rebecca Painter, Johnny Pau, Owen Peyton Jones, Marilou Prokopiou, Samantha Richiardi

Senior Technical Editor Phil Hunt

Senior Editor Julie Ferris

Senior Art Editor Philip Letsu

Managing Editor Linda Esposito

Managing Art Editor Diane Thistlethwaite

DTP Coordinators Siu Chan, Andy Hilliard

Publishing Manager Andrew Macintyre
Category Publisher Laura Buller

Picture Research Jenny Baskaya, Julia Harris-Voss, Jo Walton
Production Lucy Baker
Jacket Design Nea Cobourne
Jacket Editor Mariza O'Keeffe
Jacket Manager Sophia M Tampakopoulos Turner

Illustrators Darren Awuah, Lee Gibbons, Kevin Jones Associates, Andrew Kerr

Consultants Roger Bridgman, Ian Graham

First published in Great Britain in 2007 by
Dorling Kindersley Limited,
80 Strand, London, WC2R 0RL

2 4 6 8 10 9 7 5 3 1
TD357 – 07/07

A CIP catalogue record for this book is available from the British Library

ISBN: 978-1-40532-643-8

Colour reproduction by MDP, United Kingdom
Printed and bound by Hung Hing, China

Discover more at
www.dk.com

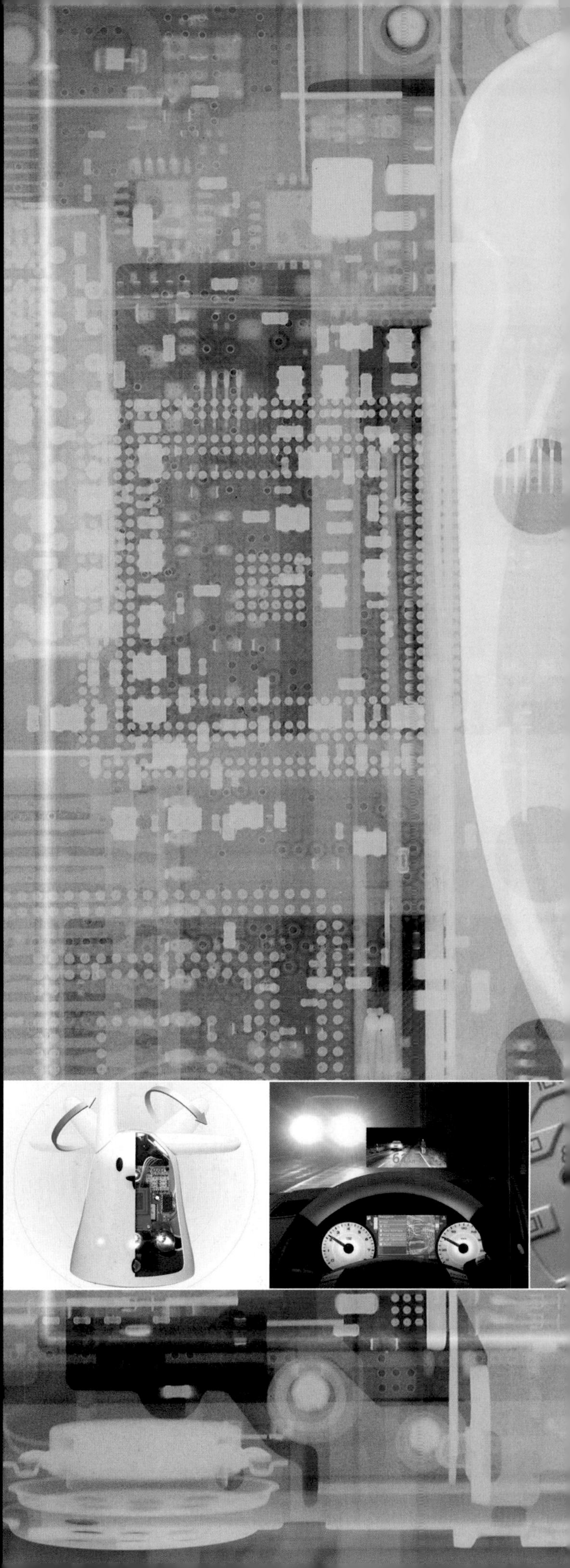

THE GADGET BOOK

AND HOW REALLY COOL STUFF WORKS

Written by Chris Woodford and Jon Woodcock

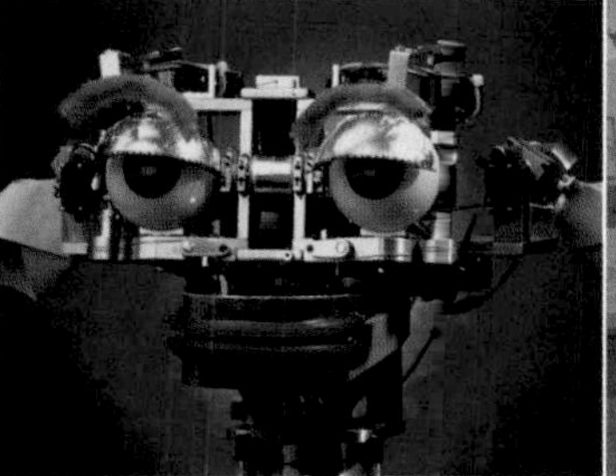

CONTENTS >>

LIVE

CONNECT

PLAY

MOVE

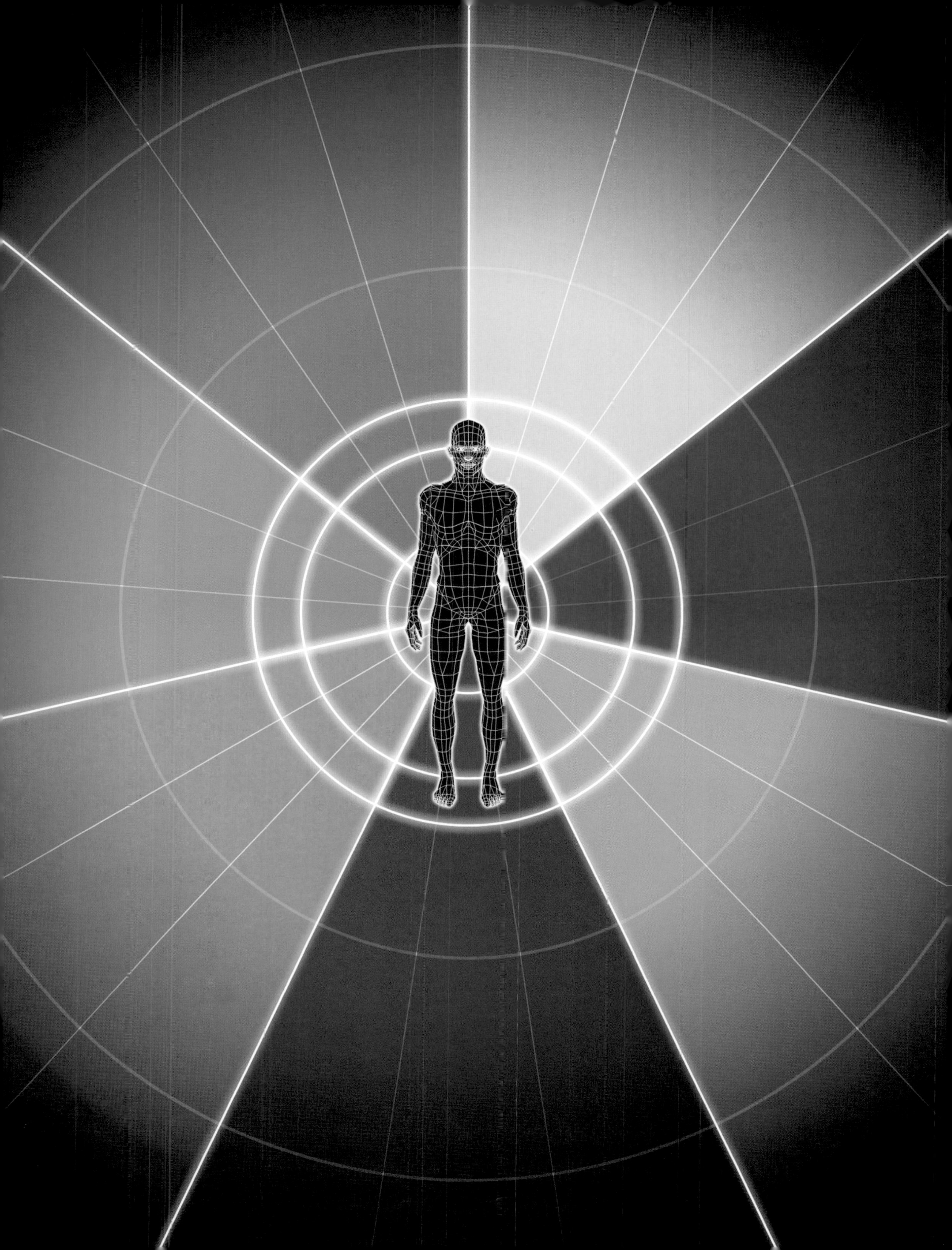

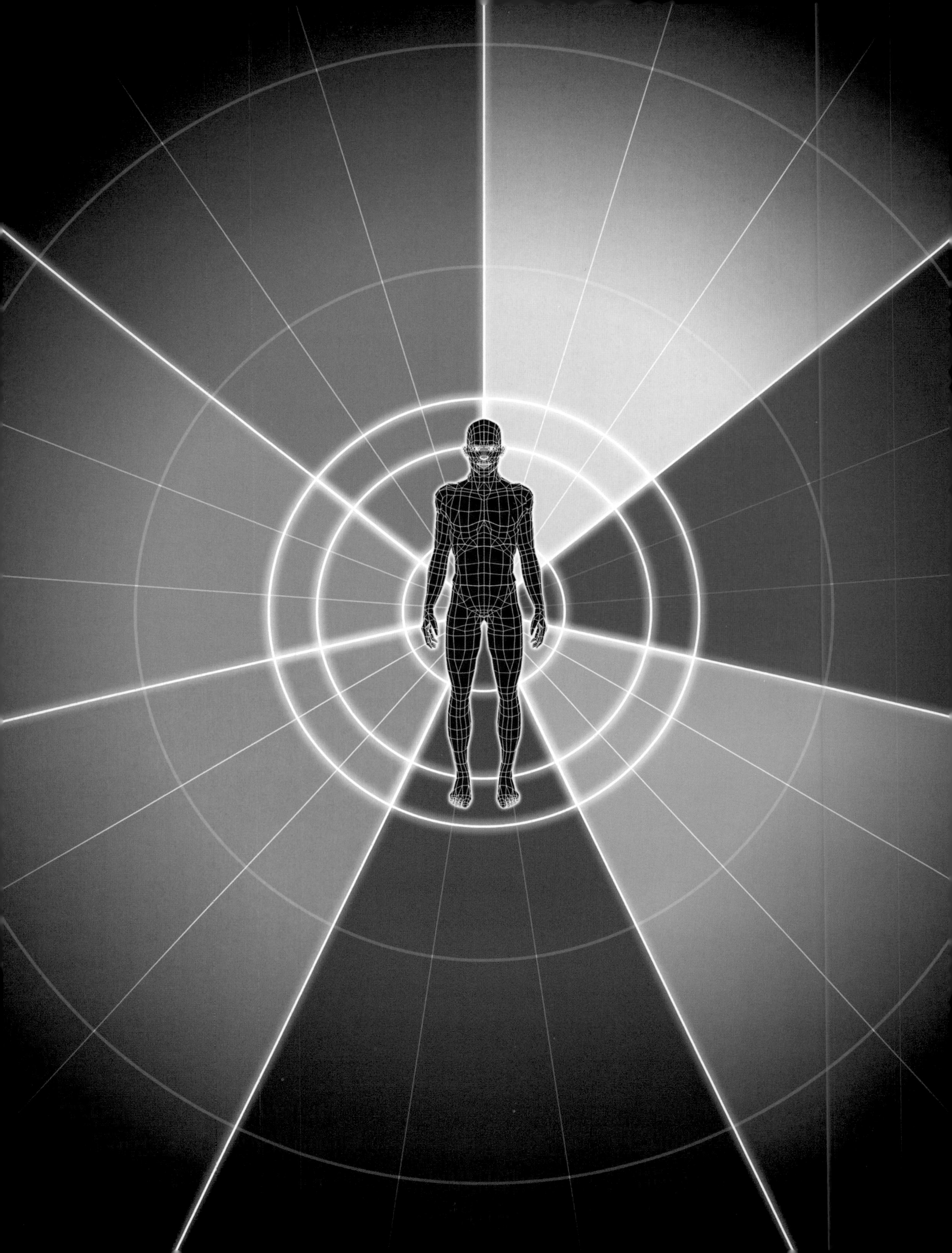

EXPLORE

CONSTRUCT

PROTECT

REFERENCE

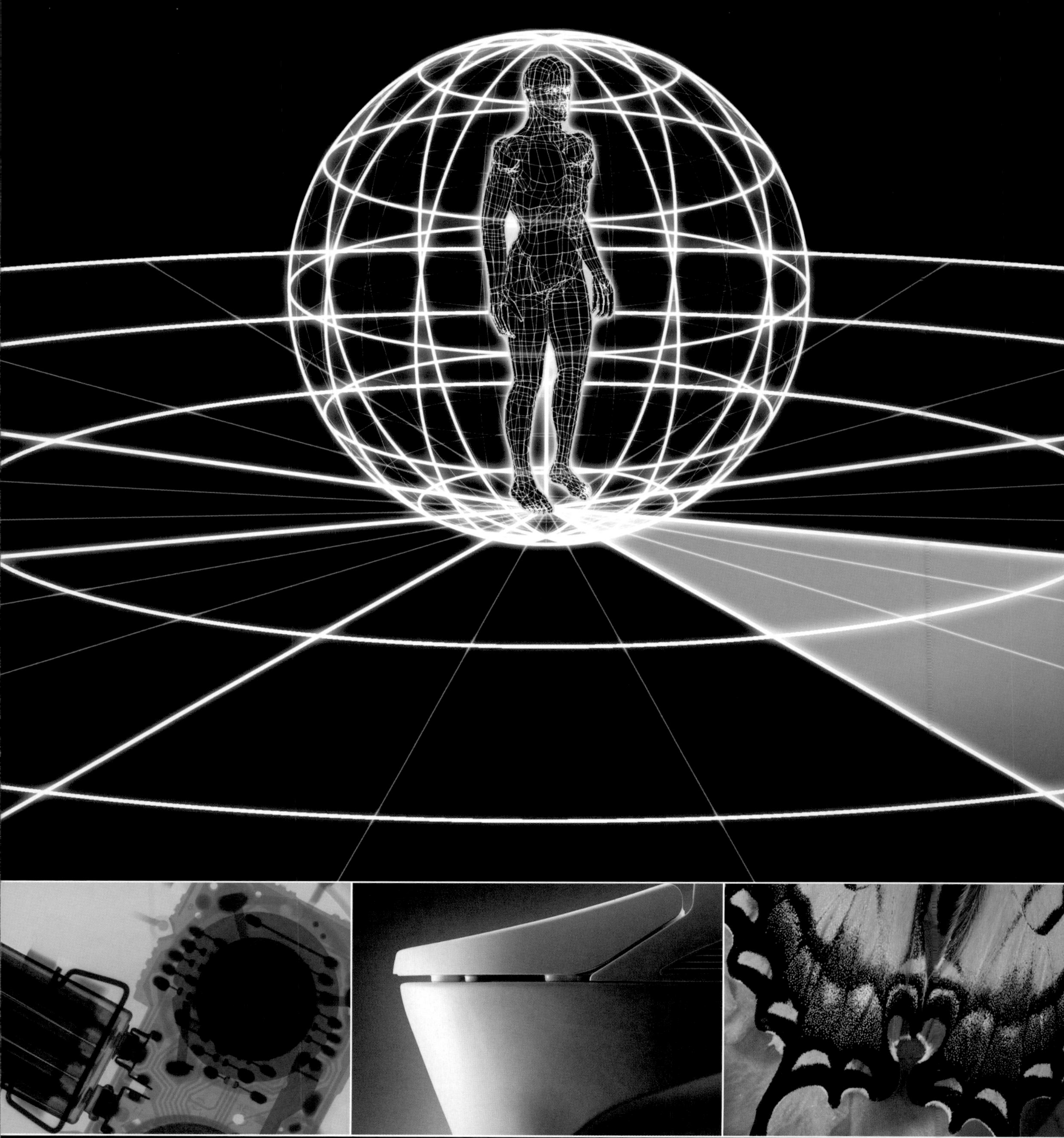

>> LIVE

Smoke detector >> Hi-tech toilet >> Floating bed >> HDTV >> Gas boiler >> Wind turbine >> Recycling >> Bioplastic >> Hydroponics >> Supermarket >> Dry shampoo >> Artificial retina >> Timepieces

What makes this picture dotty? p18
Where would you stick this? p12

▶▶ Our lives are packed with gadgets, but cool technology doesn't just make things easy and fun, it's useful too. Did you know that some shampoos get your hair microscopically clean? Or that you can grow plants without any soil? Cool technology has cool science behind it – and both are all around us. As people become more worried about the environment, technology has never been more vital. Whether we're making electricity from wind or using plastic bags that break down in soil, technology helps us to live smarter and protect the planet. ▶▶

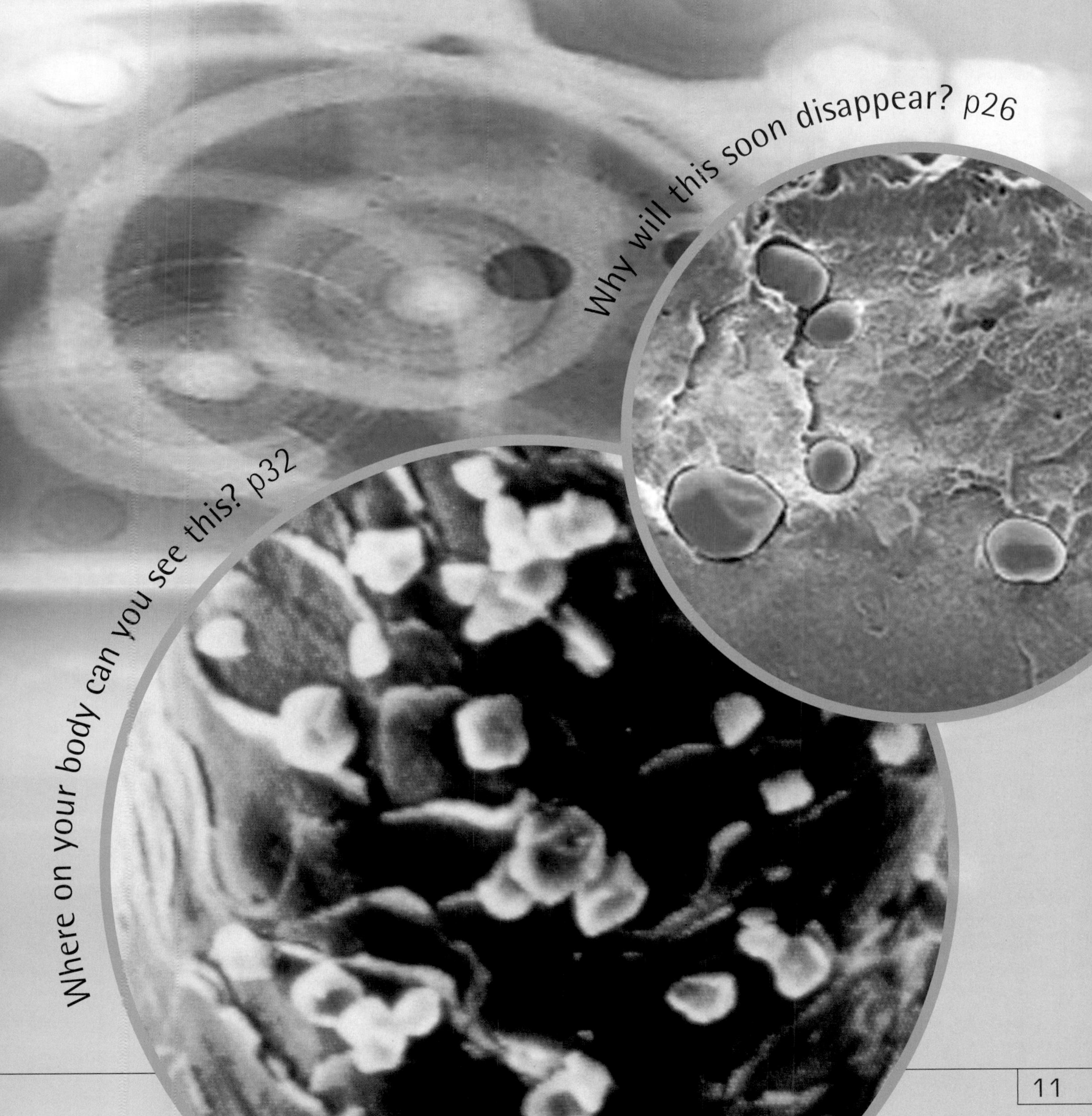

Why will this soon disappear? p26
Where on your body can you see this? p32

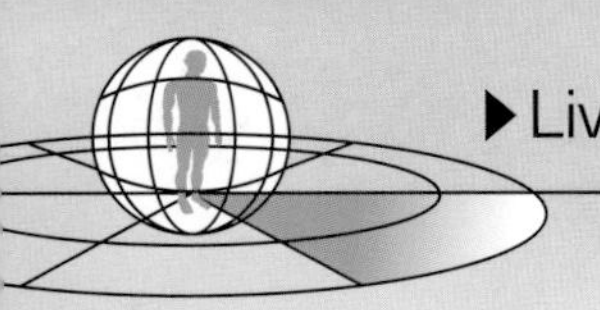

SMOKE DETECTOR

▶▶ Smoke particles are too small to see: you could fit 10,000 on a pinhead. Our noses can normally detect one particle of smoke in a million particles of air, but smoke detectors help to keep us safe, especially when we sleep. ▶▶

▶ Smoke detectors like this one are triggered by the particles of carbon (soot) in smoke. Carbon is a chemical element found in wood, paper, plastics, and other common materials. When things burn, the chemical compounds they are made from break up and the carbon is released.

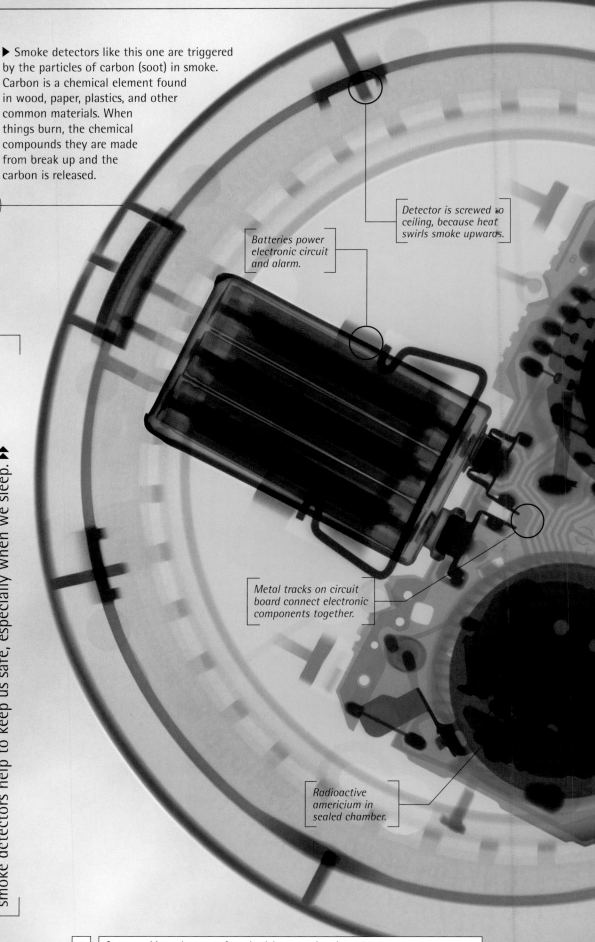

Detector is screwed to ceiling, because heat swirls smoke upwards.

Batteries power electronic circuit and alarm.

Metal tracks on circuit board connect electronic components together.

Radioactive americium in sealed chamber.

Image: X-ray image of an ionizing smoke detector

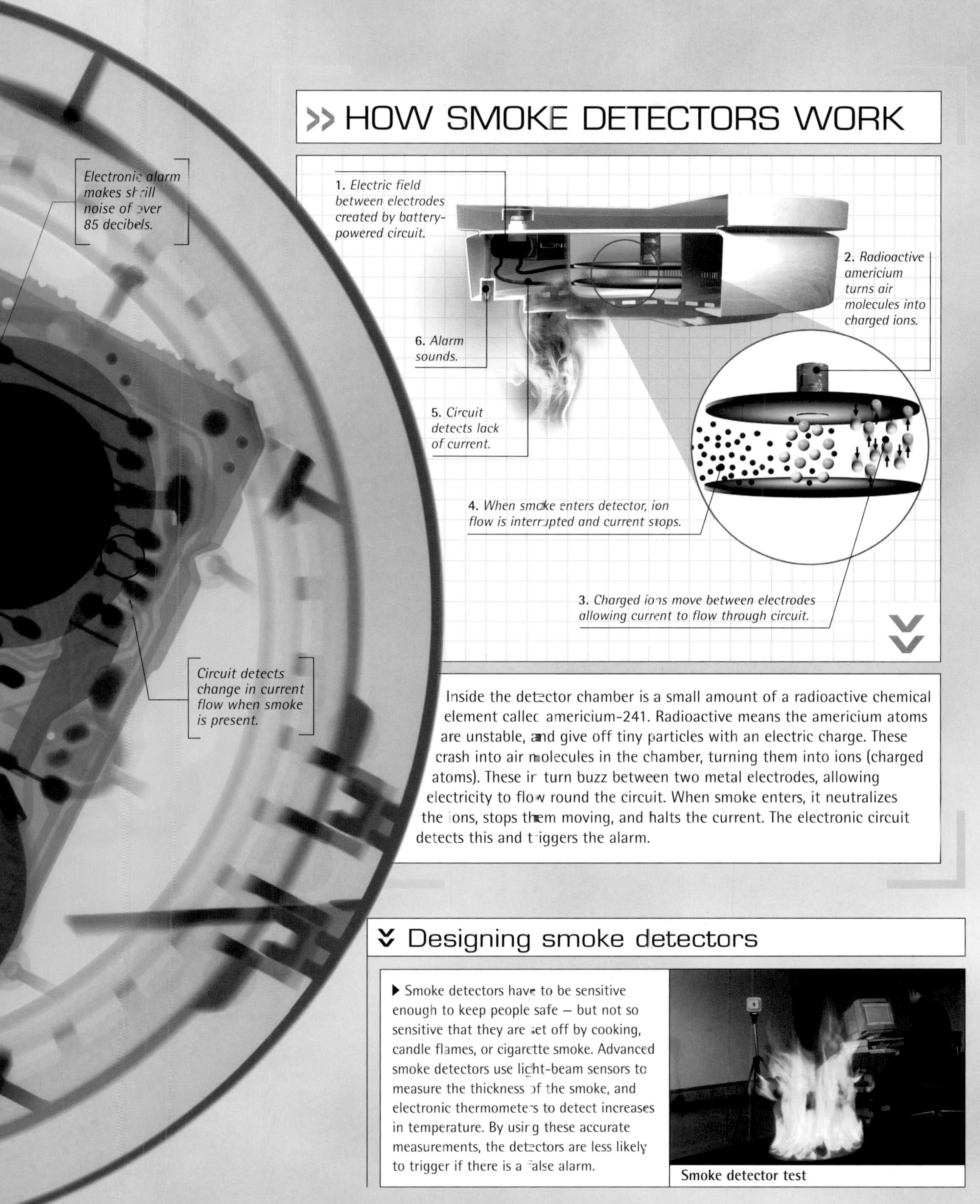

Electronic alarm makes shrill noise of over 85 decibels.
Circuit detects change in current flow when smoke is present.
1. Electric field between electrodes created by battery-powered circuit.
2. Radioactive americium turns air molecules into charged ions.
3. Charged ions move between electrodes allowing current to flow through circuit.
4. When smoke enters detector, ion flow is interrupted and current stops.
5. Circuit detects lack of current.
6. Alarm sounds.

» HOW SMOKE DETECTORS WORK

Inside the detector chamber is a small amount of a radioactive chemical element called americium-241. Radioactive means the americium atoms are unstable, and give off tiny particles with an electric charge. These crash into air molecules in the chamber, turning them into ions (charged atoms). These in turn buzz between two metal electrodes, allowing electricity to flow round the circuit. When smoke enters, it neutralizes the ions, stops them moving, and halts the current. The electronic circuit detects this and triggers the alarm.

Designing smoke detectors

▶ Smoke detectors have to be sensitive enough to keep people safe – but not so sensitive that they are set off by cooking, candle flames, or cigarette smoke. Advanced smoke detectors use light-beam sensors to measure the thickness of the smoke, and electronic thermometers to detect increases in temperature. By using these accurate measurements, the detectors are less likely to trigger if there is a false alarm.

Smoke detector test

▶▶ See also: Hard wear p224, Fire extinguisher p228

HI-TECH TOILET

▶▶ The world's most expensive toilet is as sleek as a sculpture, packed with gadgets, and comes with a 48-page instruction manual. The Toto Neorest® is a tankless, one-piece toilet that opens the lid when someone approaches, and closes it when they leave. ▶▶

▼ This striking luxury toilet is "green" as well as clean. It uses a quarter as much water as a traditional toilet – just 4.5 litres (1.2 gallons) per flush. Energy-saving features include a "fuzzy logic" microchip, which learns to recognize when the toilet is not being used and allows the seat to cool to save power.

Built-in air purifying system uses chemicals to remove all odours.

Discreet manual flush for use during power failure or lightning storm.

Image: Toto Neorest® 600

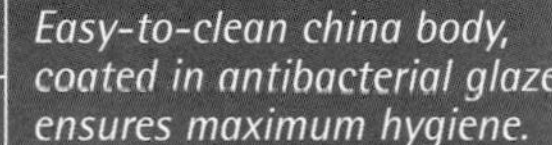

Easy-to-clean china body, coated in antibacterial glaze, ensures maximum hygiene.

» HI-TECH TOILET FEATURES

Sensors

The toilet has built-in sensors that detect when someone is nearby. The lid swings up automatically as he or she approaches, and the seat lifts at the touch of a button on the remote control. Both close silently when the person walks away. The hands-free flush rinses the bowl at the same time.

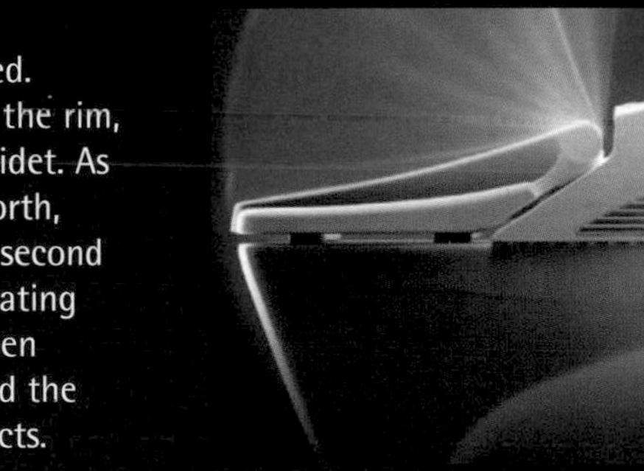

Nozzle

No toilet paper is needed. A discreet nozzle glides from the rim, converting the toilet into a bidet. As the nozzle moves back and forth, water jets cycling 70 times a second offer a gentle cleanse or pulsating massage. A warm air dryer then switches on automatically and the nozzle cleans itself as it retracts.

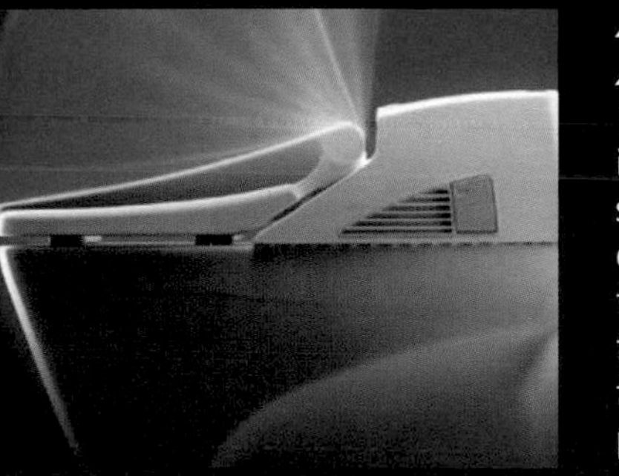

Remote control

The wireless remote operates 13 different functions of the toilet, including lifting and lowering the seat and lid, flushing the bowl, and operating the bidet. Every feature of the Neorest can be customized to the owner's preference, from the temperature of the seat to the pressure of the bidet jets.

▶▶ See also: Gas boiler p20, Wi-Fi toy p46, Bluetooth® p50, Convergence p56

FLOATING BED

Image: Artist's impression of the floating bed

▶▶ For many people, a good night's sleep is nothing but a dream. This radical new bed could change all that. Instead of resting on springs and wood, the mattress floats in mid-air using the invisible force of magnetism. ▶▶

Bed platform with built-in magnets floats above magnets buried in apartment floor.

Bed tethered to floor with wire ropes to stop it moving about.

Maglev technology

Maglev train in Shanghai, China

▲ Future trains may float on magnets instead of rolling on wheels. Trains using a system called maglev (magnetic levitation) glide above guide rails using only magnets to balance their weight. With no wheels or friction to slow it down, this maglev unit in China can reach 430 km/h (267 mph), making it the world's fastest commercial train.

▶▶ See also: Hi-tech toilet p14, ULTra® p114

>> HOW THE BED "FLOATS"

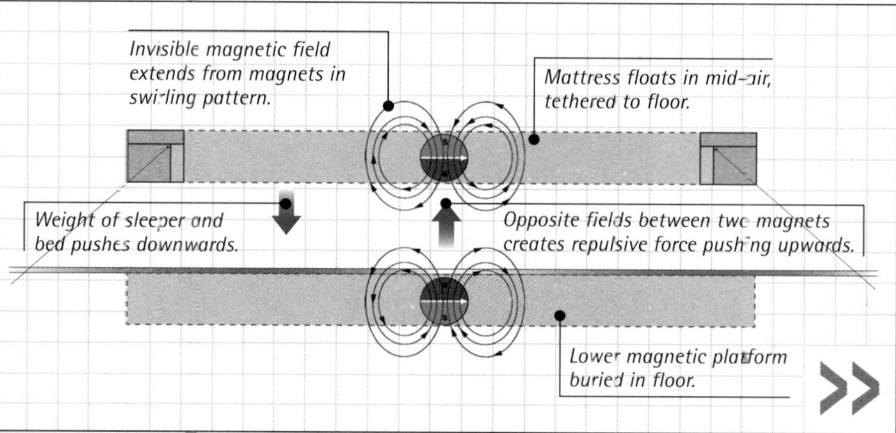
Invisible magnetic field extends from magnets in swirling pattern.
Mattress floats in mid-air, tethered to floor.
Weight of sleeper and bed pushes downwards.
Opposite fields between two magnets creates repulsive force pushing upwards.
Lower magnetic platform buried in floor.

Magnets create a magnetic field all around them. Place two magnets near one another, so one is inside another's field, and a force either pulls them together (if their neighbouring poles are different) or pushes them apart (if their poles are the same). One magnet can float on another, its weight balanced by the repulsive force between them. In the floating bed, this magnetic repulsion balances the weight of the person and mattress.

Bed is reflected in highly polished floor surface.

▲ This magnetic bed floats in mid-air, but still needs ropes to hold it to the floor. It is almost impossible to balance one magnet on top of another without one of them turning over or shooting to the side. Without the guide ropes, the magnetic bed could flip over or fly sideways through a window!

Image: Contrast in picture quality between HDTV and SDTV

▲ An HDTV picture can be made up of more than two million pixels. This means that much more detail can be seen.

▶ The picture on a digital television screen is made up of tiny dots called pixels. When a scene is captured by a TV camera it is broken down into a fixed number of pixels. The more pixels the better the picture looks, and the larger it can be shown without it becoming fuzzy. HDTV gives a much better picture because it can break a picture down into four times as many pixels as SDTV.

HDTV

▶▶ High Definition Television (HDTV) is a method of broadcasting that provides an extremely high-quality picture. Unlike its predecessor, Standard Definition Television (SDTV), HDTV can be shown on very large screens because the picture shows much finer detail. ▶▶

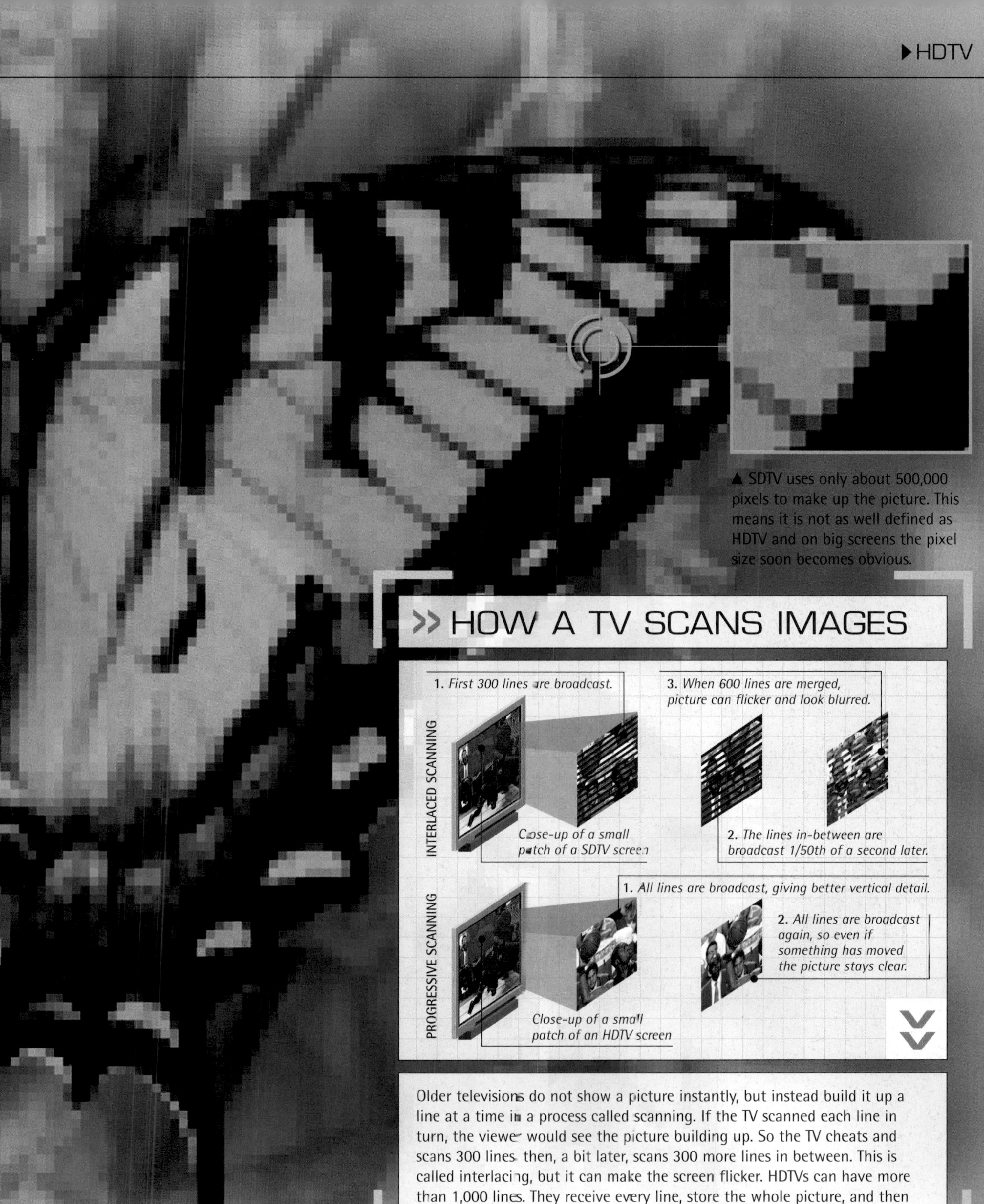

▲ SDTV uses only about 500,000 pixels to make up the picture. This means it is not as well defined as HDTV and on big screens the pixel size soon becomes obvious.

>> HOW A TV SCANS IMAGES

INTERLACED SCANNING
1. First 300 lines are broadcast.
3. When 600 lines are merged, picture can flicker and look blurred.
Close-up of a small patch of a SDTV screen
2. The lines in-between are broadcast 1/50th of a second later.
PROGRESSIVE SCANNING
1. All lines are broadcast, giving better vertical detail.
2. All lines are broadcast again, so even if something has moved the picture stays clear.
Close-up of a small patch of an HDTV screen

Older televisions do not show a picture instantly, but instead build it up a line at a time in a process called scanning. If the TV scanned each line in turn, the viewer would see the picture building up. So the TV cheats and scans 300 lines then, a bit later, scans 300 more lines in between. This is called interlacing, but it can make the screen flicker. HDTVs can have more than 1,000 lines. They receive every line, store the whole picture, and then show it all at once. This is called progressive scanning.

▶▶ See also: E-book p48, Games console p68, Simulators p70

Image: X-ray of a gas combination boiler

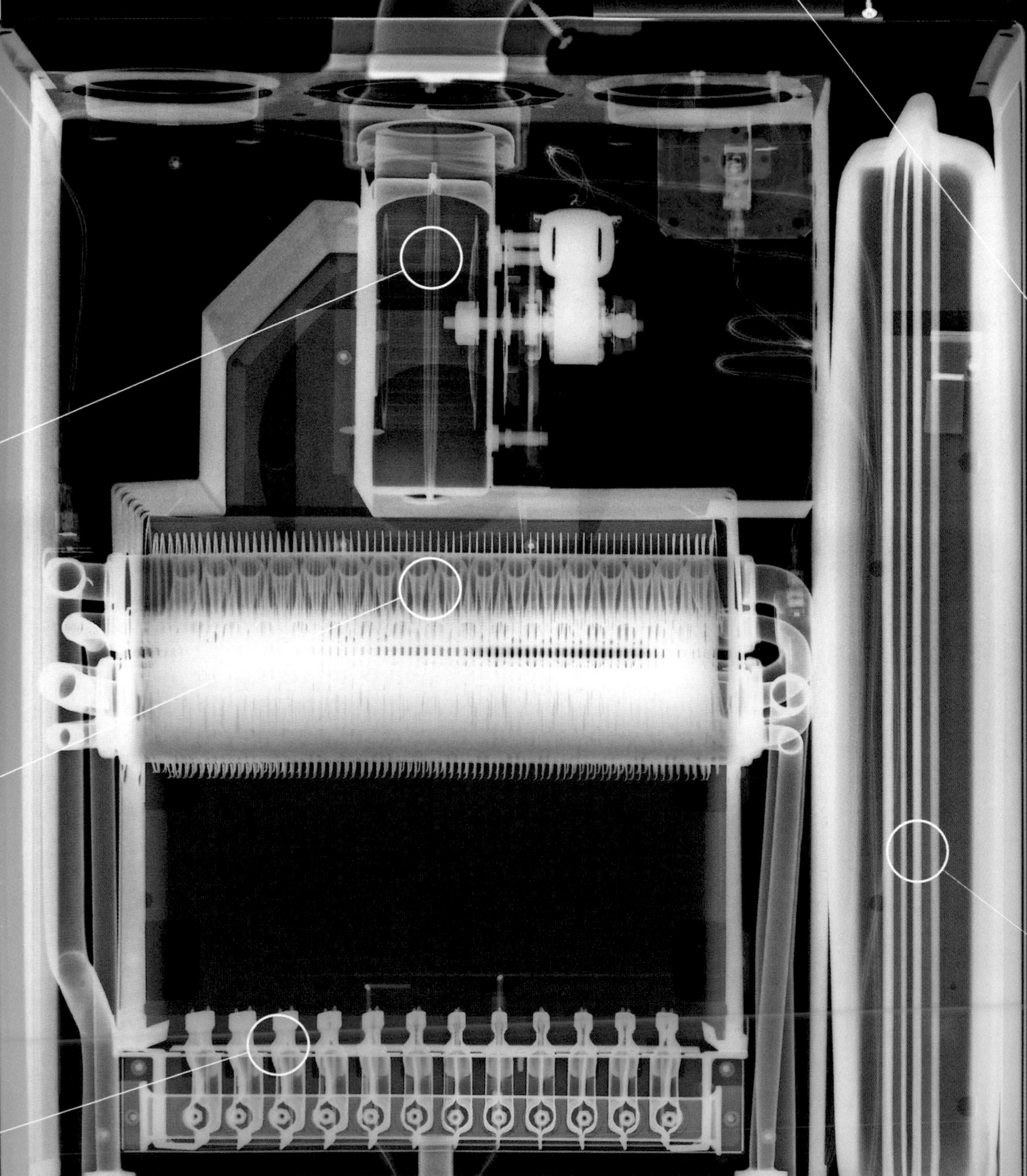

Air intake supplies air to burner.
Flue (chimney) takes gases away from burner and releases them outside building.
Fan ensures enough air passes through, preventing creation of deadly carbon monoxide gas.
Heat exchanger enables water to be heated as it runs back and forth through pipes suspended in hot gases.
Expansion vessel allows central heating water to expand as it warms to prevent pipes from bursting.
Electric spark-ignited gas burners provide hot gases that heat water in heat exchanger.

▶ This X-ray (enhanced with false colours) shows the inner workings of a gas combination boiler. This is an appliance that combines a water heater with a central heating boiler. The large pipe at the top goes outside through a wall to act as a chimney as well as an air intake. Water and gas pipes connect at the bottom.

▶▶ See also: Smoke detector p12, Hi-tech toilet p14

GAS BOILER

▶▶ A warm house and hot water are taken for granted, but it takes a sophisticated piece of engineering, such as a gas boiler, to deliver a reliable source of heat. Inside, the parts must work together for safe operation – gas cannot be allowed to escape, gas burners must be prevented from making deadly carbon monoxide, and the boiler has to shut down if the water supply is cut off. ▶▶

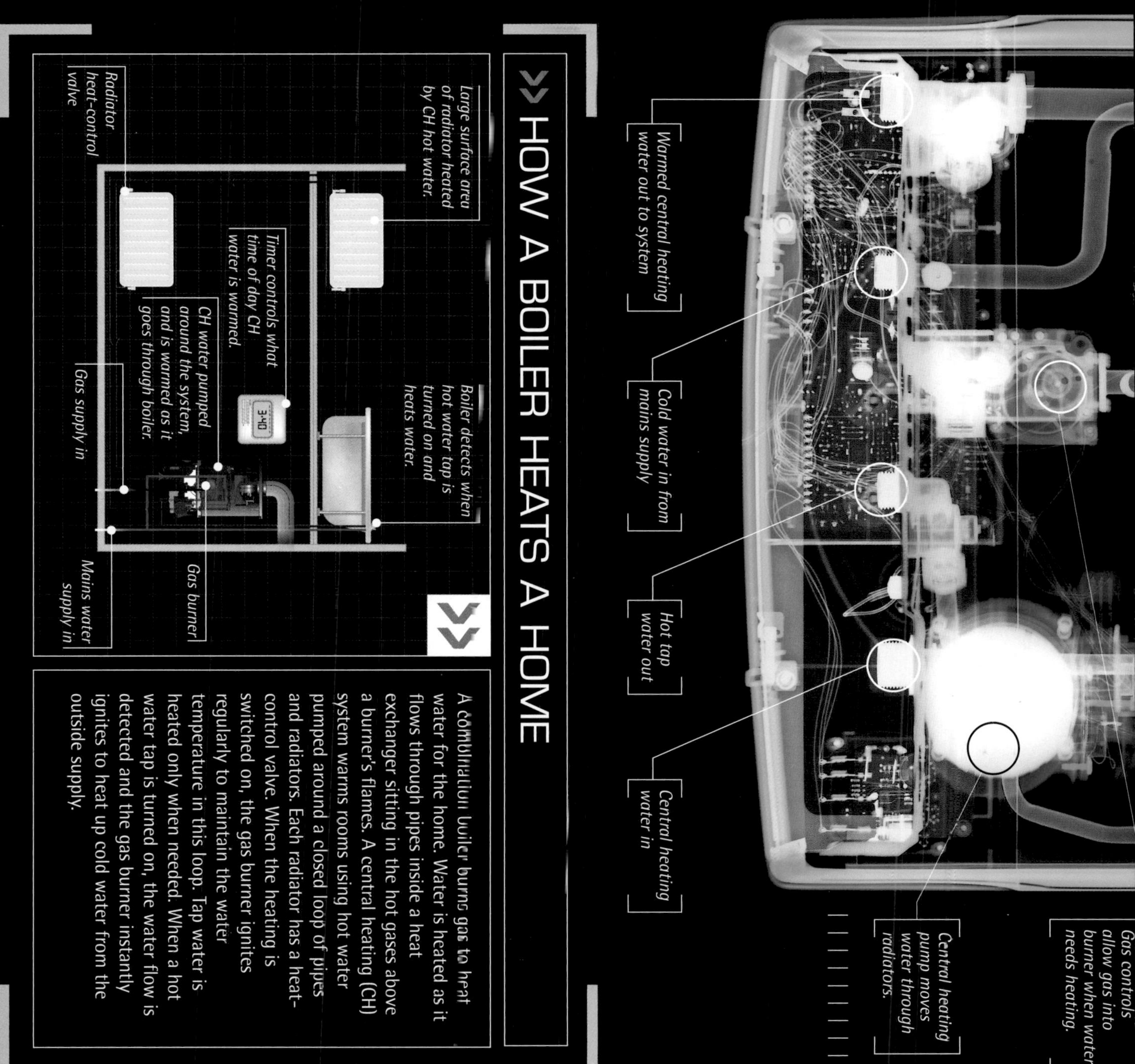

HOW A BOILER HEATS A HOME

A combination boiler burns gas to heat water for the home. Water is heated as it flows through pipes inside a heat exchanger sitting in the hot gases above a burner's flames. A central heating (CH) system warms rooms using hot water pumped around a closed loop of pipes and radiators. Each radiator has a heat-control valve. When the heating is switched on, the gas burner ignites regularly to maintain the water temperature in this loop. Tap water is heated only when needed. When a hot water tap is turned on, the water flow is detected and the gas burner instantly ignites to heat up cold water from the outside supply.

Large surface area of radiator heated by CH hot water.

Boiler detects when hot water tap is turned on and heats water.

Timer controls what time of day CH water is warmed.

CH water pumped around the system, and is warmed as it goes through boiler.

Gas burner

Gas supply in

Mains water supply in

Radiator heat-control valve

WIND TURBINE

▸▸ Giant wind turbines are the windmills of the future – they can make clean, green energy out of thin air. A single turbine can generate electricity for about 1,000 homes. In one year, it will produce enough power to run a computer for more than 1,600 years. ▸▸

Anemometer and vane measure wind speed and direction to keep turbine facing into wind.
Generator produces electricity at 690 volts.
Gearbox magnifies rotor speed so electricity can be generated in light breeze.
Rotor blades are 71 m (233 ft) in diameter – the length of 15 family cars.
250 kg

Image: Maintenance work being carried out on a wind turbine

>> HOW A WIND TURBINE WORKS

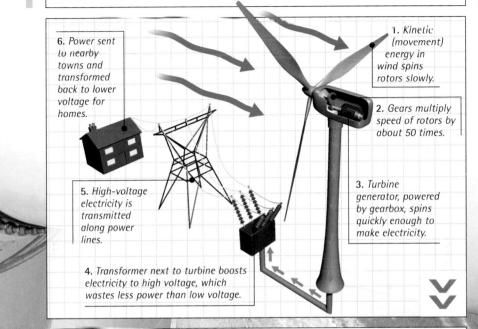

1. *Kinetic (movement) energy in wind spins rotors slowly.*

2. *Gears multiply speed of rotors by about 50 times.*

3. *Turbine generator, powered by gearbox, spins quickly enough to make electricity.*

4. *Transformer next to turbine boosts electricity to high voltage, which wastes less power than low voltage.*

5. *High-voltage electricity is transmitted along power lines.*

6. *Power sent to nearby towns and transformed back to lower voltage for homes.*

Wind turbines capture the energy of the wind and convert it into electricity. A wind turbine works the opposite way to an aeroplane's propeller engine, which converts fuel into a moving gust of air. A wind turbine is static, so air moving past spins the rotors. These drive a generator, similar to a bicycle dynamo, that produces electricity. The rotors are angled so they spin as the wind blows into them. Their enormous length means they act like levers: even a breeze can spin them round.

▶ The massive rotors of a wind turbine are positioned 80 m (262 ft) above the ground to capture as much wind energy as possible. Even though one turbine makes 2 megawatts of electricity, it takes about 1,000 turbines to make as much power as a large coal or nuclear power station.

▶▶ See also: Bodyflight p86, Weather balloon p164

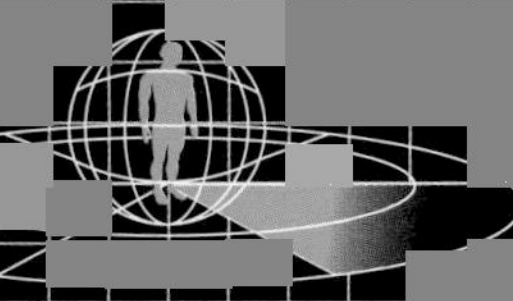

RECYCLING

We throw away our own weight in rubbish every seven weeks. Most of what we throw away is made from resources that the Earth is running out of. Recycling what we use reduces the demand for raw materials. With a little imagination, today's old trash can be born again in funky new products.

« Sweet papers These handbags are made by weaving together sweet wrappers so, like most recycled products, each one is unique. Mexican designer Olga Abadi took her inspiration from ancient weaving techniques used by the Maya civilization. The Mayans made bags by binding everyday items together.

» Telephone wire These colourful bowls are made from telephone cables no-one wants anymore. They were made in South Africa using traditional techniques for weaving grass. Wires of various colours are woven together round a wooden drum to make a beautiful, intricate, but extremely practical object.

Pipe lamps

Buried plastic can take over 500 years to disintegrate, so if plastic pipes are replaced it makes sense to recycle them rather than throwing them away. Made from recycled sewer pipes, these stunning lamps were inspired by bird bones, which are similarly strong and lightweight.

3D wallpaper

The paper you recycle today could come back to life in these 3D wall tiles. They are 100 per cent recycled and, when they are no longer wanted, can be recycled into something else. Paper represents a third of the rubbish we throw away, but it is possible to recycle paper up to five times.

Recycled cycle

This chair was made by recycling steel and aluminium parts from bicycle wheels, handlebars, and frames. The arm rests are fashioned from old bike tyres and the inner tubes from the tyres are used to make the seat's upholstery.

See also: Bioplastic p26, Grand designs p184, Shelters p234

Image: SEM image of biodegradeable plastic

BIOPLASTIC

▶▶ Plastic and nature do not mix. Some plastics take decades to disintegrate in landfill sites, while others will survive 500 years or more. However revolutionary bioplastics have been developed, using natural ingredients such as cornstarch, which will break up and harmlessly biodegrade in as little as three months. ▶▶

HOW THE PLASTIC BREAKS DOWN

1. Bioplastics contain starch, a chemical that plants use to store energy. When a plant grows, it captures the energy from sunlight and makes a sugar called glucose. The plant cannot always use all the glucose immediately, so it stores some for later in the form of starch. In this slice of potato, magnified 10–20 times, the egg-shaped starch grains are stored inside the plant cells.

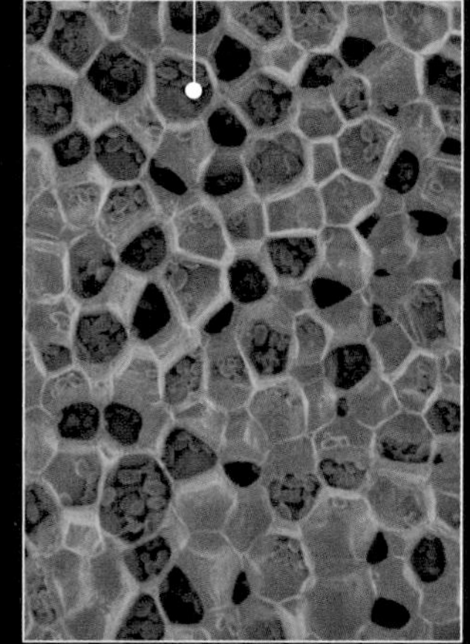

Starch grains can be seen inside cells.

2. When you boil starchy foods such as potato or pasta in water, water molecules are attracted to the starch grains and make them swell up. In this cooked potato, the starch grains have expanded and smashed the plant cells apart. This is how bioplastic works. When bioplastic is buried, the starch grains inside absorb water from the soil, swell up, and break the plastic into bits.

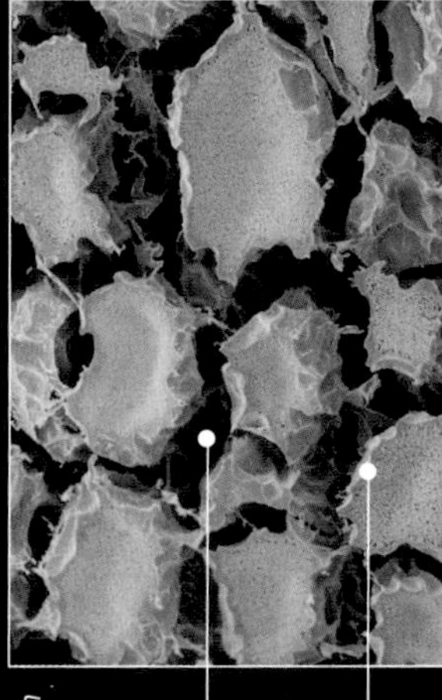

Bacteria can penetrate the gaps between the cells.

Cell walls have collapsed.

▼ Many stores now wrap foods, such as this watermelon, in bioplastic. Most foods contain water, and there is always water in the atmosphere, so bioplastic wrapping starts to break down even when it is on the supermarket shelf. However, it will take months to disintegrate completely.

▼ Bioplastic, magnified more than 1,000 times with a scanning electron microscope (SEM), reveals cornstarch granules (orange) embedded in its structure. Once buried, water in the ground causes the granules to swell. This helps break up the plastic so soil bacteria can digest it into harmless organic materials.

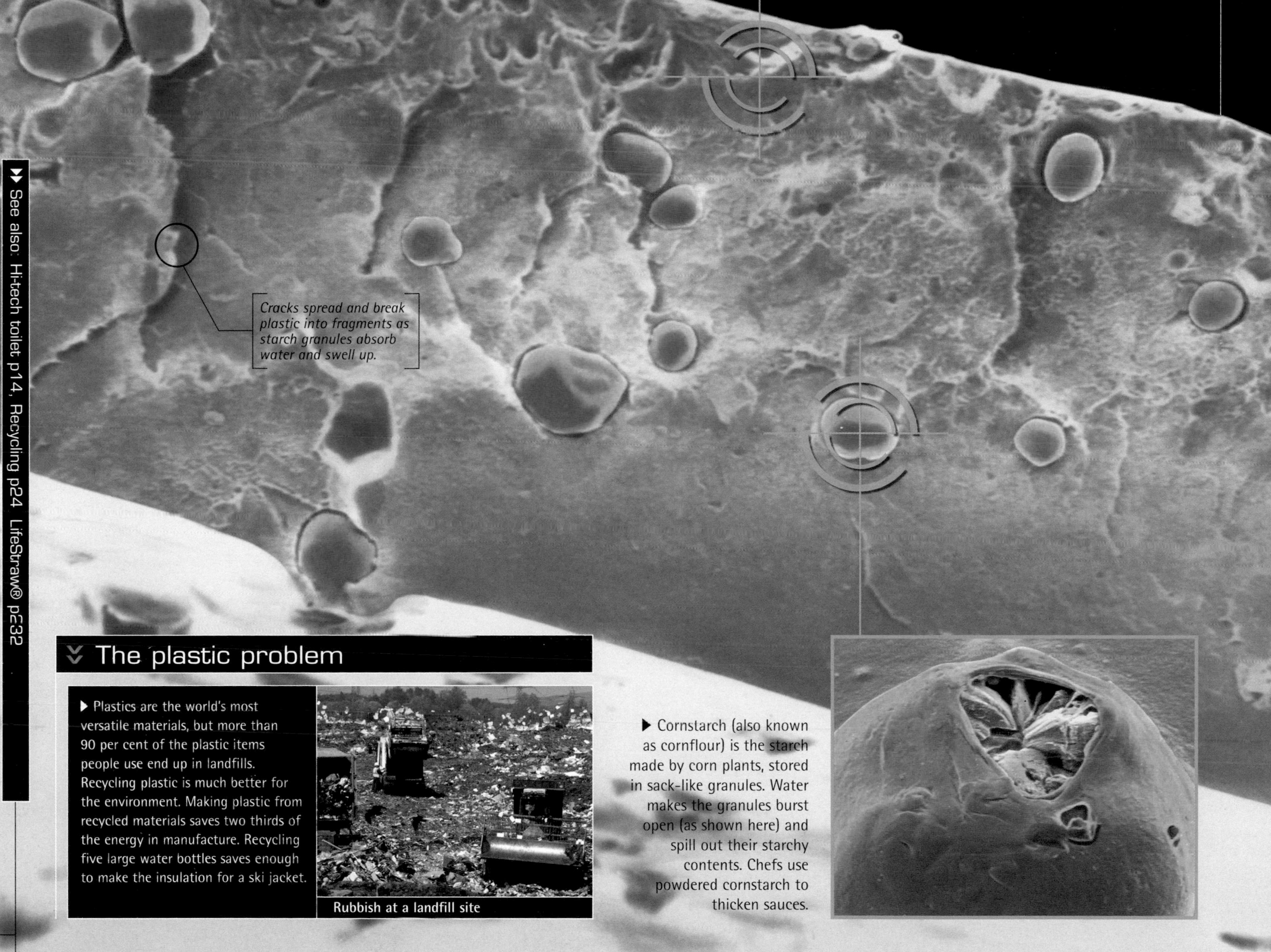

Cracks spread and break plastic into fragments as starch granules absorb water and swell up.

▶ Cornstarch (also known as cornflour) is the starch made by corn plants, stored in sack-like granules. Water makes the granules burst open (as shown here) and spill out their starchy contents. Chefs use powdered cornstarch to thicken sauces.

The plastic problem

▶ Plastics are the world's most versatile materials, but more than 90 per cent of the plastic items people use end up in landfills. Recycling plastic is much better for the environment. Making plastic from recycled materials saves two thirds of the energy in manufacture. Recycling five large water bottles saves enough to make the insulation for a ski jacket.

Rubbish at a landfill site

▶▶ See also: Hi-tech toilet p14, Recycling p24 LifeStraw® p232

HOW HYDROPONICS WORKS

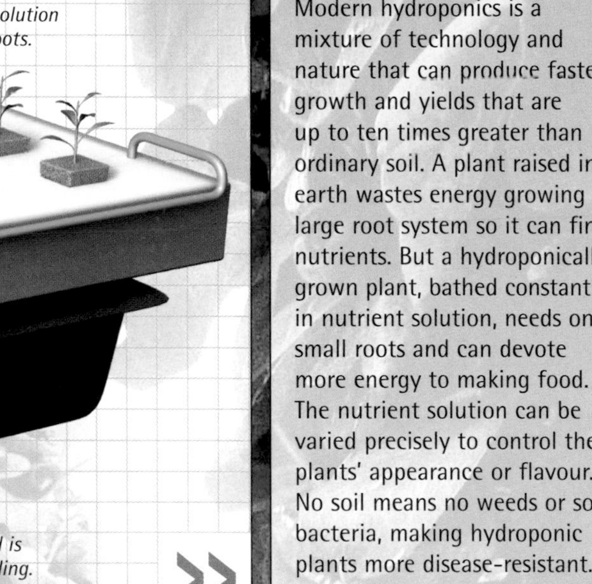
Pump cycles nutrient solution only during daytime, when plants grow.
Roots grow through many holes in the base of grow cups.
Thin film of nutrient solution trickles past plants' roots.
Air pump aerates nutrient solution, providing steady oxygen supply to roots.
Nutrient solution drips through to bottom and is pumped back for recycling.

Modern hydroponics is a mixture of technology and nature that can produce faster growth and yields that are up to ten times greater than ordinary soil. A plant raised in earth wastes energy growing a large root system so it can find nutrients. But a hydroponically grown plant, bathed constantly in nutrient solution, needs only small roots and can devote more energy to making food. The nutrient solution can be varied precisely to control the plants' appearance or flavour. No soil means no weeds or soil bacteria, making hydroponic plants more disease-resistant.

▶▶ See also: Supermarket p30, Eden Project p186, LifeStraw® p232

Image: Inside a hydroponicum

Plants trained upwards to maximize growing space.

Plants grown close together to increase yields.

Bright white top-sheet reflects light onto leaves, increasing growth.

Aeroponics

AeroGarden growing herbs

▲ Aeroponics is like hydroponics, only the plants grow in air instead of water. This AeroGarden™ can grow plants five times faster than ordinary soil. The roots are in a sealed container where the air's humidity (water content) is 100 per cent, oxygen levels are high, and a computer controls the topping up of nutrients. A daylight bulb above provides virtual sunshine.

HYDROPONICS

▶▶ If people ever live permanently in space, they will need ways of growing food without soil. One approach is to use hydroponics, which is a way of raising plants in nutrient-rich water instead of earth. ▶▶

▲ Inside this hydroponicum, plants are growing with their roots in water trays instead of beds of earth. The soil's main function is to provide plants with nutrients. If these are supplied in water, soil is no longer needed. Used as a growing method since ancient times, hydroponics is now of great interest to space scientists.

SUPERMARKET

Internet shopping Shoppers can order their groceries 24 hours a day from the comfort of their own homes. Supermarket websites list all the goods available in the store. Shoppers can browse and select what they want, then arrange a time for delivery. Around two-thirds of Internet users currently shop online, but 95 per cent of shopping is still done in actual stores.

Self-service These customers are scanning their own shopping with help from a recorded voice and prompts on the computer screen. Checkouts like this are cost-effective for stores because they save the wages of checkout operators. Built-in TV cameras help deter theft.

A typical person will spend eight and a half years of their life in stores, so gadgets that make shopping less of a chore must be welcome. Since the first piece of supermarket technology, the mechanical cash register, appeared in the 1880s, stores have become increasingly hi-tech. Today, you can find microchips in everything from trolleys to chiller cabinets.

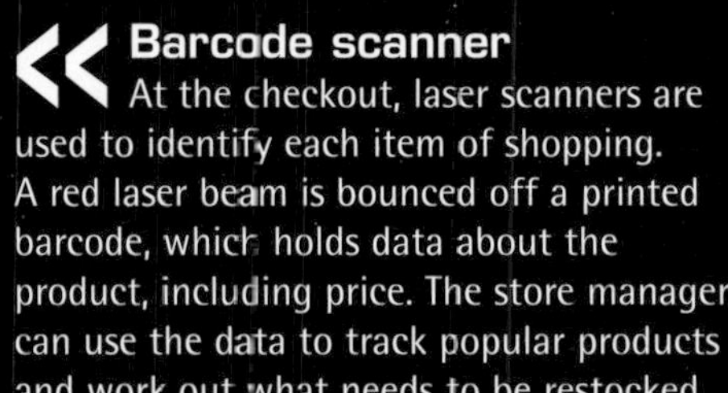

« Barcode scanner

At the checkout, laser scanners are used to identify each item of shopping. A red laser beam is bounced off a printed barcode, which holds data about the product, including price. The store manager can use the data to track popular products and work out what needs to be restocked.

» CCTV security

Around 10 per cent of shoppers steal from stores. Closed-circuit TV (CCTV) cameras, like this ceiling-mounted pod, slowly rotate to monitor large areas of the shop. Images are recorded on tape or disk for use as evidence in court cases.

^ Smart cart

This trolley's computer tracks you through the store using wireless signals from ceiling transmitters. The computer remembers what you buy each week. As you wander the aisles, it reminds you what you need and points out special offers.

▶▶ See also: Convergence p56, Money p208, DataDot p216

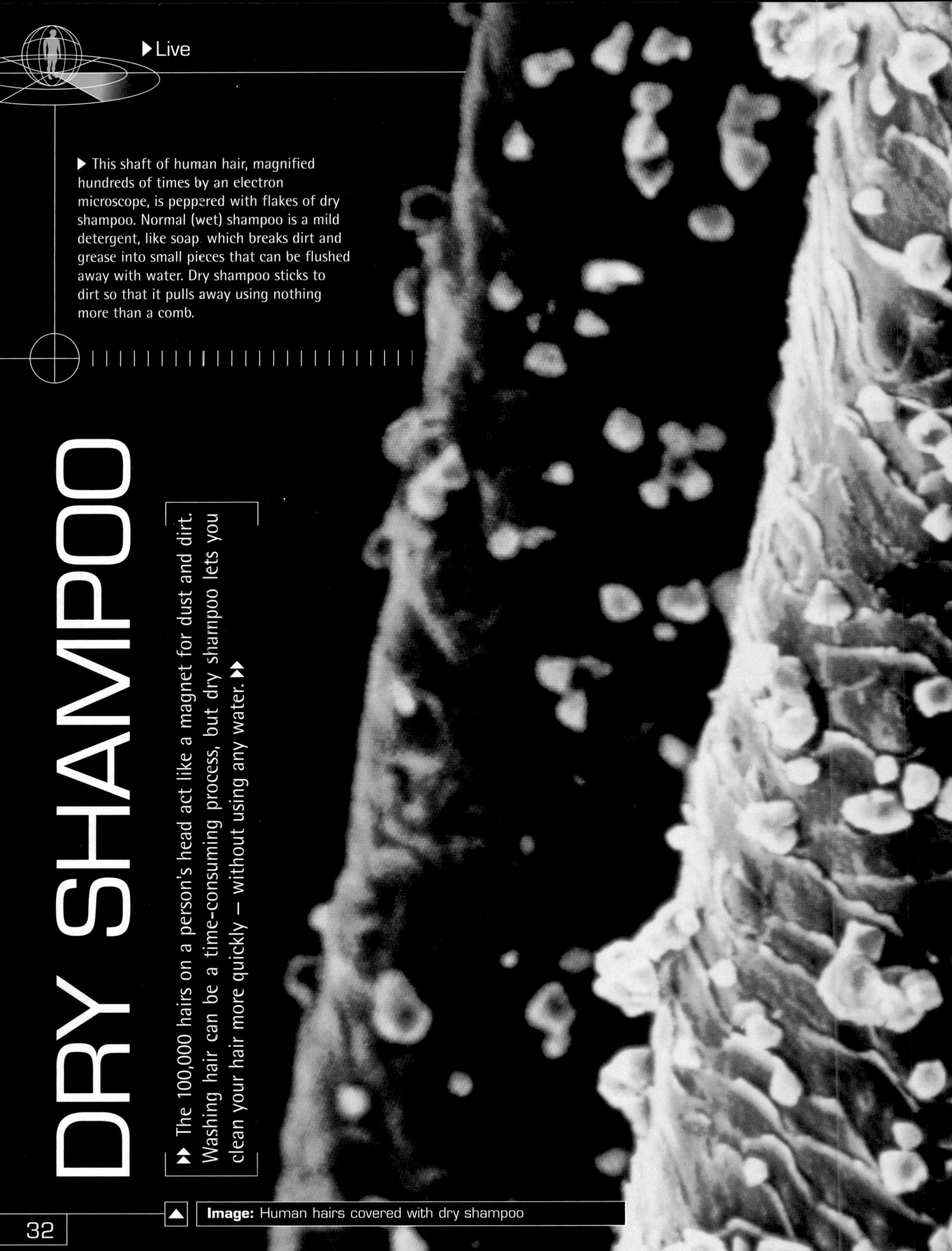

▶ This shaft of human hair, magnified hundreds of times by an electron microscope, is peppered with flakes of dry shampoo. Normal (wet) shampoo is a mild detergent, like soap, which breaks dirt and grease into small pieces that can be flushed away with water. Dry shampoo sticks to dirt so that it pulls away using nothing more than a comb.

DRY SHAMPOO

▸▸ The 100,000 hairs on a person's head act like a magnet for dust and dirt. Washing hair can be a time-consuming process, but dry shampoo lets you clean your hair more quickly – without using any water. ▸▸

▲ **Image:** Human hairs covered with dry shampoo

▶▶ See also: Microscope p162, Micro machines p200

Cuticle (outer layer) of hair shaft is covered in overlapping scales and is made entirely of dead cells.

Flakes of dry shampoo bind chemically to grease and dirt on hair shaft.

Bad hair day

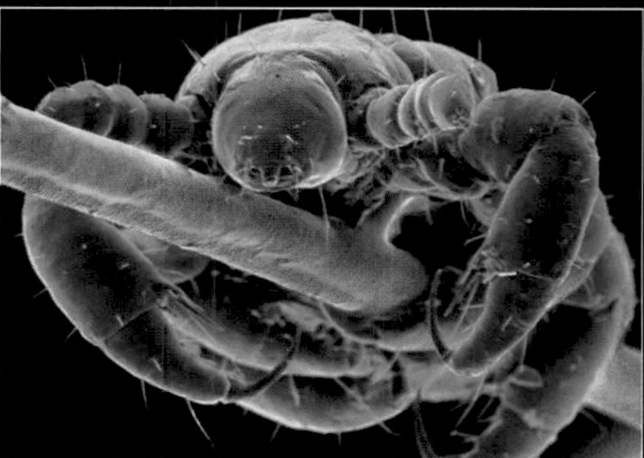

Head louse

▲ No amount of ordinary shampoo will stop head lice. These tiny, wingless insects crawl through human hair, feeding on blood from the scalp. Although they live for only one day, they lay up to 10 eggs before they die. The only way to remove them is by applying a special shampoo and running a fine comb through the hair.

HOW DRY SHAMPOO WORKS

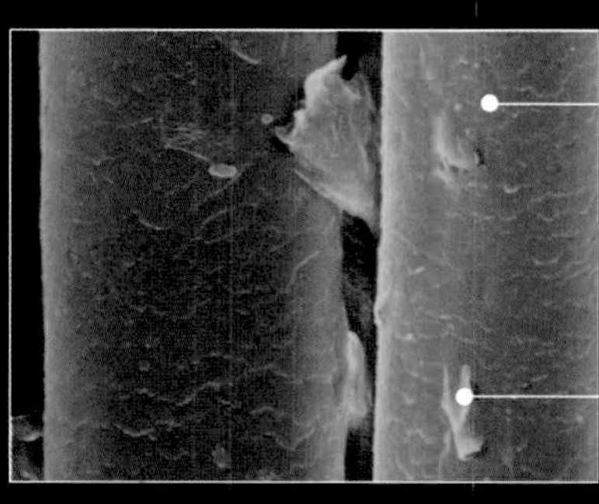

1. Glands around the follicles (hair pits) in your scalp secrete a greasy substance called sebum, which waterproofs and protects hairs. If you do not wash your hair, the sebum builds up, trapping dirt and making your hair feel lank and unpleasant. Short hair is often more greasy than long hair.

2. Dry shampoo attaches firmly to patches of grease and dirt that cling to a human hair. When you comb through the hair, the shampoo flakes are too big to pass through the comb's teeth. The comb tugs the shampoo flakes away, pulling the dirt away too.

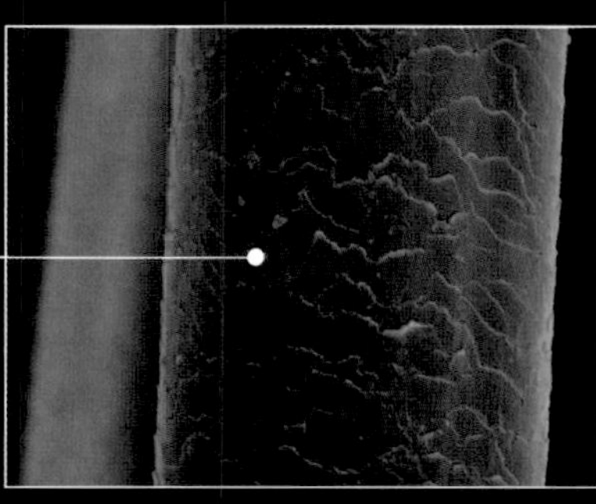

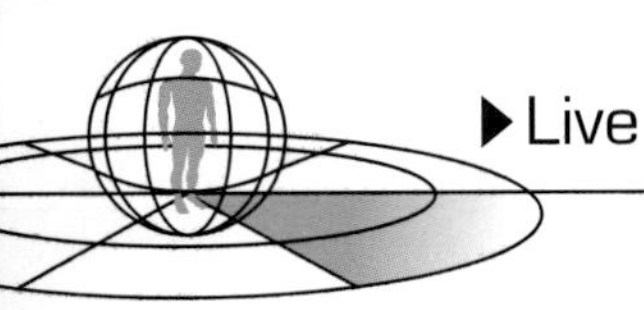

ARTIFICIAL RETINA

▶▶ The blind live in a world of darkness, but new technology could help them "see". Artificial retinas, similar to digital cameras, can carry pictures from the outside world directly to a blind person's brain, bypassing the parts of their visual system that do not work. ▶▶

▶ The artificial retina developed at the University of Southern California takes just 90 minutes to implant surgically. After surgery, vision is crude but good enough to make out simple shapes and detect movement. As blind people get used to the system, their brains "fill in" some missing information and their vision improves.

Eye implant receives from the microchip the processed images captured by the camera.

Digital camera built into glasses captures image in place of blind person's damaged retina.

▲ **Image:** Model of a retinal implant

▶▶ See also: Bluetooth® p50, Simulators p70, Eyewear p230

>> HOW AN ARTIFICIAL RETINA WORKS

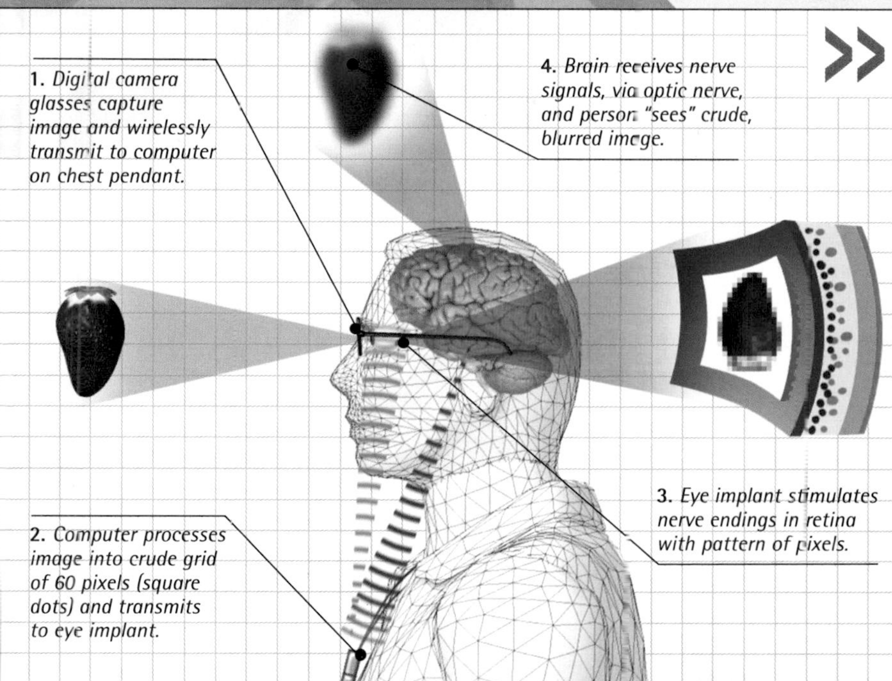

1. Digital camera glasses capture image and wirelessly transmit to computer on chest pendant.
2. Computer processes image into crude grid of 60 pixels (square dots) and transmits to eye implant.
3. Eye implant stimulates nerve endings in retina with pattern of pixels.
4. Brain receives nerve signals, via optic nerve, and person "sees" crude, blurred image.

People are blind because the path between their cornea (the protective outside of the eye) and visual cortex (part of the brain that processes visual things) is damaged. The optic nerve, which carries signals from eye to brain, is usually intact. Scientists are working to restore sight by sending images directly into the optic nerve. A microchip connected to electronic glasses captures a digital image, which is beamed to an eye implant. This stimulates the optic nerve to send images to the brain.

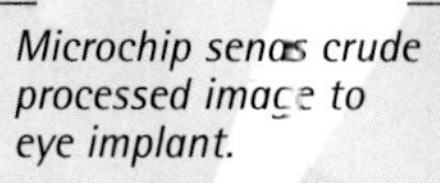

Microchip sends crude processed image to eye implant.

Robot vision

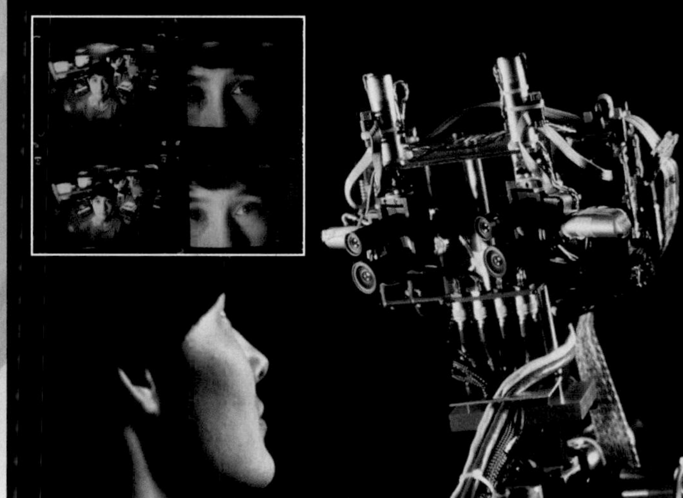

Kismet robot "seeing" a subject

▶The Kismet robot has an artificial head with four digital cameras for eyes. Two of these cameras see wide angles and two see objects close-up. A computer uses the four images to detect faces of people nearby and then automatically swivels the robot's head towards them. Turning to face people is only one of the ways in which Kismet tries to seem more human. It can also close its eyelids independently, and it raises or furrows its eyebrows to express sadness, frustration, or surprise.

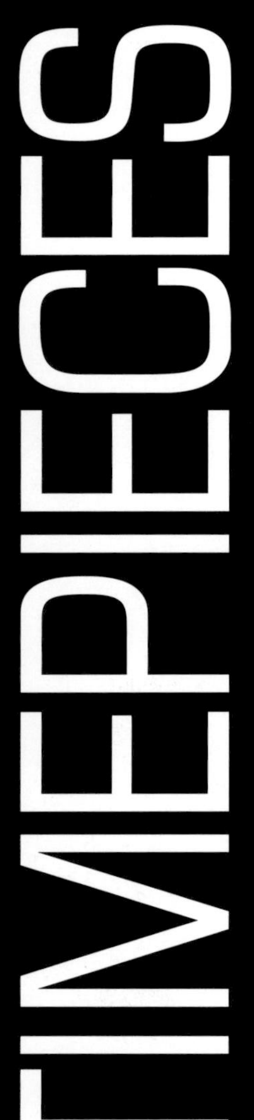

TIMEPIECES

For hundreds of years, clocks and watches all had hands driven by complex mechanical workings. They needed winding regularly or they would stop. Modern timepieces come in all shapes and sizes. Some keep time with radio broadcasts. Others use pulsating crystals. There are even watches that display a new form of time designed for the Internet age.

Binary wristwatch Computers use binary to store numbers using just two numerals: "0" (off) and "1" (on). This watch does the same. The first light is worth one, then each light is worth double the one before. Adding up you can see this watch says it is 3:25.

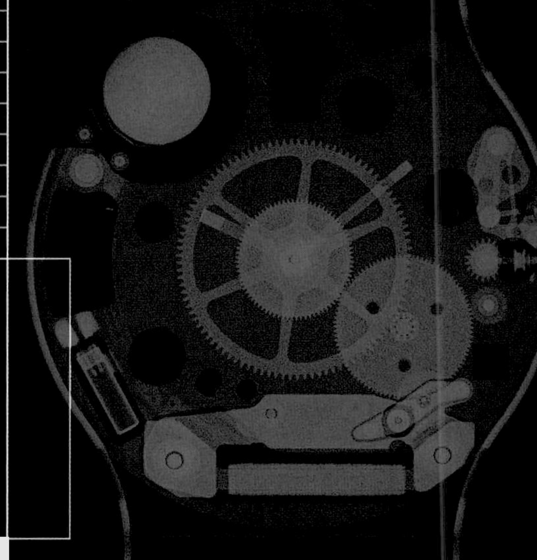

Quartz watch X-ray Electricity can make a quartz crystal (seen lower left) wobble at a very precise rate. This is used to accurately control each tick of this watch.

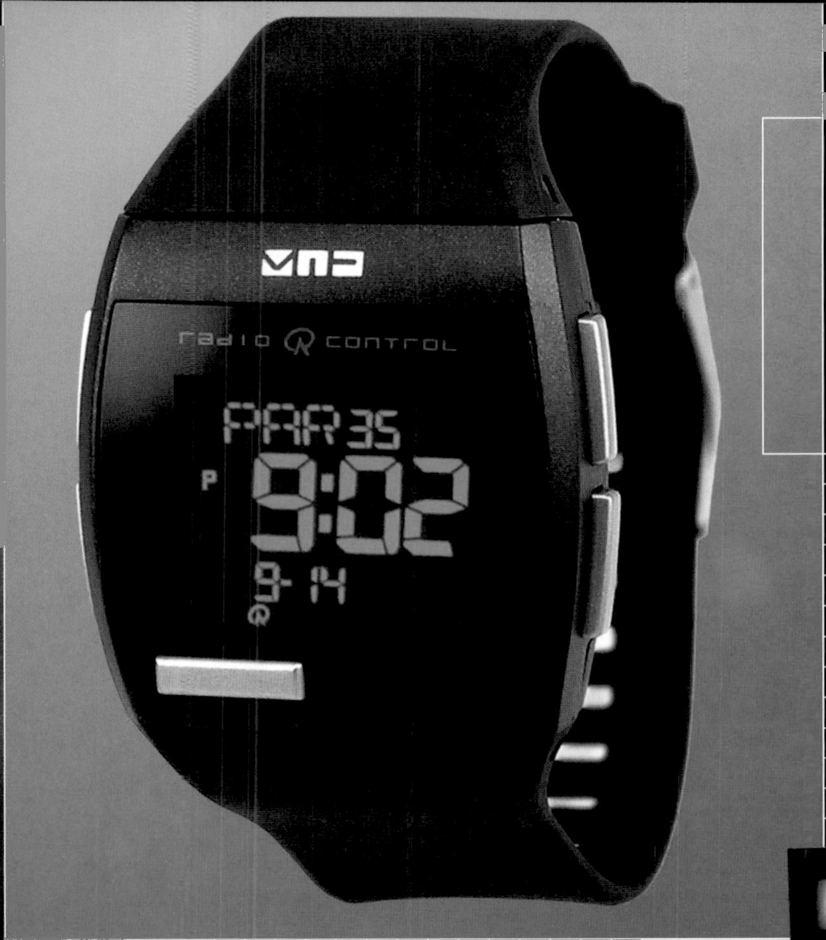

Atomic watch

The best clocks in the world are atomic clocks. They can keep time to less than a billionth of a second – but they're far too large to fit on your wrist. This watch stays accurate by receiving regular radio broadcasts, which synchronize it with atomic time.

LED clock

Can you tell what time these two TIX LED (light-emitting diode) clocks show? It's 12:34. All you need to do is count the number of lit LEDs in each section of the clock face in turn. Easy when you know how!

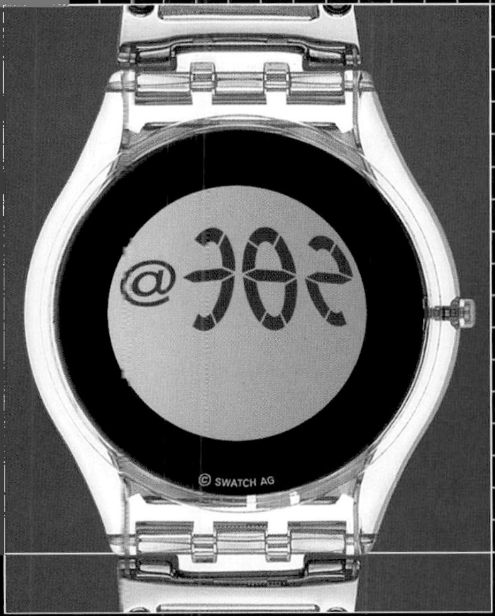

Internet time

Arranging events on the Internet can get very confusing around the world because people set their watches according to the time zone they live in. To try to solve this problem "Internet time" is the same everywhere. It splits the day into 1,000 ".beats", each about 1.5 minutes long.

▶▶ See also: Bluetooth® p50, Convergence p56, Supercomputer p60, Spy p214

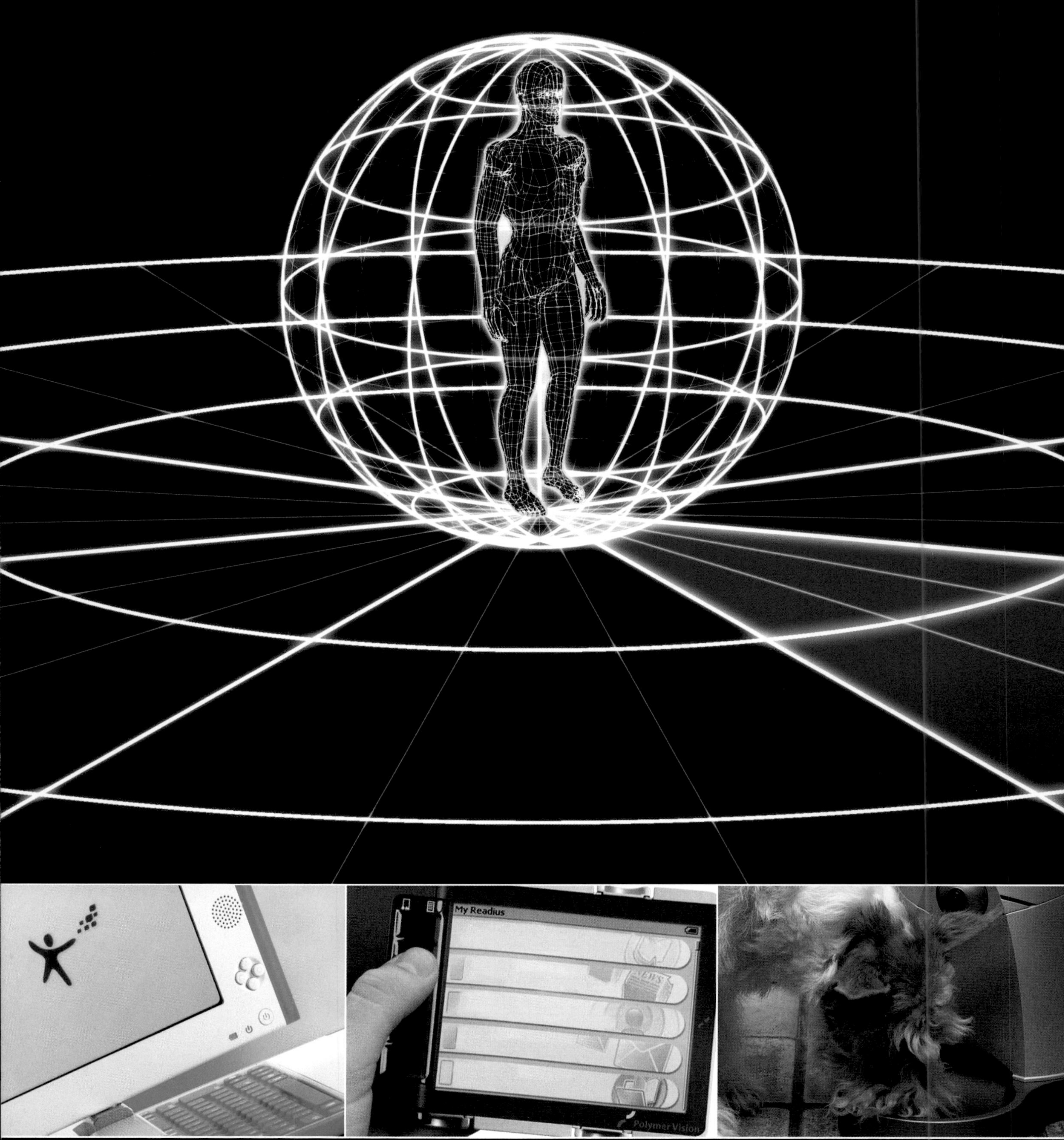
My Readius
NEWS
Polymer Vision

>>CONNECT

Laptop for all >> Mouse >> Wi-Fi toy >> E-book >> Bluetooth >> Petcam >> Head up >> Convergence >> E-voting >> Supercomputer >> Seti@Home

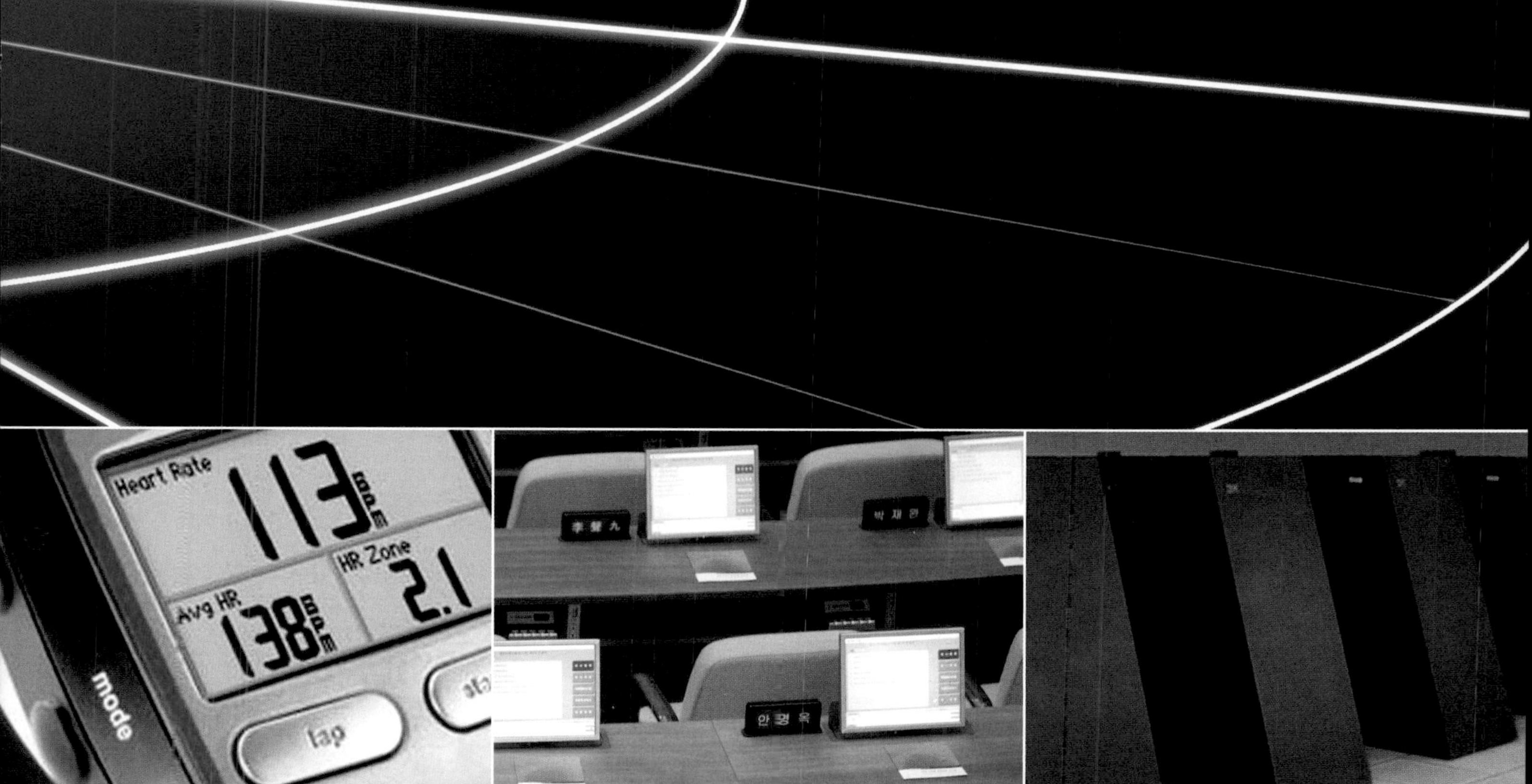

What makes this rabbit wiggle its ears? p46

In the 21st century there is no such thing as far away. Mobile phones are commonplace, and computers around the globe swap data over the Internet. Most gadgets are designed to perform more than one function and some to communicate with other gadgets. The wires and cables that have been so essential to getting us connected will soon be a thing of the past as technology becomes increasingly wireless and data is transmitted via radio or infrared waves.

How does this thumb-sized robot communicate? p50

Why hasn't this rodent got a ball to play with? p44

>> HOW THE XO LAPTOP WORKS

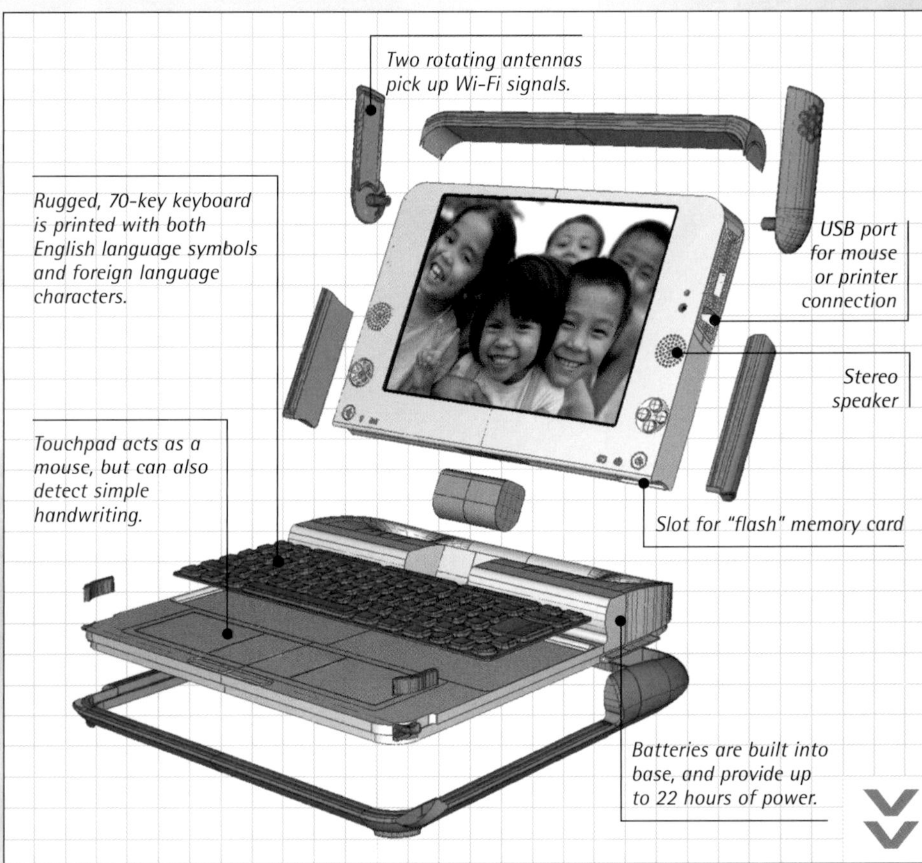

Two rotating antennas pick up Wi-Fi signals.
Rugged, 70-key keyboard is printed with both English language symbols and foreign language characters.
USB port for mouse or printer connection
Stereo speaker
Touchpad acts as a mouse, but can also detect simple handwriting.
Slot for "flash" memory card
Batteries are built into base, and provide up to 22 hours of power.

Port for headphones
Directional mouse pad can scroll text on screen.

The XO laptop is designed to be powerful but affordable. It has an inexpensive processor chip running a simplified operating system (the main software that controls a computer and the programs that run on it). It has no mechanical hard drive. Instead, the XO's memory is provided by "flash" cards like those used in digital cameras. There is a port for connecting the laptop to the mains, but since electricity is not widely available in some developing countries, the battery on later models will be recharged by using a hand-crank, a pedal, or a pull-cord. Built-in Wi-Fi (wireless networking) chips allow the laptop to connect automatically with nearby machines as well as to the Internet.

LAPTOP FOR ALL

▶▶ More than 80 per cent of the world's population has no Internet access. The XO has been designed to bring information power to all. Costing just £50 each, the laptops will be sold to governments in developing countries for use in schools. ▶▶

▶▶ See also: Wi-Fi toy p46, E-book p48, Convergence p56

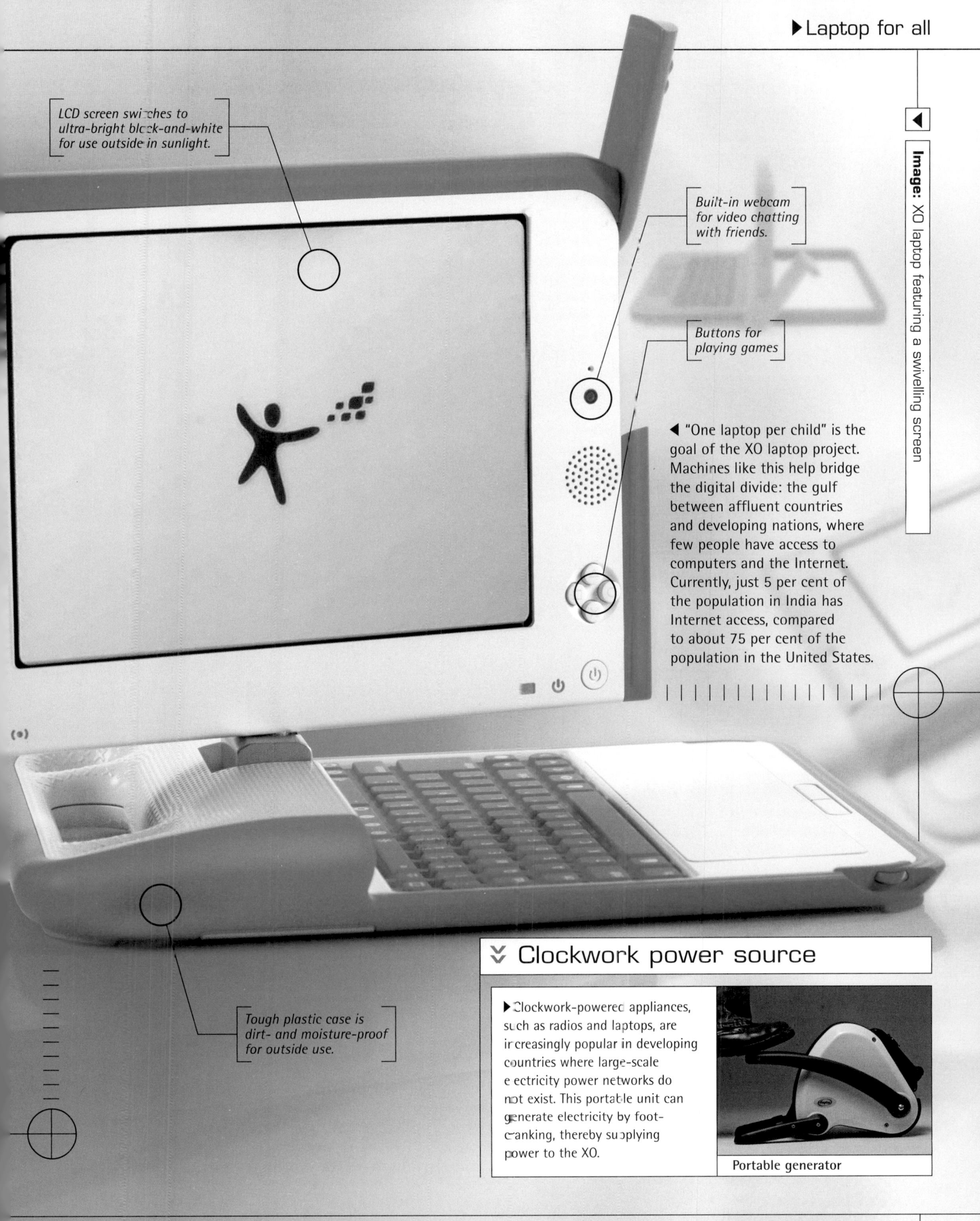
LCD screen switches to ultra-bright black-and-white for use outside in sunlight.
Built-in webcam for video chatting with friends.
Buttons for playing games
Tough plastic case is dirt- and moisture-proof for outside use.

Image: XO laptop featuring a swivelling screen

"One laptop per child" is the goal of the XO laptop project. Machines like this help bridge the digital divide: the gulf between affluent countries and developing nations, where few people have access to computers and the Internet. Currently, just 5 per cent of the population in India has Internet access, compared to about 75 per cent of the population in the United States.

Clockwork power source

Clockwork-powered appliances, such as radios and laptops, are increasingly popular in developing countries where large-scale electricity power networks do not exist. This portable unit can generate electricity by foot-cranking, thereby supplying power to the XO.

Portable generator

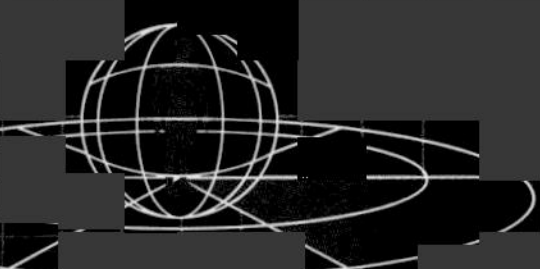

MOUSE

Space Navigator 3D controller

Pressure sensing technology inside the SpaceNavigator™ means that the user can simply push, pull, twist, or tilt the cap to move around, zoom into, and rotate 3D images. Increasing pressure makes the mouse operate faster.

Bluetooth mouse

This Bluetooth® mouse doesn't need a wire – it connects to a computer using coded radio signals. Its power comes from an internal rechargeable battery, so it does have to be plugged in occasionally for the battery to be charged. The latest wireless mouse can recharge without cables when left on a special mouse mat.

A conventional computer mouse consists of a curved plastic case with a click ability, a ball underneath to sense movement, and a wire connecting it to the computer. But the ball collects dust and the wire keeps the mouse prisoner on the desk. In recent years, the mouse has mutated into many more flexible forms.

Shape-changer mouse

This sleek mouse is designed to combat repetitive strain injuries. It can change shape so that it can be operated in a variety of ways. The shell is sculpted to be grip-friendly and the mouse is wireless so it can be held away from a desk.

periric™

Optical mouse

This ball-less mouse uses a camera to detect faint surface details below it. The computer tracks the speed and direction of the mouse by interpreting the moving picture.

Braille mouse

Many blind people use a writing system of raised dots, called braille, which they read by touching the dots with their fingers. This mouse converts computer output to braille by mechanically raising and lowering pins to form patterns of dots. A rotating disc moves the characters beneath the fingers of the reader.

See also: Wi-Fi toy p46, Bluetooth® p50, Supercomputer p60, Seti@Home p62

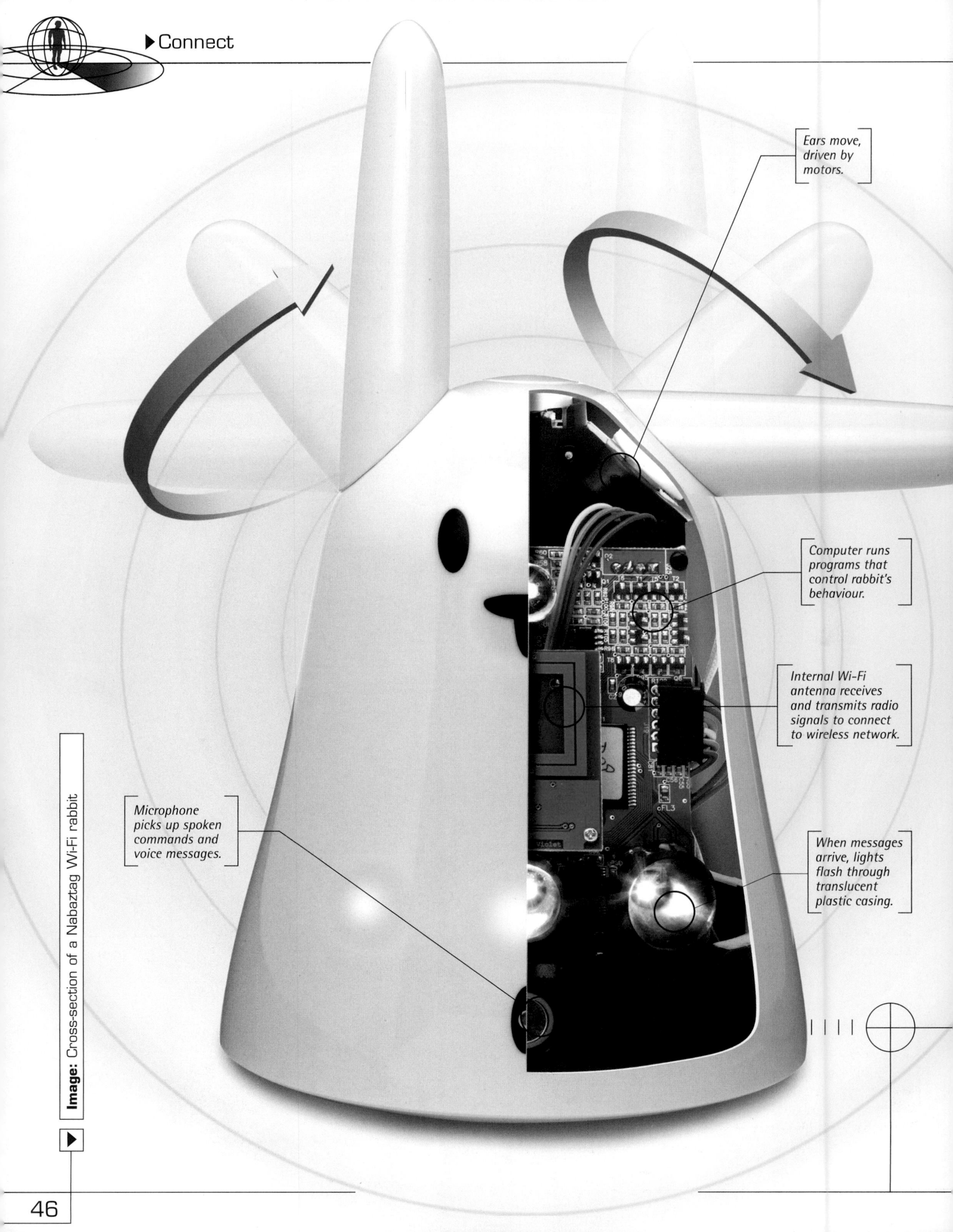

Ears move, driven by motors.
Computer runs programs that control rabbit's behaviour.
Internal Wi-Fi antenna receives and transmits radio signals to connect to wireless network.
When messages arrive, lights flash through translucent plastic casing.
Microphone picks up spoken commands and voice messages.

Image: Cross-section of a Nabaztag Wi-Fi rabbit

▶▶ See also: Mouse p44, E-book p48, Bluetooth® p50, Spy p214

WI-FI TOY

▶▶ The Nabaztag robot rabbit waggles its ears if a new email arrives from a friend, then reads out the latest news. Using radio signals it can connect to any nearby wireless (Wi-Fi) network linked to the Internet. It is controlled by a central computer that its owner can access via the manufacturer's website. ▶▶

>> HOW THE WI-FI TOY COMMUNICATES

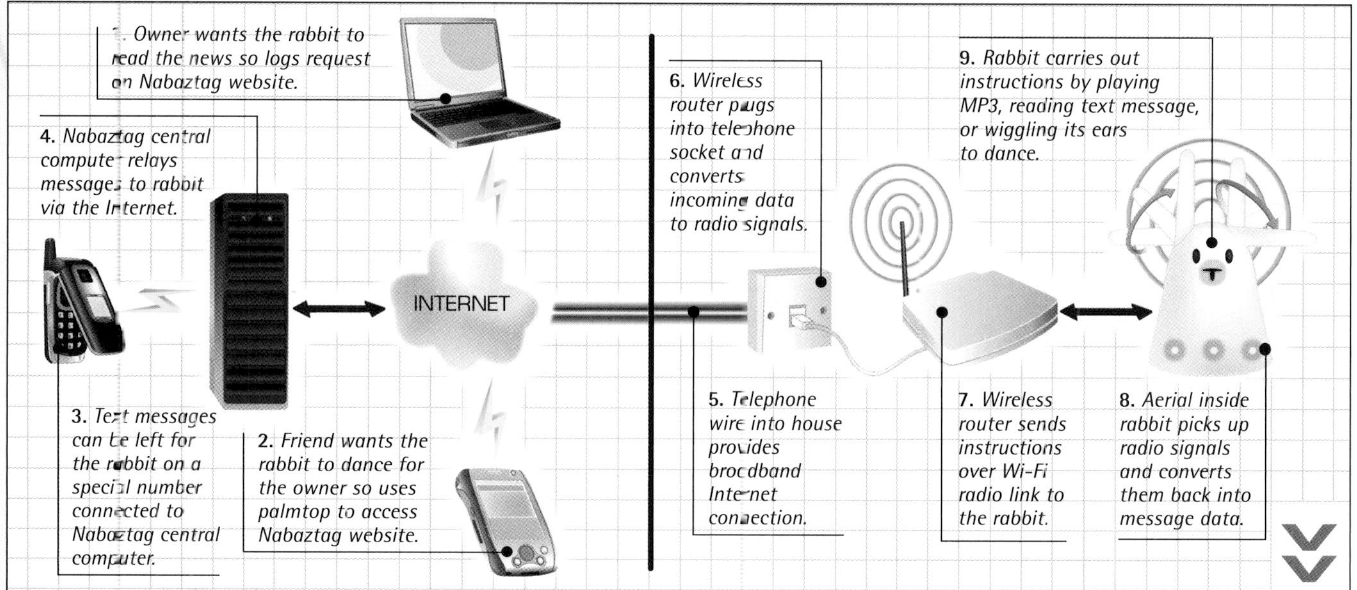

1. Owner wants the rabbit to read the news so logs request on Nabaztag website.
4. Nabaztag central computer relays messages to rabbit via the Internet.
INTERNET
3. Text messages can be left for the rabbit on a special number connected to Nabaztag central computer.
2. Friend wants the rabbit to dance for the owner so uses palmtop to access Nabaztag website.
6. Wireless router plugs into telephone socket and converts incoming data to radio signals.
9. Rabbit carries out instructions by playing MP3, reading text message, or wiggling its ears to dance.
5. Telephone wire into house provides broadband Internet connection.
7. Wireless router sends instructions over Wi-Fi radio link to the rabbit.
8. Aerial inside rabbit picks up radio signals and converts them back into message data.

All messages for the rabbit must first go to the Nabaztag central control computer at the manufacturer's offices. The owner and friends can communicate with the rabbit by contacting this central computer. This can be done over the Internet from a laptop or palmtop by typing the message into the rabbit manufacturer's website, or by mobile phone using a special number linked directly to the central computer. The computer works out what data is being requested – maybe an MP3 file of the news being read or an ear-waggling program – and then sends it over the Internet to the rabbit.

◀ Inside the Nabaztag rabbit is a computer to process the data it receives plus electronics to connect to Wi-Fi, play sounds, and control the lights and motorized ears.

Apple TV

▶ Apple TV is a box that plugs into a television and connects wirelessly to a home computer. This means that the television can be used to watch films and programmes that are stored on the computer's hard drive.

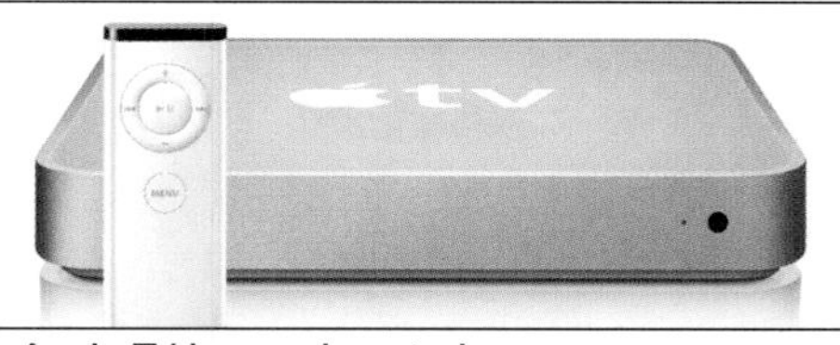

Apple TV box and control

▲ **Image:** Readius® e-book

E-BOOK

▶▶You can carry thousands of music tracks on an MP3 player – so why shouldn't you do the same with books? Convenient, easy-to-read e-books (electronic books) promise to put whole libraries in your pocket. ▶▶

High-contrast black-and-white display is readable even in bright sunlight.

▲ This Readius® e-book has a four gigabyte memory – enough to store 5,000 books the size of the Bible. It can also store emails and music, and receive Internet news updates using a system called RSS feeds.

>> HOW E-INK WORKS

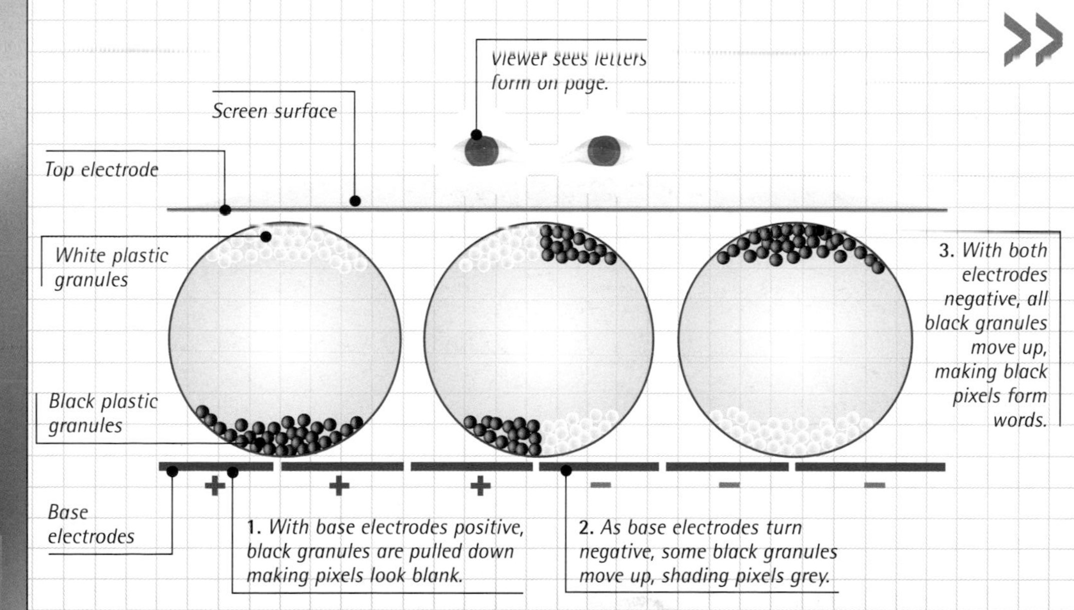
Viewer sees letters form on page.
Screen surface
Top electrode
White plastic granules
Black plastic granules
Base electrodes
1. With base electrodes positive, black granules are pulled down making pixels look blank.
2. As base electrodes turn negative, some black granules move up, shading pixels grey.
3. With both electrodes negative, all black granules move up, making black pixels form words.

Laptops, mobile phones, and calculators display words and pictures using millions of tiny dots called pixels. A typical LCD display uses only 35 pixels per cm (90 pixels per inch), one-sixth as many as a typical computer printer. That is why printed text is clearer and easier to read. An e-book display uses tiny plastic capsules the width of a human hair to make a sharp display with about 60–80 pixels per cm (150–200 pixels per inch). Each capsule contains black and white granules. The granules move to the top or the bottom of the capsules, under precise electrical control, to form letters, words, and pictures on the flexible screen. Displays like this are not just sharper than computer screens, they are easier to read in bright sunlight and use less battery power.

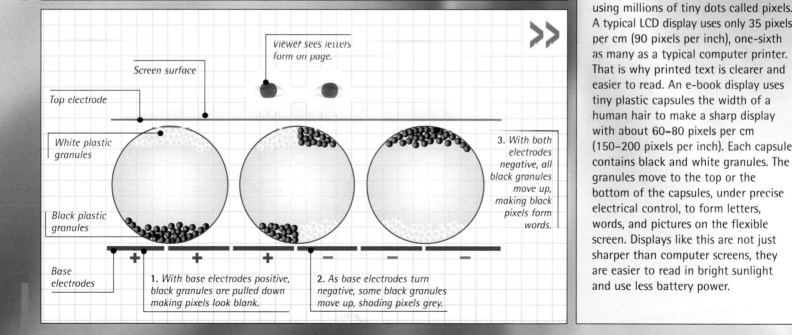

▶▶ See also: Wi-Fi toy p46, Convergence p56, Games console p68

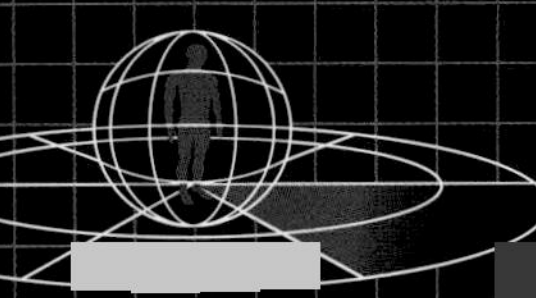

BLUETOOTH

Bluetooth® is dramatically changing the way that machines exchange information. It is a short-range wireless connection that can securely link electronic equipment – and it's gradually replacing the use of wires to connect gadgets such as printers, headphones, and video-game consoles. Bluetooth creates an intelligent radio link that changes frequency 1,600 times a second to avoid radio interference problems.

Microrobots
Bluetooth gadgets – such as these thumb-sized microrobots – can be very small. Unlike many other radio control systems, Bluetooth connects devices using a digitally coded link. This means that several connections can share one frequency without problems.

Microcopter
This tiny helicopter, weighing about 12 g (0.4 oz), uses Bluetooth to receive its instructions and transmit aerial photographs back to base. Bluetooth normally has a maximum range of about 10 m (33 ft), but longer range connections can be made with higher power transmitters.

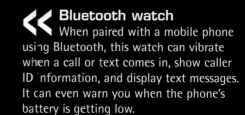

Bluetooth watch

When paired with a mobile phone using Bluetooth, this watch can vibrate when a call or text comes in, show caller ID information, and display text messages. It can even warn you when the phone's battery is getting low.

Glasses phone

These glasses have a built-in Bluetooth hands-free kit for mobile phones. A tiny speaker fits the ear and a microphone picks up speech. A single touch on the glasses answers a call – and the kit can be hidden under hair or a hat.

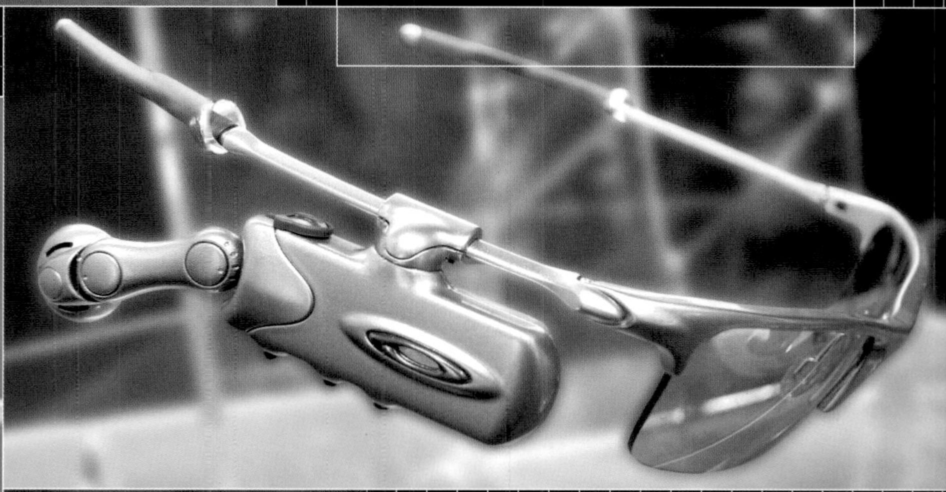

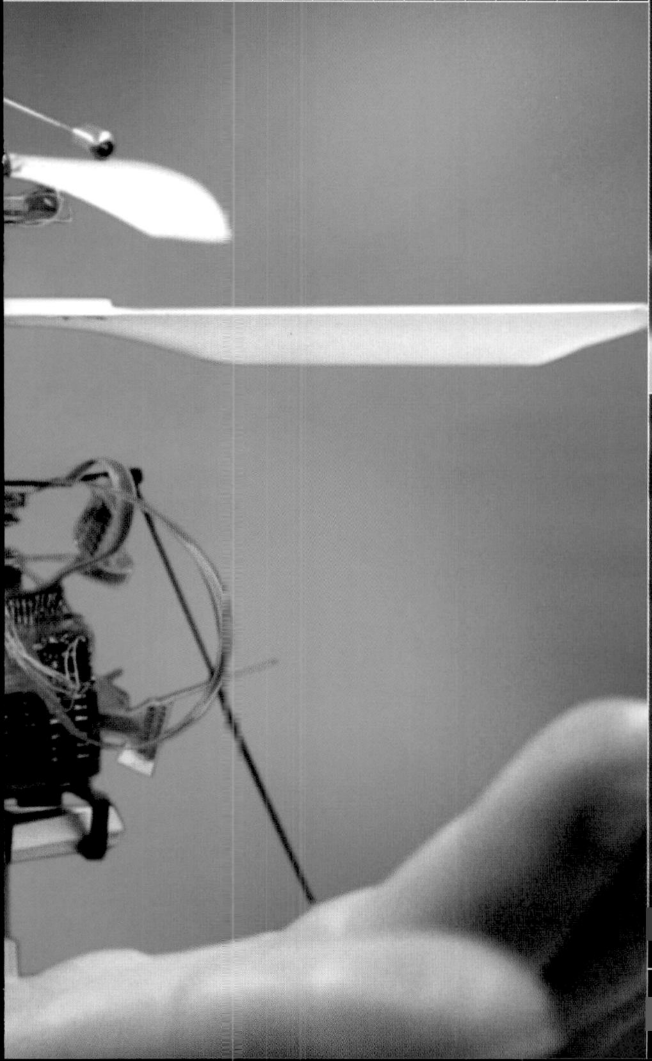

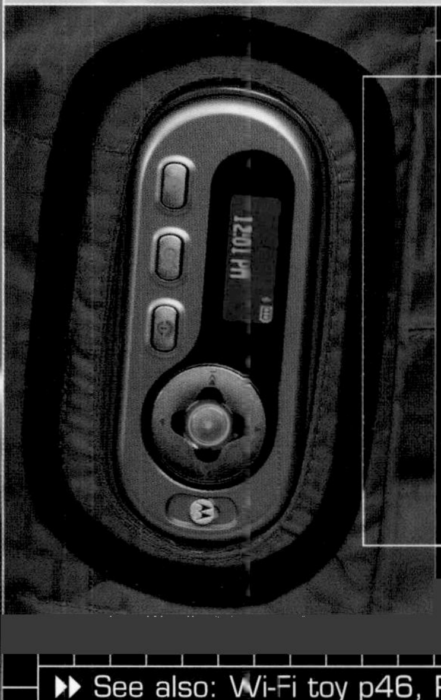

Skiing MP3 player

This Bluetooth controller sits within a ski jacket sleeve, and is connected to speakers built into the hood with a microphone in the collar. It connects wirelessly to a phone and MP3 player, and allows hands-free calling as well as non-stop music as the wearer skis down the slopes.

▶▶ See also: Wi-Fi toy p46, Petcam p52, Robots p90

PETCAM

▶▶ Conscientious pet owners can check up on their pets when they are away from home, and feed them with just a click of a mouse. The iSeePet™ is a special feeder unit rigged with a camera and connected to the Internet. ▶▶

▼ The iSeePet feeder allows pet owners to contact their pampered pooches. Via a web link they can instruct the feeder to ring for their pets' attention. They can then view their animals using the webcam.

Unit is connected to the Internet to relay webcam pictures and receive commands.

Camera eye allows owner to see pet via the Internet.

Image: The iSeePet™ pet communication system

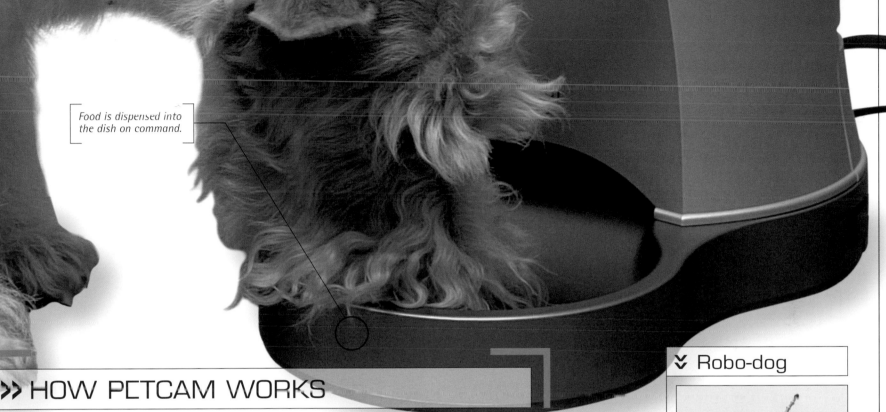

Food is dispensed into the dish on command.

» HOW PETCAM WORKS

« When a pet owner logs onto the petcam website, a live video from the camera eye in the feeder unit is shown. The feeder can be instructed via the website to sound an electronic noise to summon the pet to the feeder unit. The pet owner can then instruct the feeder to drop a portion of food into the bowl. They can even adjust the amount. It is also possible for more than one person to check on the same pet at the same time from different computers.

» Robo-dog

Aibo robot dog at play

▲ If feeding and exercising a real pet seems like too much effort, then a robot dog may be the answer. The Aibo™ is not as warm and soft as the real thing, but it can be programmed to behave just like a real dog.

▶▶ See also: Wi-Fi toy p46, Convergence p56, E-voting p58, Spy p214

HEAD UP

▶▶ Extra care needs to be taken when driving at night and it is important that drivers keep their eyes on the road. With a head-up display (HUD) glowing data appears superimposed on the windscreen, so the driver does not need to look down at instrument displays on the dashboard. ▶▶

>> HOW A HEAD UP DISPLAY WORKS

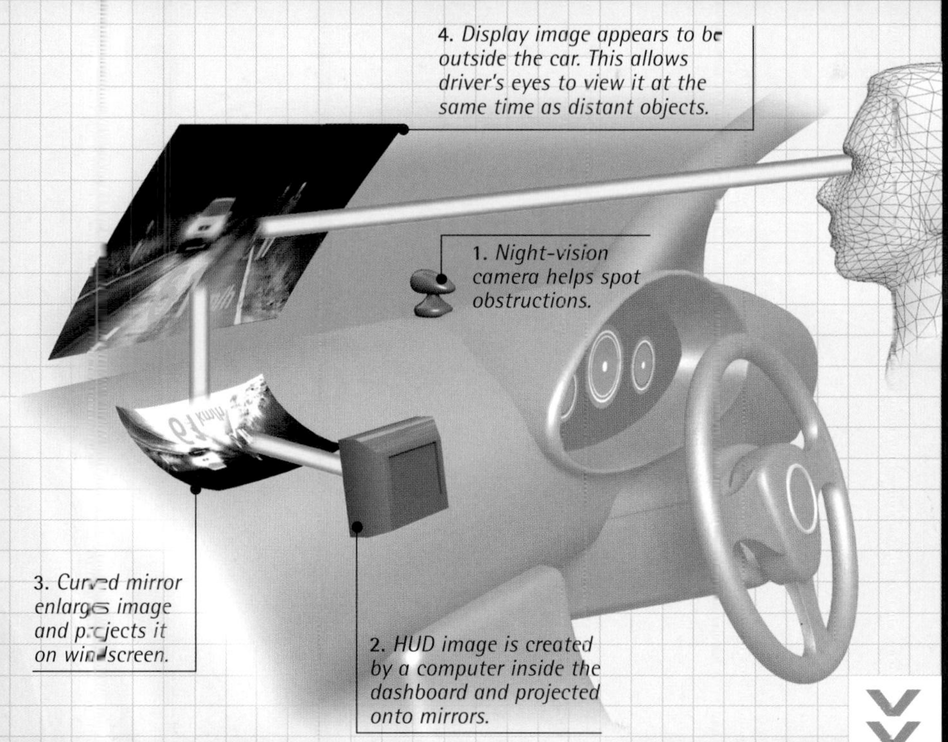

4. Display image appears to be outside the car. This allows driver's eyes to view it at the same time as distant objects.
1. Night-vision camera helps spot obstructions.
3. Curved mirror enlarges image and projects it on windscreen.
2. HUD image is created by a computer inside the dashboard and projected onto mirrors.

Head-up displays can be projected onto the vehicle windscreen or a special transparent screen mounted in front of it. A computer creates an image that is then projected via a series of lenses and mirrors onto the windscreen. Curved mirrors bend the light rays to create the illusion that the display is beyond the windscreen – this prevents users having to refocus their eyes, which is both tiring and distracting. In a night-vision system, a view looking ahead is picked up by an infrared camera and fed to the HUD.

▲ This car's HUD shows both current speed and a night-vision camera's view of the road. The driver can select what information appears in the HUD, tailoring it to different driving conditions.

Aircraft HUD

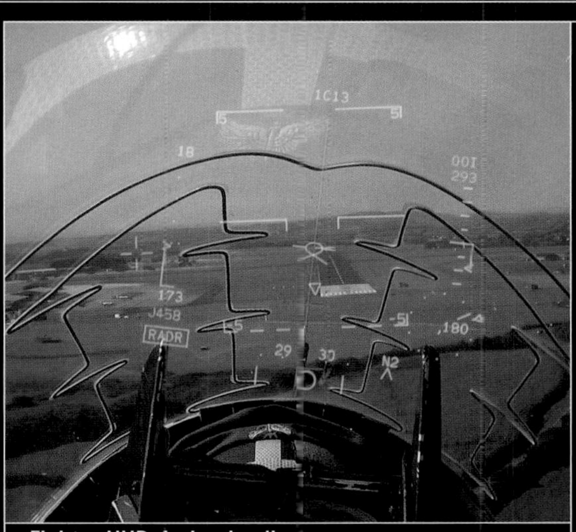
Fighter HUD during landing

◀ HUDs were first used by military pilots. Military jets fly fast and low, so any time the pilot spends checking instruments and not looking out of the cockpit could result in a crash. Many aeroplanes are now equipped with HUDs for use when landing in bad weather, such as fog. In the near future, there could be HUDs in eyeglasses projecting maps, reminders, and shopping lists.

▸▸ See also: Robot car p104, Silent flight p126, Binoculars p158

CONVERGENCE

Convergence is all about combining useful technologies into one package. Most mobile phones can take photographs and store and play music as well as make phone calls. Games consoles can also play CDs and DVDs. There are some real surprises in familiar-looking packages.

Pussycat PC The head of this conceptual robot cat is a touch-screen computer. The robot pet is capable of looking for its owner and can play games and patrol its territory. It will seek out its owner when an email arrives. It even sprays air freshener from its bottom!

Mobile projector This prototype mobile phone incorporates a built-in projector. A laser inside the phone is deflected by tiny mirrors to draw a display on an adjacent flat surface. Using a special pen that is wirelessly linked to the phone, the user can interact with the virtual screen. The pen can be used like a conventional computer mouse or as a drawing tool.

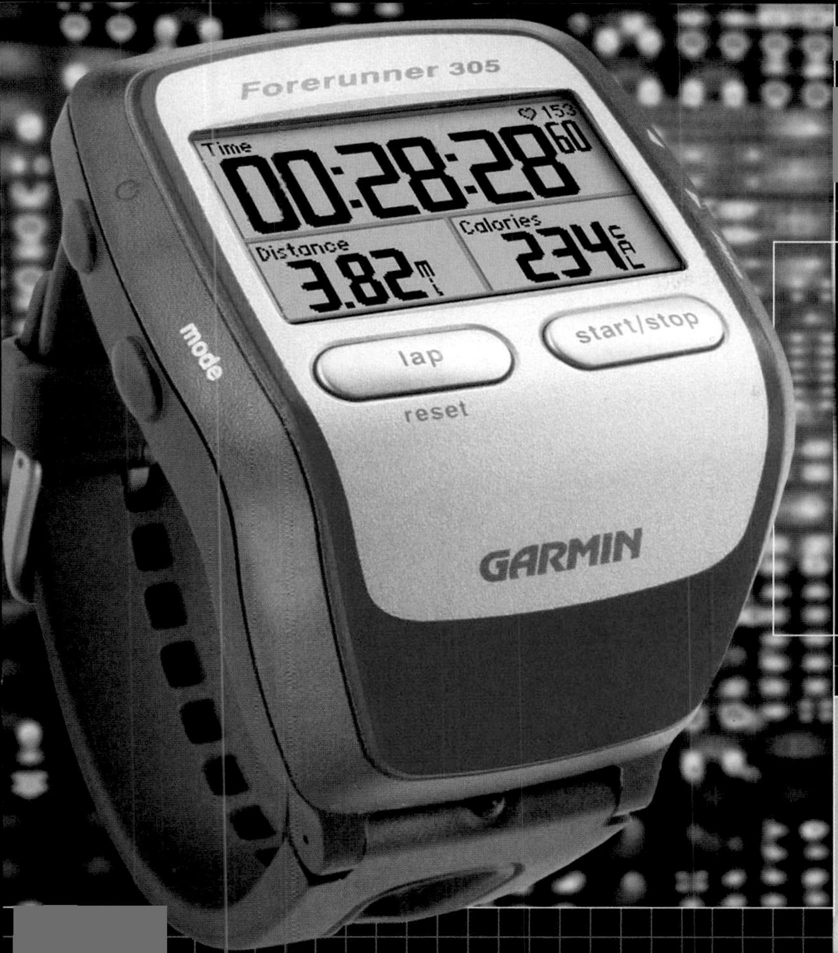

Personal trainer

This is not just a stopwatch, but a complete analysis of your fitness – a personal trainer on your wrist. Using built-in GPS (Global Positioning System), this watch knows where you are and how fast you are going. At the same time, it monitors your heart rate. All this information is stored and can be downloaded to your computer for analysis at the end of a training session.

Waterproof music

The SwiMP3 underwater MP3 player is built into swimming goggles to provide music as you swim. Normal headphones do not work if they get wet, so there are no earphones. Instead, the SwiMP3 transmits sound to the inner ear using vibrations passed through the cheekbones. Transducers (which convert electrical energy into sound energy) rest on each cheek.

Office in your pocket

No more typing on a tiny keypad or getting annoyed when predictive text picks the wrong word. This mobile camera phone and pocket PC has a slide-out keyboard and a large colour touch screen. It can be used to surf the web, check email, or edit documents – just about anything a desktop computer can do.

▸▸ See also: Wi-Fi toy p46, E-book p48, Bluetooth® p50

E-VOTING

▶▶ Democracy (in which people choose their government) is the bedrock of many societies, but it is impossible to ask everyone what they feel about everything that affects them. New electronic voting machines could give people more say in important issues. ▶▶

Screen shows several voting options.

Image: Electronic voting in the South Korean parliament

» HOW E-VOTING WORKS

Touch screen
People are voting electronically in many countries. This e-voting system in the United States uses a large touch screen. Its simple instructions mean voters do not need to know how to operate a computer.

Picture symbols
E-voting machines in India display picture symbols to help people who cannot read. More than 100,000 machines were used in a recent election by 650 million people.

Votes are cast by pressing buttons on the side of the screen.

◀ This politician in the Seoul parliament, South Korea, is passing new laws using a computerized console. Instead of time-consuming ballot papers or queuing in person, politicians vote electronically and the results are counted instantly by a central computer.

▶▶ See also: Laptop for all p42, E-book p48, Biometric ID p210

SUPERCOMPUTER

▶▶Humming with vast electronic brainpower, supercomputers help us understand atoms, predict global warming, and cure disease. The world's biggest supercomputer contains as many processor chips as 131,000 laptops. ▶▶

>> HOW A SUPERCOMPUTER WORKS

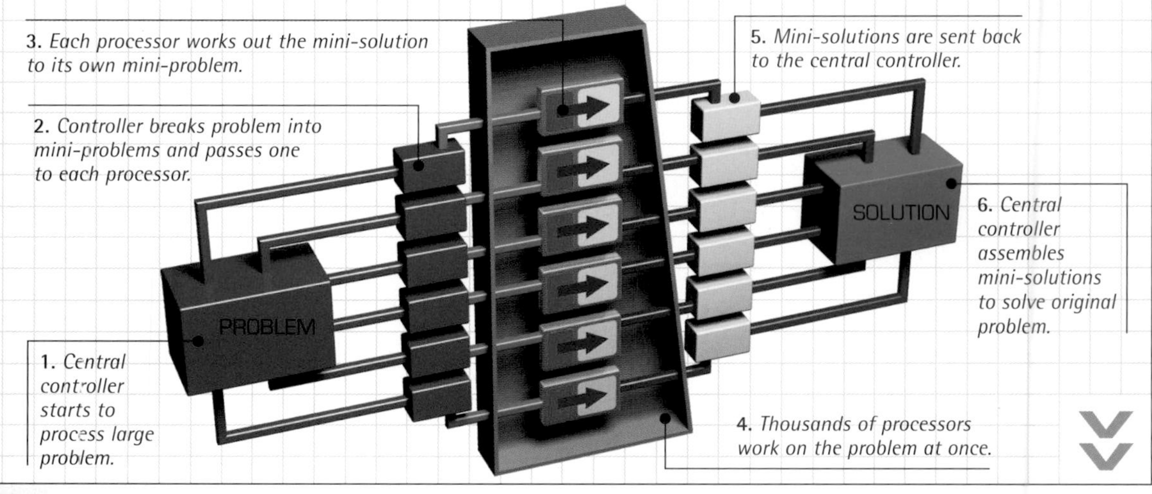

3. *Each processor works out the mini-solution to its own mini-problem.*
2. *Controller breaks problem into mini-problems and passes one to each processor.*
1. *Central controller starts to process large problem.*
PROBLEM
5. *Mini-solutions are sent back to the central controller.*
SOLUTION
6. *Central controller assembles mini-solutions to solve original problem.*
4. *Thousands of processors work on the problem at once.*

An ordinary computer has one processor (main microchip). It breaks a problem into pieces and processes them one at a time using instructions called a program. Later steps cannot be completed until earlier ones have finished. This way of problem-solving is called serial processing.

A supercomputer has thousands of processors, coordinated by a central controller. This breaks a problem into chunks and passes one chunk to each processor. The problem is solved quickly because the processors tackle many parts of it at once. This is called massively parallel processing.

▶▶ See also: Laptop for all p42, SETI@Home p62

▲ The world's most powerful supercomputer, BlueGene/L, at the Lawrence Livermore National Laboratory in California, USA, is used for atomic research. Its 64 separate cabinets have unusual slanted fronts to allow air to circulate through them. This stops the machine from overheating when it works at speeds up to two million times faster than a desktop PC.

Processing power

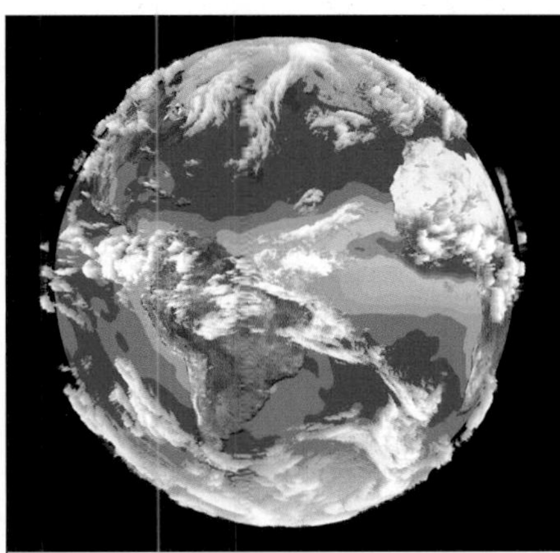

Computer model of Earth's climate

◀ Scientists study problems like climate change using computer models. A computer model is simply a collection of mathematical equations. By trying different numbers in the equations, scientists can predict how climate change will develop in future. Although this problem is complex, massively powerful supercomputers can predict what Earth's climate will be like 1,000 years from now.

▶ Each BlueGene cabinet contains 2,048 processors that work in pairs. The processors are mounted on large circuit boards called cards, which slot together into massive racks. Each rack uses 27.5 kilowatts of power – about the same as ten electric toasters burning full-time.

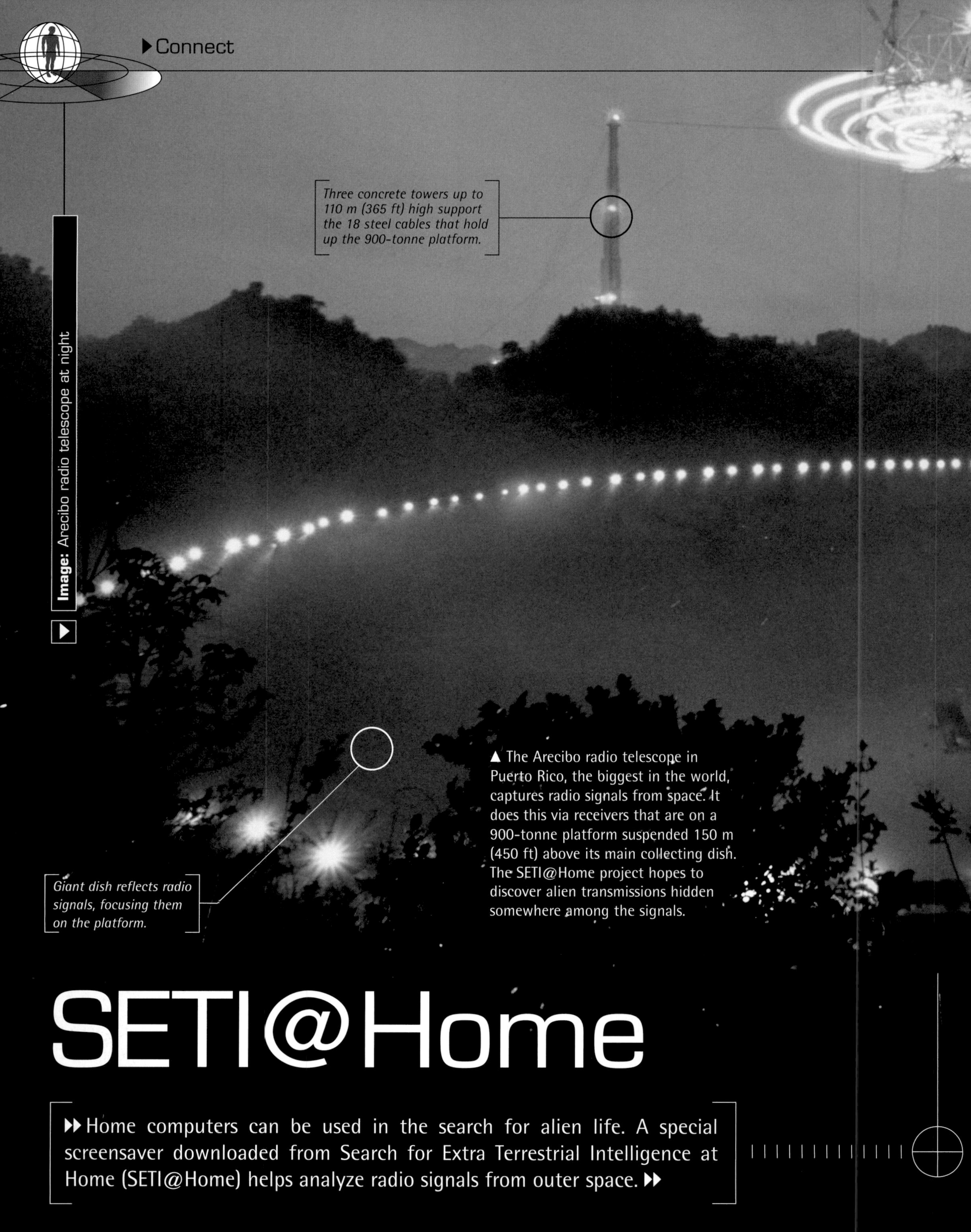

Image: Arecibo radio telescope at night
Three concrete towers up to 110 m (365 ft) high support the 18 steel cables that hold up the 900-tonne platform.
Giant dish reflects radio signals, focusing them on the platform.

▲ The Arecibo radio telescope in Puerto Rico, the biggest in the world, captures radio signals from space. It does this via receivers that are on a 900-tonne platform suspended 150 m (450 ft) above its main collecting dish. The SETI@Home project hopes to discover alien transmissions hidden somewhere among the signals.

SETI@Home

▶▶ Home computers can be used in the search for alien life. A special screensaver downloaded from Search for Extra Terrestrial Intelligence at Home (SETI@Home) helps analyze radio signals from outer space. ▶▶

Red lights warn low-flying aircraft of tower's presence.

Flatform for radio receiver and antennae. Moving the antennae slightly "points" the telescope at different parts of the sky.

World's largest dish

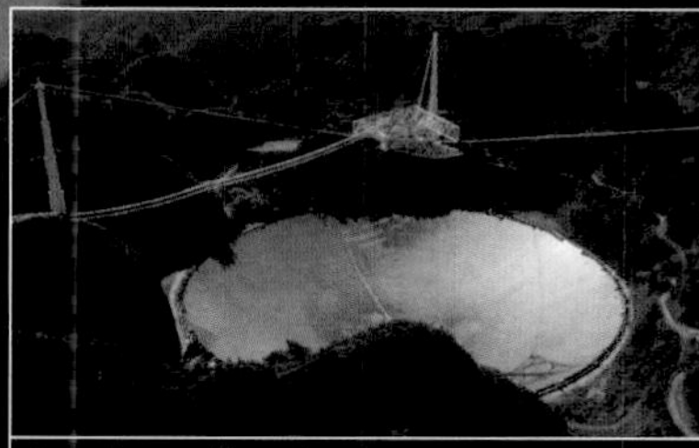
Arecibo radio telescope

◀ The Aceribo radio telescope's main reflector dish is 51 m (167 ft) deep and 305 m (1,000 ft) across – the equivalent of 10 football fields. It is constructed from nearly 39,000 aluminium panels supported by a network of cables.

Lights mark the top of the dish.

HOW SETI@HOME WORKS

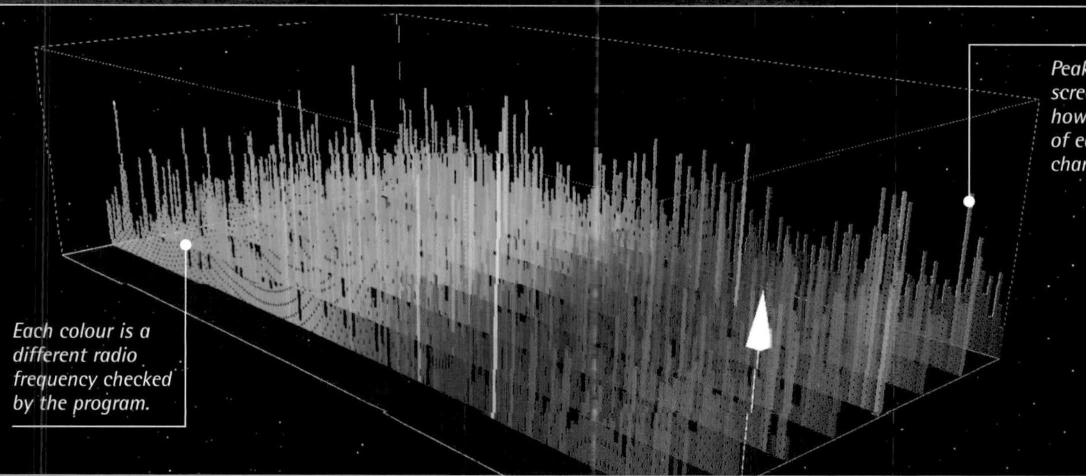
Peaks in the screensaver show how the signal of each frequency changes over time.

Each colour is a different radio frequency checked by the program.

The SETI@Home screensaver runs on your computer when it is not in use. The signals received by the Arecibo dish are split into chunks and sent to SETI@Home members. More than a million computers worldwide are running the screensaver. The program separates out all the frequencies contained in the signal (like listening to lots of radio stations at once) and then looks at how they change over time. An alien signal could be a single large peak, or a string of short blips, like Morse code. If such a signal is found, the program sends a message to SETI@Home headquarters so the data can be investigated more carefully. No alien messages have appeared yet.

▶▶ See also: Supercomputer p60, Space probes p144, Telescope p150

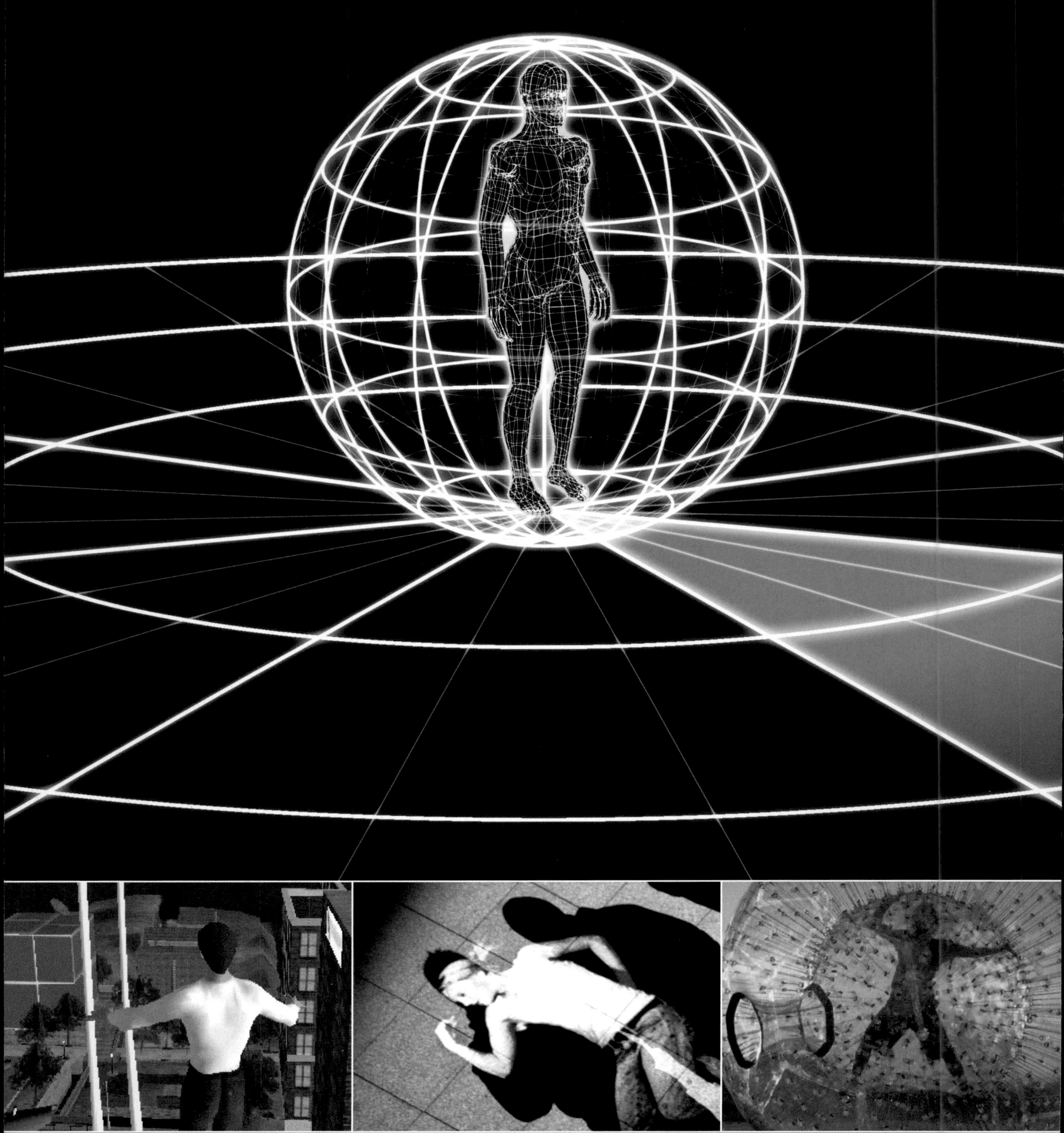

PLAY

Games console » Simulators » Second Life » Under Scan » Weird music » Roller coaster » X-sports » Flybar » Gekkomat » Bodyflight » Hawk-Eye » Robots » Lego Mindstorms » Cube World

▸▸ Technology has taken fun to a new level. Computers can immerse us in a virtual online world, and pocket-sized games consoles utilize the latest computer graphics. Machines help us move, jump, and climb in ways our ancestors could only dream of, and extreme sports and stomach-churning roller-coaster rides provide extra thrills. Even art has become an interactive adventure, with video projections that dance with the shadows of passers-by. ▸▸

What makes this robot happy? p90

Is this a tube or a tuba? p76

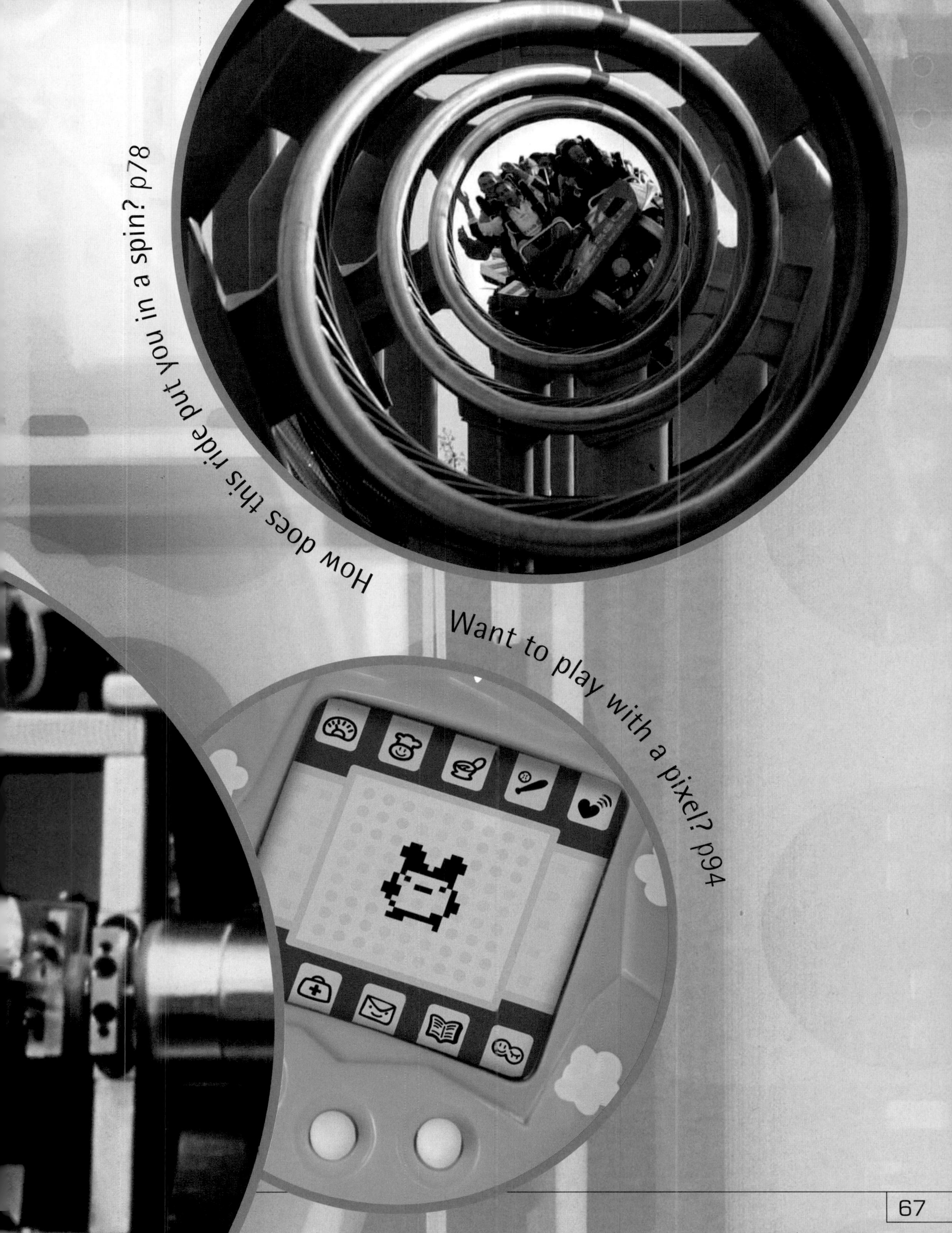

How does this ride put you in a spin? p78

Want to play with a pixel? p94

GAMES CONSOLE

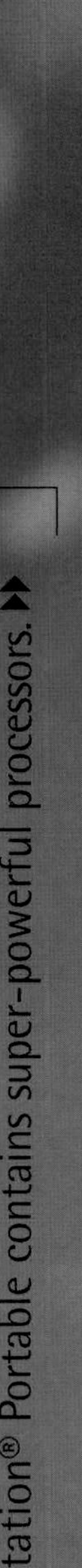

▸▸ The amount of computer power that can fit into a small box has increased dramatically over the last few decades. Games consoles in particular are now full of state-of-the-art technology – the pocket-sized PlayStation® Portable contains super-powerful processors. ▸▸

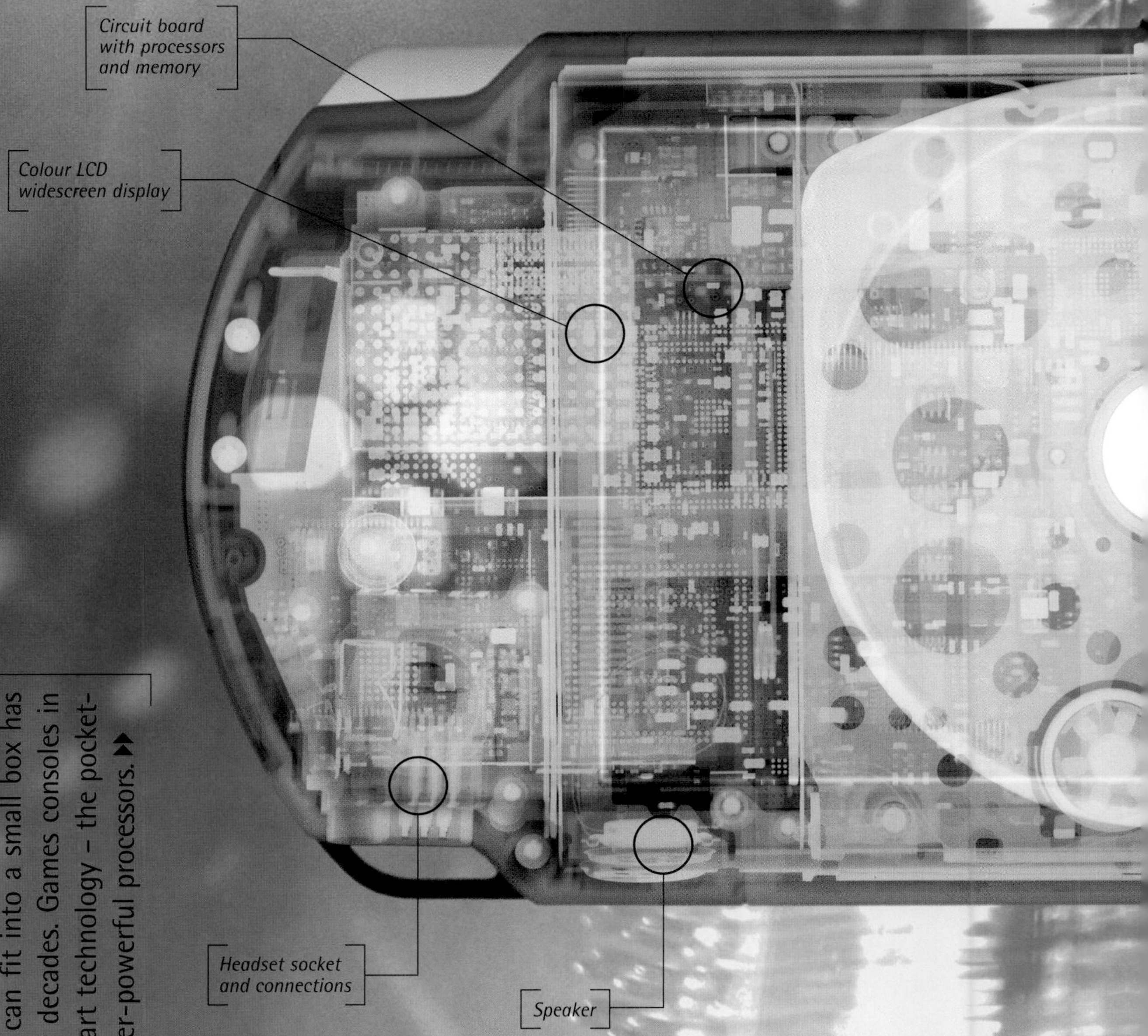

Circuit board with processors and memory

Colour LCD widescreen display

Headset socket and connections

Speaker

▲ In a single package, the PlayStation Portable (PSP) combines a powerful computer, an LCD display, an optical disk reader, and a Wi-Fi connection that links it to the Internet or other PSP players nearby. Despite containing all these different features, the PSP is small enough to be carried in your pocket.

Games arcade

▸ Games arcades, such as this one in Osaka, Japan, are often open 24 hours a day, appealing to the most dedicated players. In Korea, around 17 million people (a third of the country's population) play computer games, many of them in Internet cafés called *baangs*.

Rows of computer games

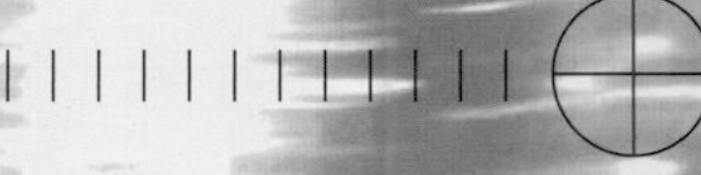

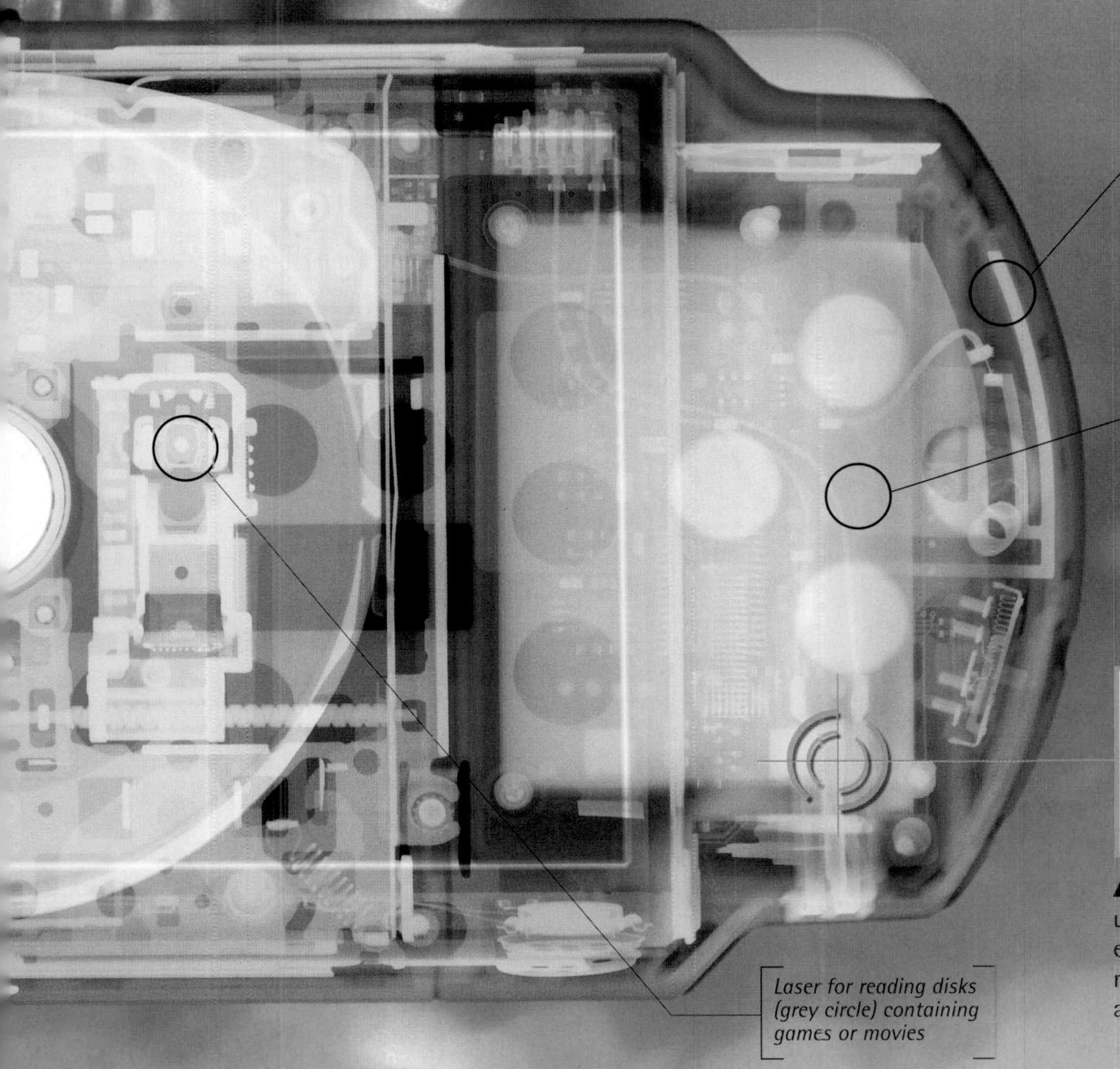

Image: X-ray image of a PlayStation® Portable

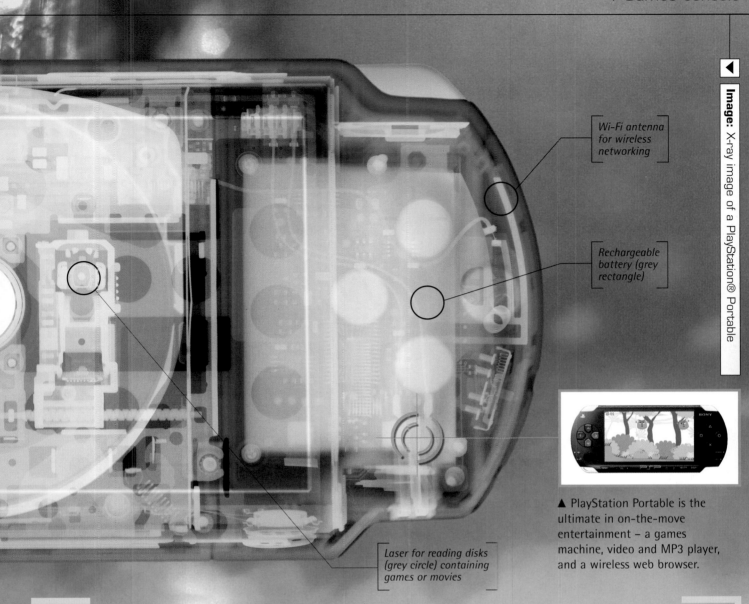

Wi-Fi antenna for wireless networking

Rechargeable battery (grey rectangle)

Laser for reading disks (grey circle) containing games or movies

▲ PlayStation Portable is the ultimate in on-the-move entertainment – a games machine, video and MP3 player, and a wireless web browser.

>> HOW CELL PROCESSORS WORK

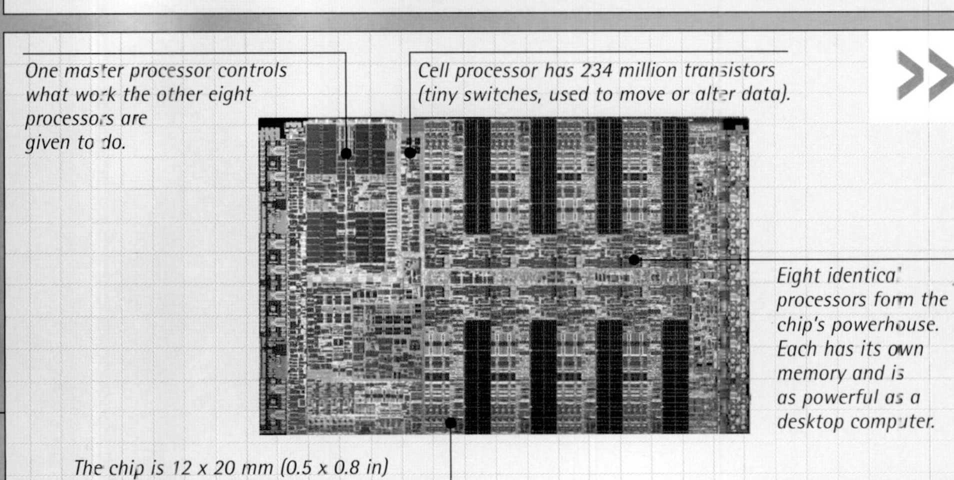

One master processor controls what work the other eight processors are given to do.
Cell processor has 234 million transistors (tiny switches, used to move or alter data).
Eight identical processors form the chip's powerhouse. Each has its own memory and is as powerful as a desktop computer.
The chip is 12 x 20 mm (0.5 x 0.8 in)

It takes artists several years to draw the scenes in an animated CGI (computer-generated imagery) movie such as *The Incredibles* or *Cars*, even with powerful computers. A games console has to draw similar scenes in "real time" (as you play), so it works like a tiny supercomputer. Nine processors, on one chip called a cell processor, share the work to carry out hundreds of billions of calculations every second.

▶▶ See also: Wi-Fi toy p46, E-book p48, Head up p54, Supercomputer p60

SIMULATORS

Virtual snowboarding The helmet's two eye-mounted screens give the impression of being on a snow-covered slope. The board has sensors that detect forces applied through the player's feet and motors to move the board in response to virtual bumps.

A simulator is a machine that copies an environment in the real world in order to train or entertain someone. Simulations are computer-controlled and if the computer creating a virtual world is fast enough and the graphics are good enough, the simulation can be very realistic.

▶▶ See also: HDTV p18, Bluetooth® p50, Head up p54, Games console p68

Flight simulator This cockpit is connected to a computer, not an aircraft. The computer recreates a real plane's responses to the pilot's control inputs, changing the instrument display and the simulated view out of the window. Modern simulators are so realistic that airline pilots use them to train for emergency procedures.

American football This trainee player is concentrating on a 3D American football virtual training game that is remotely controlled by a football coach. The trainee is inside a room-sized cube with 3D stereo viewing – special glasses are used to create the illusion of 3D. He is being trained to observe situations and will be able to react quickly when confronted with them in real life.

Body control The Nintendo Wii™ is a motion-sensitive game controller that enables the user to control game characters that respond to the player's body movements. The sensors in the controller cause different onscreen results as they sense and interpret the player's movements. In the future, the sensors could be attached to the body to allow full body control of games.

The Sims In this computer game you can follow – and control – the simulated lives of a group of people. The Sims™ interact with each other and their environment. You can instruct them to do things, but they may not obey.

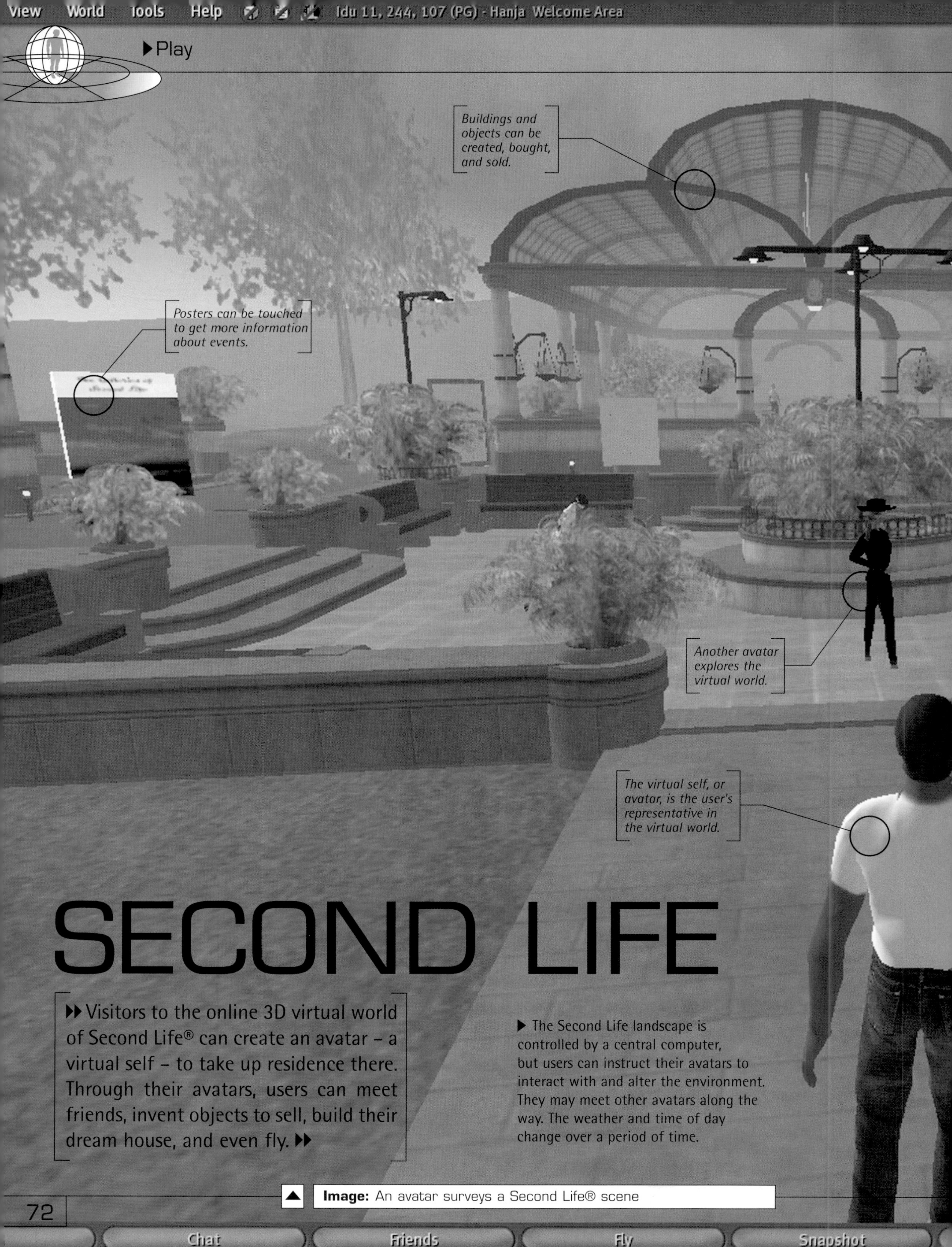
View World Tools Help Idu 11, 244, 107 (PG) - Hanja Welcome Area
Buildings and objects can be created, bought, and sold.
Posters can be touched to get more information about events.
Another avatar explores the virtual world.
The virtual self, or avatar, is the user's representative in the virtual world.
Chat
Friends
Fly
Snapshot

SECOND LIFE

▶▶ Visitors to the online 3D virtual world of Second Life® can create an avatar – a virtual self – to take up residence there. Through their avatars, users can meet friends, invent objects to sell, build their dream house, and even fly. ▶▶

▶ The Second Life landscape is controlled by a central computer, but users can instruct their avatars to interact with and alter the environment. They may meet other avatars along the way. The weather and time of day change over a period of time.

▲ **Image:** An avatar surveys a Second Life® scene

▶▶ See also: HDTV p18, Simulators p70, Hawk-Eye p88, Cube World p94

>> HOW SECOND LIFE WORKS

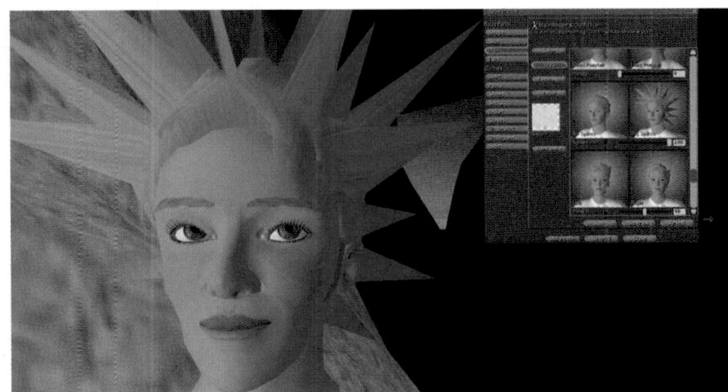

<< Each Second Life resident exists as an avatar – a virtual self. Avatars can be customized to look however the user wishes to appear within the virtual world. Every aspect of the avatar can be changed – looks, height, clothes, colour, and shape. It is even possible to become an animal! Users can also create all kinds of objects, including cars, ships, and aeroplanes. The virtual world has its own money, and real-world companies have set up shops in Second Life to sell virtual versions of their products to the residents.

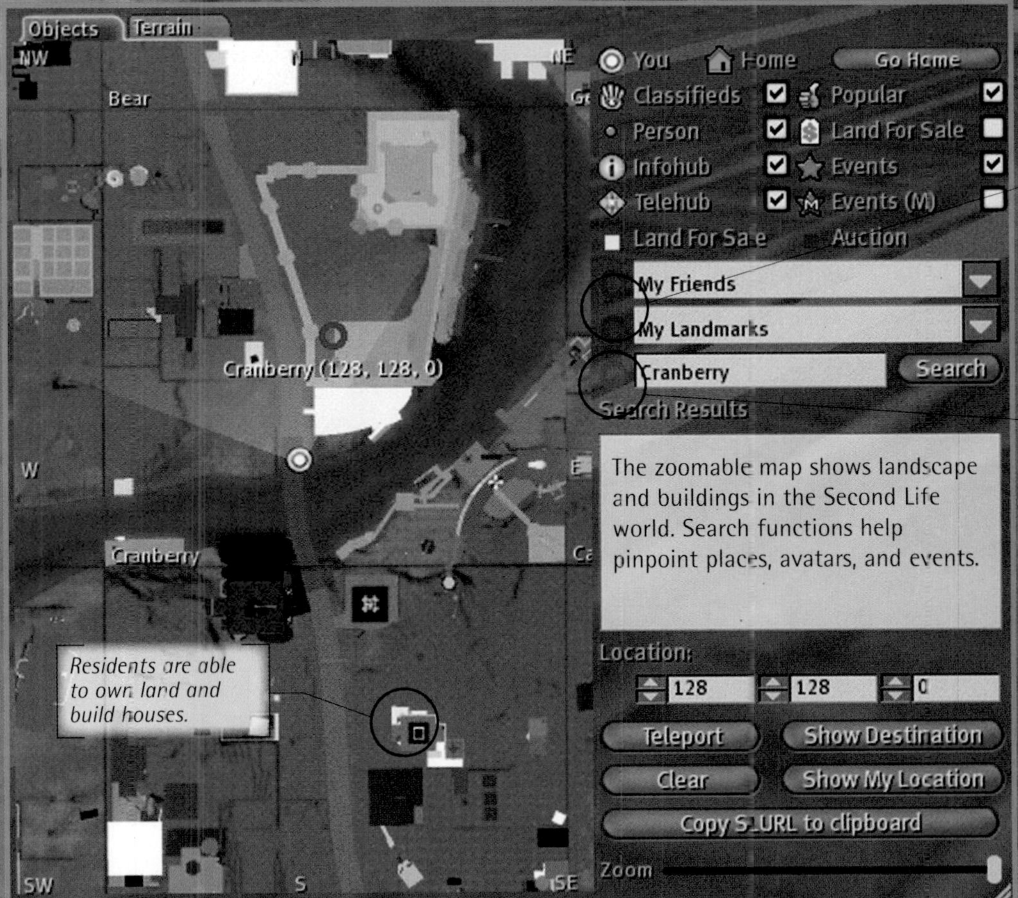

The zoomable map shows landscape and buildings in the Second Life world. Search functions help pinpoint places, avatars, and events.

Favourite locations and avatars can be bookmarked so they can be located easily later on.

Instant teleportation is available to anywhere in Second Life. The map shows we are in Cranberry.

Residents are able to own land and build houses.

UNDER SCAN

▶▶Artists try to make people look at familiar experiences in new ways. Modern video and computer technologies give them a new set of mind-bending tools. In the Under Scan art installation, shadows come to life. Other artists make ghostly dancers who invite us to follow. ▶▶

▼ Under Scan is an interactive artwork by artist Rafael Lozano-Hemmer. As people walk across a brightly lit public space at night figures appear within their shadows, reacting to the shadows' movements and apparently wanting to interact. In reality, the shadow people are just video clips.

▶▶ HOW UNDER SCAN WORKS

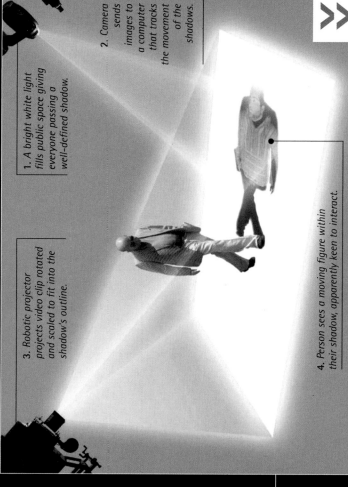

1. *A bright white light fills public space giving everyone passing a well-defined shadow.*

2. *Camera sends images to a computer that tracks the movement of the shadows.*

3. *Robotic projector projects video clip rotated and scaled to fit into the shadow's outline.*

4. *Person sees a moving figure within their shadow, apparently keen to interact.*

Light floods an area throwing crisp shadows. A camera feed enables a computer to track these shadows, determining their movements and passing this information to other computers in control of robotic projectors. Each projector turns and tilts to display a video clip of a moving figure inside a shadowed area. If the shadow is stationary, the computer uses a part of the video where the figure shows friendly behaviour, apparently interacting. When the shadow moves away, the computer switches seamlessly to a clip where the figure loses interest and looks away.

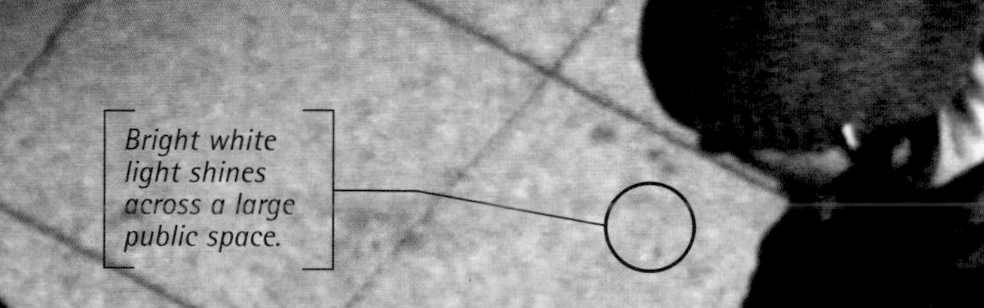

Bright white light shines across a large public space.

Image: Under Scan interactive art installation

A moving image of a person appears in the shadows.

People cast shadows as they stand or walk around.

» Flock ghost dance

Shadow dancers perform

◀ Another installation, Flock, turns a dark space into an impromtu ballet, with the audience as the dancers. An infrared (heat) camera detects where people are and illuminates them with their own spotlight containing a projected shadow –their own personal "ghost dancer". The dancers move as music plays, inviting people to follow them. The ghost dancers' paths are coordinated by a computer.

▶▶ See also: Petcam p52, Simulators p70, Cube World p94

WEIRD MUSIC

Überorgan
The Überorgan is so big that it is spread over several rooms when displayed in museums. Bus-size plastic balloons, each with a horn tuned to a different note in the octave, are controlled by computerized valves and blow compressed air through reeds to make the sounds. Optical sensors read music from a long scroll of dots and dashes. Timers and motion sensors mix up the notes to make each performance unique.

Backpack tubulum
The Blue Man Group created the extraordinary tubulum from plastic pipes, which are hit with sticks to make an echoing sound. The length of each pipe determines the note produced. This version even allows the player to launch rockets!

The words "musical instrument" are likely to conjure up conventional images of a guitar, piano, or trumpet. But just about anything can be used to make a sound. In this gallery, there is a selection of the strangest and most unusual musical instruments ever built.

See also: Recycling p24, Convergence p56, Under Scan p74, Laser p202

The Pikasso

This 42-stringed guitar weighs nearly 7 kg (15 lb). Its structure has to be super-strong because the enormous tension of the strings stresses it in all directions. It can be played acoustically or as an electric guitar, and some of the strings can also control sounds created by a synthesiser. It was specially designed for musician Pat Metheny and took two years to build.

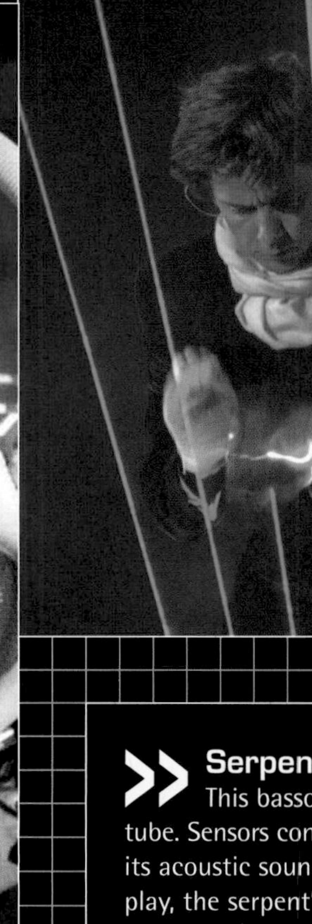

Laser harp

More of a keyboard than an instrument in its own right, beams of laser light projected in the air act as strings for different notes. The harp is played by breaking these beams with the hands. Light sensors detect which beams are broken and send this information to a synthesiser or computer, which in turn creates the sounds.

Serpentine bassoon

This bassoon is made from leather tube. Sensors connect it to a computer, mixing its acoustic sound with artificial sounds. To play, the serpent's tail must be disconnected and a bassoon mouthpiece attached.

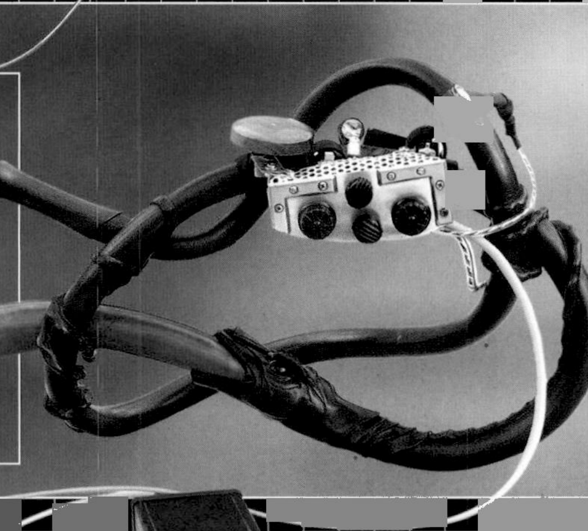

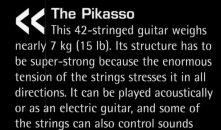

Car rolls down from start point under force of gravity.
Steel tubes are gripped by the car's wheels.
Image: Photograph of roller-coaster track

ROLLER COASTER

▶▶The computer design of roller coasters enables all the forces at work on the structure, cars, and riders to be calculated in advance. This means that every thrilling twist and turn of the track on a new roller coaster can be fully tested before a single piece of steel is bent into shape. ▶▶

▼ When roller-coaster cars set off, they travel down the track with enough momentum to climb to the high point of the first incline. Gravity's pull turns this height into speed, allowing the car to climb the next incline. Roller coasters trade energy between speed and height like this all the way around the track.

Series of reversing loops means the forces on riders change rapidly.

>> HOW A ROLLER COASTER PROVIDES THRILLS

Acceleration

Traditional roller coasters use only gravity to accelerate their cars, but this ride in New Jersey, USA, catapults the cars from the start using a detachable cable. Riders are launched from 0–206 km/h (128 mph) in 3.5 seconds – the same acceleration as a Formula 1 racing car. It is the fastest roller coaster in the world.

Turns and loops

Changes in direction create G-forces on the riders. On a tight turn the riders' momentum wants to carry them in a straight line, but the car is forcing them along a curved path and so they feel pressed down into their seats. On a sharp descent, rider and car fall together giving a feeling of weightlessness.

Psychology

Some roller coasters play on psychology to increase the thrill of the ride. Taking away the floor so legs dangle in the air makes riders feel more at risk of falling out and so makes the ride seem more dangerous. Roller coasters that turn upside down and have seats without reassuring shoulder bars also up the fear factor.

▶▶ See also: Formula 1 p100, Vomit comet p140, Ejector seat p220

X-SPORTS

Many extreme sports (x-sports) are only possible because of modern technology. Ingenious devices magnify our physical abilities using springs and levers. Special materials keep us safe in dangerous situations by absorbing energy without tearing or snapping. However, we still rely on our basic human fears of speed and height to give us that all important adrenaline rush.

Bungee jumping A bungee jumper falls with only a latex rubber rope (the bungee) connecting his ankles to a high bridge. At the end of the fall, the bungee becomes tight and begins to stretch like a giant elastic band. It absorbs the energy of the jump, slows the jumper to a momentary stop, then bounces him up and down a few more times.

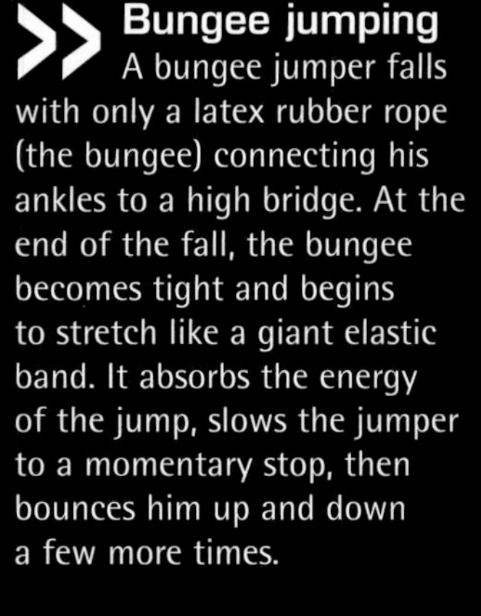

PowerBocks PowerBocks enable you to jump 3 m (10 ft) in the air and run at 30 km/h (20 mph). The technology is based on hopping kangaroos, who store jump energy in springy tendons as they land, releasing it again as they leap. PowerBocks let you do the same by storing energy in curved fibreglass springs.

Street luge

Gravity accelerates a type of large skateboard called a street luge and its rider downhill at speeds of up to 115 km/h (70 mph). The luge is steered by leaning sideways and has no brakes. Wind resistance that would slow the luge down is minimized by the aerodynamic riding position.

Zorbing

A Zorb® is a 3-m (10-ft) diameter inflatable sphere, constructed from tough PVC plastic, with a smaller sphere suspended inside by hundreds of nylon strands. Riders (Zorbonauts) are strapped inside for a downhill roll.

Kiteboarding

A large powerkite can easily lift a person into the air. The rider's feet are strapped to a landboard with wheels. Steering and speed are controlled by a combination of leaning and adjusting the angle between the kite and the wind.

See also: Roller coaster p78, Flybar® p82, Bodyflight p86

FLYBAR

This hi-tech pogo-stick certainly puts a spring in the step. As the giant elastic thrusters inside the Flybar® stretch and pull back into shape, the bounce produced is an amazing 1.5 m (5 ft), into the air.

A fusion of pogo stick, bungee jump, and trampoline, the Flybar was developed by the company behind the original pogo stick, with help from physicist Bruce Middleton and eight-times world skateboarding champion Andy Macdonald, who is shown here in action.

Handlebars covered with roughened grip tape for improved control.

Image: Andy Macdonald rides the Flybar®

Footpegs covered with grip tape.
Piston length can be increased up to 46 cm (18 in) for higher bounces.

HOW A FLYBAR WORKS

1. Tip of flybar hits the ground.
2. Force of gravity (rider's weight) pushes foot pegs down.
3. Twelve elastic thrusters (rubber rods) stretch downwards.
4. Thrusters stretch until elastic force is greater than rider's weight.
5. Thrusters pull foot pegs back up again.
6. Flybar and rider pogo up into the air.

The Flybar works like a giant elastic band, using the science of elasticity to bounce the rider into the air. When a rider jumps onto the footpegs, their weight stretches the 12 elastic thrusters. When elastic things stretch, long tangled molecules inside straighten and pull apart. The energy used in stretching the elastic is stored inside the elastic as potential energy. The forces between molecules grow as the elastic stretches. When these forces are bigger than the weight of the rider, the potential energy stored in the elastic is converted into kinetic (movement) energy as the rider springs upwards.

The original pogo stick, shown above, used a strong metal spring where the Flybar uses rubber thrusters.

▶▶ See also: Simulators p70, X-sports p80, Gekkomat p84

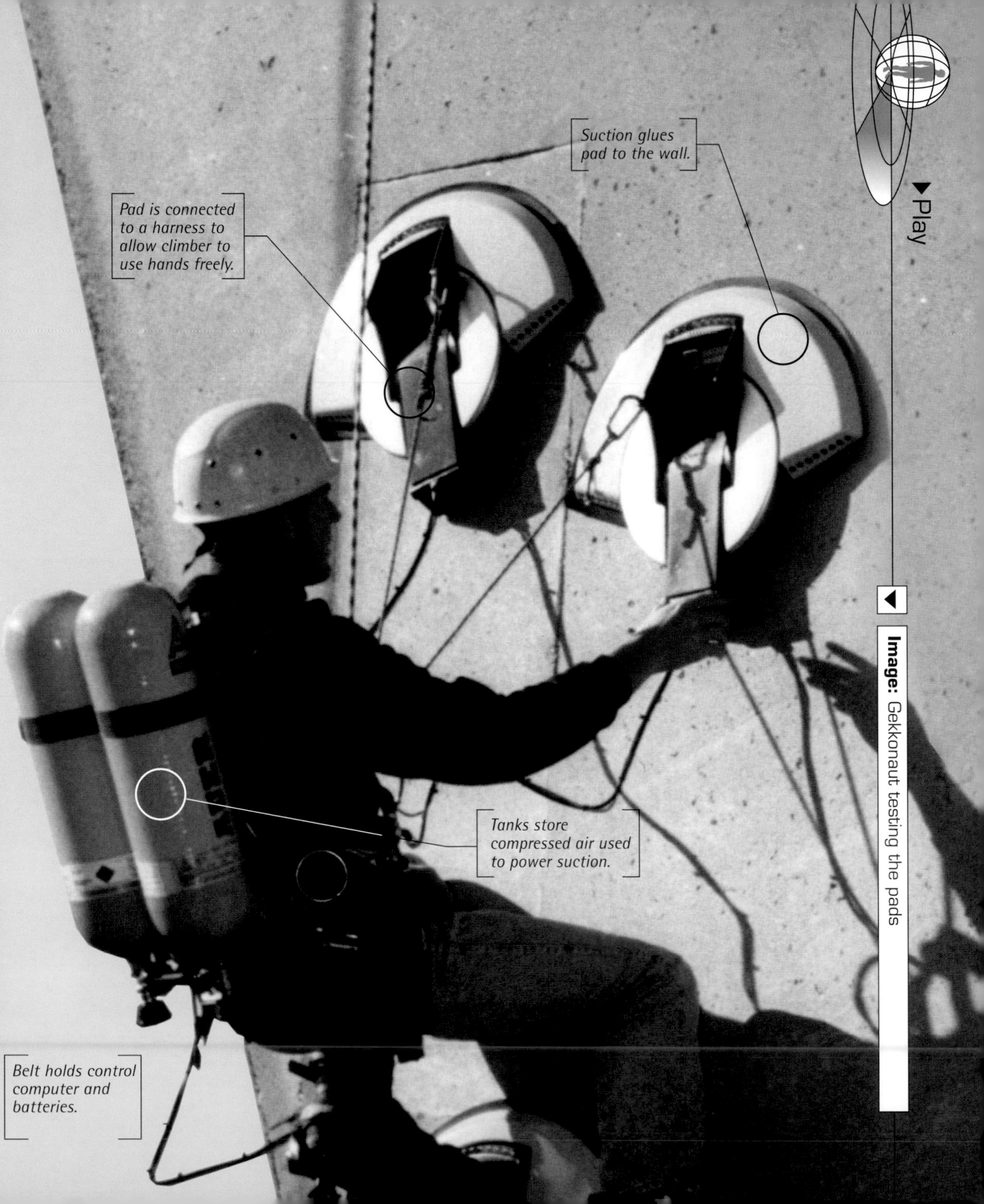

Image: Gekkonaut testing the pads

Pad is connected to a harness to allow climber to use hands freely.

Suction glues pad to the wall.

Tanks store compressed air used to power suction.

Belt holds control computer and batteries.

» Gekko "glue" magic

▶ **1.** Geckos can climb almost any surface. Their feet do not produce suction or make sticky goo – in fact their feet are dry. So how do they do it? The secret lies in the millions of microscopic hairs found on their feet called setae, each of which is split into fine branches.

Green gecko on a tree

Underside of a gecko's foot

◀ **2.** On average, a gecko has 6.5 million setae on the soles of its feet. These setae help to "glue" the lizard to virtually any surface – smooth, rough, dry, or even wet. The glueing strength of all these setae combined is enough to hold the weight of two adult men. Scientists have now made artificial gecko hairs that stick strongly to surfaces.

▶ **3.** At the end of each seta are tiny structures called spatulae. These attract the molecules of the surface that the gecko is climbing by using electrostatic attractions called Van der Waals forces. No chemical reaction takes place. It is simply that, on a minute scale, molecules are pulled towards each other.

Setae under a microscope

▶▶ See also: Simulators p70, Bodyflight p86, Robots p90

GEKKOMAT

▶▶ The Gekkomat allows the intrepid to follow in the footsteps of Spiderman. Suction pads enable the user to climb vertical surfaces such as walls. It is named after the gecko, an insect-eating lizard that not only walks vertically on smooth surfaces, but can also walk across ceilings. ▶▶

▶ The Gekkomat is a self-contained climbing system. The climber has four suction pads that can be attached to the wall – one for each hand and foot. By placing each pad higher on the wall in turn, the "Gekkonaut" can slowly climb up. Any surface on which the pads can get a good enough seal to form a vacuum – including concrete, stone, plaster, wood, glass, and metal – can be scaled.

▶▶ HOW THE GEKKOMAT WORKS

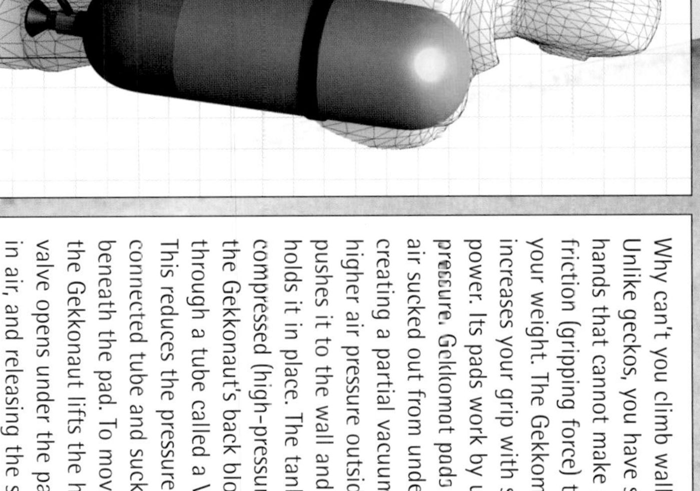

Soft rim to help achieve an airtight seal on the wall.

Exhaust holes to allow air under pad to break suction.

Gekkonaut pulls up on handle to tell computer which pad to release.

Computer controls valves inside pad to switch suction on and off.

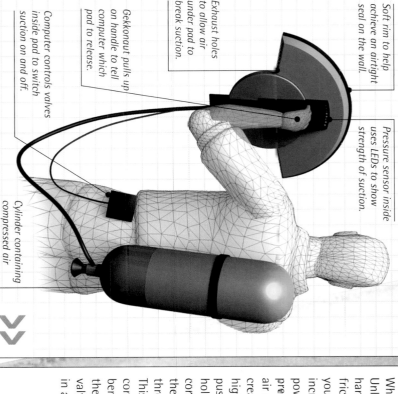

Pressure sensor inside uses LEDs to show strength of suction.

Cylinder containing compressed air

Why can't you climb walls? Unlike geckos, you have smooth hands that cannot make enough friction (gripping force) to hold your weight. The Gekkomat increases your grip with suction power. Its pads work by using air pressure. Gekkomat pads have the air sucked out from underneath, creating a partial vacuum. The higher air pressure outside the cup pushes it to the wall and friction holds it in place. The tank of compressed (high-pressure) air on the Gekkonaut's back blows air through a tube called a Venturi. This reduces the pressure in a connected tube and sucks air from beneath the pad. To move a pad, the Gekkonaut lifts the handle. A valve opens under the pad, letting in air, and releasing the suction.

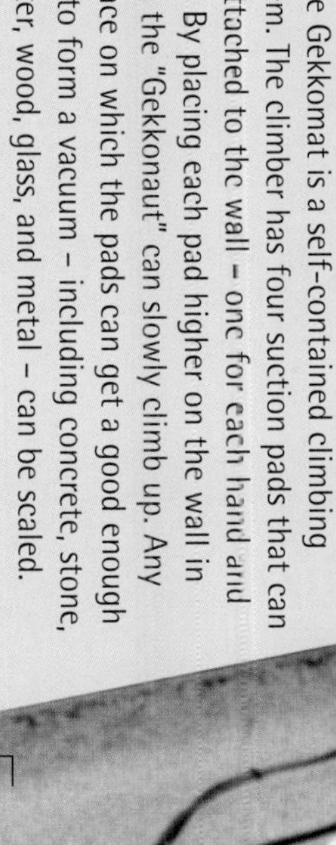

Each pad can hold up to 250 kg (550 lb) in weight.

BODYFLIGHT

▶▶ Bodyflying in a vertical wind tunnel enables the brave to get an experience of skydiving and practise moves in a controlled environment. Air rushes upwards at 190 km/h (120 mph), exactly the speed at which a person freefalls. ▶▶

Bodyfliers float suspended in the fast, upwards moving airflow.

Windows allow spectators to watch the action at close range.

Mesh floor allows air through, while protecting fliers if they drop.

▲ Bodyfliers can practise tricky manoeuvres in the flight chamber of the vertical wind tunnel. Changing body position alters the drag forces (see below) on a flier, moving them around in the air. Vanes at the bottom of the wind tunnel help to reduce turbulence in the airflow so that fliers get a smooth ride.

Image: Bodyfliers in a vertical wind tunnel

HOW BODYFLIGHT WORKS

Powerful electric motor drives fan.

3. Large fan drives air circulation around wind tunnel.

Mesh prevents fliers coming into contact with fan.

Flight chamber is padded to prevent injury if fliers crash into it.

2. Air speeds up through narrow flight chamber due to Venturi effect.

4. Air circulates around outer section of wind tunnel.

1. Smooth-shaped channel for air reduces turbulence.

TYPICAL VERTICAL WIND TUNNEL

Bodyflying is all about drag. Drag is the force that resists the movement of a solid object through the air. So, when you fall, still air slows your fall. Fast-moving air, however, tries to pull you along with it. In a vertical wind tunnel, drag force is used to balance your weight, so you neither fall nor rise. A large fan pushes air past you fast enough to hold you up, and the airspeed is controlled to prevent fliers either shooting up or falling down. Fliers move around by increasing or decreasing the drag of their bodies, using their arms and legs as rudders. The flying area (flight chamber) is the narrowest part of the wind tunnel. Air flowing through a tube speeds up as it narrows – this is called the Venturi effect.

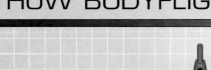

There are two main types of vertical wind tunnels. The fan can be above you (see left) or below (as with these outdoor fliers above).

See also: Aerobatics p128, Vomit comet p140, Ejector seat p220

Image: Flight path of a ball during a tennis game

HAWK-EYE

▶▶ Umpires and referees at sporting events sometimes get things wrong. In sports such as tennis and cricket, Hawk-Eye cameras are used to pinpoint the ball so a computer can work out its exact path and where it bounced. ▶▶

▲ In tennis, Hawk-Eye is used to determine whether a ball has landed in the correct part of the court. This is especially useful when the ball bounces on a line. Television viewers get 3D pictures of the ball's path and instant displays of game statistics.

HOW HAWK-EYE WORKS

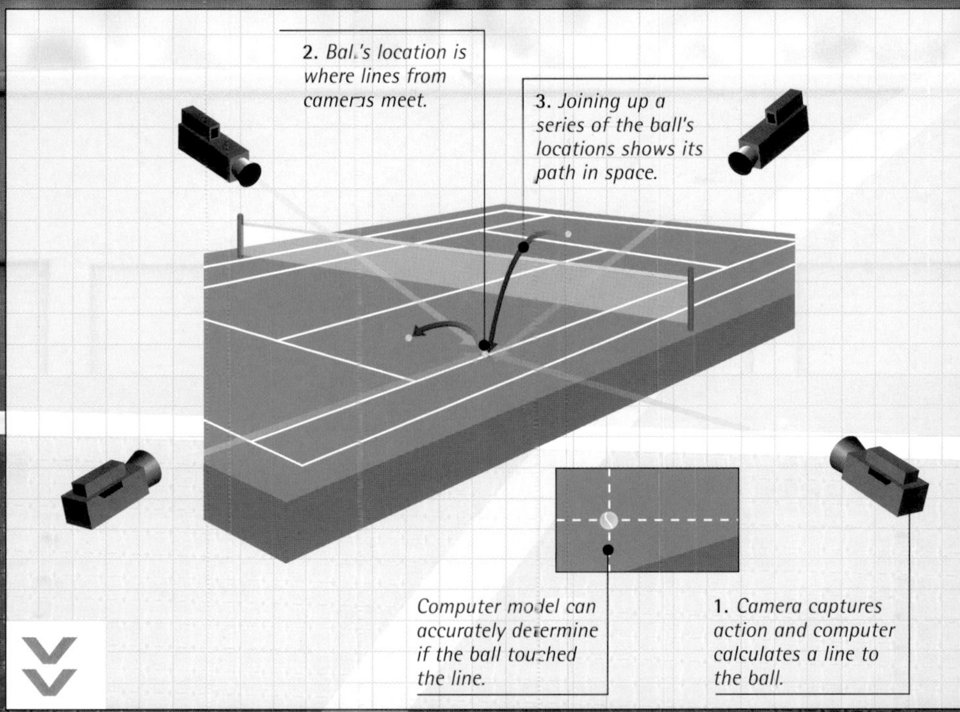

2. Ball's location is where lines from cameras meet.
3. Joining up a series of the ball's locations shows its path in space.
Computer model can accurately determine if the ball touched the line.
1. Camera captures action and computer calculates a line to the ball.

Multiple video cameras point at the tennis court. Each camera has a different viewpoint of the court. By electronically plotting a line from each camera to the ball, the exact location of the ball on the court can be calculated by the Hawk-Eye computer – it is the point where the lines from all the cameras cross. The ball's location can be plotted with just two cameras, but players can block a camera's view so more are used. To show the ball's path, the computer joins together the complete series of the ball's positions.

Path of the ball calculated by a computer from camera images.

Imprint of the ball on court tells the umpire exactly where the ball bounced.

Cricket

▶ In cricket it's not only interesting where the ball went, but for the Leg Before Wicket (LBW) rule, whether the ball would have hit the stumps if the batsman had not got in the way. Hawk-Eye uses a computer program to calculate where the ball would have ended up.

Every ball's path is tracked

▶▶ See also: Head up p54, Simulators p70, Under Scan p74

ROBOTS

Our bodies are the most remarkable "machines" on the planet. Muscles and bones work together like levers, reducing the effort we need to move ourselves and other objects. Our brains, packed with 100 billion nerve cells, are more versatile than any computer. Developing machines that can rival this all-round flexibility is a tough challenge.

>> ASIMO The only robot in the world that can walk independently, ASIMO can also run around corners and climb stairs. During a brisk walk, human leg joints experience forces nearly twice our body weight. The same is true of ASIMO, who wears padded shoes to cushion the impact. ASIMO's arms are complex enough to carry trays, push carts, and even hold hands.

<< Robo doctor This RP-6 robot is a walking video-link that allows doctors to talk to patients at a moment's notice, even when they are in hospitals far away. The robot's "head" carries a live TV image of the doctor, while a built-in TV camera and microphone sends the patient's picture and voice back to the doctor's office.

Ubiko

Robots already do factory jobs, such as spray-painting and welding cars – but they could soon be commonplace in shops as well. With its friendly cat-like face, this 1.13-m (3.7-ft) tall Ubiko robot has been greeting customers and helping to sell mobile phones in Japanese stores.

Kismet

Robots are also learning to express emotions. Kismet's mechanical head is packed with sensors and motors that help it react to people nearby. When Kismet goes from calm (left) to happy (right), its ears prick up, it smiles, and its eyes open wide. Kismet was developed to study the way people react with machines.

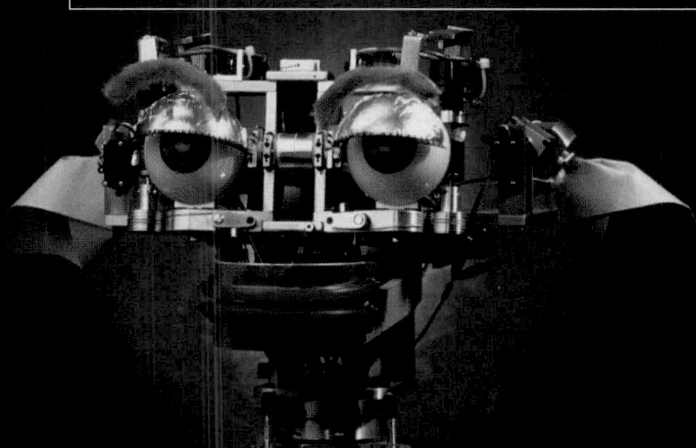

Plen

Today's factory robots are just remote-controlled machines wired to the wall, but future robots will be more mobile and independent. This wireless robot, controlled by a Bluetooth® mobile phone, is a step closer. It can walk, wave, and move in response to commands sent from the keypad.

See also: Petcam p52, Lego® Mindstorms™ p92, Robot car p104, Mars rover p142

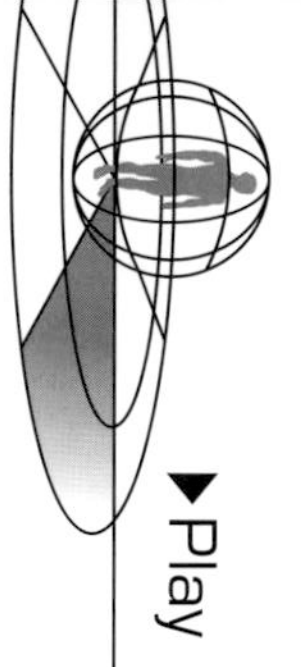

LEGO MINDSTORMS

▶▶ If designing a robot was easy, you would already have one buzzing around your bedroom tidying up. A great way to learn the skills is with a kit like Lego® Mindstorms™, which has all you need to build and program a moving robot. ▶▶

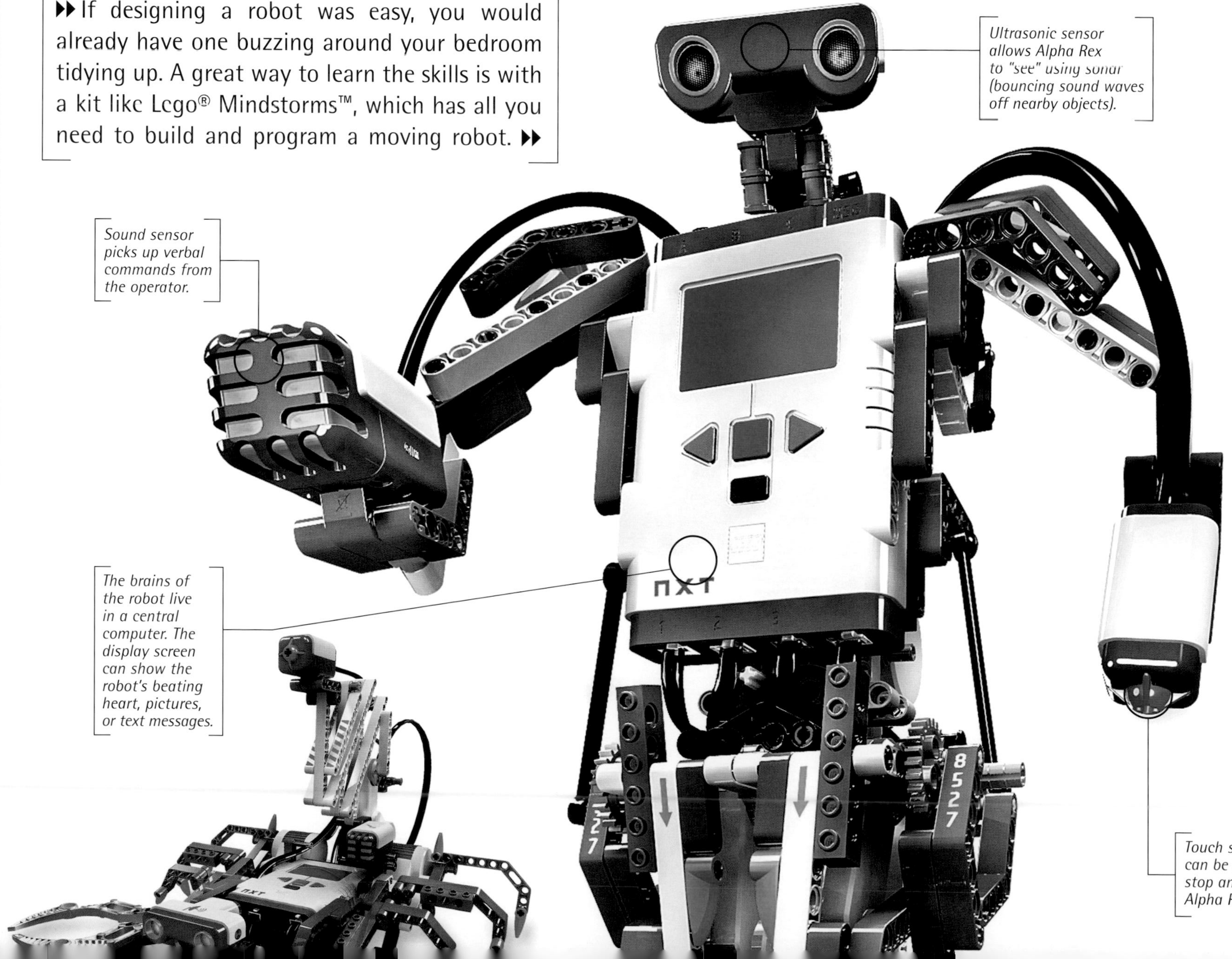

Ultrasonic sensor allows Alpha Rex to "see" using sonar (bouncing sound waves off nearby objects).

Sound sensor picks up verbal commands from the operator.

The brains of the robot live in a central computer. The display screen can show the robot's beating heart, pictures, or text messages.

Touch sensor can be used to stop and start Alpha Rex.

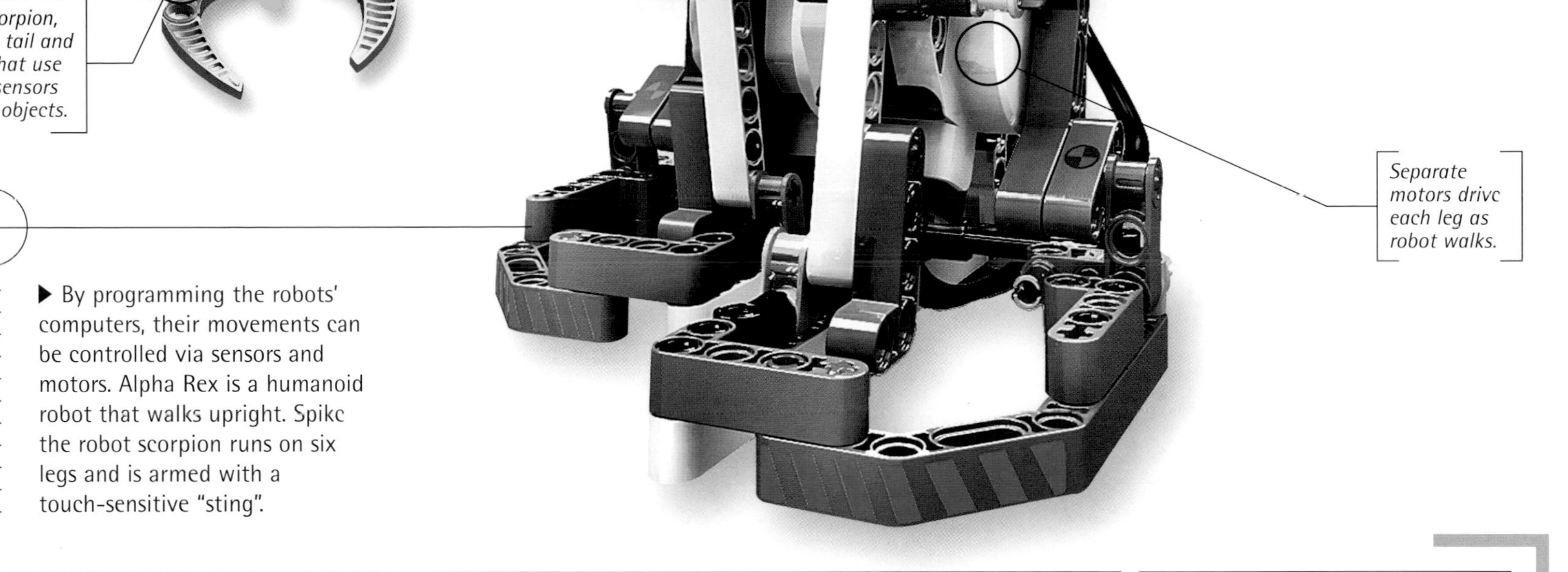

Spike, a robotic scorpion, has an extendable tail and grasping pincers that use sound and touch sensors to detect external objects.

Separate motors drivc each leg as robot walks.

▶ By programming the robots' computers, their movements can be controlled via sensors and motors. Alpha Rex is a humanoid robot that walks upright. Spikc the robot scorpion runs on six legs and is armed with a touch-sensitive "sting".

>> HOW LEGO MINDSTORMS WORK

NXT Intelligent Brick – the brains of the robot – contains a computer and the robot's control panel.

Three motors with rotation sensors work together to move and turn the robot with great precision.

Touch sensor detects a push, a release, or a bump.

Sound sensor detects sound and can be used to recognize sound patterns.

Light sensor measures light intensity.

Ultrasonic sensor uses sound waves to measure distances and detect movement, enabling robot to "see" its surroundings.

At the heart of all these robots is a small computer called the NXT Intelligent Brick. It can control three motors and take input from four sensors. The Brick can be programmed to make a robot react to sensor data about its surroundings and perform tasks. Programs are written using a menu of options or with conventional programming languages.

Programming Alpha Rex

▶▶ See also: Wi-Fi toy p46, Robots p90, Mars rover p142

CUBE WORLD

▶▶ These small plastic cubes can be piled on top of one another or set side by side. The individual stickmen inside play games and interact with one another, travelling between the cubes. ▶▶

This cube's resident is out – he is visiting the cube below.

The symbol on the front of the cube indicates the inhabitant's activity.

Image: A stack of Cube World characters interacting

>> HOW CUBE WORLD WORKS

CUBE WORLD
SLIM
Inside cube is a computer that controls display and can connect to another cube's computer.
LCD display shows in-cube activity.
Buttons allow games to be played with the cube dweller.
Electrical contacts connect cube computers to swap data and coordinate activities.
Magnets stick cubes together so that electrical connection is maintained.
Motion sensors allow cube's occupant to respond when cube is turned or shaken.

Inside each cube is a battery-powered computer that is connected to the LCD display and the buttons. This computer runs a program that displays the animated stickman and controls his actions. On four sides of the cube are electrical connectors that can magnetically attach to another cube's connectors when the cubes are stacked together. When cubes are connected, the computers communicate by passing digital data to each other. If two cubes' computers agree that a stickman should visit his neighbour, then signals can be passed between them to exactly match the time of his departure from one cube to his arrival in the next. Once multiple stickmen are in one cube, that cube's computer uses data from the other computers to determine their behaviour.

◀ Each Cube World stickman has an activity it performs, such as playing a musical instrument or lifting weights. When cubes are stacked together, the stickmen interact. Without external prompting, they visit other cubes to play or dance together. Up to four stickmen can gather together in a single cube.

✓ Tamagotchi

The pet in your pocket

◀ Tamagotchi™ is a virtual pet that can be carried around in a pocket. A tiny creature is shown on the screen of a plastic box with buttons. These allow the owner to feed the pet or play games with it. Over time, the Tamagotchi grows up and changes its appearance and behaviour. Forget to feed it, and it will die! The latest Tamagotchi can connect to each other and interact through an infrared link.

▶▶ See also: Wi-Fi toy p46, Petcam p52, Games console p68, Lego® Mindstorms™ p92

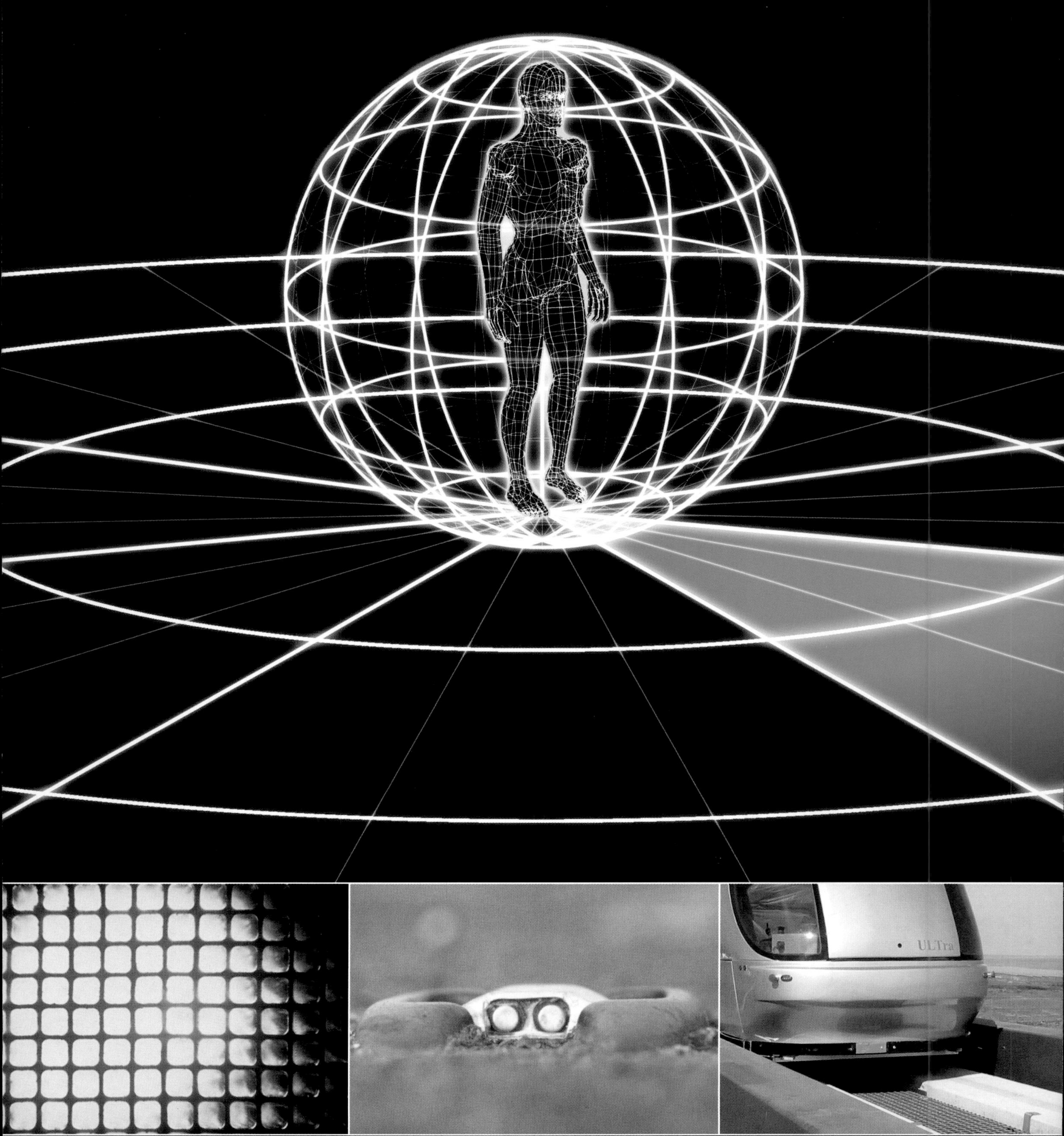
ULTra

>> MOVE

Formula 1 >> Converter >> Robot car >> Road >> Catseyes >> VentureOne >> Segway PT >> ULTra >> Water craft >> FLIP ship >> Jet Ski >> SailRocket >> Glider >> Silent flight >> Aerobatics >> Helicopter >> Trainers >> Escalator

How can you lean and not fall over? p112

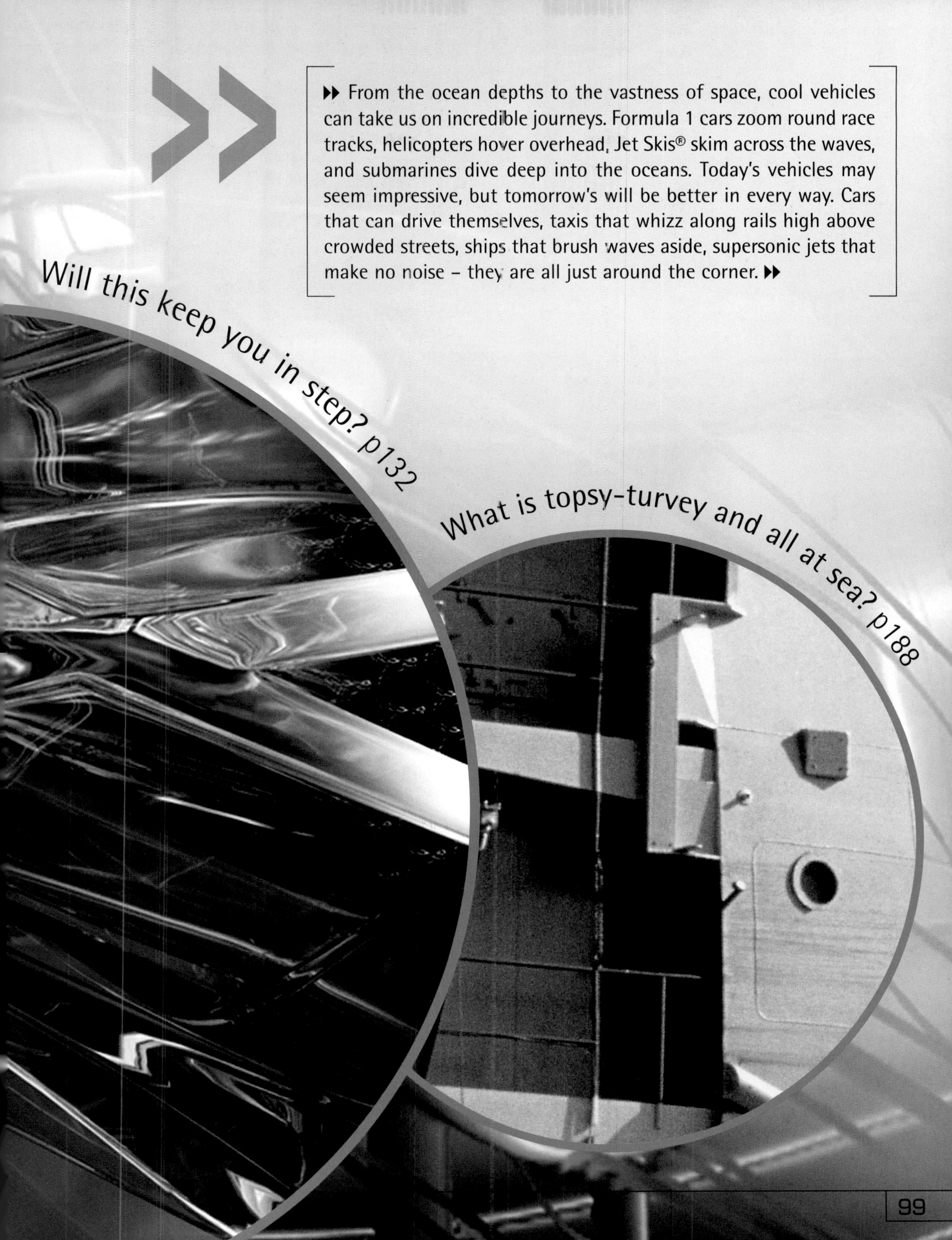
▸▸ From the ocean depths to the vastness of space, cool vehicles can take us on incredible journeys. Formula 1 cars zoom round race tracks, helicopters hover overhead, Jet Skis® skim across the waves, and submarines dive deep into the oceans. Today's vehicles may seem impressive, but tomorrow's will be better in every way. Cars that can drive themselves, taxis that whizz along rails high above crowded streets, ships that brush waves aside, supersonic jets that make no noise – they are all just around the corner. ▸▸
Will this keep you in step? p132
What is topsy-turvey and all at sea? p188

FORMULA 1

Wind-tunnel testing

▶ Racing cars are made more aerodynamic (enabling air to pass over smoothly) by testing them in wind tunnels. In this test, a 50 per cent scale model car is held steady by four arms while air is forced past it at high speed.

Model of an F1 car in a wind tunnel

Rear wing can be set at 20 different angles and provides 35 per cent of car's down force.

Air intake provides 650 litres (172 gallons) of air – about 120 deep adult breaths – to the engine each second.

Lines indicate path of air over car.

Diffusers on either side of the cockpit direct air under car to generate suction that produces 40 per cent of vehicle's total down force.

▶▶ A Formula 1 (F1) car drives like a ground-hugging aeroplane, with a sleek body designed to grip the race track at high speeds. Its engine is five times more powerful than one found in a typical family car. ▶▶

"Wishbone" suspension clamps tyres on to road during high-speed cornering.

Image: Computer simulation of air pressure and airflow on an F1 car

» HOW FORMULA 1 TECHNOLOGY WORKS

Cockpit

The driver's cockpit is as close to the ground as possible so the car can corner at high speed. The snug cockpit is heavily reinforced for safety and a fighter-pilot's seatbelt secures the driver.

Button controls

Drivers have no time to reach for levers, so buttons on the steering wheel operate all controls except the brake and accelerator. Traditional dials are replaced by a single LCD display.

Tyres

F1 car tyres are made from soft rubber reinforced with polyester and nylon. Forces five times that of gravity and 100°C (212°F) temperatures wear them out after only 200 km (125 miles).

◀ Air resistance or drag creates pressure on the surface of a Formula 1 car. On this computer simulation of a Sauber BMW being driven at 180 km/h (112 mph), areas coloured red and yellow have the greatest air pressure. The pressure is higher above the Sauber than beneath it, creating a down force that makes the car "stick" to the track. The lines on the simulation show airflow over the car.

Front wing redirects incoming air to cool the brakes and also provides 25 per cent of car's down force.

▶▶ See also: Head up p54, Vomit comet p140

Image: View through a catalytic converter

CONVERTER

▶▶ From Athens to Moscow and Beijing to Mumbai, smog blights the world's biggest cities. Air pollution chokes our lungs, kills trees, and turns buildings to dust. Catalytic converters are chemical cleaners that scrub the filth from vehicle exhausts, reducing the pollution from motor engines. ▶▶

HOW A CATALYTIC CONVERTER WORKS

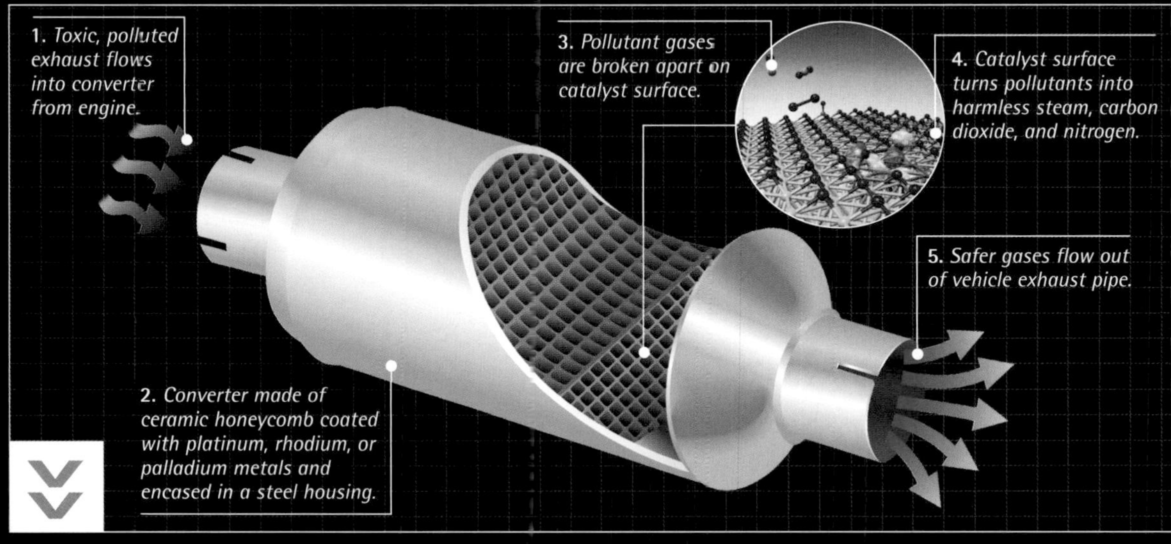

1. Toxic, polluted exhaust flows into converter from engine.
2. Converter made of ceramic honeycomb coated with platinum, rhodium, or palladium metals and encased in a steel housing.
3. Pollutant gases are broken apart on catalyst surface.
4. Catalyst surface turns pollutants into harmless steam, carbon dioxide, and nitrogen.
5. Safer gases flow out of vehicle exhaust pipe.

Vehicle engines burn fuel with air in a chemical reaction that produces power. However, the hydrocarbons from which petroleum fuel is made never burn completely cleanly so engines make a mixture of pollution, too. The toxic cocktail in exhaust fumes includes nitrogen oxides (which cause lung problems), poisonous carbon monoxide, and unburnt hydrocarbons.

A catalytic converter looks like a three-dimensional sieve. But instead of straining out the pollutants, its large surface area encourages chemical reactions to happen. These reactions break apart the harmful molecules of nitrogen oxide, carbon monoxide, and hydrocarbons. Their atoms then rearrange on the catalyst to make cleaner and safer substances – water (steam), carbon dioxide, and nitrogen.

◀ As exhaust fumes flow through this catalytic converter, a pair of back-to-back catalysts strip away pollution. A reduction catalyst removes nitrogen oxides (converting them to nitrogen and oxygen), while an oxidation catalyst converts carbon monoxide and hydrocarbons into carbon dioxide and water.

▶▶ See also: Head up p54, Road p106

ROBOT CAR

▶▶ Some unusual car races have taken place in a US desert. There are no drivers and no remote controls. Using cameras, radar, and lasers, the robot cars must navigate the 212-km (132-mile) course themselves. ▶▶

▶ Entrants, such as Sandstorm pictured here, must race across sand dunes, through rocky terrain, and over dry river beds, avoiding any obstacles in their paths. The engineers designing these vehicles aim to develop a robot car that can drive to remote and dangerous destinations and deliver supplies or equipment without putting a driver's life at risk.

Steerable long-range laser scanner can turn to look around corners.

Camera surveys terrain to spot obstacles.

GPS antenna calculates position to within a few metres.

Computer plans where to go next and controls all systems.

Special suspension cushions electronics and sensors over uneven terrain.

Riderless motorbike

Ghostrider riderless motorbike

◀ One team entered a riderless motorbike in the 2005 race. As well as navigating the course, Ghostrider also faced the challenge of remaining upright. Every 1/100th of a second, its computer determined the bike's lean and directed the front wheel to steer in the opposite direction to keep it balanced. The bike didn't get through the qualifying rounds, so never got a shot at the £1 million prize.

▶▶ See also: Head up p54, Hawk-Eye p88, Robots p90, Road p106

>> HOW SANDSTORM NAVIGATES

Sandstorm gets data from many onboard sensors. GPS (Global Positioning System) provides detailed location information so it can follow the race route, but that's not accurate enough to allow Sandstorm to stay on narrow roads or deal with obstacles encountered en route. To work out exactly where to steer, Sandstorm's computer combines data about its surroundings from long-range radar, camera images, and laser scanners (LIDAR). LIDAR gives the most detail as it scans a laser across the terrain around the vehicle, returning the exact shape of the ground and any obstacles.

Long-range LIDAR scans in stripes up to 50 m (164 ft) ahead and can be turned to look around corners.

Computer combines LIDAR data with information from other sensors to control speed, steering, and brakes.

Short-range LIDAR collects data all round vehicle.

Time taken for laser light to travel from car to terrain in front, then back again is used to calculate distance.

Radar is less accurate than lasers but senses obstacles further ahead and is unaffected by dust in the air.

Fixed laser scanners help build map of surrounding terrain.

Image: Sandstorm robot car in the 2005 race

ROAD

▶▶ Roads can be buzzing channels of urban life or quiet ribbons of asphalt snaking through rural landscapes. The busiest motorways are built to survive 150,000 vehicles driving over them per day, including trucks that can weigh as much as seven elephants. ▶▶

Asphalt lake

La Brea, Trinidad

▲ Most roads look black because they are surfaced with asphalt. This lake in La Brea, Trinidad, is the world's largest asphalt deposit. The asphalt here is so soft that a car would quickly sink. Asphalt has to be mixed with gravel or other rocks to make a hard-wearing, waterproof suface strong enough to support cars.

▼ This road in Lofoten, Norway, is inside the Arctic Circle and has to withstand a huge range of temperatures between winter and summer. Additives ensure the upper layer of asphalt can expand and contract as the temperature changes. This stops it cracking and letting in water, which would unsettle the layers beneath.

HOW ROADS ARE CONSTRUCTED

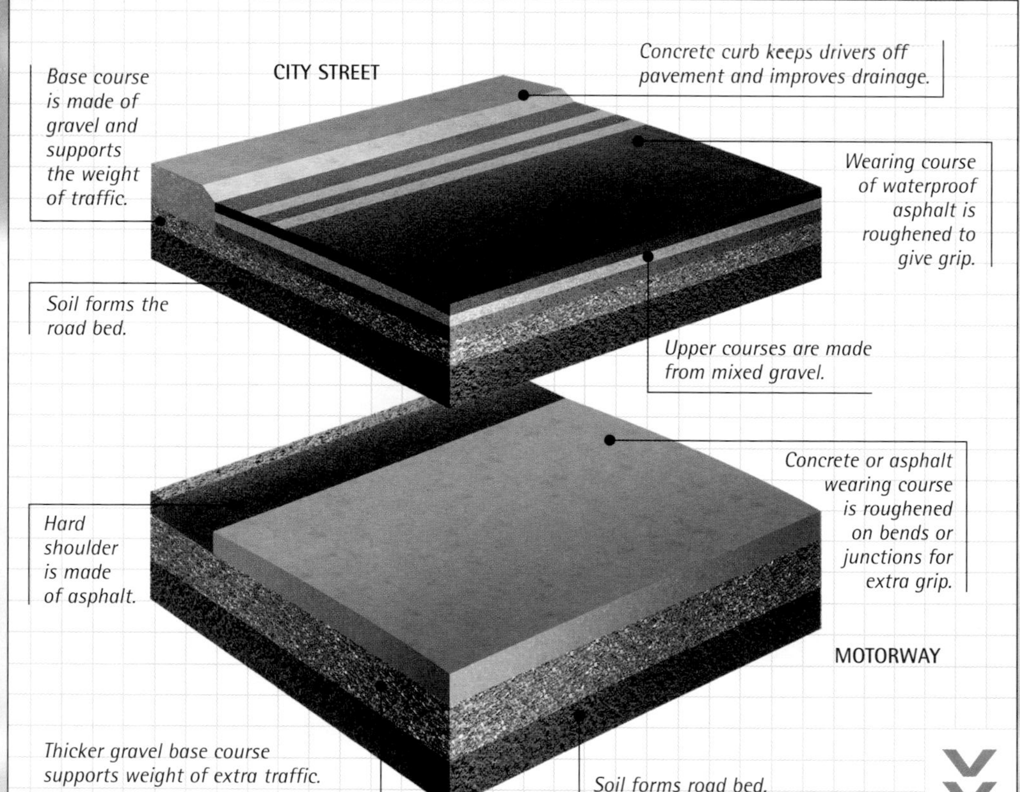

CITY STREET
Base course is made of gravel and supports the weight of traffic.
Concrete curb keeps drivers off pavement and improves drainage.
Wearing course of waterproof asphalt is roughened to give grip.
Soil forms the road bed.
Upper courses are made from mixed gravel.
MOTORWAY
Hard shoulder is made of asphalt.
Concrete or asphalt wearing course is roughened on bends or junctions for extra grip.
Thicker gravel base course supports weight of extra traffic.
Soil forms road bed.

Rough rocks on the bottom layer of a road provide strength to carry weight, while a smooth upper layer is designed for speed and comfort. The top layer (wearing course) is waterproof to protect layers beneath. Friction from tyres rubs it away, so it has to be replaced every few years. Motorways are often surfaced with roughened concrete, which wears out less quickly than asphalt. Over 90 per cent of roads are surfaced with asphalt, which is easier to lay around curved streets, manholes, drains, and other obstacles.

Image: Surface of road in Lofoten, Norway

Asphalt surface is roughened by powerful water jets or hammering during construction to improve grip.
Titanium dioxide road-marking paint has tiny glass beads embedded in it to reflect headlights more effectively.

▶▶ See also: Formula 1 p100, Robot car p104, Catseyes® p108

CATSEYES

Drivers are ten times more likely to have an accident at night, but tiny light reflectors squatting in the road help reduce the risk. Catseyes®, as they are known, have saved countless lives since they were invented in 1934.

Image: A road's-eye view of Catseyes®

Streams of night traffic flow safely thanks to Catseyes between the lanes. Catseyes are usually white, but they can also be red, amber, or green to indicate roads that should not be crossed, slip roads, or other special roads. The raised bumper of a Catseye makes a noise if it is driven over, which helps to warn drivers if they stray out of lane.

Bumpers on iron surround protect Catseye from impact damage.

Invention of Catseyes

Percy Shaw (1890–1976) invented Catseyes after driving down a dangerous hill one foggy night. A strange light that he spotted in the road turned out to be a cat's eyes reflecting his headlights back at him. Shaw suddenly realized that he was on the wrong side of the road and heading for a precipice and certain death. The cat had saved his life.

Percy Shaw in his Catseyes factory

» HOW CATSEYES WORK

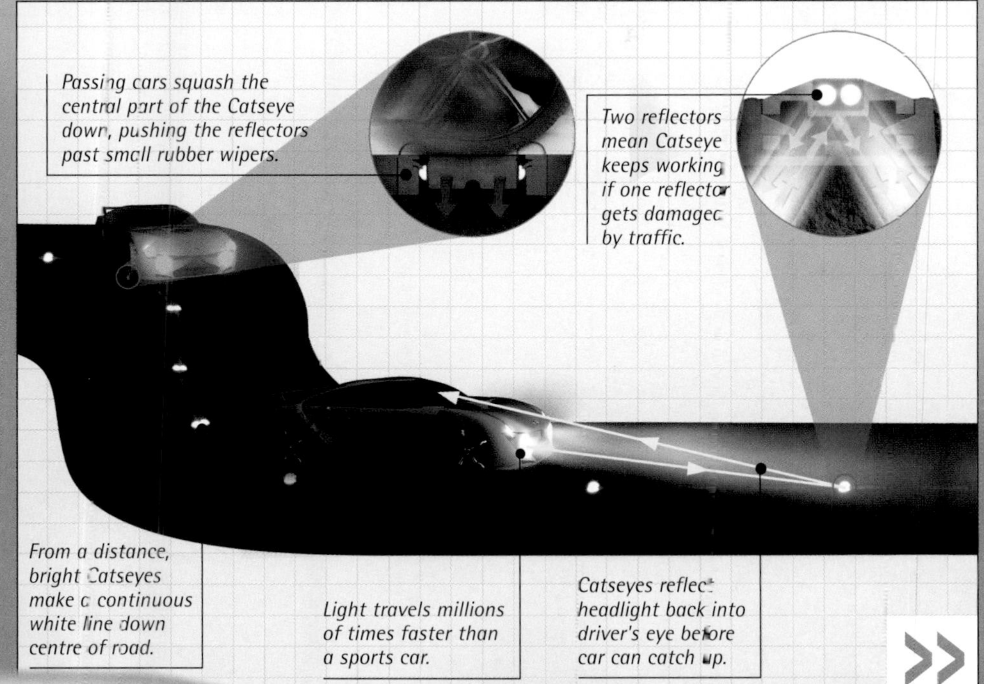

Passing cars squash the central part of the Catseye down, pushing the reflectors past small rubber wipers.
Two reflectors mean Catseye keeps working if one reflector gets damaged by traffic.
From a distance, bright Catseyes make a continuous white line down centre of road.
Light travels millions of times faster than a sports car.
Catseyes reflect headlight back into driver's eye before car can catch up.

Car headlights dip down so they light the road surface, while the reflectors in Catseyes tilt upwards to reflect oncoming light back to the driver's eyes. On a typical road, the Catseyes are placed 6–18 m (20–60 ft) apart. They are spaced more widely on faster roads, and more closely on bends, in dips where fog or mist can gather, and on the brows of hills where dazzle from oncoming vehicles is a problem. Catseyes would soon become dirty and useless were it not for their unique, self-wiping design. The rubbery white centre bobs up and down every time a car drives over one, wiping the reflector studs clean in the process.

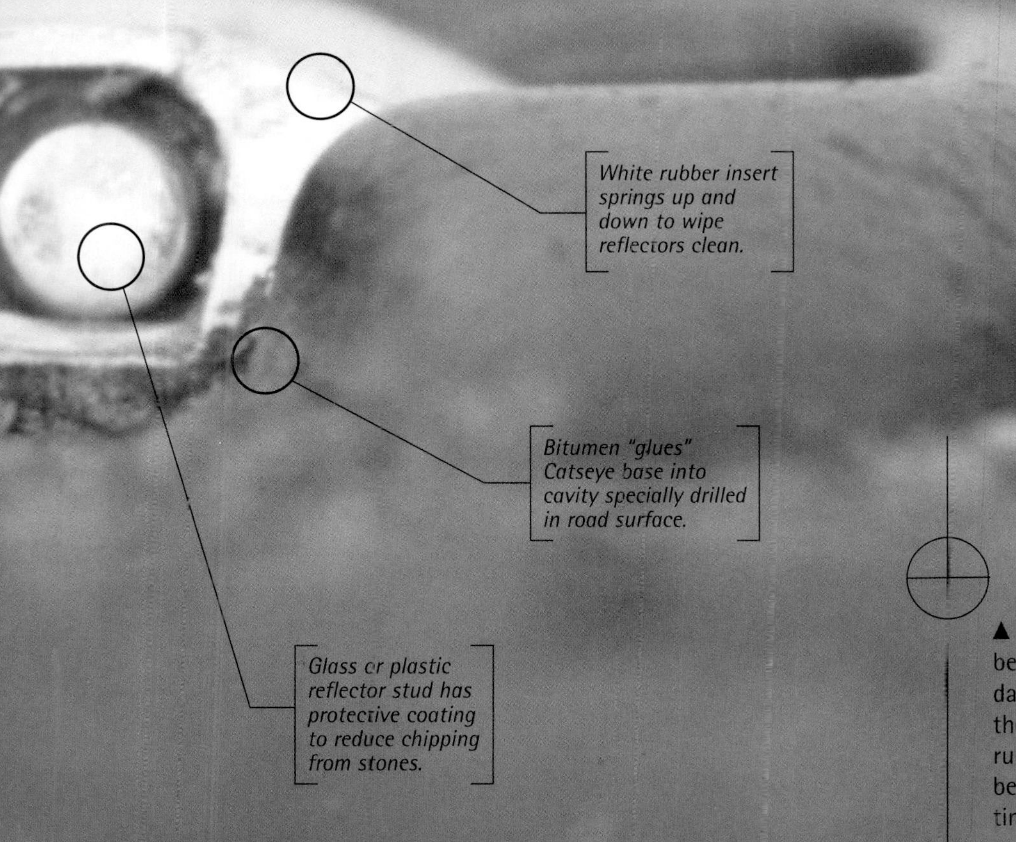

White rubber insert springs up and down to wipe reflectors clean.
Bitumen "glues" Catseye base into cavity specially drilled in road surface.
Glass or plastic reflector stud has protective coating to reduce chipping from stones.

▲ Catseyes must be high enough to be seen, but low enough not to get damaged by, or damage, traffic. With their sturdy iron surrounds and tough rubber insides, Catseyes can survive being driven over more than one million times and will last for 10 to 20 years.

▶▶See also: Head up p54, Road p106, Night vision p160

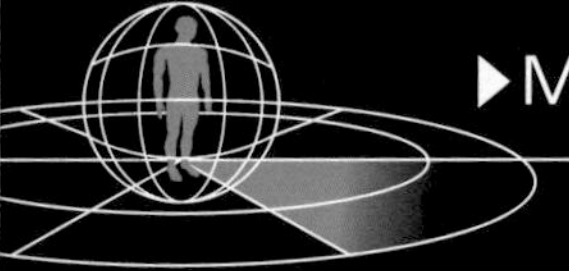

VENTUREONE

▶▶ Picture a vehicle as safe as a car but as exhilarating and economical as a motorbike. This electric- and petrol-powered three-wheeler offers the best of both worlds. It is 30 times safer than a motorbike, just as fast, and uses half as much petrol. ▶▶

▼ VentureOne™ uses hybrid power (petrol and electricity). A compact petrol engine at the back drives an electricity generator and batteries, which power two electric motors inside the wheels. When the vehicle brakes, the energy normally wasted is captured and used to recharge the batteries, increasing efficiency.

High-strength molybdenum steel cage protects occupants in a collision or rollover.

Tilting mechanism under rear engine.

Body is sculpted inwards so it does not scrape on the ground when the vehicle tilts over.

▲ **Image:** VentureOne™

▶▶ See also: Segway® PT p112, Silent flight p126

▼ Motorbikes go faster when riders lean into corners – VentureOne tilts. At low speeds, steering turns the front wheel and the car stays upright. At higher speeds, the whole vehicle tips instead.

>> HOW VENTUREONE PROTECTS

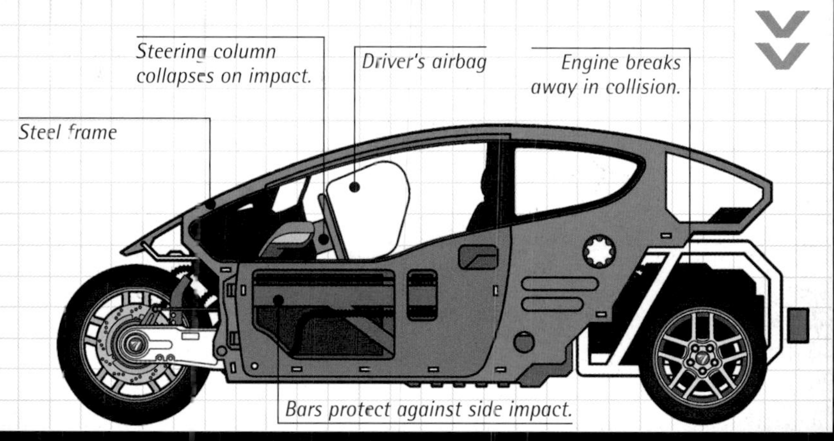
Steering column collapses on impact.
Driver's airbag
Engine breaks away in collision.
Steel frame
Bars protect against side impact.

The open design of a motorbike offers little protection in a crash, but VentureOne's passengers are heavily defended by a closed, steel-framed safety cage that can withstand the impact of an accident. In a head-on collision, the impact is transmitted from the front wheel to the steel frame, so the energy flows away from the passengers. In a rear collision, the engine at the back snaps away from the frame to stop it from crushing the occupants. Safety glass, anti-skid brakes, and airbags all combine to make VentureOne much safer than a motorbike.

"Capture collar" transfers energy from front wheel to safety cage in a collision.

Tilting technology

Pendolino tilting train

▲ This Italian-designed Pendolino train tilts to go around corners at higher speeds. The wheels remain securely on the tracks, while the coaches swing from side to side above the tracks.

SEGWAY PT

▶▶ Simply lean forward on a Segway® Personal Transporter and it glides you down pavements up to three times faster than you can walk. Powered by electric motors and batteries, this quiet, zero-emission device could be the urban transport of the future. ▶▶

>> HOW THE SEGWAY PT MOVES

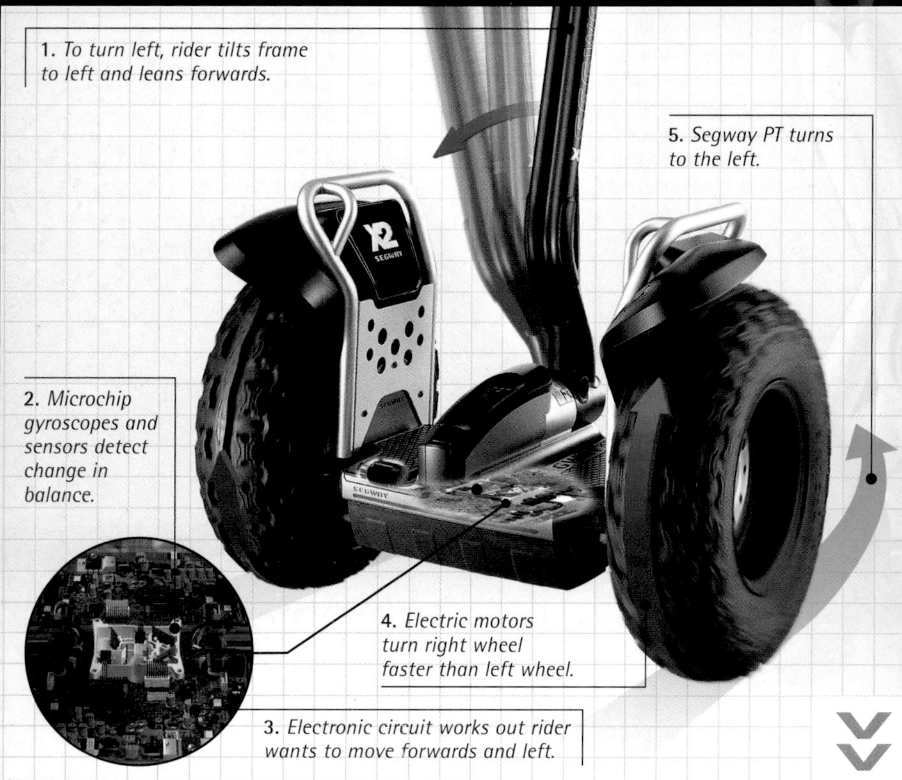

1. *To turn left, rider tilts frame to left and leans forwards.*
2. *Microchip gyroscopes and sensors detect change in balance.*
3. *Electronic circuit works out rider wants to move forwards and left.*
4. *Electric motors turn right wheel faster than left wheel.*
5. *Segway PT turns to the left.*

Lean forward while you are standing and your body will start to topple. Before this happens, balance sensors in your ear detect the problem, and your brain sends signals to your muscles to make you step forward. Segway PTs also work like this, only with electronic gyroscopes and electric motors in place of your brain and muscles. The gyroscopes are electronic sensors just 6 mm (0.25 in) across. When you shift your position, these microchips detect the tilt of the Segway PT, and the motors compensate to keep you balanced.

▲ A removable wireless key turns the device on and monitors battery life, speed, and distance travelled. It also doubles as an anti-theft alarm.

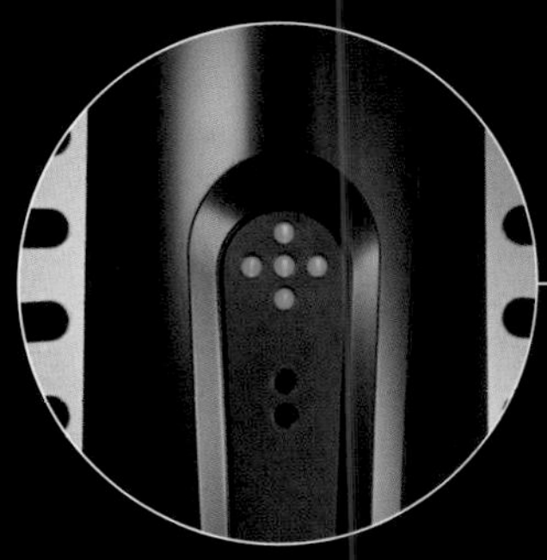

▲ Indicator lights pulse gently when the Segway PT is balanced and safe to ride. Five built-in gyroscopes check and correct the Segway PT's balance.

▲ A heavy-duty lock allows the Segway PT to be secured to immovable objects. When the anti-theft alarm is activated, the wheels lock automatically.

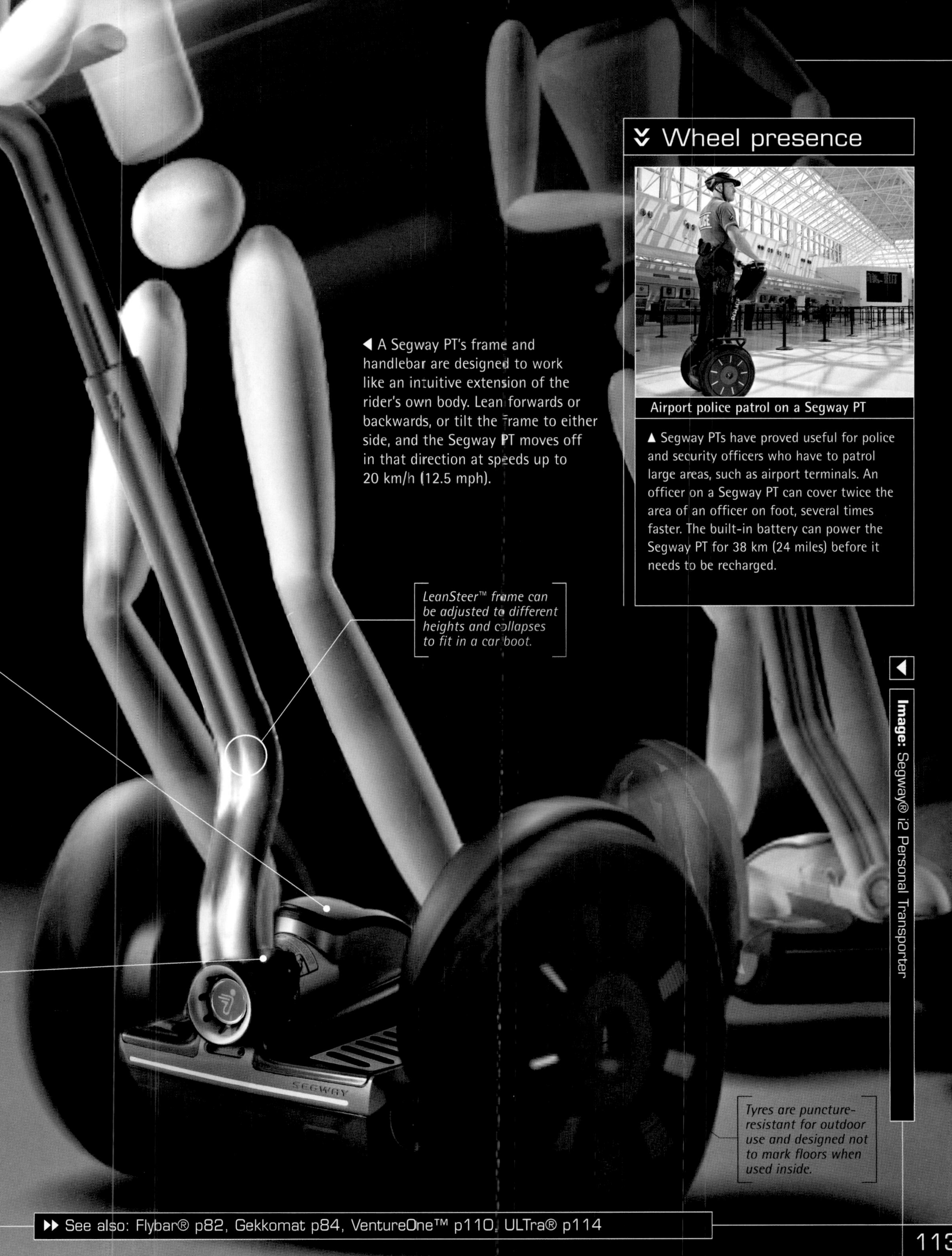

◀ A Segway PT's frame and handlebar are designed to work like an intuitive extension of the rider's own body. Lean forwards or backwards, or tilt the frame to either side, and the Segway PT moves off in that direction at speeds up to 20 km/h (12.5 mph).

LeanSteer™ frame can be adjusted to different heights and collapses to fit in a car boot.

Tyres are puncture-resistant for outdoor use and designed not to mark floors when used inside.

Wheel presence

Airport police patrol on a Segway PT

▲ Segway PTs have proved useful for police and security officers who have to patrol large areas, such as airport terminals. An officer on a Segway PT can cover twice the area of an officer on foot, several times faster. The built-in battery can power the Segway PT for 38 km (24 miles) before it needs to be recharged.

▶▶ See also: Flybar® p82, Gekkomat p84, VentureOne™ p110, ULTra® p114

Image: ULTra® cab travelling on raised guide rails ▶

ULTra

▶▶ There are 600 million cars in the world – one for every 11 people on our planet. As traffic grows steadily worse, driverless electric ULTra® taxis could help to relieve congestion and pollution. ▶▶

>> ULTra: KEY FEATURES

◀ Tram meets car: ULTra is two to three times faster for getting around cities because it runs on its own special rails, up to 6 m (20 ft) above the ground and separate from other traffic. Instead of a driver, each cab has on-board sensors that enable a central computer system to guide it.

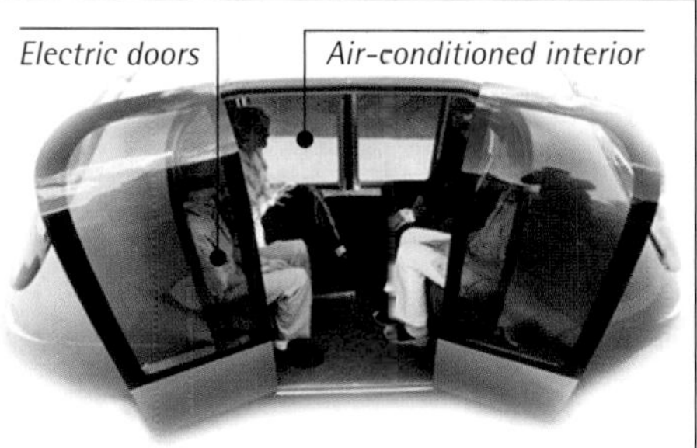

Passenger access
Each cab is 3.7 m (12 ft) long (the same as a small car) and carries four passengers, or loads up to 500 kg (1100 lb). Wide doors and low floors make it accessible to the elderly, parents with pushchairs, and the disabled. ULTra cabs are designed to be at least 10 times safer than cars.

Boarding platforms
Although ULTra's top speed is a modest 40 km/h (25 mph), journeys run non-stop between special boarding platforms so trip times are short. A fleet of these cabs keeps average waiting times to less than 10 seconds. The cabs can travel faster through urban areas than street traffic.

Electric motor
Instead of petrol engines, ULTra cabs use electric motors and batteries, so they are almost silent and virtually pollution-free. They use one-tenth as much energy as a car at rush hour and are several times more efficient than buses, trains, and trams.

▶▶ See also: Robot car p104, Road p106, Segway® PT p112

WATER CRAFT

Earthrace

This eco-powerboat was built to attempt a round-the-world trip in record time. It runs on biodiesel made from sources like soya beans or waste cooking oil. The boat can travel more than 6,000 km (3,730 miles) on a tank of fuel at up to 90 km/h (56 mph).

WAM-V

The eye-catching WAM-V™ craft doesn't force its way through the waves – it adapts and flexes with the sea. The "pod" suspended over the ocean can be luxury accommodation, a cargo hold, or a marine lab.

Never before has there been such a variety of ways to take to the water. Today's cutting-edge water craft come in all shapes and sizes – some don't even look like boats. Aerodynamic design and lightweight materials make for maximum speed and manoeuvrability, while submarine technology allows pleasure boats to dive beneath the waves.

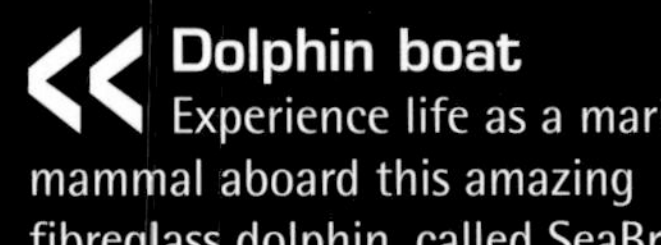

Dolphin boat

Experience life as a marine mammal aboard this amazing fibreglass dolphin, called SeaBreacher. Capable of travelling at 48 km/h (30 mph) and diving 3 m (10 ft) below the surface, this boat can mimic dolphin tricks such as leaping from the water and rolling in mid-air.

M 80 Stiletto

The Stiletto is built from lightweight carbon-fibre. As a result, it can operate in very shallow water. Its 24-m- (79-ft-) long twin M-shaped hull is very efficient as it creates almost no wake, giving top speeds of more than 100 km/h (62 mph).

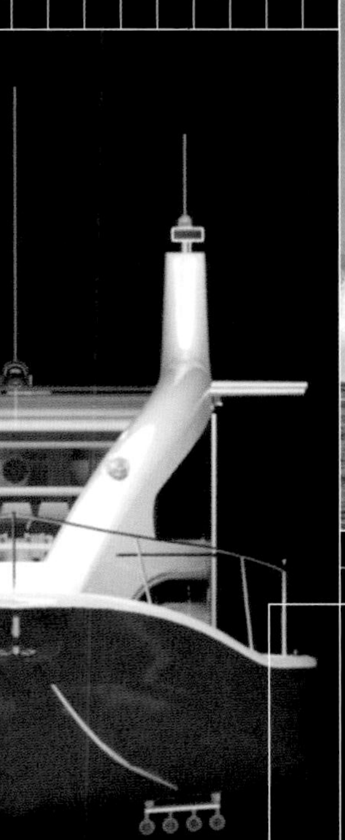

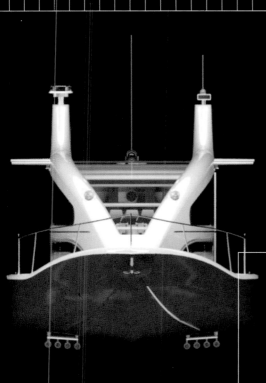

Exomos submersible

This luxury yacht is also a submarine that can dive 20 m (66 ft) below the waves. Up to 14 divers can sit on deck while the 21-m- (69-ft-) long boat submerges, and there's a waterproof cabin for another eight passengers who can stay dry and enjoy the view.

▶▶ See also: FLIP ship p118, Jet Ski® p120, SailRocket p122

FLIP SHIP

▶▶ Some things sink, others float, but this amazing laboratory can do both. Half ship and half submarine, FLIP (Floating Instrument Platform) floats out to sea then sinks beneath the surface to study the ocean. ◀◀

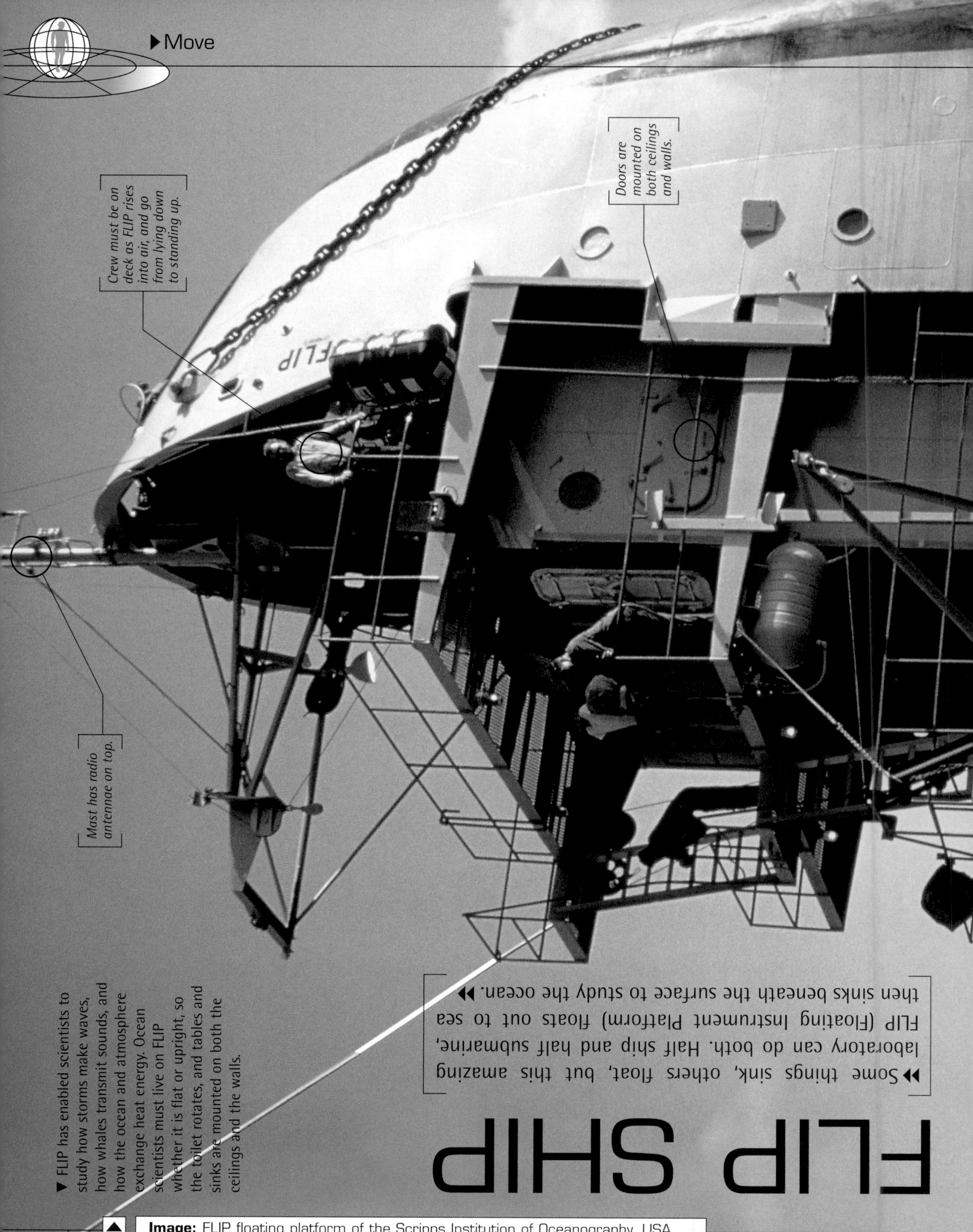

FLIP
Crew must be on deck as FLIP rises into air, and go from lying down to standing up.
Doors are mounted on both ceilings and walls.
Mast has radio antennae on top.

▼ FLIP has enabled scientists to study how storms make waves, how whales transmit sounds, and how the ocean and atmosphere exchange heat energy. Ocean scientists must live on FLIP whether it is flat or upright, so the toilet rotates, and tables and sinks are mounted on both the ceilings and the walls.

▲ **Image:** FLIP floating platform of the Scripps Institution of Oceanography, USA

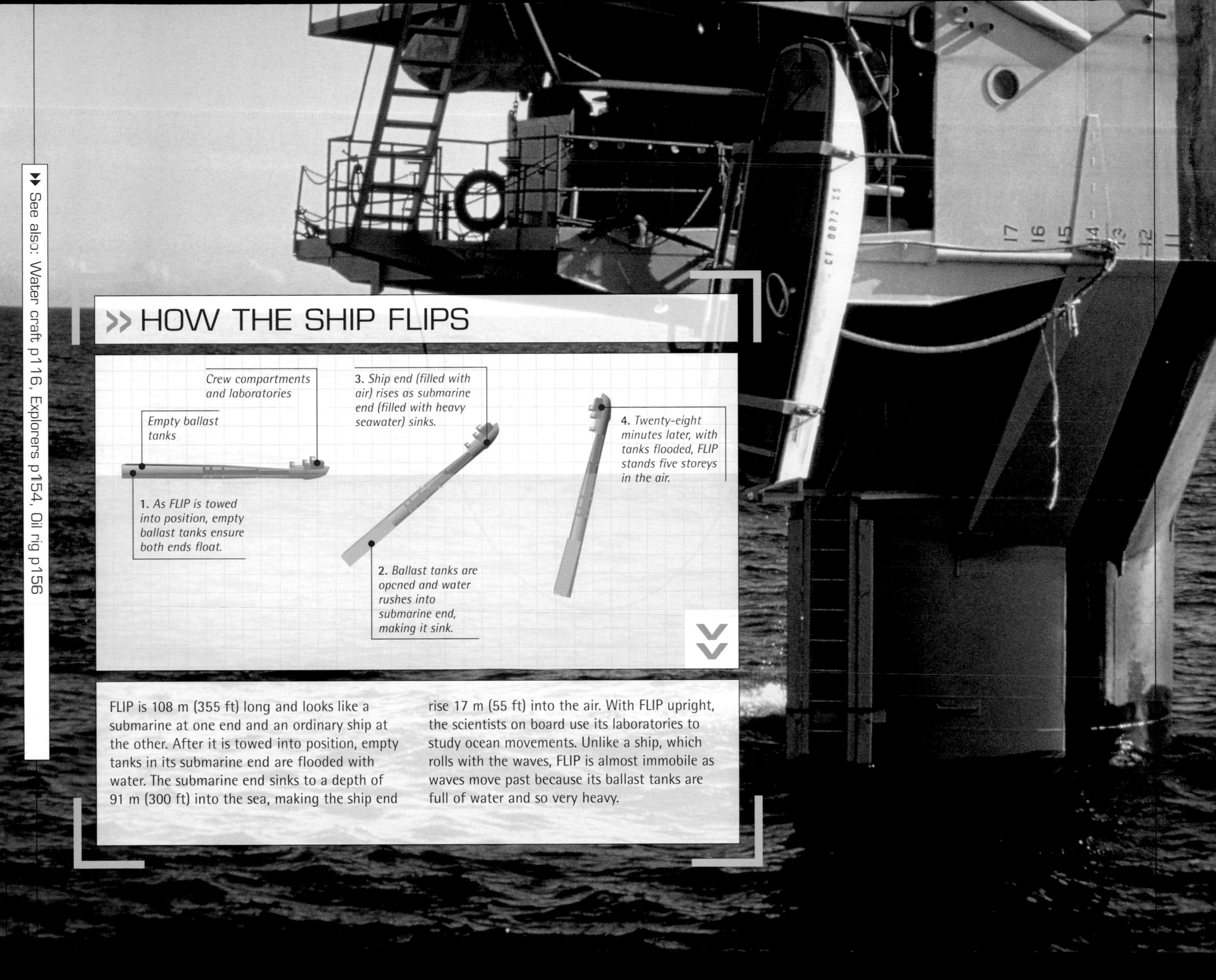

HOW THE SHIP FLIPS

Crew compartments and laboratories
Empty ballast tanks
1. As FLIP is towed into position, empty ballast tanks ensure both ends float.
3. Ship end (filled with air) rises as submarine end (filled with heavy seawater) sinks.
2. Ballast tanks are opened and water rushes into submarine end, making it sink.
4. Twenty-eight minutes later, with tanks flooded, FLIP stands five storeys in the air.

FLIP is 108 m (355 ft) long and looks like a submarine at one end and an ordinary ship at the other. After it is towed into position, empty tanks in its submarine end are flooded with water. The submarine end sinks to a depth of 91 m (300 ft) into the sea, making the ship end rise 17 m (55 ft) into the air. With FLIP upright, the scientists on board use its laboratories to study ocean movements. Unlike a ship, which rolls with the waves, FLIP is almost immobile as waves move past because its ballast tanks are full of water and so very heavy.

See also: Water craft p116, Explorers p154, Oil rig p156

JET SKI

▶▶ A Jet Ski® is a sea "motorbike" that can thump across waves at speeds of more than 80 km/h (50 mph). Unlike motorboats powered by propellers, Jet Skis are driven by powerful, backward-pumping jets of water. ▶▶

Cushioned rider area provides crash protection.

Hull is made from light but strong fibreglass-reinforced plastic.

Image: Kawasaki Jet Ski® 800 SX-R™

Jet-propelled animals

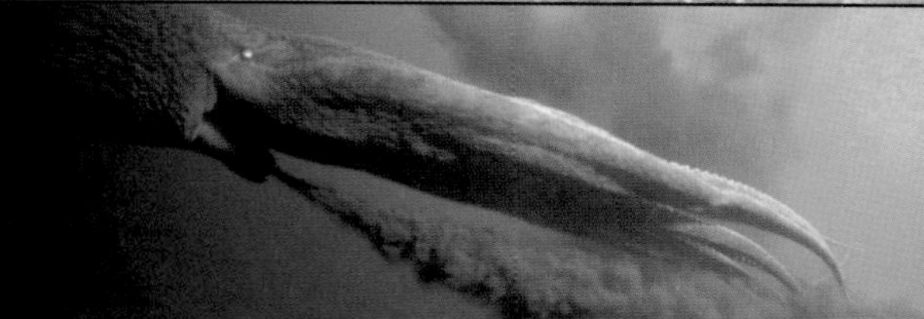

An octopus shoots through the water

▲ When an octopus gets into danger, it uses the same physics as Jet Ski technology to escape. First it pumps out a cloud of ink to hide it from its enemy, then the octopus propels itself away by squeezing water quickly from its body.

▲ The two-cylinder engine is 70 hp and 781 cc – as powerful as a large Grand Prix racing motorbike.

▲ The Jet Ski's ignition is electric and controlled by a built-in computer chip.

▶▶ See also: Water craft p116, FLIP ship p118, SailRocket p122

>> HOW A JET SKI MOVES

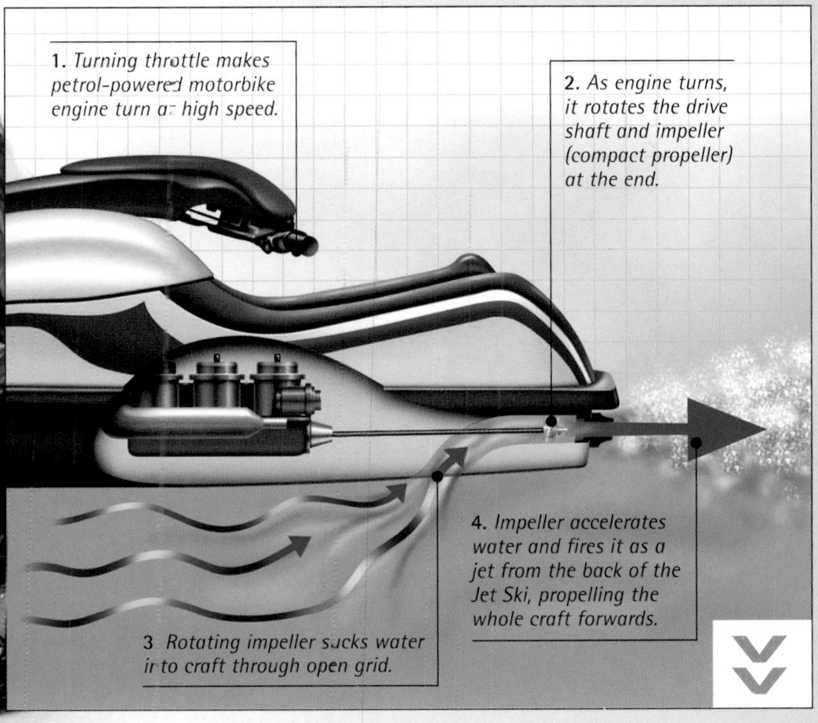

1. *Turning throttle makes petrol-powered motorbike engine turn at high speed.*

2. *As engine turns, it rotates the drive shaft and impeller (compact propeller) at the end.*

3. *Rotating impeller sucks water into craft through open grid.*

4. *Impeller accelerates water and fires it as a jet from the back of the Jet Ski, propelling the whole craft forwards.*

Jet Skis use science explored more than 300 years ago by English physicist Sir Isaac Newton (1643–1727). When the Jet Ski's powerful engine squirts a jet of water backwards, the whole craft shoots forwards. This is known as "action and reaction" because an action force (the backward-squirting water) produces an equal and opposite reaction force (moving the Jet Ski forwards). Motorboats power themselves with propellers and steer with a rudder. In a Jet Ski, turning the handlebars steers the craft.

◀ Jet Skis are as heavy and powerful as motorbikes, but float just like boats. Built-in foam panels make them virtually unsinkable, while a curved plastic hull helps to minimize water resistance and maximize speed. The sharply curved nose cuts through waves, providing a smooth ride in even the choppiest seas.

▲ A red button shuts down the engine and can be activated by a cable attached to the rider's arm.

▲ The impeller pipe shoots a water jet backwards and swivels to steer the craft when the handlebars are turned.

SAILROCKET

▶▶ Skimming gracefully over the waves, perfectly balanced between sea and air, SailRocket aims to smash a world sailing record. Under the right conditions, it can reach 90 km/h (56 mph). ▶▶

Powering over the waves

▶ Like SailRocket, this surfboard has a curved front edge where it meets the water. As the wave pushes the surfer along, the curved edge makes the front of the board plane (lift upwards). This reduces water resistance so the board skims quickly over the waves rather than dragging slowly through them.

A surfer rides towards the shore

▶ The highly streamlined SailRocket works like a cross between a windsurfer (a board with a sail) and a small sailing boat. Entirely powered by the wind, it is steered and controlled, using hand and foot ropes, by a pilot who lies snugly inside the cockpit.

Lightweight sail is made from Kevlar® and carbon fibre.

Main hull, built from lightweight carbon composite, is streamlined for low wind and water resistance.

Crossbeam is 8.3 m (20 ft) long and connects sail rig to main hull.

▶▶ See also: FLIP ship p118, Jet ski® p120, Kevlar® p222

>> HOW SAILROCKET MOVES IN THE WATER

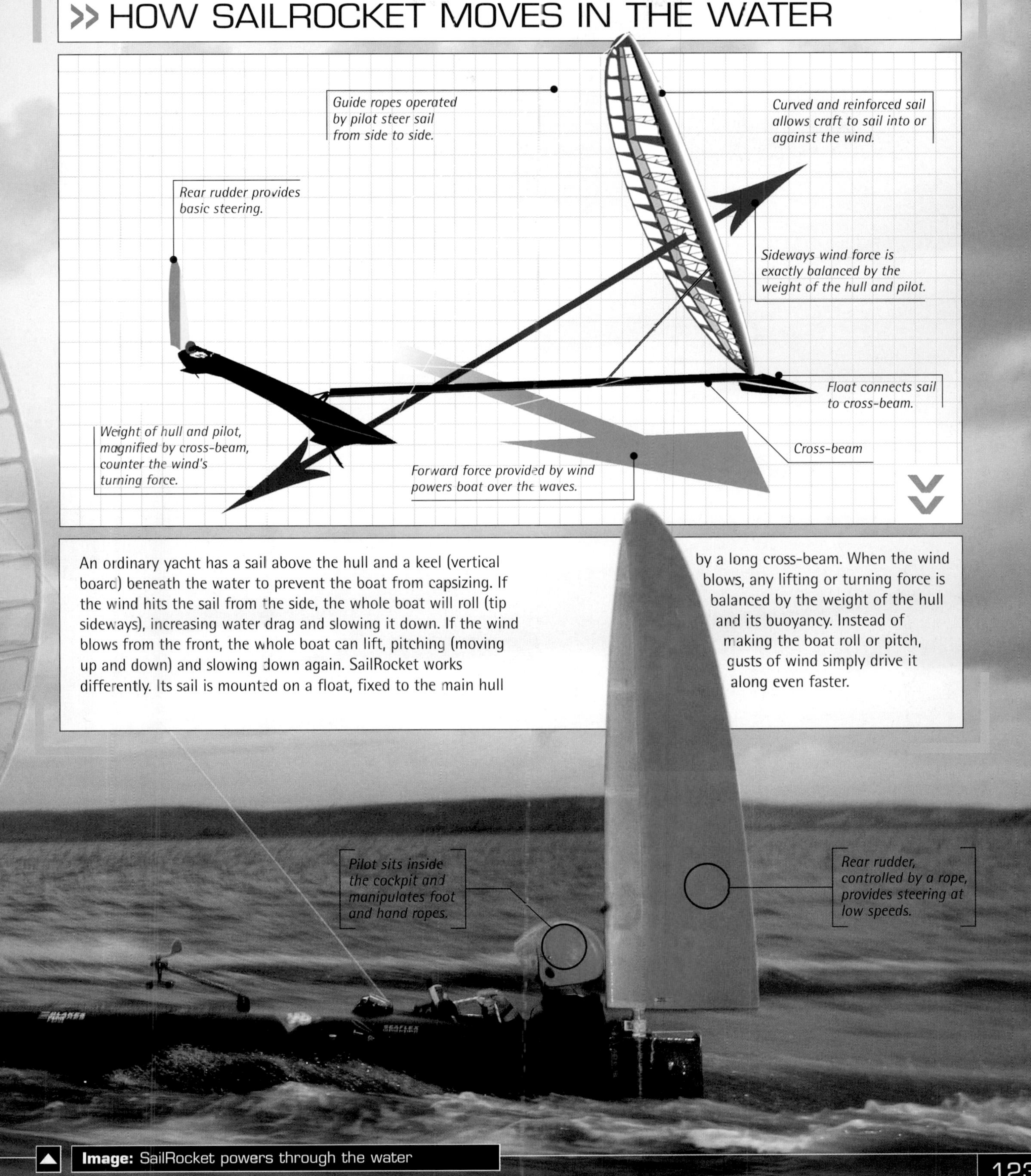

Guide ropes operated by pilot steer sail from side to side.
Curved and reinforced sail allows craft to sail into or against the wind.
Rear rudder provides basic steering.
Sideways wind force is exactly balanced by the weight of the hull and pilot.
Float connects sail to cross-beam.
Cross-beam
Weight of hull and pilot, magnified by cross-beam, counter the wind's turning force.
Forward force provided by wind powers boat over the waves.
Pilot sits inside the cockpit and manipulates foot and hand ropes.
Rear rudder, controlled by a rope, provides steering at low speeds.

An ordinary yacht has a sail above the hull and a keel (vertical board) beneath the water to prevent the boat from capsizing. If the wind hits the sail from the side, the whole boat will roll (tip sideways), increasing water drag and slowing it down. If the wind blows from the front, the whole boat can lift, pitching (moving up and down) and slowing down again. SailRocket works differently. Its sail is mounted on a float, fixed to the main hull by a long cross-beam. When the wind blows, any lifting or turning force is balanced by the weight of the hull and its buoyancy. Instead of making the boat roll or pitch, gusts of wind simply drive it along even faster.

Image: SailRocket powers through the water

GLIDER

▶▶ Imagine flying 3,000 km (1,864 miles) in a day, circling like a bird on rising air currents or surfing the wind as it travels up a mountain slope. Modern high-performance gliders can soar through the sky without an engine. ▶▶

Long, thin wings stretch to 18 m (60 ft) and reduce drag (forces resisting movement of glider through air).

▶ To get into the air, a glider is towed by a small plane or launched from a large winch on the ground. As there is no engine to produce thrust (driving force), the pilot generates speed and keeps the glider aloft by angling the wings downwards and hitching lifts on currents of warm air.

Surface of wings polished to reduce friction with air.

Record-breaking glider flight

▶ Most passenger planes fly at about 1,067 m (35,000 ft) above the ground. In 2006, the Perlan glider with two pilots on board reached 15,447 m (50,680 ft). At this height the temperature is -60°C (-76°F) and the crew needed spacesuits and oxygen masks. The glider used waves of moving air that exist in the high atmosphere. Height was gained by "surfing" the rising side of these air currents.

Perlan glider and pilots

Image: Motion photograph of a glider

D-2929
Low height area of the cockpit reduces drag but means that the pilot has to lie down.
Wheel retracts when airborne to improve streamlining.
Weight is kept to a minimum by the the use of super-strong lightweight materials.

HOW A GLIDER STAYS AIRBORNE

Clouds are created by rising air called thermals.

Wind pushes rising air along, so thermals tend to tilt.

Flying from thermal to thermal lets glider make progress over the ground and keep airborne longer.

Glider circles in thermal to gain height.

However streamlined its design, a glider will lose energy to drag and slow down when it flies along at a constant height. To gain speed, it must travel downwards. So, to maintain a constant speed, the glider must gradually descend. To travel really long distances a glider must somehow gain height. It does this by hitching a ride on rising air currents called thermals. In some terrain, such as car parks and fields, the air is warmer than average and will rise. If a glider can circle in these pockets of rising air it will be carried along with it, gaining height.

▶▶ See alsc: Silent flight p126, Aerobatics p128

SILENT FLIGHT

Image: Artist's impression of the SAX-40, the silent plane of the future

▶▶ The next generation of aircraft will be radically different from today's planes. Virtually silent, fuel-efficient aircraft will operate 24 hours a day – and the research that will make this a reality is already well underway. ▶▶

Engine has air intakes on top of wing to direct noise upwards, so less is heard on the ground. Sound insulation lines the engine to further reduce noise levels.

Exhaust from engine can be steered to give thrust (driving force) in best direction, which reduces the power needed to fly.

Winglets stop air leaking around wing ends, reducing drag (forces resisting movement of aircraft through the air).

Wing design lets aircraft land at lower speed, so makes less noise.

▲ This aircraft does not yet exist, but it could be a reality by 2030. It is the result of a research project investigating how quieter, more efficient aircraft might be built. Blended body shapes and new engine designs are being tested using wind tunnels and computer simulations. Quieter methods of take-off and landing are also being explored.

Earlier "flying wing" technology

▶ The idea of blended wing-body aircraft is not new. In the 1940s, the US Air Force tried to develop a flying wing bomber. This shape gives high lift (upwards force) and low drag, so can carry heavy loads over long distances. Several experimental aircraft were built, but the project was scrapped after a major crash.

Northrop N-9M early flying wing prototype

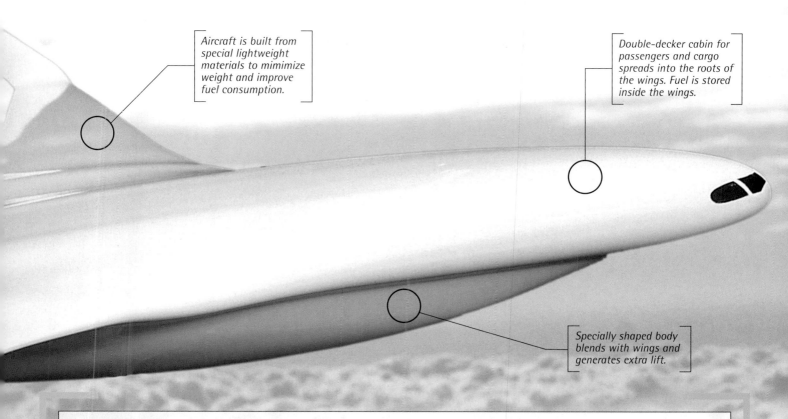

Aircraft is built from special lightweight materials to mimimize weight and improve fuel consumption.

Double-decker cabin for passengers and cargo spreads into the roots of the wings. Fuel is stored inside the wings.

Specially shaped body blends with wings and generates extra lift.

>> HOW SILENT FLIGHT IS DEVELOPED

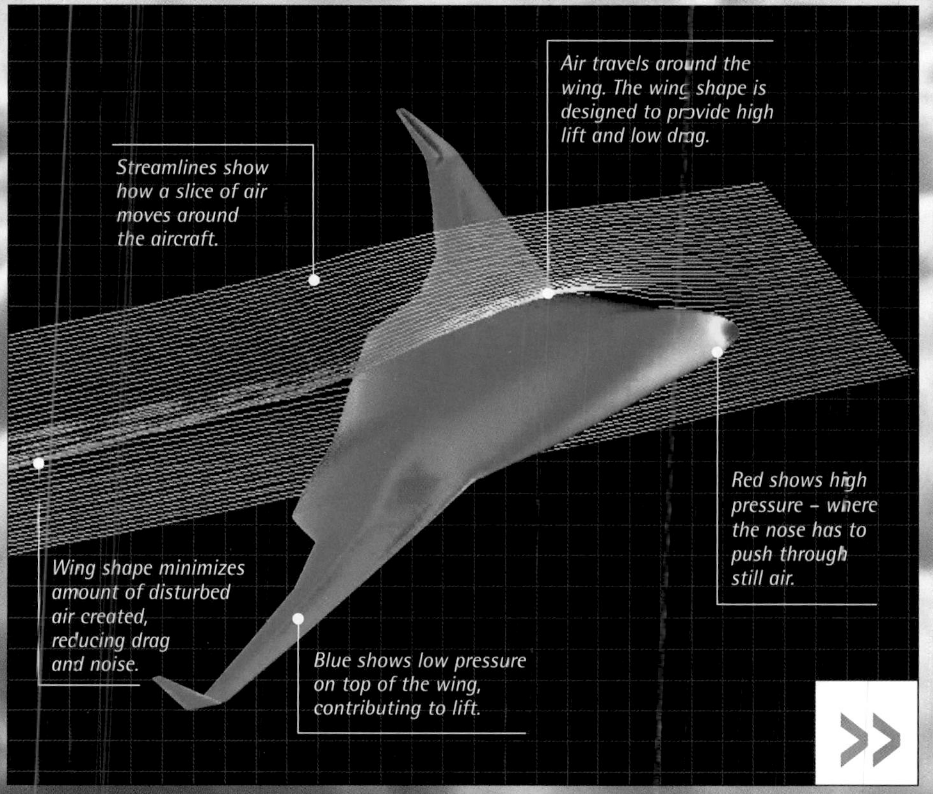

Air travels around the wing. The wing shape is designed to provide high lift and low drag.
Streamlines show how a slice of air moves around the aircraft.
Red shows high pressure – where the nose has to push through still air.
Wing shape minimizes amount of disturbed air created, reducing drag and noise.
Blue shows low pressure on top of the wing, contributing to lift.

Designs for new aircraft are tested and refined using computer simulations. This diagram shows the output from a virtual wind tunnel – revealing how the aircraft's body shape is shown as a 3D, colour-coded, digital display. From this, designers can analyze air flow around the aircraft under varying conditions. Adjustments to the design can then be made and tested without the time and expense of building a new model to re-test in a wind tunnel. Most aircraft are kept in the air by lift from their wings alone. Combining wings and body into a single, streamlined shape can create lift across the whole surface of the aircraft, reducing drag. As a result, the aircraft is more efficient and so uses less fuel, and it is also quieter, as less energy is lost as noise.

▶▶ See also: Bodyflight p86, Glider p124, Aerobatics p128, Helicopter p130

Image: A Zivko Edge 540 in a steep climb

AEROBATICS

▶▶Sitting inside the snug cockpit of a modern aerobatic plane is the ultimate thrill ride. As the plane twists and turns in the sky, the pilot has to work hard to remain conscious because the incredible forces applied to the body drain blood from the brain. ▶▶

▼ The Zivko Edge 540 is a tiny, lightweight aerobatic plane with big control surfaces (flaps on the wings and tailplane used to manoeuvre) that take up more space than most planes. Hence, it is able to change direction very quickly, which is perfect for executing aerobatic manoeuvres, and can roll its wings a full 360° in less than one second.

Propeller driven by powerful engine that works whichever way up the aircraft is.

Wheels have streamlined cowlings (coverings to reduce drag.

Pilot flies from reclined seat to reduce effect of G-forces on body.

Rudder is a flap on the fin that turns the nose left or right.

Elevator is a flap on the tailplane that pitches nose up or down.

Ailerons are flaps at the rear of each wing that roll the wings.

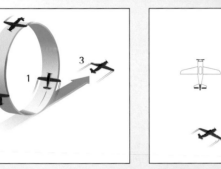

» HOW AEROBATIC FIGURES ARE FLOWN

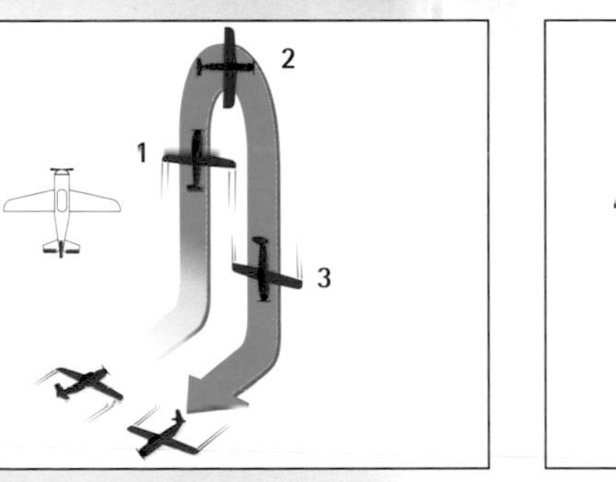

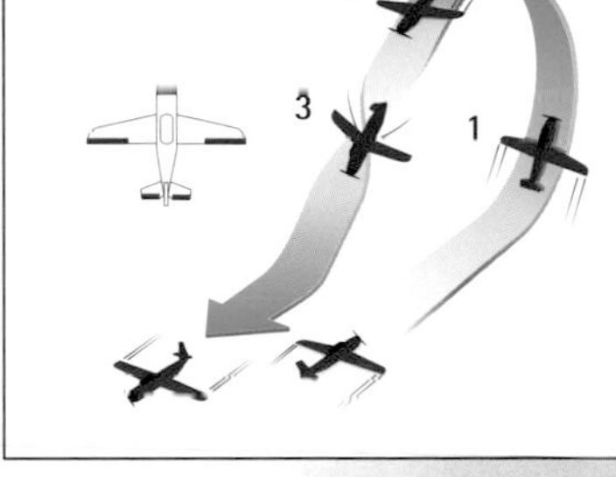

Inside loop

The plane climbs at an ever-steeper angle (1), reaching an upwards vertical position, but continuing until upside down (2), then vertically down. It eventually returns to a horizontal position (3). The elevator on the tailplane is used to keep raising the nose of the plane higher and higher.

Stall turn ("Hammerhead")

Here the elevator is used to raise the nose until the plane is climbing vertically (1). The plane slows to a stop and the rudder turns the plane sideways (2), so its nose now points straight down and it goes into a dive (3). The elevator is then used to pull the plane out of its vertical dive.

Half Cuban

This manoeuvre starts like a loop (1) until the plane is upside down with nose tipping downwards (2). At this point the pilot stops applying the elevator, so the plane keeps flying but upside down. The ailerons are then used to roll the wings (3) until the plane is the right way up once more.

▶▶ See also: Formula 1 p100, Glider p124, Ejector seat p220

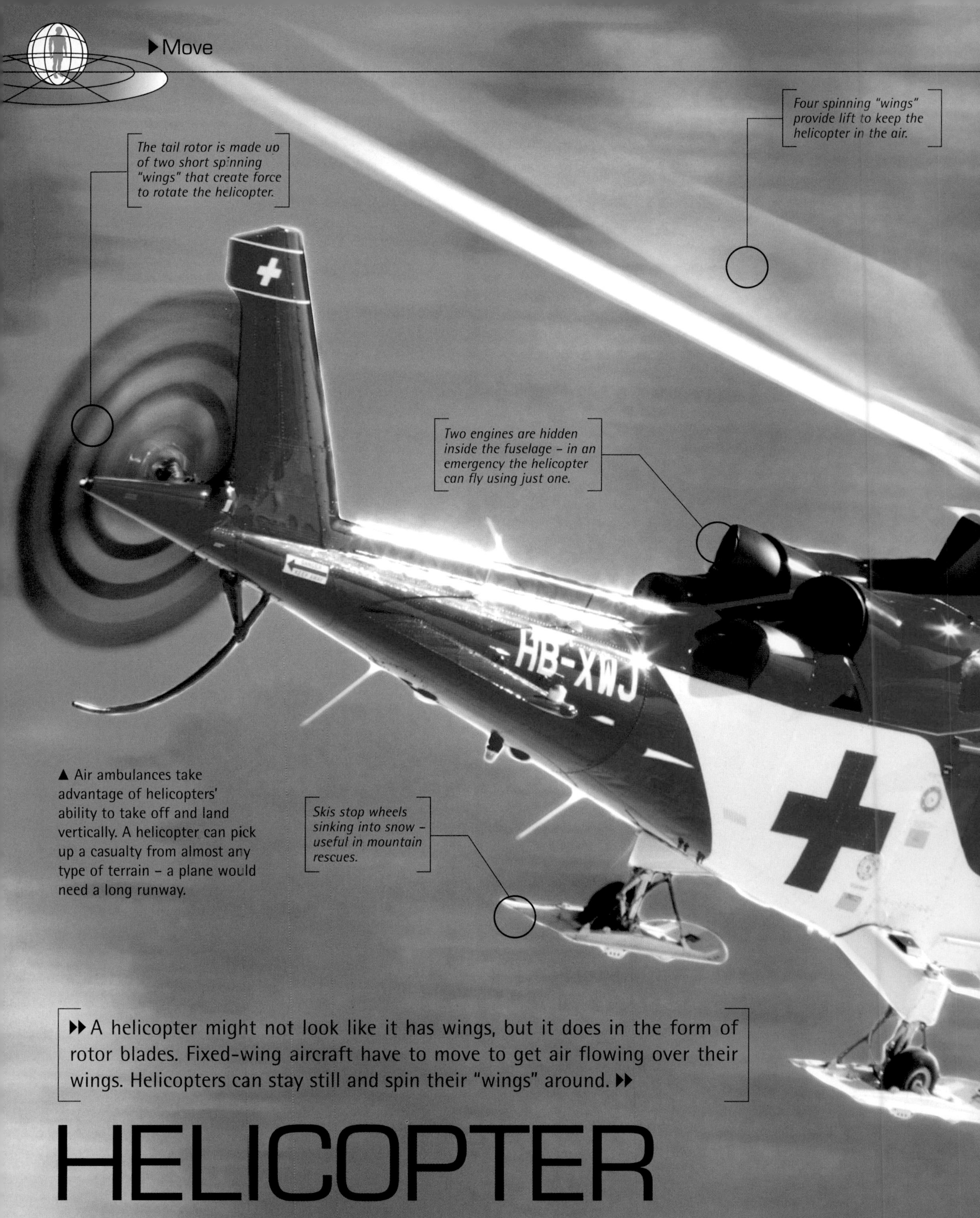

Four spinning "wings" provide lift to keep the helicopter in the air.
The tail rotor is made up of two short spinning "wings" that create force to rotate the helicopter.
Two engines are hidden inside the fuselage – in an emergency the helicopter can fly using just one.
HB-XWJ
Skis stop wheels sinking into snow – useful in mountain rescues.

▲ Air ambulances take advantage of helicopters' ability to take off and land vertically. A helicopter can pick up a casualty from almost any type of terrain – a plane would need a long runway.

▸▸ A helicopter might not look like it has wings, but it does in the form of rotor blades. Fixed-wing aircraft have to move to get air flowing over their wings. Helicopters can stay still and spin their "wings" around. ▸▸

HELICOPTER

▲ **Image:** Air ambulance of the Swiss Red Cross

>> KEY FEATURES OF A HELICOPTER

Tail rotor blades

Without a tail rotor, a helicopter's fuselage (body) would rotate in the opposite direction to the main rotor. Two short blades are mounted sideways and create thrust that counteracts this rotation. The tail rotor can be used to spin the fuselage left or right by altering the tilt of the rotor blades to change the amount of force generated.

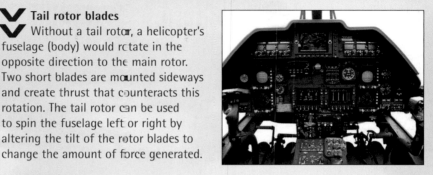

Main rotor blades

Each rotor blade is a wing that spins to create the lift needed to keep the helicopter aloft. To steer, the angle of the blade can be adjusted to create more tilt – and therefore lift – on one side of the main rotor and less on the other. This tips the helicopter in one direction, causing it to move that way.

Controls and pedals

Moving the joystick controls the main rotor and its tilt angle to direct the helicopter. The pedals control the tail rotor, adjusting the fuselage position without changing course. Another lever in the middle, the collective (throttle), controls the engine power and overall lift of the main rotor.

Large windows give pilots good all-round view – essential in search-and-rescue work.

Rotor-wing hybrid

▶ The CarterCopter prototype aircraft is a cross between a plane with wings and a helicopter. It is designed to test ideas for aircraft that use a rotor for vertical take off and landing, and wings for fast flight once in the air. The combination of the two technologies means that at high speeds the rotor blades can be slowed right down, as the wings create the lift to hold the aircraft up.

CarterCopter prototype

▶▶ See also: Glider p124, Aerobatics p128

TRAINERS

Funky footwear that does more than just protect your feet is now big business. Science and technology have combined to design specialist shoes to suit a whole range of sporting activities. There are shoes that keep the whole body healthy, trainers that "grow" to larger sizes, trainers with wheels in the heels, and eco-trainers that will reduce your carbon footprint.

Tribal influences The Masai Barefoot Technology (MBT®) system used in these trainers recreates the action of walking barefoot in the style of the Masai people of east Africa. It encourages healthy muscles and joints. The secret lies in the curved soles, which make the shoes slightly unstable. This forces the wearer to make constant small adjustments, which tones muscles and burns extra calories.

Inchworm Kids' feet grow very quickly, so Inchworm shoes are designed to grow with a child's feet. Simply press a button on the side, pull the toe, and the shoe will increase in half-size increments. A tiny window displays the current size.

Wheelies with Heelys®

There's no longer any need to carry a skateboard when you own a pair of these trainers – they have a wheel concealed in each heel. To bring the wheel into operation, wearers simply shift their weight back onto their heels and they're rolling along. To stop, they drop the soles of the feet back on the ground.

Night moves

The BrightWalk 2 trainers were designed for walking or running at night. Energy from the impact of each stride is converted into electricity. This powers patches of a special polymer on the trainer, which then glows to illuminate the road ahead – and can be seen by cars behind.

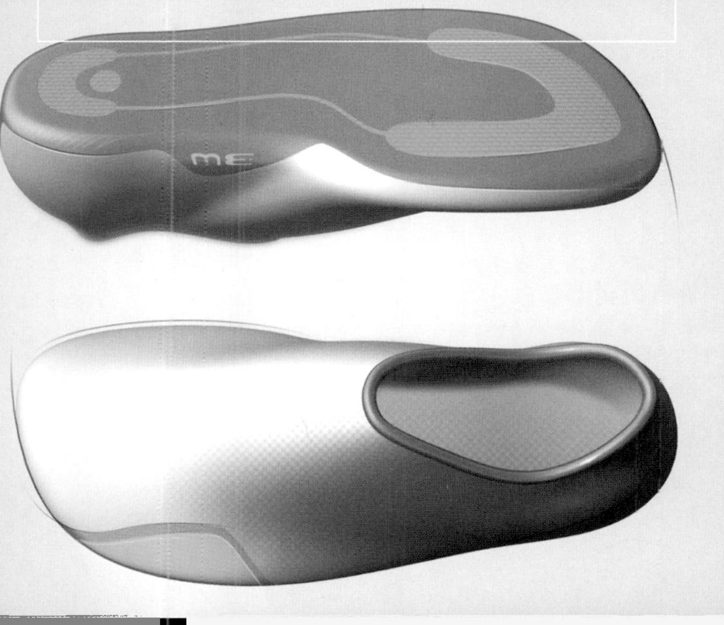

Recycled trainers

These Worn Again trainers are made from 99 per cent recycled materials – anything from scrap car seats to old clothes. To minimize fuel use, the shoes are assembled using unwanted items found near the factory. Additionally, any CO_2 emissions produced during the manufacturing process are balanced by tree planting and support for eco-projects.

▶▶ See also: X-sports p80, Flybar® p82, Gekkomat p84

Handrails move at exactly the same speed as the steps to keep travellers steady.
A step can make the same journey up the escalator 3,000 times a day.

Image: Multiple escalators in a shopping centre

ESCALATOR

▶▶Escalators are efficient people-movers. A lift can only carry a small group at a time, but an escalator moves people in a continuous cycle. As some people are stepping on, others are riding, and some are stepping off. ▶▶

▲ Sets of escalators are often arranged to make people follow indirect routes through shops. In this way a customer might notice something and buy it. A more direct route would not have led to that extra sale.

▶▶ HOW ESCALATORS WORK

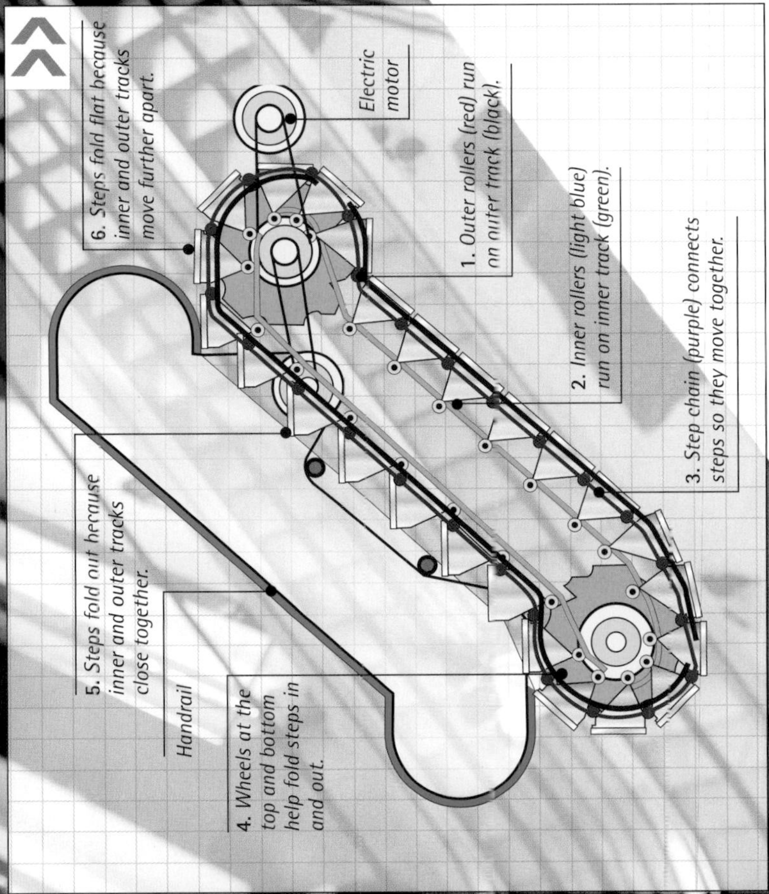

1. Outer rollers (red) run on outer track (black).

2. Inner rollers (light blue) run on inner track (green).

3. Step chain (purple) connects steps so they move together.

4. Wheels at the top and bottom help fold steps in and out.

5. Steps fold out because inner and outer tracks close together.

6. Steps fold flat because inner and outer tracks move further apart.

Electric motor

Handrail

An escalator's metal steps fold out into a staircase as they travel on the side where people stand, and fold flat underneath the escalator on their journey back. Each step has two rollers to make it alternately fold out and flatten as it moves around. One roller is fixed to the top of the step and the other is fixed to the bottom. The rollers travel on two separate tracks. When the tracks come together, on top of the escalator, the steps fold out. When the tracks separate, underneath the escalator, the steps fold flat. The folding steps also make it easier to get on and off the escalator both at the top and bottom.

▶▶ See also: Roller coaster p78, ULTra® p114

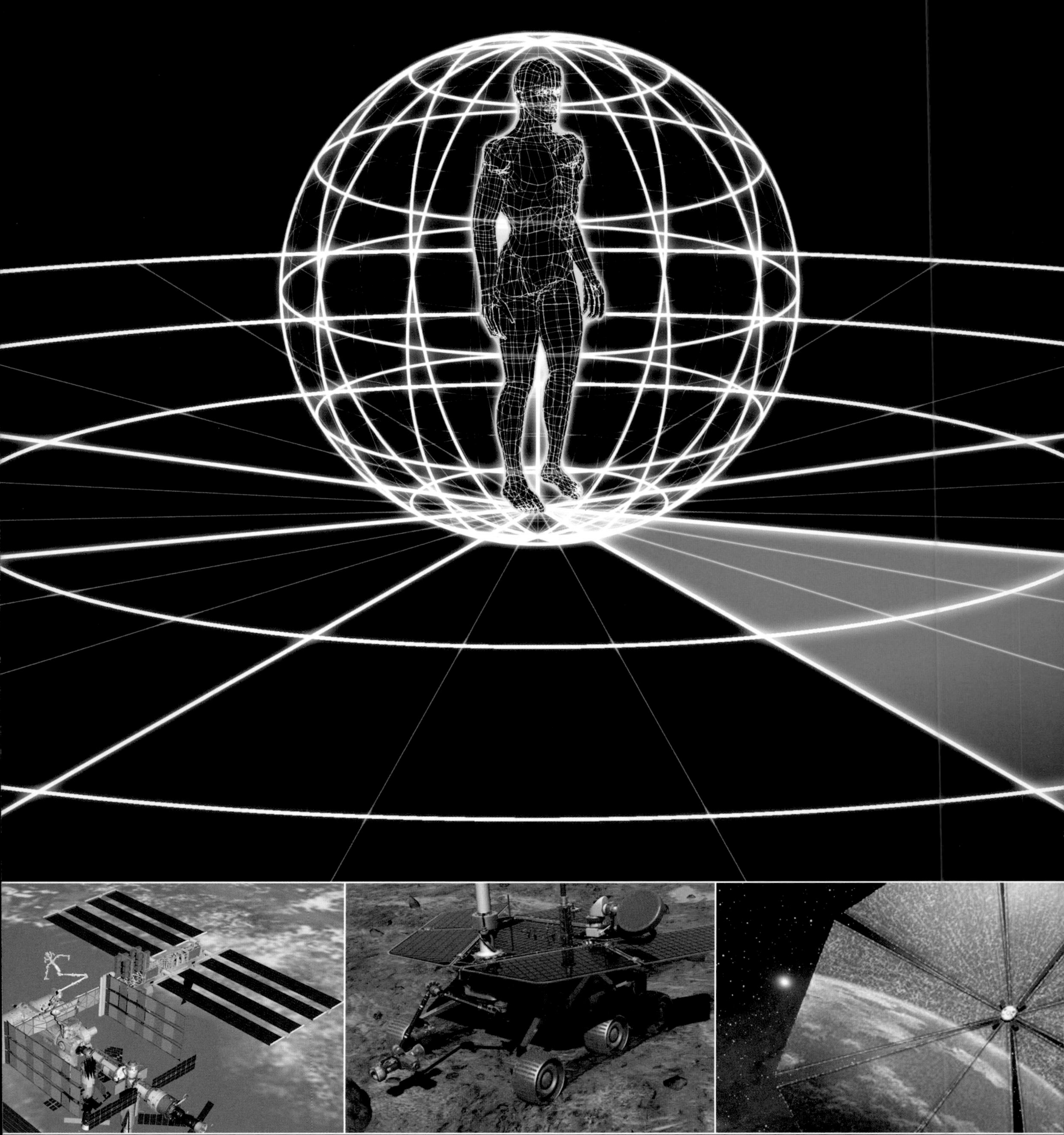

>> EXPLORE

Vomit comet >> Mars rover >> Space probes >> Solar sail >> SpaceShipOne >> Telescope >> Space station >> Explorers >> Oil rig >> Binoculars >> Night vision >> Microscope >> Weather balloon >> Atlas >> Neutrino tank >> Fusion reactor

A big machine to look at the tiny? p166
Want a fish-eye view? p154

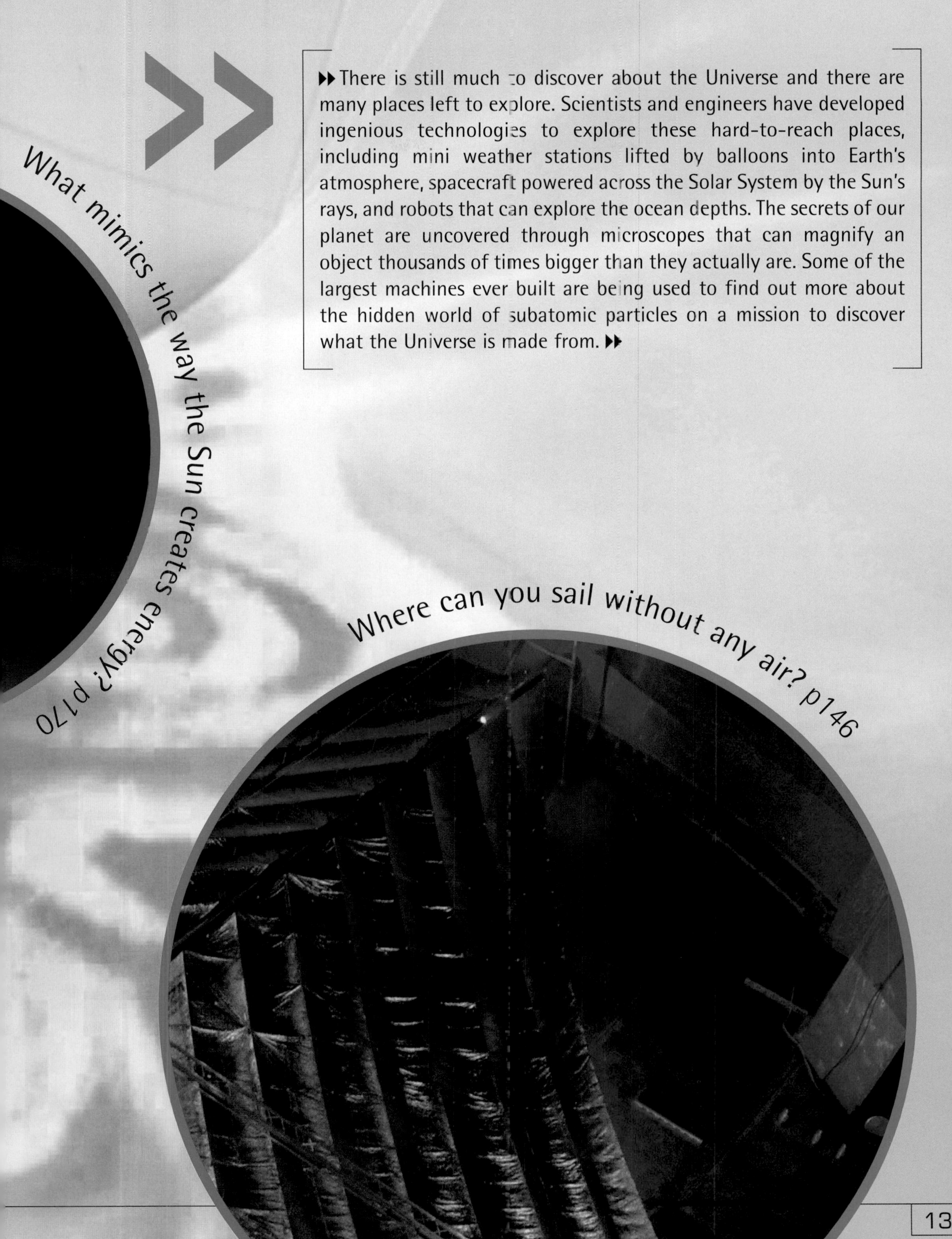

What mimics the way the Sun creates energy? p170
Where can you sail without any air? p146

▸▸ There is still much to discover about the Universe and there are many places left to explore. Scientists and engineers have developed ingenious technologies to explore these hard-to-reach places, including mini weather stations lifted by balloons into Earth's atmosphere, spacecraft powered across the Solar System by the Sun's rays, and robots that can explore the ocean depths. The secrets of our planet are uncovered through microscopes that can magnify an object thousands of times bigger than they actually are. Some of the largest machines ever built are being used to find out more about the hidden world of subatomic particles on a mission to discover what the Universe is made from. ▸▸

VOMIT COMET

Astronauts link arms to stay together as they float weightless.

▲ During the vomit comet's unusual flight path it enters a weightless section that lasts 25 seconds. It feels as if gravity has been turned off inside the aeroplane. People float in mid-air. Dropped objects no longer fall to the floor, but simply hang in one place.

▶▶ Want a taste of outer space? The flight path of a specially adapted "vomit comet" plane gives trainee astronauts a stomach-turning ride in zero-G. Perfect practice for the weightlessness they will experience on space missions in Earth's orbit. ▶▶

▲ **Image:** Crew experience weightlessness on vomit comet flight

▶▶ See also: Roller coaster p78, Bodyflight p86, SpaceShipOne p148

>> HOW THE VOMIT COMET WORKS

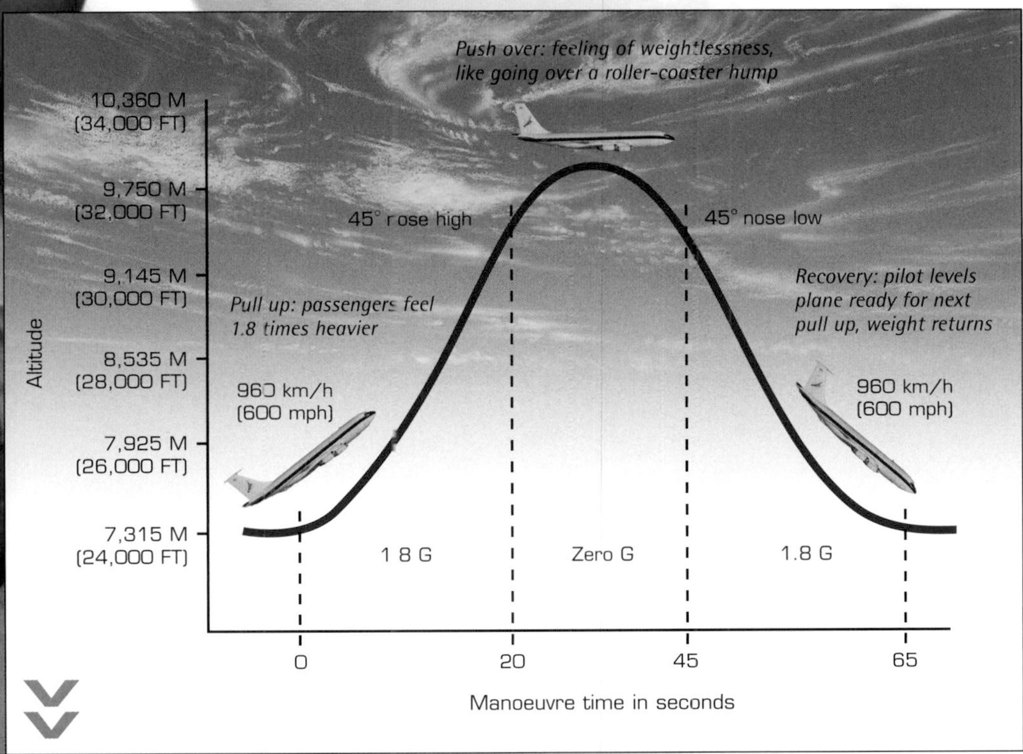

When the vomit comet flies straight and level, gravity feels just like it does on the ground. As the plane pulls up into a 45° climb, the trainee astronauts are pressed into their seats and feel like their weight has increased – this is positive "G". Then, very slowly, the pilot begins to push the plane's nose down again, flying a very special path called a parabola. This is exactly the path a stone thrown up in the air takes as it approaches the top of its arc and then starts to come down again. For just 25 seconds, the plane falls away from those on board at exactly the same speed that they fall towards it. They hang in one spot but can feel themselves falling – this is weightlessness.

Astronauts push off from the floor to float to the ceiling.

Water tank training

▶ The vomit comet can only provide short periods of weightlessness and room is limited by the size of the aircraft. When astronauts need to train for long or complex space walks, such as mending the Hubble Space Telescope, water tanks are used. Astronauts wear weighted spacesuits to practise procedures in the tank. It is not quite the same as being in space as they do not feel weightless and water is harder to move through than space.

Astronaut trains for Hubble mission

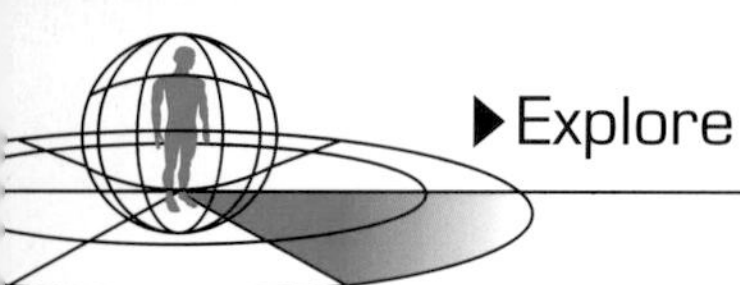

MARS ROVER

▶▶ Two vehicles, *Spirit* and *Opportunity*, have been exploring the surface of the planet Mars since January 2004. These robot geologists have been designed to be autonomous, working on their own to find water and signs of life. ▶▶

>> HOW A MARS ROVER TRAVELS

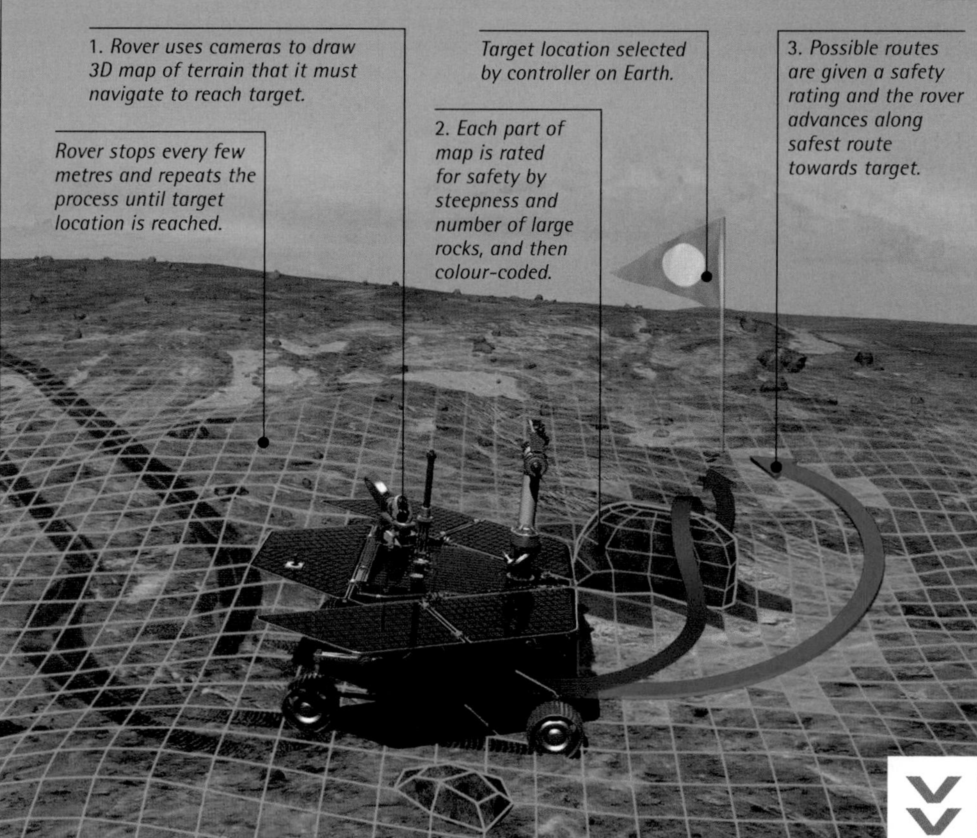

1. Rover uses cameras to draw 3D map of terrain that it must navigate to reach target.
Target location selected by controller on Earth.
3. Possible routes are given a safety rating and the rover advances along safest route towards target.
Rover stops every few metres and repeats the process until target location is reached.
2. Each part of map is rated for safety by steepness and number of large rocks, and then colour-coded.

Signals take several minutes to travel between Earth and Mars, so it is impossible to control the rover in real time like a model car. The rover must be able to navigate to a goal over rough terrain on its own, without getting into trouble. An operator on Earth informs the rover of its target location. The rover's hazard-avoidance and navigation cameras enable the rover's computer to map the surrounding terrain in 3D. The computer then picks the most direct safe route, and the rover travels up to 2 m (6.5 ft) before re-examining the route. Rovers have reached targets more than 1 km (0.5 miles) away without further guidance.

▶ Each Mars Exploration Rover is self-sufficient. It can generate power, navigate rough terrain, conduct experiments, and communicate with Earth. The two rovers will never meet as they landed on opposite sides of the planet. They have found evidence that liquid water flowed on Mars long ago.

Solar arrays convert sunlight to electricity to provide power.

Pair of hazard-avoidance cameras for navigation

Robot arm to manoeuvre science instruments

▶▶ See also: Space probes p144, SpaceShipOne p148, Space station p152

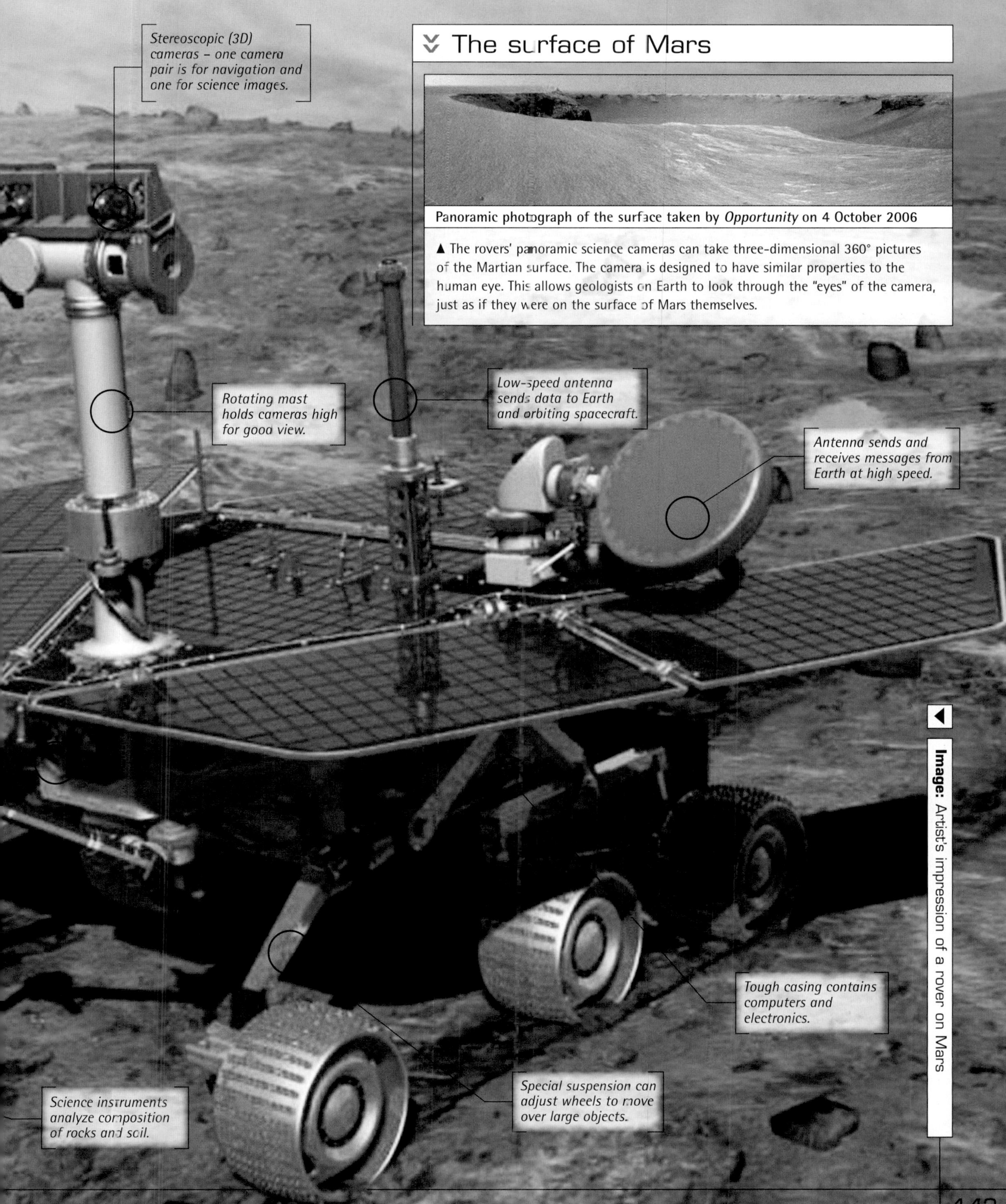

Stereoscopic (3D) cameras – one camera pair is for navigation and one for science images.
Rotating mast holds cameras high for good view.
Low-speed antenna sends data to Earth and orbiting spacecraft.
Antenna sends and receives messages from Earth at high speed.
Tough casing contains computers and electronics.
Special suspension can adjust wheels to move over large objects.
Science instruments analyze composition of rocks and soil.

The surface of Mars

Panoramic photograph of the surface taken by *Opportunity* on 4 October 2006

▲ The rovers' panoramic science cameras can take three-dimensional 360° pictures of the Martian surface. The camera is designed to have similar properties to the human eye. This allows geologists on Earth to look through the "eyes" of the camera, just as if they were on the surface of Mars themselves.

Image: Artist's impression of a rover on Mars

SPACE PROBES

As yet, humans have travelled no further than the Moon, but scientists are able to send space probes to further explore the Solar System. Some probes observe planets, moons, or comets from a distance to take pictures and collect scientific data. Others land to analyze alien soils and atmospheres. The most ambitious probes collect samples of gases or rocks and return them to Earth for study.

Voyager
In 1977, NASA lauched two Voyager space probes to explore Jupiter, Saturn, Uranus, and Neptune. Voyager 1 is now exploring the edge of the Solar System. It is the furthest human-made object from Earth and travels more than 1.5 million km (900,000 miles) a day.

Solar probe
The Sun still holds many mysteries and scientists are keen to understand it better. NASA is developing a solar probe that will travel into the Sun's corona (outer atmosphere). The probe will have a sophisticated heat shield to prevent its structures and systems melting in the Sun's intense heat.

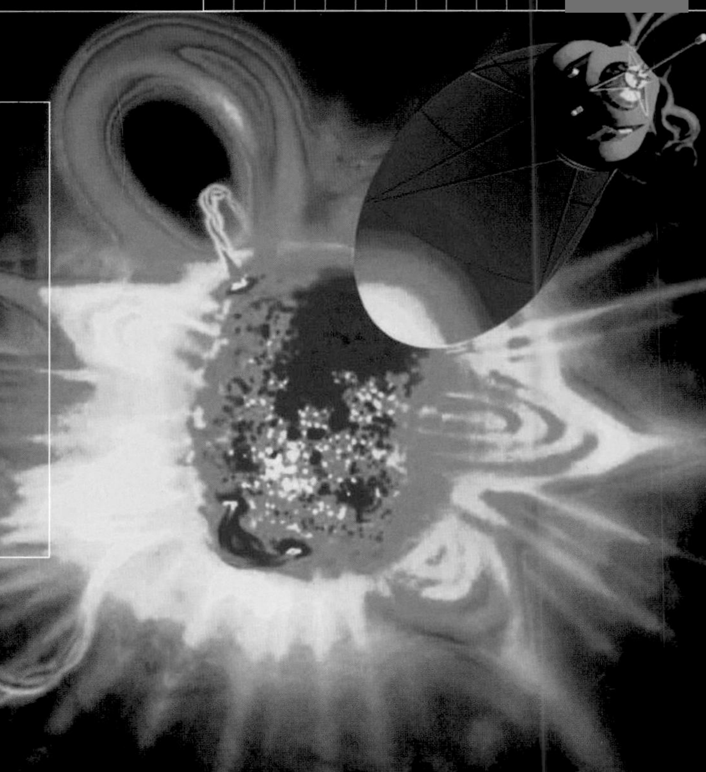

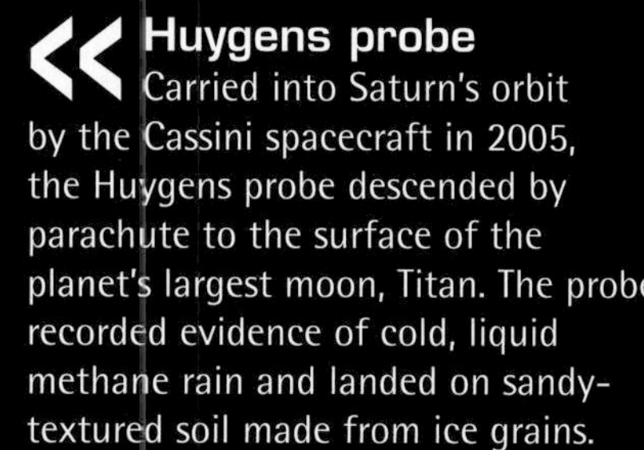

Huygens probe

Carried into Saturn's orbit by the Cassini spacecraft in 2005, the Huygens probe descended by parachute to the surface of the planet's largest moon, Titan. The probe recorded evidence of cold, liquid methane rain and landed on sandy-textured soil made from ice grains.

Cluster mission

Four Cluster probes orbit the Earth in formation, exploring the connection between the Sun and the Earth. The Sun emits streams of particles – known as the solar wind – which interact with Earth's magnetic field. Using information from several probes enables scientists to create a 3D image of the solar wind's activity.

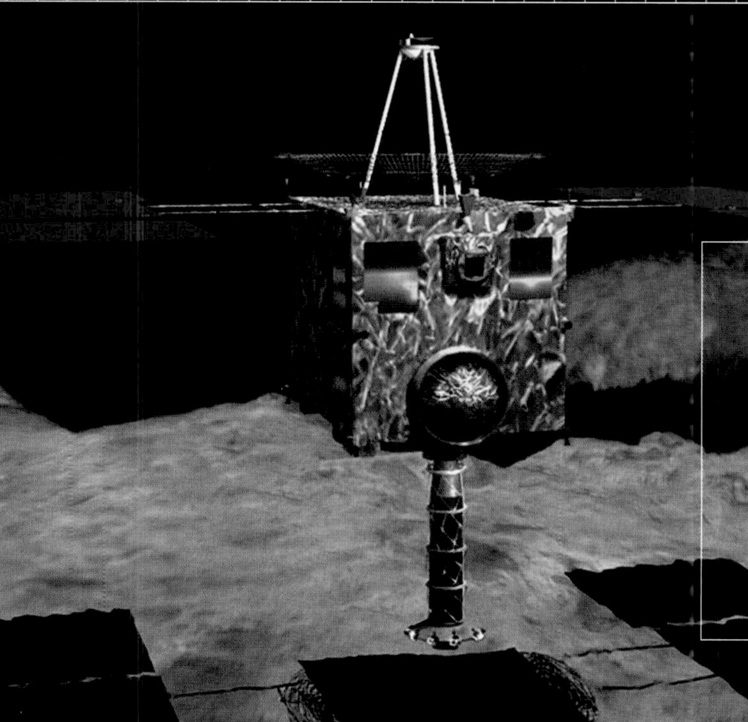

Hayabusa

The Hayabusa probe, launched by the Japan Aerospace Exploration Agency, landed on an asteroid for 30 minutes in November 2005. Its purpose was to collect samples and return them to Earth in 2010, using a capsule dropped by parachute. However, the landing encountered problems and it is not yet certain whether samples were successfully collected.

See also: Mars rover p142, Solar sail p146

SOLAR SAIL

Solar sails harness light from the Sun to move spaceships. They do not use any fuel. Solar sails will change the way we explore our Solar System and may one day carry us to the most distant stars.

The Cosmos 1 solar sail was designed to fly in Earth orbit. Its mirrored sails, the area of three tennis courts, fold away for launch. Instead of being powered by an engine, the force of sunlight bouncing off the sail pushes the spacecraft forwards. Unfortunately, Cosmos 1 was never tested because it was destroyed by a problem with the launch rocket.

Inflatable plastic tubes unfold sails and keep them flat.

Structure is ultra-lightweight plastic with metal coating.

HOW A SOLAR SAIL MOVES

Sunlight made of particles called photons.

Photons push sail as they bounce off, giving it a tiny nudge.

Sail moves in this direction.

Sail panels can be tilted to change direction of photon push.

Light is made from particles called photons. When photons bounce off a mirror they give it a tiny push – this push is the sum of the force of the impact and the recoil as the photon bounces off. A solar sail is a large mirror that reflects photons. It feels a force that is the sum of a great many photons bouncing off. In the vacuum of space, there is no air resistance and these tiny pushes will slowly but constantly accelerate the sail and any connected spacecraft. The larger the area of the sail and the lower the overall weight, the bigger the acceleration will be. The sail can tilt to steer the spacecraft.

Image: An artist's impression of Cosmos 1 in space

▶▶ See also: Mars rover p142, Space probes p144, SpaceShipOne p148

Payload includes computer, sensors, and motors to tilt sails.

Solar sail testing

Scientists test a prototype

▲ A prototype solar sail (smaller than Cosmos 1) is unfolded inside a space environment simulation chamber. In this room, solar sails can be exposed to realistic space vacuum and temperature conditions to test their reliability, unpacking methods, and control systems.

Image: Artist's impression of SS1 in flight

SPACESHIPONE

▶▶ The idea of space travel has fascinated people for thousands of years and, in 1961, Russian cosmonaut Yuri Gagarin became the first person to turn this dream into reality. Today, space tourists pay millions of dollars to travel to the International Space Station, but in the not too distant future, spaceships like SpaceShipOne will take many more people to the edge of space. ◀◀

▶▶ HOW SPACESHIPONE REACHES SPACE

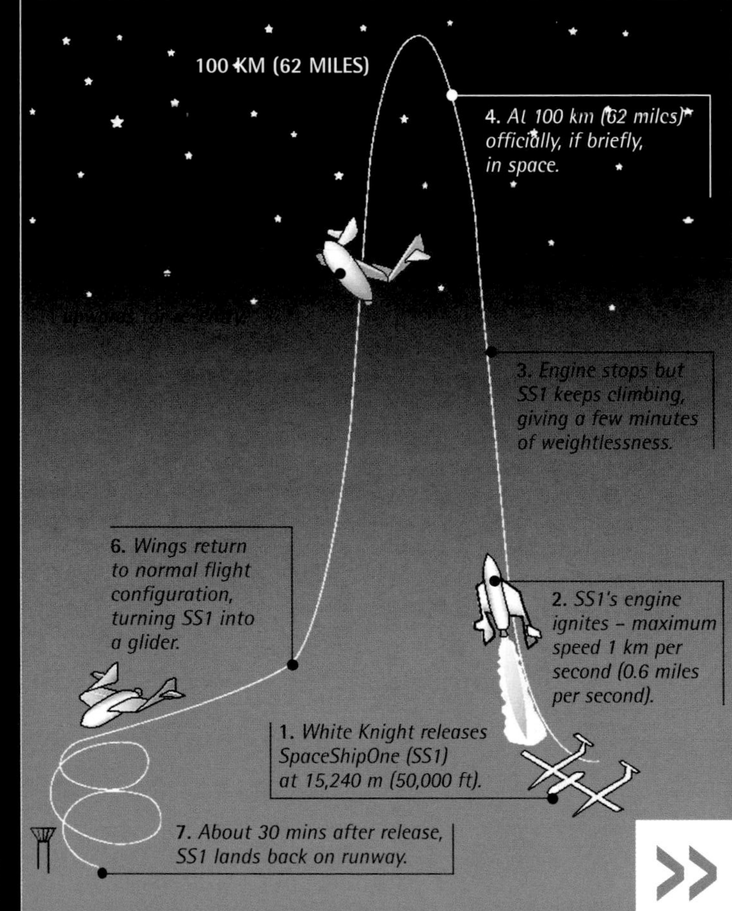

100 KM (62 MILES)
1. White Knight releases SpaceShipOne (SS1) at 15,240 m (50,000 ft).
2. SS1's engine ignites – maximum speed 1 km per second (0.6 miles per second).
3. Engine stops but SS1 keeps climbing, giving a few minutes of weightlessness.
4. At 100 km (62 miles) officially, if briefly, in space.
6. Wings return to normal flight configuration, turning SS1 into a glider.
7. About 30 mins after release, SS1 lands back on runway.

To get off the ground SpaceShipOne (SS1) is carried under a launch vehicle called White Knight, which takes off like a normal plane and drops off SS1 at 15,240 m (50,000 ft). SS1 then fires its rocket engine, climbing at more than three times the speed of sound. Once its fuel is all used, SS1's momentum continues to carry it upwards, like a thrown stone. This gives a period of weightlessness and, at the top of its flight path, SS1 briefly enters space. The tail section hinges upwards to give a stable and safe re-entry. Once lower in the atmosphere, the tail hinges back down to allow SS1 to glide back to Earth, landing in the same way as a normal plane.

▶ For a slower, safer re-entry to the atmosphere, the tail and rear sections of SpaceShipOne's wing hinge upwards to give much higher drag.

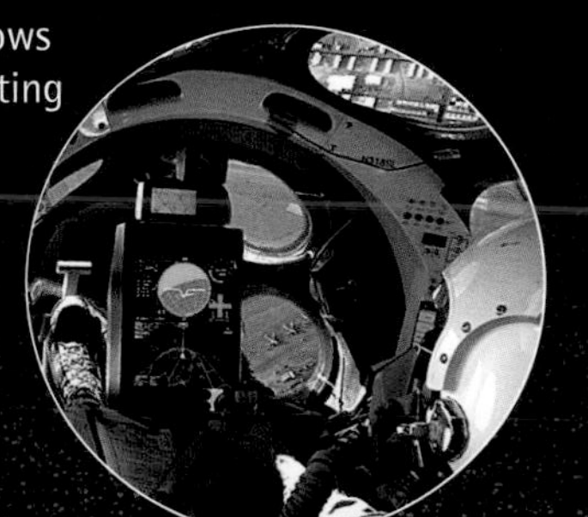

▶ Many small round windows provide good visibility. Cutting holes for larger windows would weaken the hull. The cabin holds three people and spacesuits aren't needed.

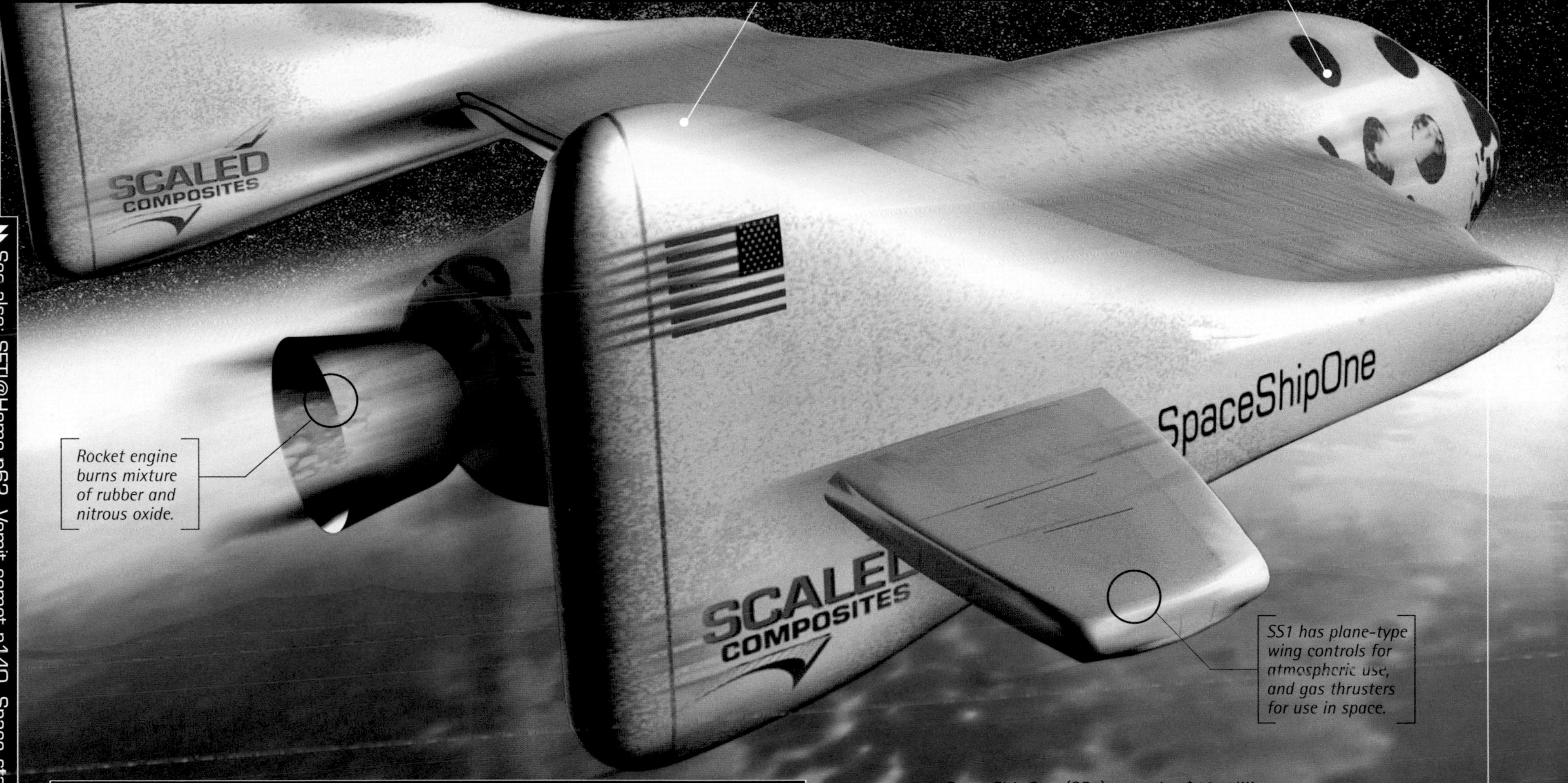
SCALED COMPOSITES
SpaceShipOne
Rocket engine burns mixture of rubber and nitrous oxide.
SS1 has plane-type wing controls for atmospheric use, and gas thrusters for use in space.

▲ SpaceShipOne (SS1) won the $10 million Ansari X-prize for the first private spacecraft capable of carrying three people into space twice in two weeks. Constructed from lightweight composite materials, SS1 was built for a fraction of the cost of most space vehicles.

≫ SpaceShipTwo

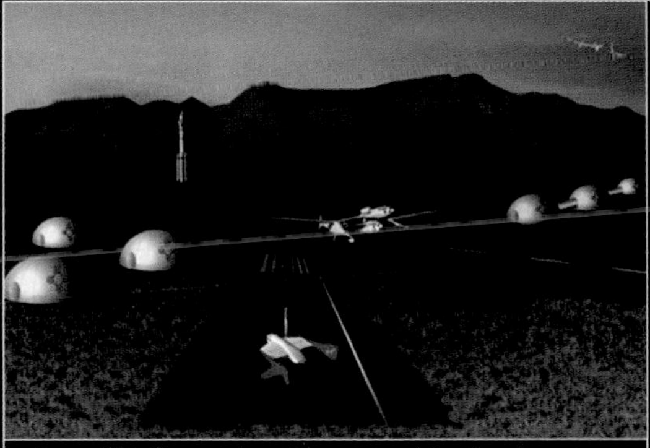

SpaceShipTwos take off and land in the desert

◀ Virgin Galactic is planning a fleet of next-generation SpaceShipTwo crafts to take fare-paying passengers into space. Although tickets cost £100,000 each, thousands of people have already applied. The flight will spend just a few minutes above 100 km (62 miles), so passengers will have officially been into space, and a slightly longer period under weightless conditions. This artist's impression shows the planned spaceport in New Mexico, USA.

▶▶ See also: SETI@Home p62, Vomit comet p140, Space station p152

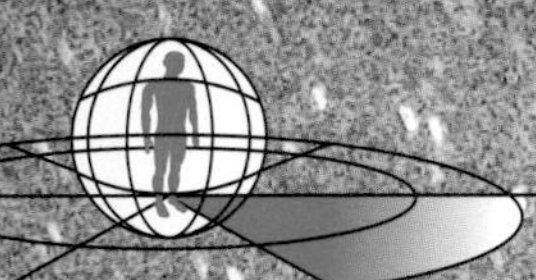

▼ The Keck I and II telescopes are sited high up on a volcano in Hawaii, USA, where the dark skies are usually cloudless and the air is clear. Big telescopes use mirrors instead of lenses. The mirrors in the Keck telescopes are 10 m (33 ft) in diameter and are some of the largest in the world. The telescopes are used to discover new planets and stars, and to seek answers to how and when galaxies formed.

Clouds on Uranus

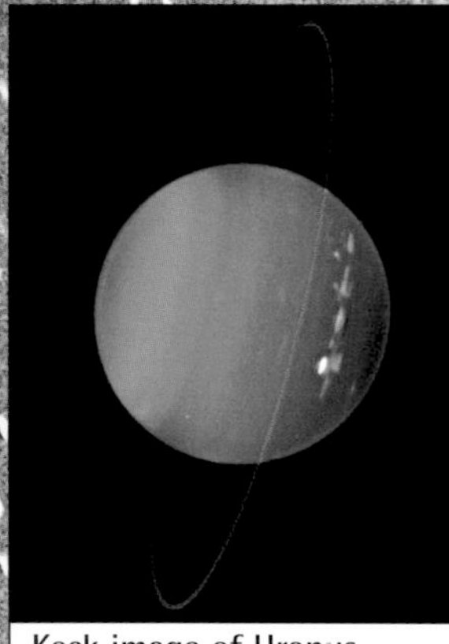

Keck image of Uranus

◀ The Keck telescope created this false-colour infrared (heat) image of the planet Uranus. Modern telescopes show details that were previously invisible, helping scientists to unravel the mysteries of the Solar System. The bright spots are fast-moving clouds high in the atmosphere. The faint ring system is also visible.

Laser beam is aimed into the atmosphere to create a false star. Tracking this "star" helps astronomers get a sharper picture of the sky.

TELESCOPE

▶▶ Large telescopes use giant curved mirrors to stare deep into space, revealing faint astronomical objects in incredible detail. Some telescopes fire lasers into the high atmosphere to improve their vision. ▶▶

Dome as tall as a ten-storey building protects telescope from the weather.

▲ Each telescope weighs 300 tonnes, but can be aimed and moved very precisely to follow a single point in the sky as the Earth turns. The two identical telescopes can work together as if they were a single, larger telescope.

» HOW A KECK TELESCOPE WORKS

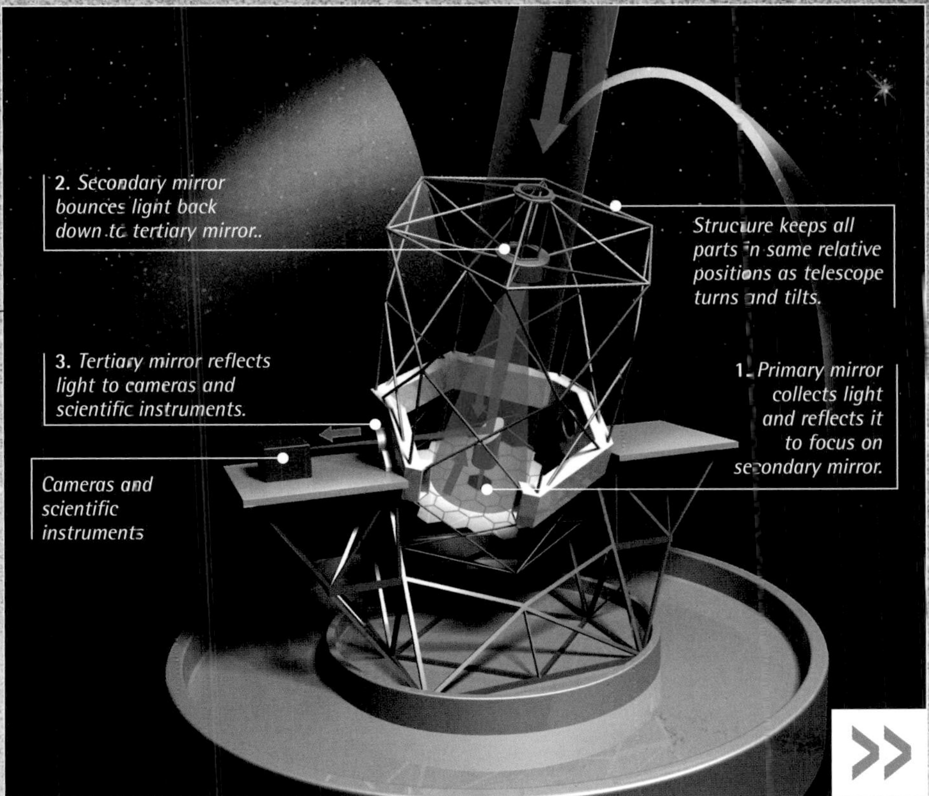

2. Secondary mirror bounces light back down to tertiary mirror.
Structure keeps all parts in same relative positions as telescope turns and tilts.
3. Tertiary mirror reflects light to cameras and scientific instruments.
1. Primary mirror collects light and reflects it to focus on secondary mirror.
Cameras and scientific instruments

The most powerful telescopes use giant mirrors instead of lenses, because these are lighter, easier to move, and more accurate. Each Keck telescope has a giant primary mirror that catches and focuses light from faint objects in space. It is made from 36 small hexagons that work like a single large mirror. Twice a second, each hexagon is adjusted by a computer to an accuracy 25,000 times smaller than a human hair. The mirror segments reflect light with amazing precision. Each one has been polished so smooth that any remaining imperfections are about 1/1000th the thickness of a piece of paper. Apart from making images, the telescope mirrors also reflect light onto scientific instruments. These help astronomers to understand what distant objects are made from.

Interior is cooled during the day so that the mirror does not heat up and warp.

Shutters open so that light can enter telescope, and can be turned to point in different directions.

▶▶ See also: Seti@Home p62, Space probes p144, SpaceShipOne p148

SPACE STATION

▶▶ The International Space Station (ISS) is a research facility orbiting more than 300 km (186 miles) above the Earth. Scheduled to be completed in 2010, it is a symbol of international cooperation with contributions from more than a dozen nations. ▶▶

▶ This is how the ISS will look when complete. Modules are constructed on Earth, transported to the space station, and assembled in orbit. Each module has a different function, from living space and laboratories to docking facilities for spacecraft bringing crew and supplies.

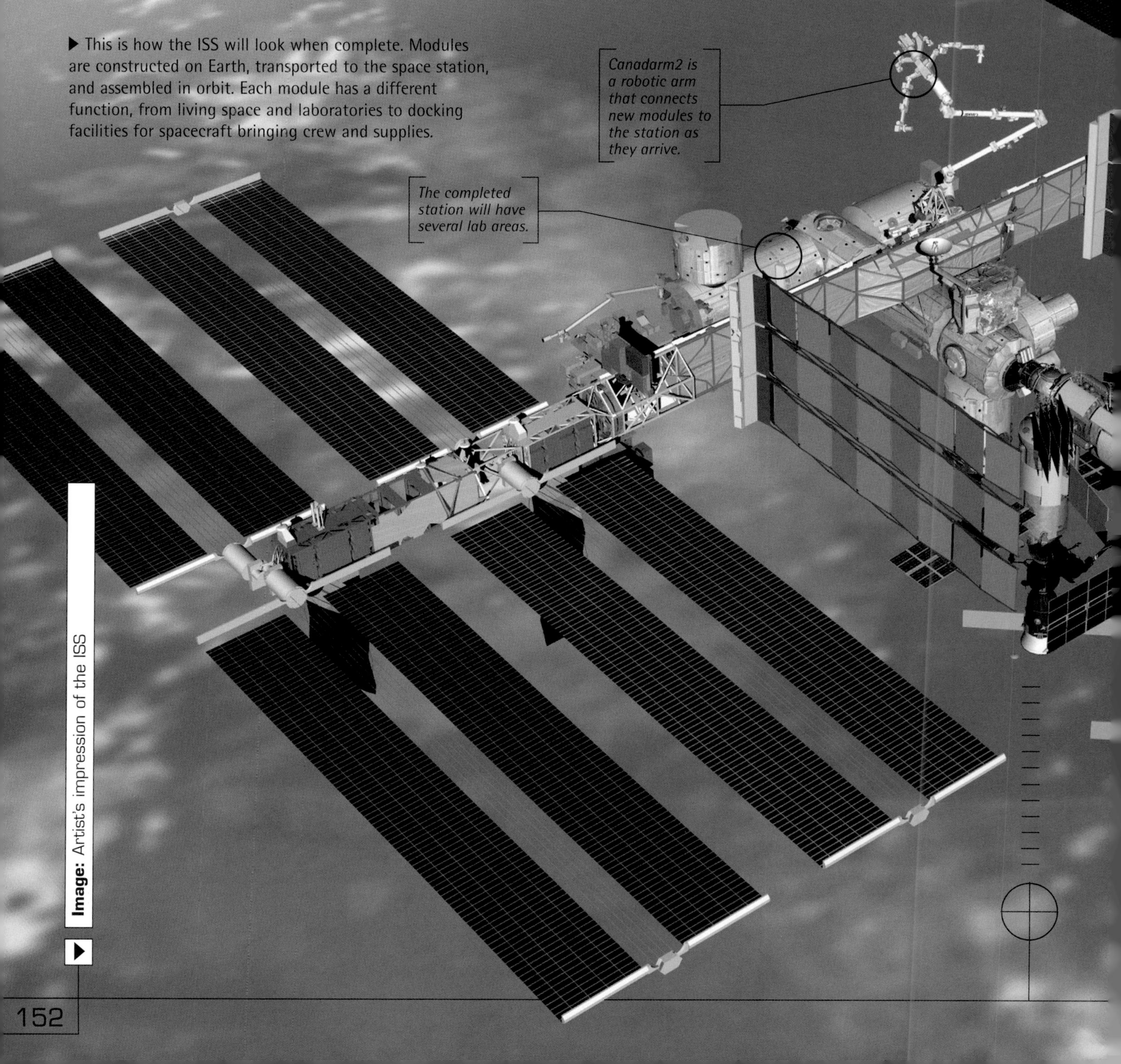

Canadarm2 is a robotic arm that connects new modules to the station as they arrive.

The completed station will have several lab areas.

Image: Artist's impression of the ISS

Solar panels convert sunlight into electricity to power the space station's systems.

Life on board

▶ The ISS orbits the Earth every 90 minutes and this means that the Sun rises 15 times a day. Astronauts have to follow an artificial 24-hour-long schedule with normal length periods of sleep and regular mealtimes. Exercise stops astronauts' muscles and bones weakening in the weightlessness of space – but runners must be tied down to avoid floating away!

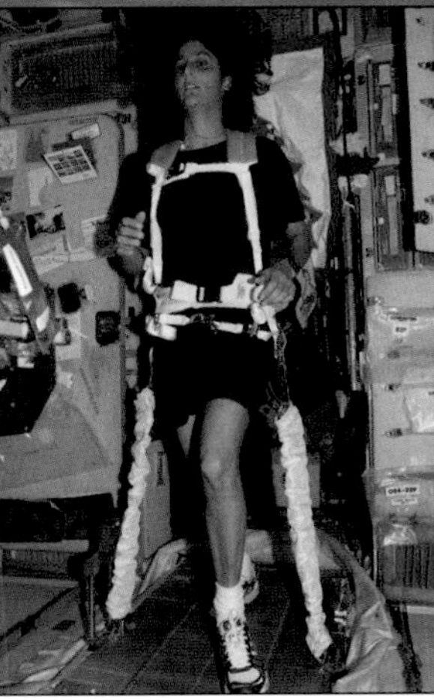
Astronaut exercising

WHAT HAPPENS ON BOARD?

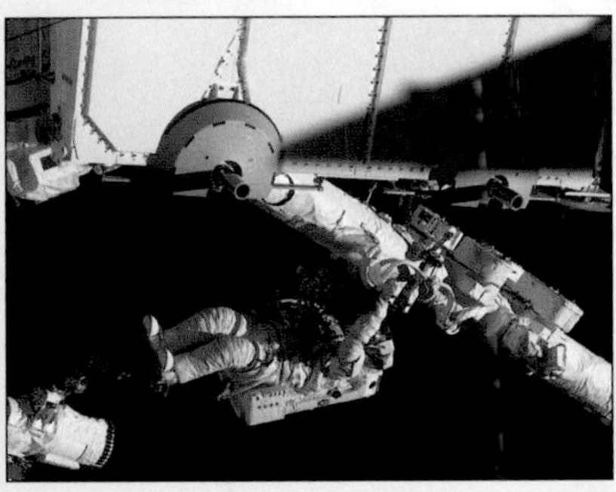

Experiments
Unlike in laboratories on Earth, on the ISS it is possible to carry out experiments in weightless conditions. This research is helping scientists to understand the long-term effects on our bodies of living without normal gravity – vital preparation for possible future missions to the Moon, Mars, and beyond.

Canadarm2
Here an astronaut is tethered to the space shuttle, carrying out work on the space station's robotic arm, Canadarm2. The arm can move around the station's framework, enabling it to work anywhere it is needed. The arm can do routine jobs outside the station without the need for astronauts to go on a spacewalk.

Visiting spacecraft can dock with the space station.

▶▶ See also: Vomit comet p140, Mars rover p142, Space probes p144, Solar sail p146

EXPLORERS

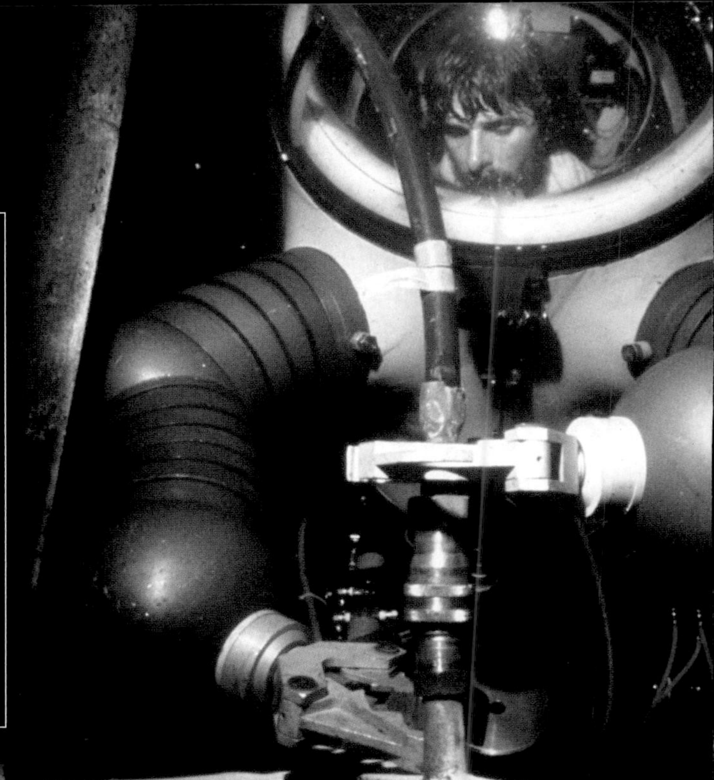

WASP suit Part diving suit, part mini-sub, this was developed for underwater pipeline maintenance and can dive to a depth of 600 m (2,000 ft). The diver's arms fit inside flexible aluminium tubes with hand-operated grabbers. Foot-operated thrusters propel the diver forward.

Explorers need to be mentally prepared for many potential hazards. They should also make sure they take the latest kit with them. These hi-tech gadgets will help them visit all those hard-to-get-to places and to survive in style once they get there.

Air camper This two-person tent simply hooks to the back of a car, acting as a comfy extension on overnight camping trips. It has no poles – it is simply held up by air pressure. It even self-inflates using a fan that connects to the car's internal electricity socket.

Robocarp

If it is deep, dark, and dangerous then why not send Robocarp? This intelligent robot fish with built-in sensors can find its own way around, avoid obstacles, and deal with changing water conditions. It could be used for seabed exploration or to detect leaks in oil pipelines.

Prometheus 1

Meals can be cooked without fuel using a fold-out reflector 1.3 m (4 ft) across. It concentrates the sun's heat on a pan placed in the centre to give cooking temperatures of up to 250°C (480°F).

Paramotoring

A great way to travel to remote areas is by a powered paraglider, also know as paramotoring. This consists of a paraglider – a parachute that inflates into a wing shape – and a large fan driven by a lawnmower engine. Pilots can take off and land almost anywhere, and fly as low or as high as they like.

See also: Robots p90, Robot car p104, Mars rover p142, Space probes p144

OIL RIG

Earth is like a giant petrol station, with more than a trillion barrels of oil stored in its rocks. Much of this lies beneath the surface of the sea. Getting the oil out requires enormous drills that screw down into the Earth's crust.

This type of oil platform or "rig" is known as a jackup. It is designed to extract oil from shallow water. With the rig in position, the legs are lowered to the seabed to keep the rig upright during drilling. When the oil deposit is exhausted, the legs are lifted and the rig is hauled to another location.

Legs made from tubular steel can support rig in water 150 m (500 ft) deep.

Cranes lift supplies from ships and haul drilling pipes into position.

Helicopter pad allows supplies and crew to be brought in by air.

Image: The Roger W Mowell jackup rig in the Mediterranean Sea

Oil tanker carries oil from rig to a refinery onshore.

HOW OIL IS EXTRACTED

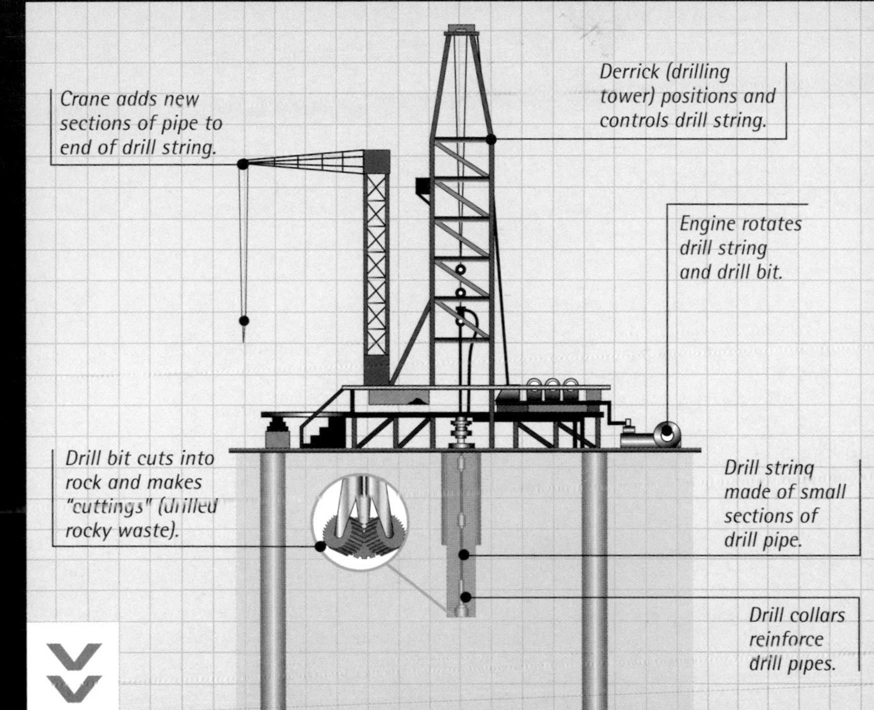
Crane adds new sections of pipe to end of drill string.
Derrick (drilling tower) positions and controls drill string.
Engine rotates drill string and drill bit.
Drill bit cuts into rock and makes "cuttings" (drilled rocky waste).
Drill string made of small sections of drill pipe.
Drill collars reinforce drill pipes.

An engine on top of the rig slowly rotates the drill bit (the cutting tool) at the bottom by turning a long pipe called a drill string. The drill string is assembled from hundreds of separate sections of pipe, each approximately 10 m (30 ft) long, making an enormous drill up to 10 km (6 miles) long. Mud is pumped down the hole to clean and cool the drill bit and remove the "cuttings" (waste rock). When the drill is removed, the oil can be pumped to the surface up the same hole using a suction pump.

▶▶ See also: Big builds p192, Mass damper p194, Power tower p196

▶ This coloured X-ray shows the internal optics of a pair of binoculars. Each side of the binoculars is identical. Together, the objective lens and the eyepiece lens present your eye with a magnified image of distant objects. The greater the magnification, the larger distant objects will appear when viewed through the binoculars.

BINOCULARS

▶▶ Binoculars are essentially two identical telescopes aligned to point in the same direction. They show each eye an image of the same magnified object, and the brain processes these two images as one 3D picture. ▶▶

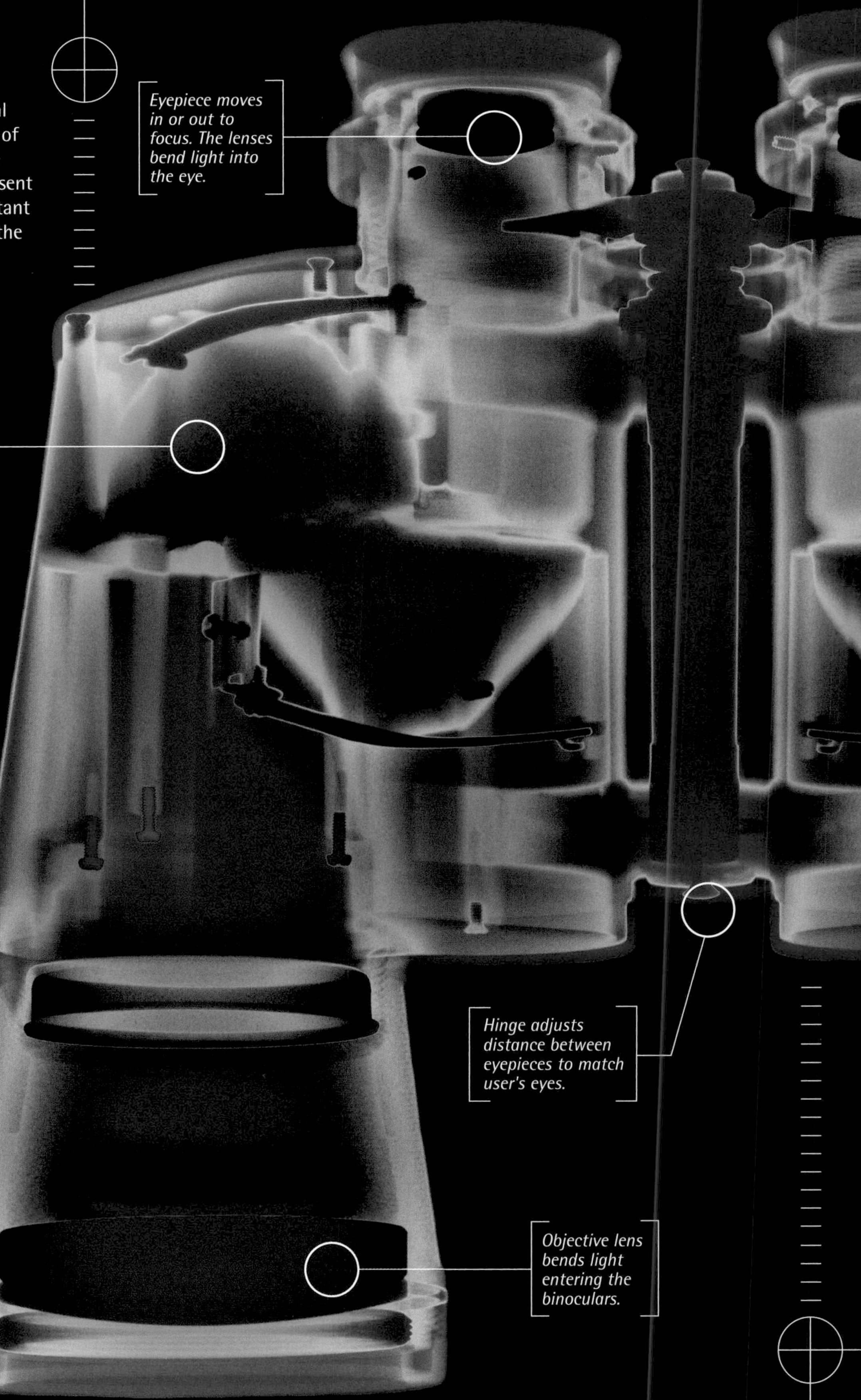

Eyepiece moves in or out to focus. The lenses bend light into the eye.
Prisms – blocks of glass – reflect light and correct upside down image from lens.
Hinge adjusts distance between eyepieces to match user's eyes.
Objective lens bends light entering the binoculars.

Image: False-coloured X-ray of binoculars

▶▶ See also: Telescope p150, Lighthouse p236

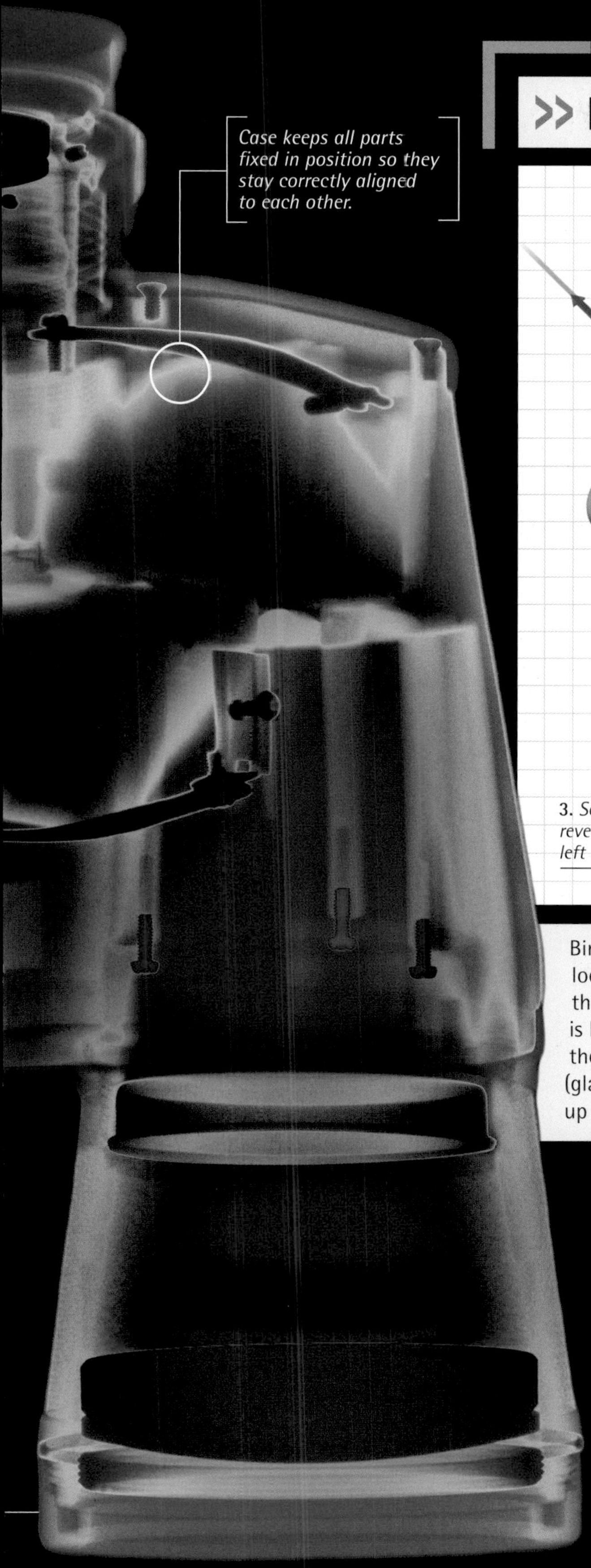

Case keeps all parts fixed in position so they stay correctly aligned to each other.

>> HOW BINOCULARS WORK

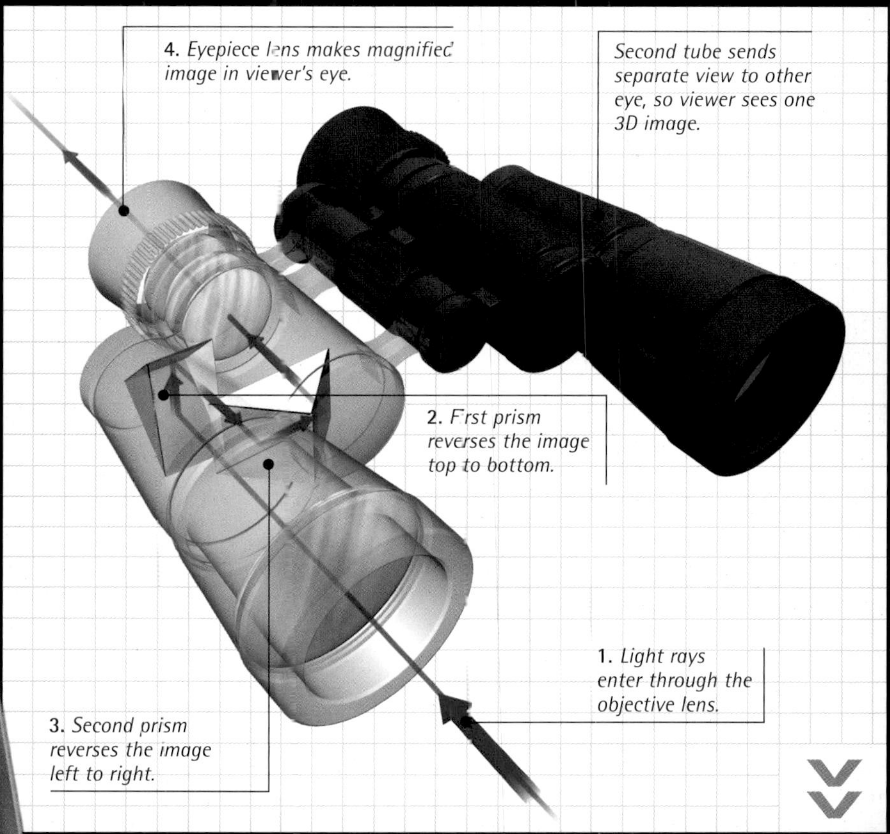

4. Eyepiece lens makes magnified image in viewer's eye.

Second tube sends separate view to other eye, so viewer sees one 3D image.

2. First prism reverses the image top to bottom.

1. Light rays enter through the objective lens.

3. Second prism reverses the image left to right.

Binoculars use lenses (curved pieces of glass) to make distant objects look bigger. Between them, the large lens at the front (the objective lens) and the small eyepiece lens at the back bend light rays from whatever the viewer is looking at into the eye to form a clear, magnified (bigger) image. However, the two lenses also turn the image upside down and back to front. Two prisms (glass wedges) in between the lenses reverse the image and turn it right side up so it looks correct.

Naval binoculars

▶ These high magnification binoculars are being used for military manoeuvres. With lenses up to 15 cm (6 in) in diameter they are very heavy, so they must be mounted to minimize image wobble. Binoculars like these are capable of magnification of up to 25 times.

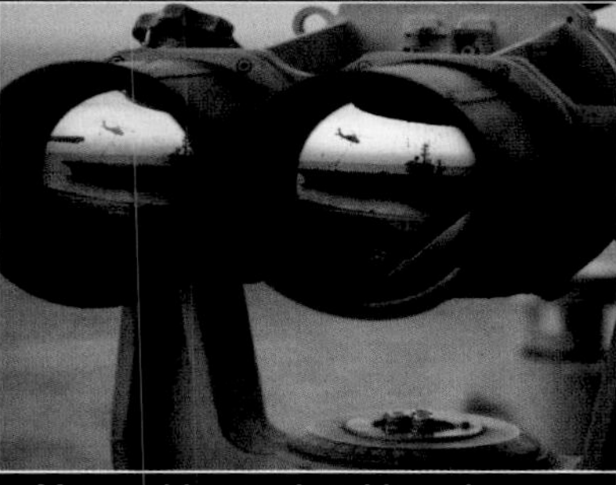

Mounted heavy-duty binoculars

NIGHT VISION

HOW NIGHT VISION WORKS

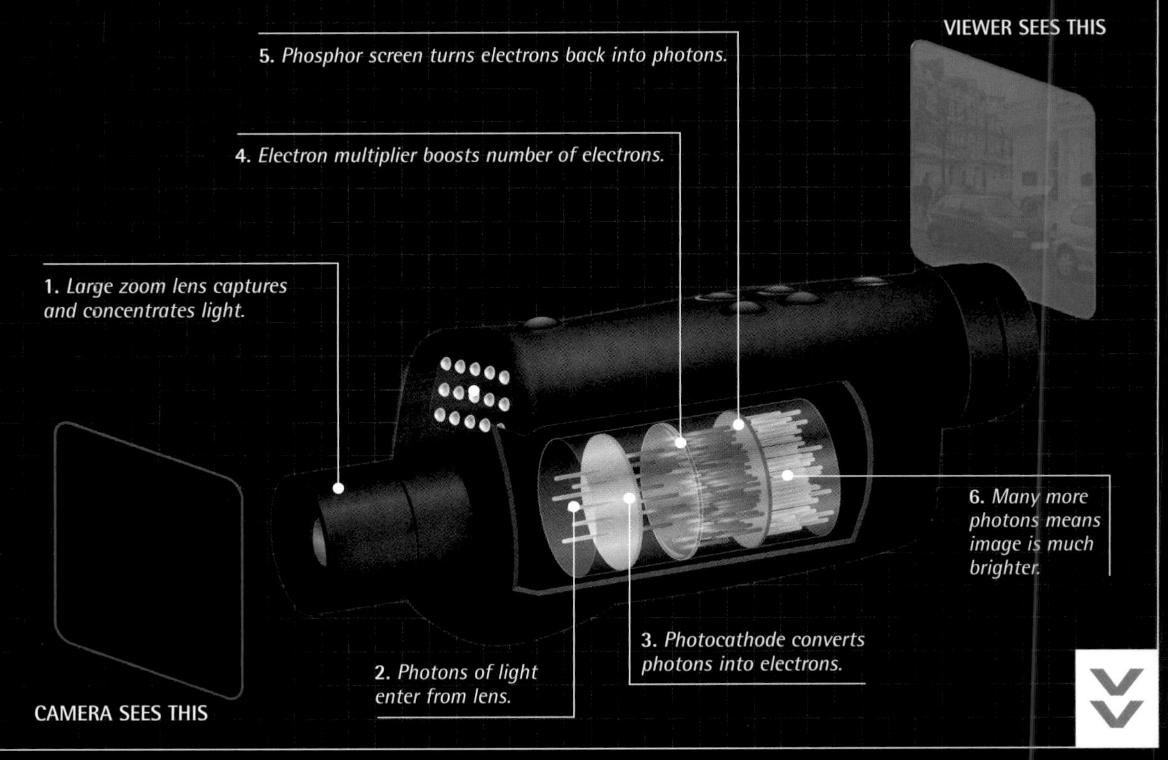
VIEWER SEES THIS
5. Phosphor screen turns electrons back into photons.
4. Electron multiplier boosts number of electrons.
1. Large zoom lens captures and concentrates light.
6. Many more photons means image is much brighter.
3. Photocathode converts photons into electrons.
2. Photons of light enter from lens.
CAMERA SEES THIS

Night-vision cameras capture dim light and intensify it to enable our eyes to see things. They work by converting light into electricity, boosting the electricity, and then turning it back into brighter light. Like ordinary cameras, night-vision instruments have a lens at the front that gathers photons (individual packets of light). Behind the lens, the photons hit a light detector called a photocathode that converts them into a trickle of electrons – the tiny particles that generate electricity.

Light photons of all colours become electrons, so any colour in the incoming light is lost. An electron multiplier unit inside the camera boosts the electron flow, turning the trickle into a flood. Hugely increased in number, the electrons fire into a glass plate covered in a chemical called phosphor. Like the screen in a television, the phosphor plate generates photons of light when electrons hit it. Because there are many more photons, our eyes have no trouble seeing them.

▶▶ Our eyes contain 126 million light-detecting cells that can paint a colourful panorama in the daytime. But at night, when human eyes barely function, we have to rely on night-vision cameras to maximize the little light available. ▶▶

Rods and cones

▶ The retinas in our eyes contain light-detecting cells called rods and cones. There are 120 million rods (green) and 6 million cones (blue). The rods detect dim light and movement and are more sensitive than the cones. Three types of cones detect red, blue, and green light.

Green rods and blue cones

Image: Night-vision image of a fox

▲ A fox can be seen up to 140 m (460 ft) away with a night-vision camera, even in total darkness. Although night vision makes things much brighter, some of the detail – and all of the colour – is lost during the enhancement process.

Phosphor plate is green because the human eye can make out more shades of this colour than any other.

▶▶ See also: Catseyes® p108, Binoculars p158, Spy p214

>> HOW AN SEM WORKS

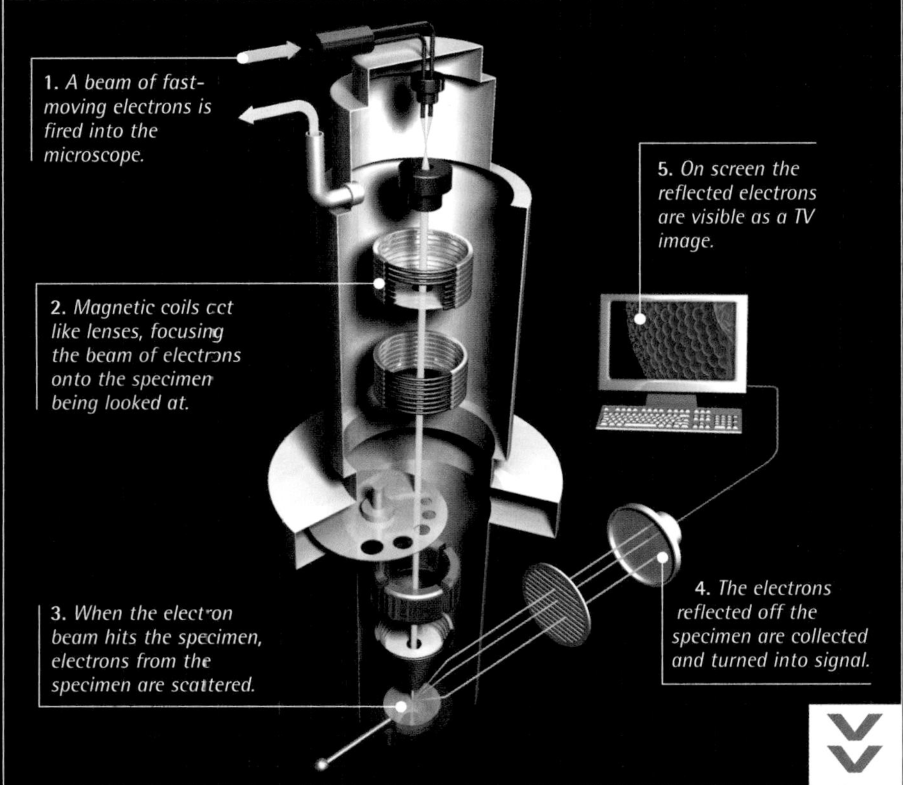

1. A beam of fast-moving electrons is fired into the microscope.
2. Magnetic coils act like lenses, focusing the beam of electrons onto the specimen being looked at.
3. When the electron beam hits the specimen, electrons from the specimen are scattered.
4. The electrons reflected off the specimen are collected and turned into signal.
5. On screen the reflected electrons are visible as a TV image.

An ordinary (optical) microscope uses a light beam, focused and magnified by a glass lens, to make tiny objects seem bigger. The light beam is made up of streams of minute particles called photons, which are about 200 times thinner than a human hair. To see anything smaller, we need an electron microscope which uses a beam of even smaller particles, called electrons, instead of light. An electron microscope can reveal details about 500–1,000 times smaller than the things we can see with an optical microscope.

Tiny hairs detect air vibrations, helping fly to control its speed and movement while airborne.

▲ A housefly is able to detect threats from any direction. Using just the naked eye, it is not obvious how the fly does this, but a close-up look reveals key details.

MICROSCOPE

▶▶ From the buzzing circuits of microchips to the hidden secrets of living cells, scanning electron microscopes (SEMs) have opened up amazing new worlds. With an electron microscope, it is possible to see objects 100,000 times smaller than a human hair. ▶▶

▶ A housefly's compound eye, magnified around 2,000 times by a scanning electron microscope, is made of approximately 6,000 segments, called ommatidia. Together, they give the fly the sensitive, almost 360° vision it needs to escape from danger.

▶▶ See also: Telescope p150, Binoculars p158, Night vision p160

Each ommatidium has its own lens and light-detecting cells inside.
Image: Coloured SEM image of a housefly's eye

OUTSIDE AND IN

Looking through an SEM

▲ A scanning electron microscope (SEM) bounces electrons off the surface of a tiny specimen (like a fly's eye) to make a bigger image of its outer appearance. A transmission electron microscope (TEM) sends electrons straight through a specimen to reveal its detailed inner structure. TEMs are used for studying living cells and can even show up atoms inside crystals.

Image: Weather balloon and radiosonde

WEATHER BALLOON

Every day, more than a thousand weather balloons are released all over the world, each carrying a mini weather station high into the atmosphere. Filled with lighter-than-air hydrogen gas, the balloons can reach altitudes of 40 km (25 miles).

Weather watchers in space

Weather satellite

Weather satellites observe the Earth from space. Some stay over one spot on the Earth while others orbit rapidly, covering the globe in strips. Cameras can photograph clouds and weather patterns, while other sensors measure ground and sea temperatures and monitor pollution levels. Information from satellites is fed into computer models of the weather and used to produce detailed weather forecasts. Satellites are a useful tool, but they can't see wind or details of the 3D structure of the atmosphere, so weather balloons are still needed to produce good forecasts.

Latex balloon expands as it rises, reaching up to 8 m (26 ft) in diameter before it bursts.

Most weather balloons are launched by hand.

Radiosonde, a disposable weather station, falls back to Earth when balloon bursts.

◀ This weather balloon is being released in Mumbai, India. The radiosonde, or mini weather station, on board will transmit measurements back to base. Weather balloons are crucial in tracking India's annual monsoon (rainy season), which affects the lives of millions of agricultural workers.

>> KEY FEATURES OF A RADIOSONDE

Lightweight polystyrene case is cheap and reduces impact when radiosonde lands.

Sensor boom holds temperature and humidity sensors away from case for more accurate readings.

GPS antenna used to calculate position.

Pressure sensor is located inside case, away from moving air that would disturb readings.

Electronic components process sensor inputs and convert data to coded radio signals.

Transmitter antenna sends data to ground station.

A radiosonde weighs just 250 g (8.8 oz) and is small enough to hold in your hand. The radiosonde is carried upwards by a weather balloon and takes measurements of key properties of the atmosphere, such as temperature and humidity, relaying the data back to a ground station using a radio transmitter. It also carries a GPS (Global Positioning System) antenna to report its exact position. As the balloon travels with the wind this information can be used to calculate the wind's speed and direction. A typical flight might last 2 hours, during which the balloon may drift 200 km (125 miles) from the release point, and encounter temperatures of -90°C (-130°F). When it gets too high the balloon bursts and the radiosonde falls to the ground.

▶▶ See also: Wind turbine p22, Power tower p196

ATLAS

▶▶ One way to understand how things work is to take them apart. That is just what scientists hope to do at CERN, a physics laboratory in Switzerland, where pieces of atoms will be smashed apart in a giant underground experiment called Atlas. ▶▶

▶ Atlas will detect and identify the new particles created when other particles collide. The huge experiment takes place in a long pipe with particles beamed in by a particle accelerator. When the particles collide, they make new particles that travel outwards. Detectors inside Atlas measure the particles so scientists can identify them.

>> HOW ATLAS WORKS

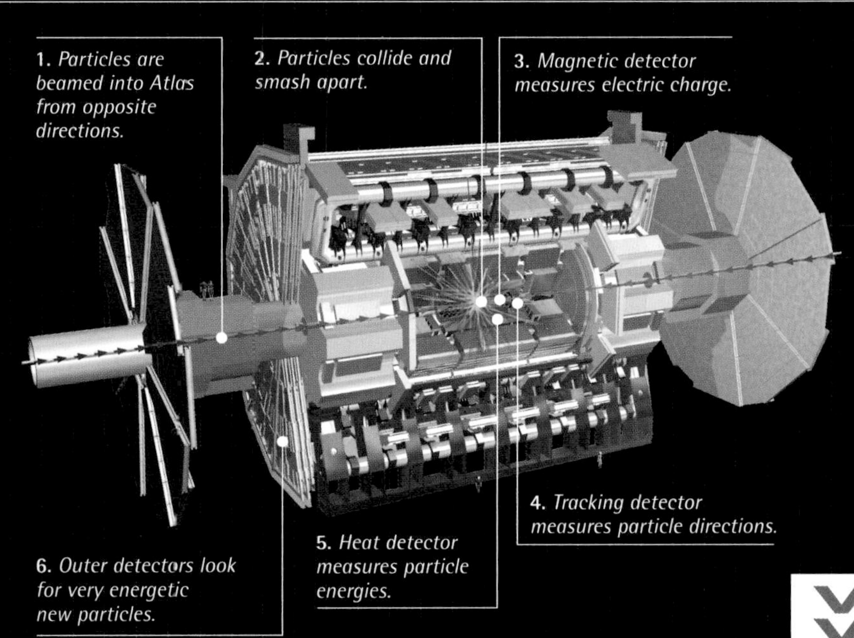

1. *Particles are beamed into Atlas from opposite directions.*

2. *Particles collide and smash apart.*

3. *Magnetic detector measures electric charge.*

4. *Tracking detector measures particle directions.*

5. *Heat detector measures particle energies.*

6. *Outer detectors look for very energetic new particles.*

Atoms, though tiny, are made of smaller particles. Scientists hope to understand how the Universe works by studying these particles in Atlas. This is a huge underground experiment using CERN's particle accelerator (a long, circular pipe that speeds particles to near the speed of light). The particles race around the pipe, going ever faster. When they collide, they smash apart and create new particles. Detectors inside Atlas measure various properties of the new particles, such as mass, electric charge, and the direction they are travelling in. These experiments could reveal the secrets of the Big Bang (when the Universe was created).

Particles entering Atlas travel at almost the speed of light.

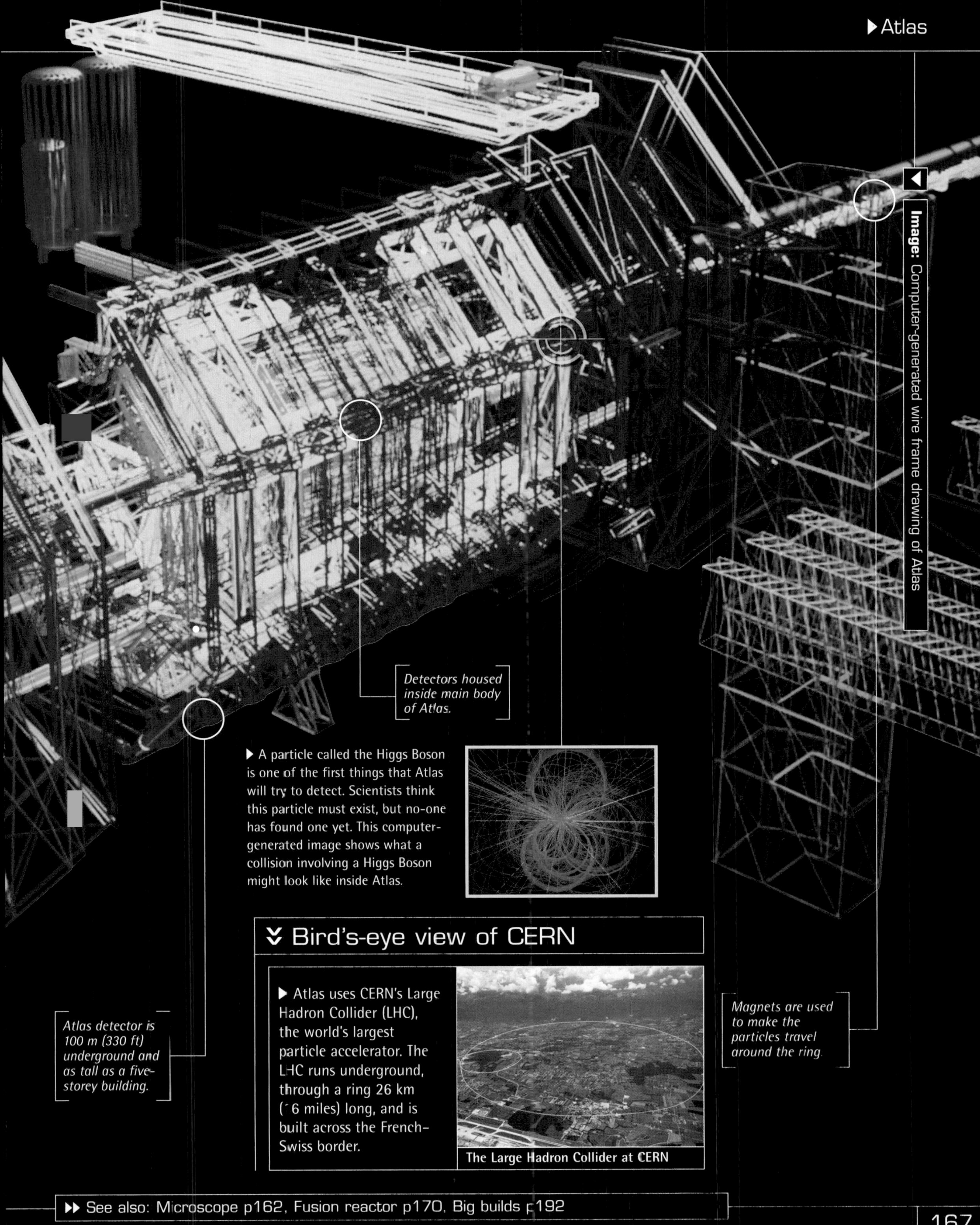

Image: Computer-generated wire frame drawing of Atlas
Detectors housed inside main body of Atlas.
Atlas detector is 100 m (330 ft) underground and as tall as a five-storey building.
Magnets are used to make the particles travel around the ring.

▶ A particle called the Higgs Boson is one of the first things that Atlas will try to detect. Scientists think this particle must exist, but no-one has found one yet. This computer-generated image shows what a collision involving a Higgs Boson might look like inside Atlas.

Bird's-eye view of CERN

▶ Atlas uses CERN's Large Hadron Collider (LHC), the world's largest particle accelerator. The LHC runs underground, through a ring 26 km (16 miles) long, and is built across the French–Swiss border.

The Large Hadron Collider at CERN

▶▶ See also: Microscope p162, Fusion reactor p170, Big builds p192

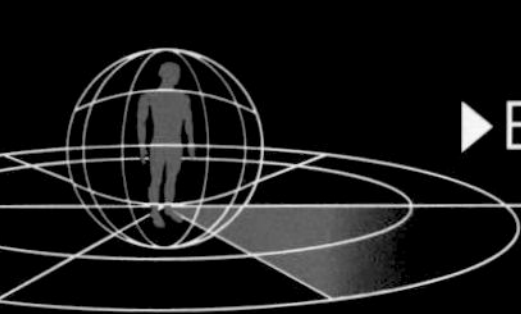

NEUTRINO TANK

▶▶ While you are reading this sentence, about 2,000 million, million neutrinos will pass harmlessly through you. Neutrinos are particles produced by nuclear reactions at the core of the Sun and other stars. Scientists study them using giant undergound detectors, to learn more about the Universe. ▶▶

▶ This tank is under construction in Japan, in a mine 1 km (0.6 mile) below the Earth's surface to screen out interference from other particles. A 10-storey building could fit inside. When operating it contains 50,000 tonnes of ultra pure water and is pitch black. The photomultiplier tubes detect occasional flashes of light left by passing neutrinos.

Light detectors, called photomultiplier tubes, look for light flashes caused by neutrinos.

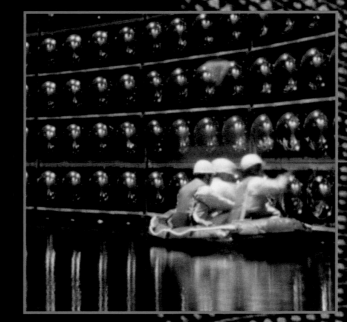

▲ **There are more than 10,000 photomultiplier tubes, each capable of detecting a single photon of light. With water in the tank, boats and divers are needed to access the tubes.**

When complete, the floor will also be covered in photomultiplier tubes.

▲ **Image:** Super-Kamiokande detector array, Japan

See also: Telescope p150, Microscope p162, Atlas p166

HOW THE TANK WORKS

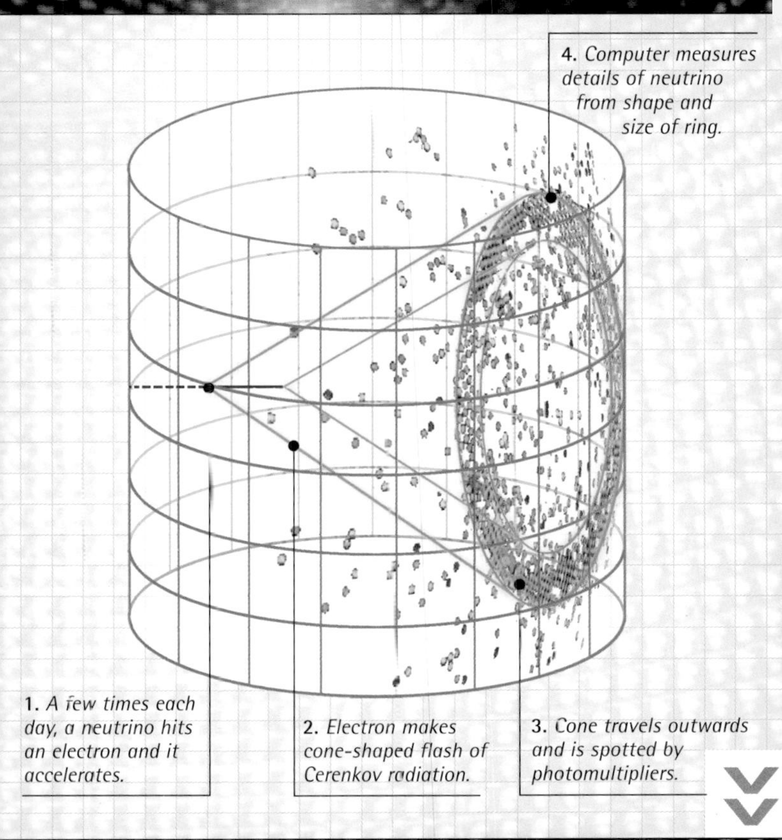

4. Computer measures details of neutrino from shape and size of ring.
1. A few times each day, a neutrino hits an electron and it accelerates.
2. Electron makes cone-shaped flash of Cerenkov radiation.
3. Cone travels outwards and is spotted by photomultipliers.

Neutrinos are hard to detect as they usually pass completely unnoticed through everything in their path. One way to detect them is in a large water tank where some neutrinos collide with water molecules, ejecting electrons (particles with a negative electric charge). The moving electrons make cone-shaped flashes of blue light, called Cerenkov radiation, which are detected by photomultiplier tubes (sensitive light detectors) on the tank walls.

Supernova activity

In 1987, neutrino observatories recorded a burst of neutrinos and an exploding star (supernova) was seen in a nearby galaxy. It is thought that these neutrinos were created during the star's last moments, and studying their properties has helped scientists to understand how supernovas work. This picture shows the tidy pattern of hot gas left after the explosion.

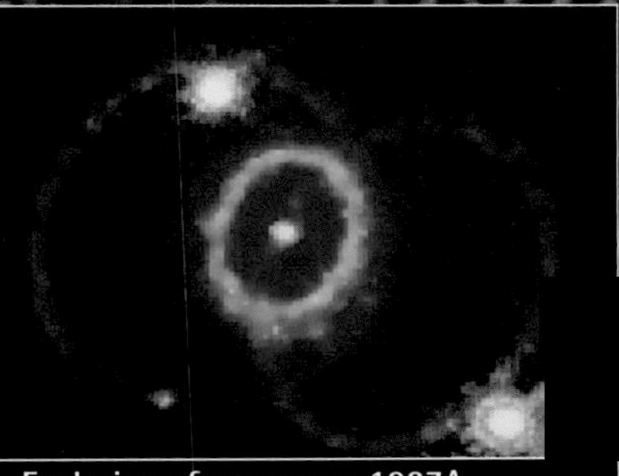

Explosion of supernova 1987A

FUSION REACTOR

Nuclear fusion is the process that powers the Sun. Within 50 years, fusion reactors on Earth should be making electricity using the same process. About 10 g (0.35 oz) of hydrogen fuel will produce enough energy to satisfy one person's lifetime needs.

The gas inside this experimental fusion reactor is so hot – up to 100,000,000°C (180,000,000°F) – that the atoms of the gas have fallen apart to become a mixture of nuclei and electrons. This is a state of matter known as a plasma.

Energy is released when two types of hydrogen nuclei (one deuterium, one tritium) bash together at high speed. The two hydrogen nuclei fuse to form one helium nucleus and emit a spare neutron. This reaction is called hydrogen fusion.

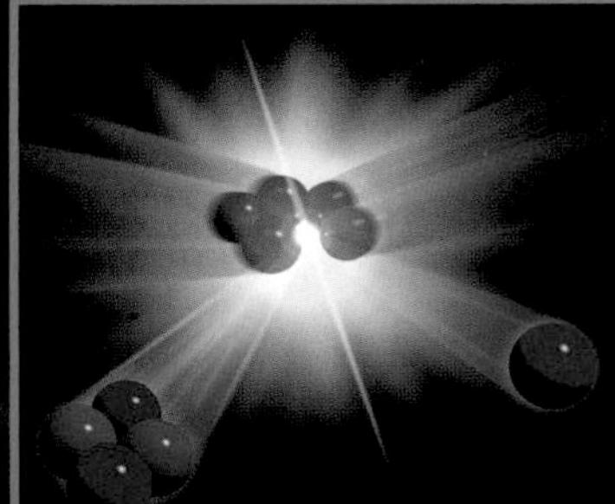

Plasma kept away from reactor walls by magnetic field.

The hottest plasma does not glow but emits invisible, super-energetic X-rays. This is the place where fusion occurs.

Cooler edges of plasma reach 10,000°C (18,000°F) and emit visible light.

Image: Plasma glow on the inside of a fusion reactor

▶▶ See also: Atlas p166, Neutrino tank p168

» HOW A FUSION REACTOR WORKS

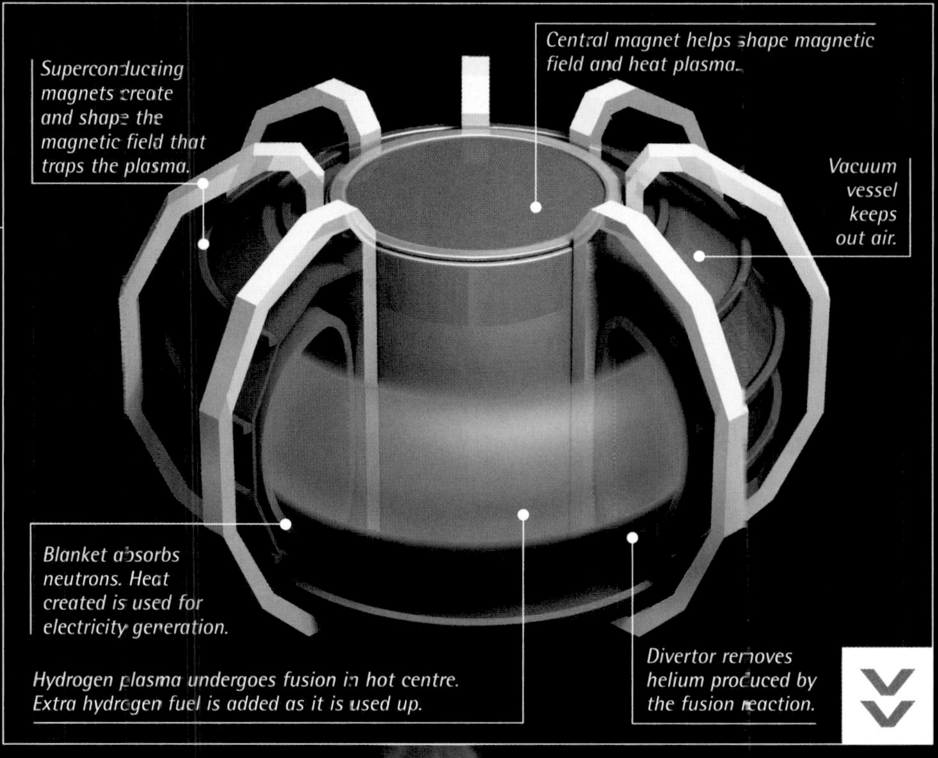

Superconducting magnets create and shape the magnetic field that traps the plasma.
Central magnet helps shape magnetic field and heat plasma.
Vacuum vessel keeps out air.
Blanket absorbs neutrons. Heat created is used for electricity generation.
Hydrogen plasma undergoes fusion in hot centre. Extra hydrogen fuel is added as it is used up.
Divertor removes helium produced by the fusion reaction.

A fusion reactor works by providing the conditions for fusion to occur and then harnessing the energy produced. The plasma – held in place by a powerful magnetic field – is first heated up using radio waves or by passing an electric current through it. However, once fusion reactions begin the process becomes self-sustaining as the energy released is enough to keep the plasma hot without outside help. The fusion reaction produces fast-moving neutrons, which escape the magnetic field and hit the blanket (reactor wall). This creates heat that can then be used to generate electricity. Helium, also produced in the reaction, is removed, and new hydrogen fuel is added to take its place.

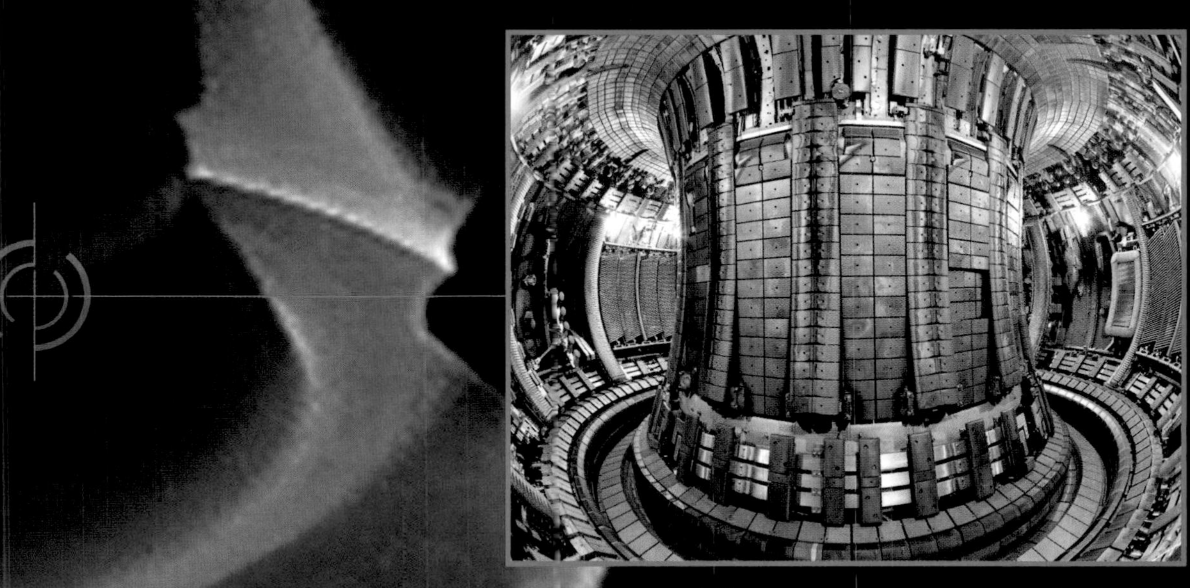

▲ The reactor vessel is the shape of a giant ring doughnut, or "torus". Air is pumped out to create a vacuum and the plasma inside is controlled by a specially shaped magnetic field. The superheated plasma cannot be allowed to touch the reactor walls as this would cool it down, stopping the fusion reaction.

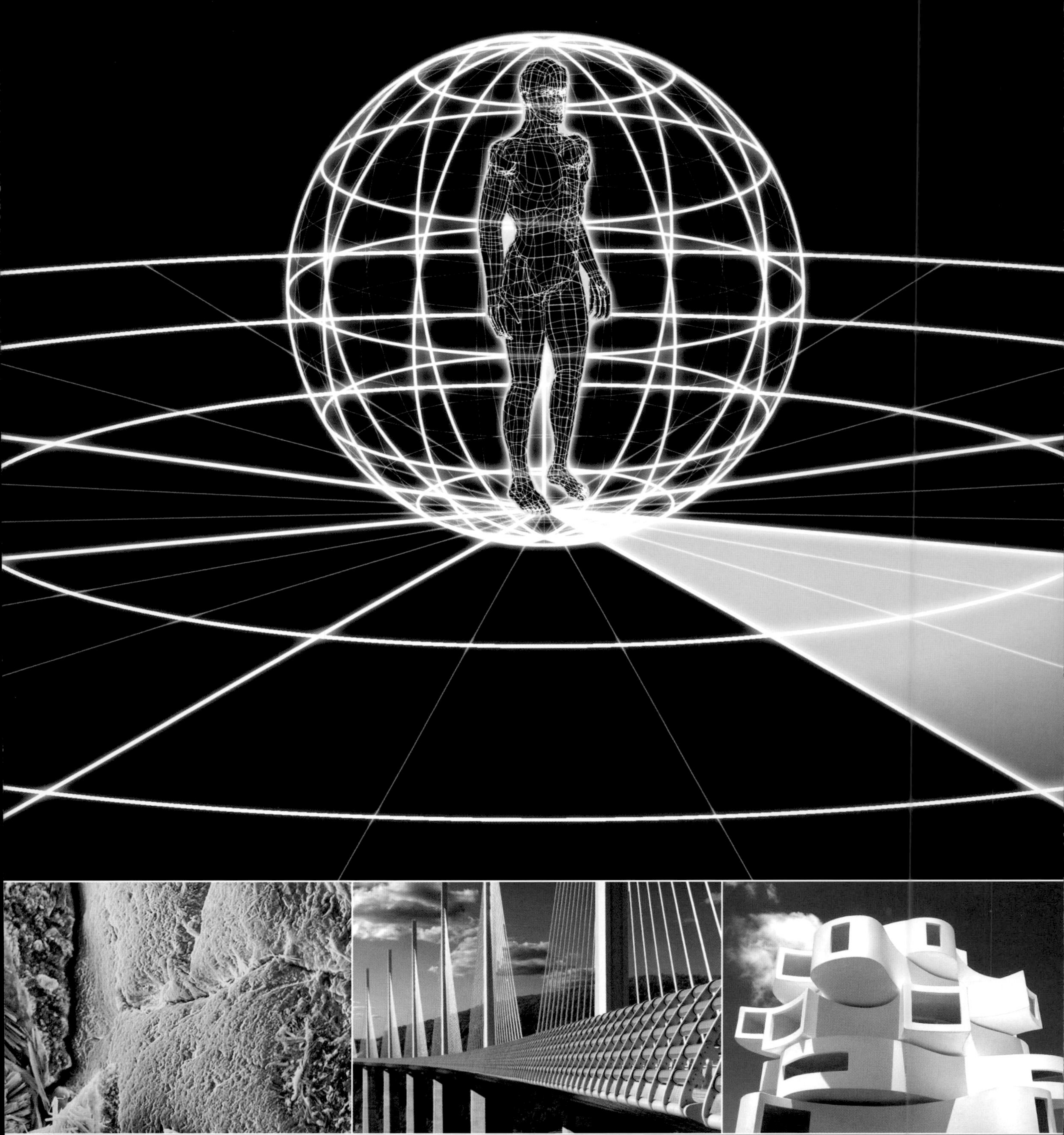

>> CONSTRUCT

Concrete >> Building blocks >> Drill >> Millau Viaduct >> Grand designs >> Eden Project >> Falkirk Wheel >> Skywalk >> Big builds >> Mass damper >> Power tower >> Stadium roof >> Micro machines >> Laser

How can cars drive through clouds? p182
What makes this shake? p194

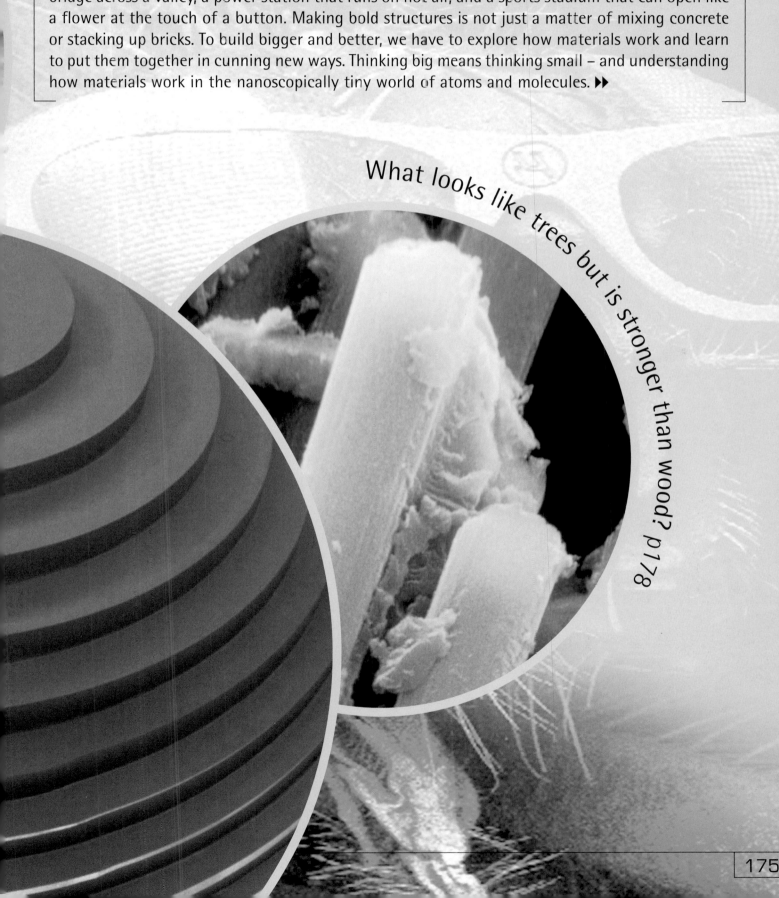

▸▸ People have certainly made their mark on the planet. Recent marvels of construction include a bridge across a valley, a power station that runs on hot air, and a sports stadium that can open like a flower at the touch of a button. Making bold structures is not just a matter of mixing concrete or stacking up bricks. To build bigger and better, we have to explore how materials work and learn to put them together in cunning new ways. Thinking big means thinking small – and understanding how materials work in the nanoscopically tiny world of atoms and molecules. ▸▸

What looks like trees but is stronger than wood? p178

CONCRETE

▶▶ From the tallest skyscrapers to the longest highways, the world's most impressive engineering structures balance on microscopic concrete crystals five times thinner than human hairs. ▶▶

▶▶ HOW CONCRETE IS MADE

Without reinforcement, concrete can resist compressive (squeezing) forces but can crack or snap when subject to tensile (bending) forces.

Steel can resist tensile forces, so concrete reinforced with steel can withstand both squeezing and bending.

Concrete is a versatile building material dating back to Roman times. It is made by mixing sand, gravel, and cement. When water is added, crystals grow in the cement, binding the sand and gravel together. The concrete becomes hard not because it dries, but because a chemical reaction forms crystals inside it. Although concrete is strong in vertical pillars, it is weaker in horizontal beams because it cracks under stress rather than bending. For this reason, concrete is often applied over a framework of steel bars or cages. Reinforced concrete, as this is known, is hundreds of times stronger than concrete alone.

Gypsum crystals grow in cement, binding concrete together.

▲ Concrete gets its strength when crystals growing in cement lock together particles of sand and gravel. Typical concrete is made from 10–15 per cent cement, 60–75 per cent sand and gravel, and 15–20 per cent water.

▶▶ See also: Millau Viaduct p182, Grand designs p184, Skywalk p190

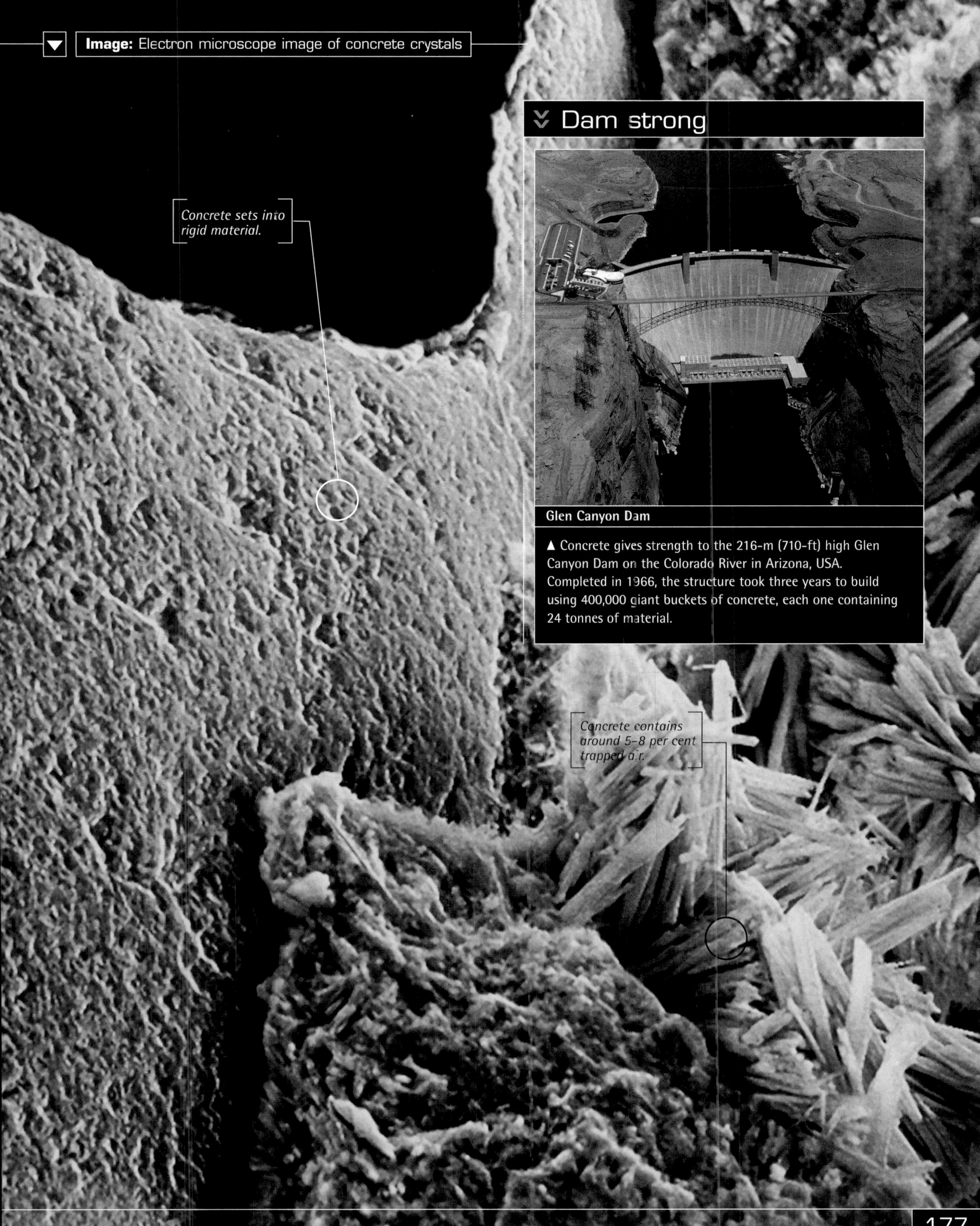
Image: Electron microscope image of concrete crystals
Concrete sets into rigid material.
Concrete contains around 5–8 per cent trapped air.

Dam strong

Glen Canyon Dam

▲ Concrete gives strength to the 216-m (710-ft) high Glen Canyon Dam on the Colorado River in Arizona, USA. Completed in 1966, the structure took three years to build using 400,000 giant buckets of concrete, each one containing 24 tonnes of material.

BUILDING BLOCKS

Why does a skyscraper have glass windows and steel walls, not the other way around? The materials we use in buildings are chosen for special properties that make them perfect for certain jobs. Using the wrong material could make a building unsafe or shorten its life. Magnify a building material hundreds of times with a microscope and you reveal the secret inner structure that makes it powerful and unique.

« Insulating fibre This Dacron® material is made from polyester filaments, themselves made from long chains of carbon-based molecules called polymers. Each filament contains up to seven air cavities. The air trapped inside and between the filaments makes Dacron perfect for insulating lofts and walls.

» Vermiculite Vermiculite (micafill) is a fireproof insulating material that is made by heating mica until it expands into lots of separate layers – very similar to puff pastry. It is fireproof because the mica is made from silicate minerals (compounds of silicon and oxygen) that do not burn. Vermiculite insulates because air is trapped between the many layers.

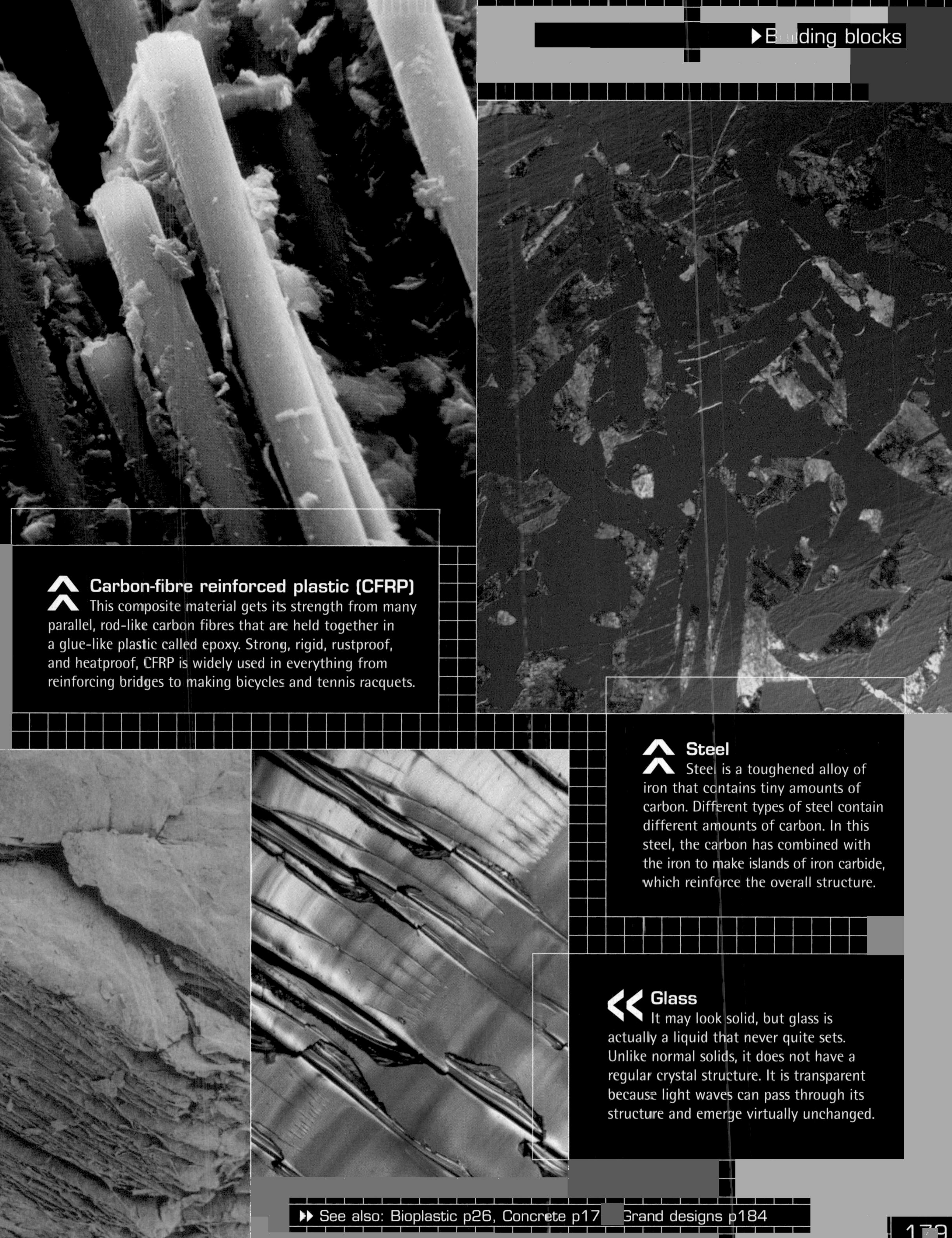

Carbon-fibre reinforced plastic (CFRP)

This composite material gets its strength from many parallel, rod-like carbon fibres that are held together in a glue-like plastic called epoxy. Strong, rigid, rustproof, and heatproof, CFRP is widely used in everything from reinforcing bridges to making bicycles and tennis racquets.

Steel

Steel is a toughened alloy of iron that contains tiny amounts of carbon. Different types of steel contain different amounts of carbon. In this steel, the carbon has combined with the iron to make islands of iron carbide, which reinforce the overall structure.

Glass

It may look solid, but glass is actually a liquid that never quite sets. Unlike normal solids, it does not have a regular crystal structure. It is transparent because light waves can pass through its structure and emerge virtually unchanged.

See also: Bioplastic p26, Concrete p17[illegible] Grand designs p184

DRILL

▶▶ Roads are built to last, so cracking them apart is a tough job. Whenever repairs are needed, pneumatic drills do the work efficiently by using the power of compressed air to pound a heavy chisel into the road surface at a rate of 25 times per second. ▶▶

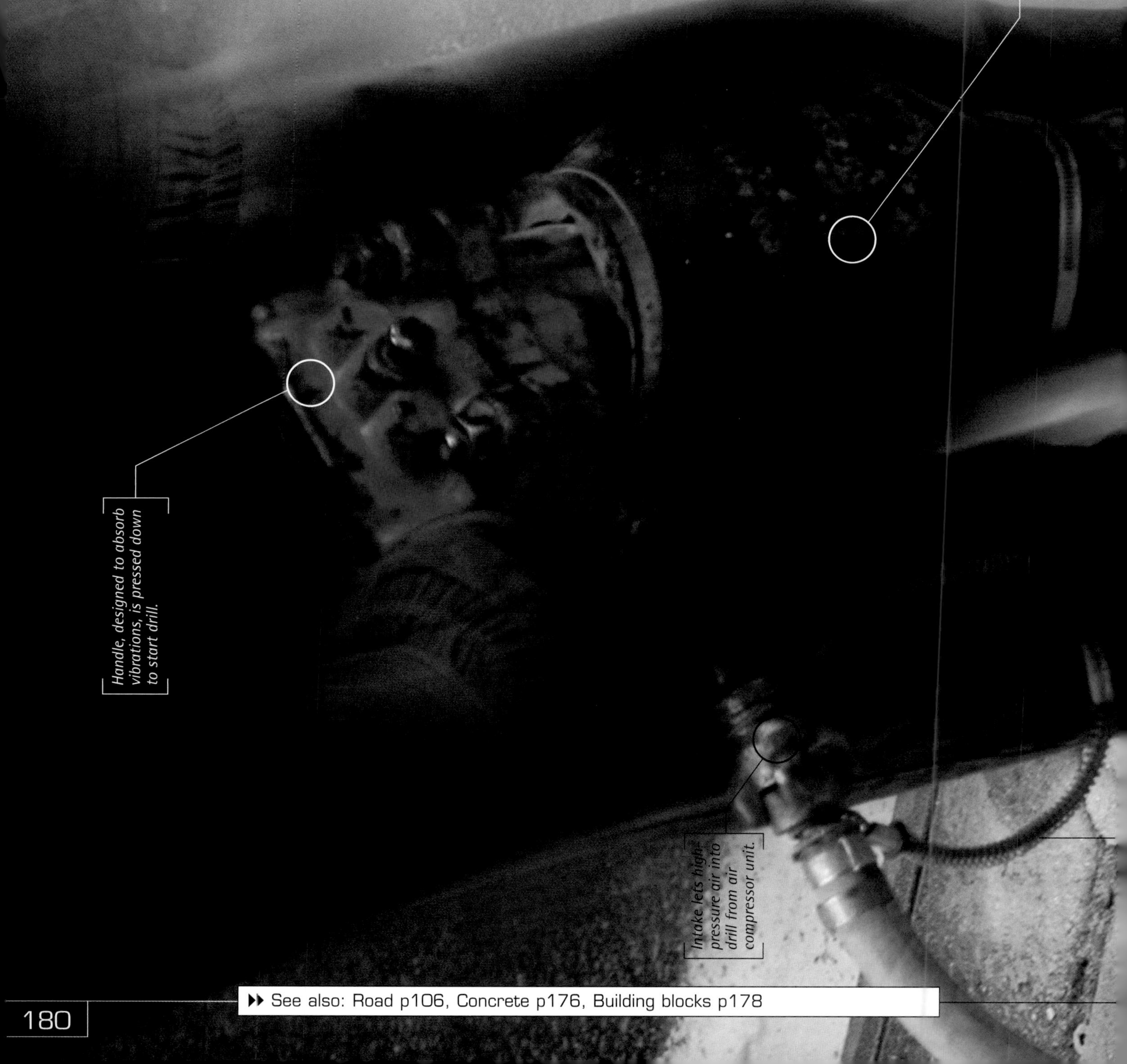

Padded silencer reduces noise and vibration from drill.

Handle, designed to absorb vibrations, is pressed down to start drill.

Intake lets high-pressure air into drill from air compressor unit.

▶▶ See also: Road p106, Concrete p176, Building blocks p178

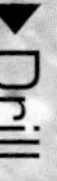

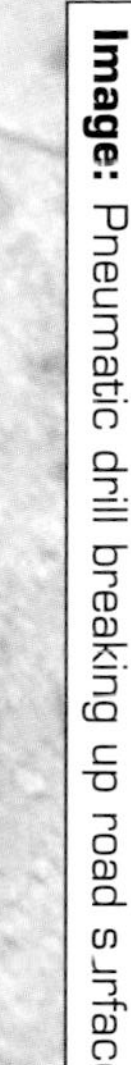

Image: Pneumatic drill breaking up road s.ırface

◀ Pneumatic drills have no petrol engine or electric motor, but operate entirely by using air. A typical drill uses about 30 litres (8 gallons) of air per second (roughly five or six deep adult breaths) and is designed to break up sections of road in just 10–20 seconds.

Drill bit is made of hardened steel.

Wide chisel can be exchanged for narrow chisel or pointed tool for making holes.

» HOW THE DRILL WORKS

1. *Operator pushes handle to let in the air.*
2. *Pressurized air (blue) enters from compressor.*
3. *Valve is flat at start of process.*
4. *Air circulates around outer tube.*
5. *Piledriver rises up main tube.*
6. *Drill bit rises up main tube.*
7. *Waste gas flows out of exhaust.*

STAGE ONE

8. *Flow of air makes valve flip over.*
9. *Air is forced down main tube.*
10. *Piledriver is forced down main tube.*
11. *Drill bit is pounded by piledriver into the ground.*
12. *Waste gas flows out of exhaust.*

STAGE TWO

When air is squeezed under pressure, it can exert a force and do useful things. This is called pneumatics. Squeezing air with a bike pump gives it enough pressure to inflate a tyre. A pneumatic drill is operated by a large, diesel-powered pump called an air compressor. The compressor squeezes the air to ten times its normal pressure. That gives it enough force to pound a piledriver inside up and down, smashing the drill bit underneath it repeatedly through the concrete, asphalt, or brick below.

MILLAU VIADUCT

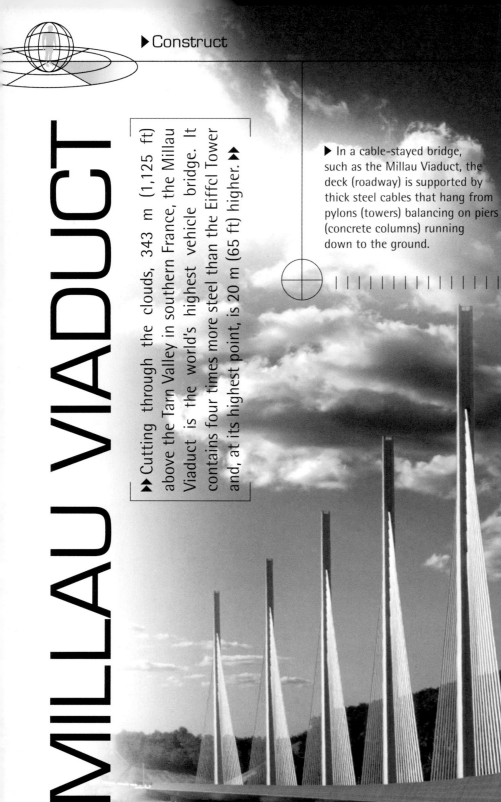

Cutting through the clouds, 343 m (1,125 ft) above the Tarn Valley in southern France, the Millau Viaduct is the world's highest vehicle bridge. It contains four times more steel than the Eiffel Tower and, at its highest point, is 20 m (65 ft) higher.

In a cable-stayed bridge, such as the Millau Viaduct, the deck (roadway) is supported by thick steel cables that hang from pylons (towers) balancing on piers (concrete columns) running down to the ground.

Cables run from the pylons to the deck.

Image: The Millau Viaduct crosses the River Tarn, France

HOW THE MILLAU VIADUCT WAS BUILT

Piers

The seven concrete piers, one of which is the tallest in the world, took two years to build. During the building work, they rose on average 1.3 m (4.4 ft) a day from foundations that sunk to a depth of 15 m (50 ft) in the ground.

Pylons

Once the piers were in place, pylons were swung into position directly above them. This was done with the help of two huge steel pincer arms (coloured blue) and hydraulic (fluid-filled) lifting jacks capable of moving 2,000 tonnes.

Cable-stays

The 22 cables were then attached to each pylon. Each cable is made from up to 91 strands, each of which is constructed from seven steel wires. So each section of the deck is effectively supported by more than 14,000 individual wires.

Deck

The steel bridge deck weighs as much as 1,000 fully laden articulated lorries and took just under two years to assemble. Once it was built, the deck was slid sideways into position, one section at a time, using 64 huge hydraulic jacks.

See also: Building blocks p178, Big builds p192, Flood barrier p240

GRAND DESIGNS

Architects today are free to let their imaginations run wild, as cutting-edge materials and construction techniques make possible buildings of all manner of weird and wonderful designs. The curves, patterns, and shapes of the natural world inspire many modern designs. Increasingly important is the impact of buildings on the environment.

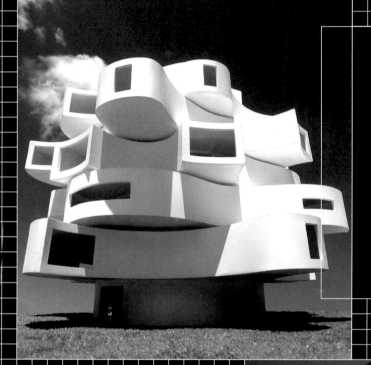

Wind-shaped pavilion
This American concept building changes shape as the wind blows. Its six vertical layers are free to rotate around a central column. The breeze gently turns each layer in a different way so the tower's outline constantly changes. This movement could drive electric generators to produce enough electricity to illuminate the pavilion at night.

Living Tomorrow
Created in Amsterdam, in the Netherlands, for an exhibition of ideas and inventions for the future home and office, the strangely shaped Living Tomorrow Pavilion is constructed from materials that can be recycled or have little environmental impact. Its energy- saving systems include a device that reclaims waste heat from shower water.

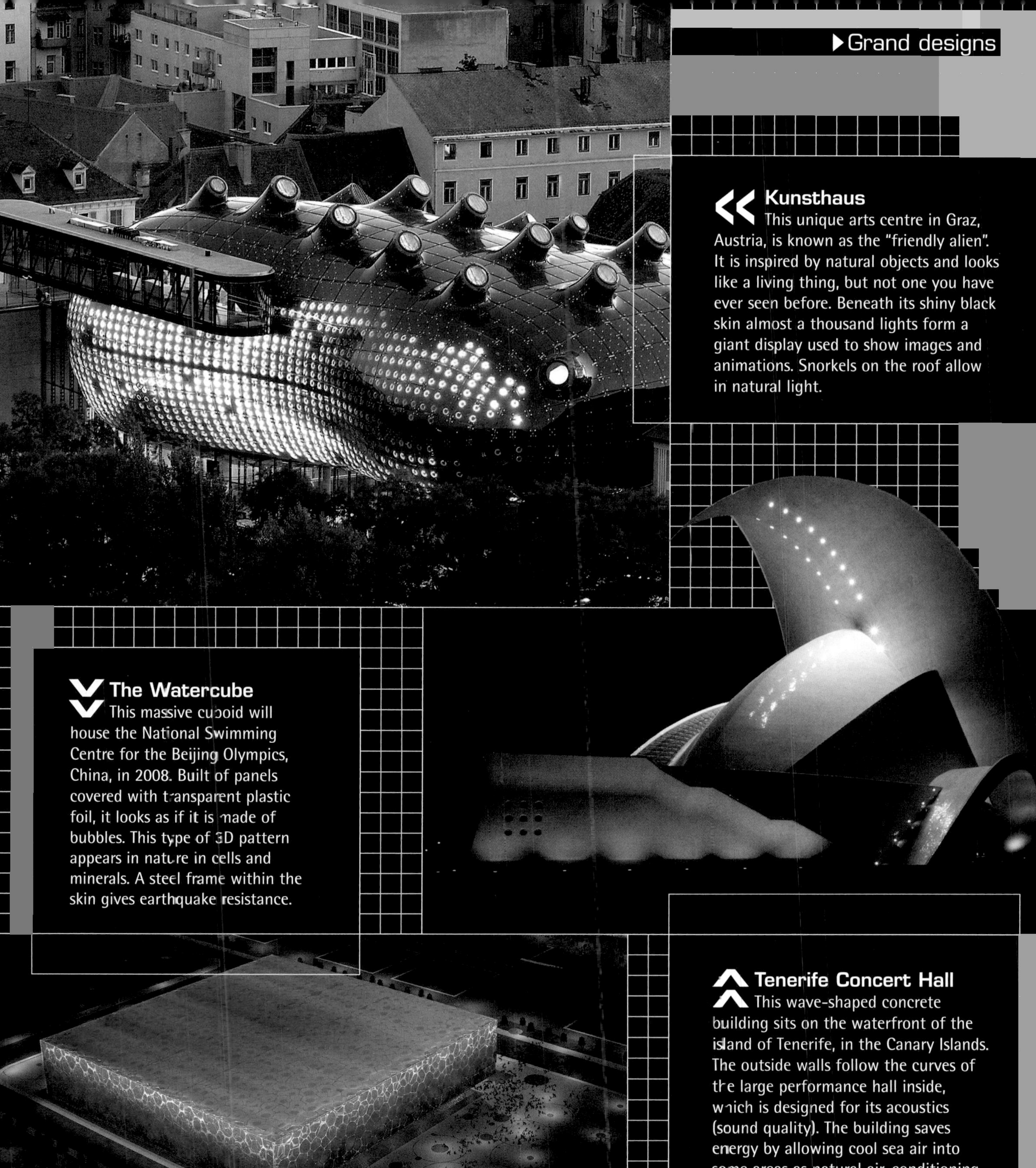

Kunsthaus
This unique arts centre in Graz, Austria, is known as the "friendly alien". It is inspired by natural objects and looks like a living thing, but not one you have ever seen before. Beneath its shiny black skin almost a thousand lights form a giant display used to show images and animations. Snorkels on the roof allow in natural light.

The Watercube
This massive cuboid will house the National Swimming Centre for the Beijing Olympics, China, in 2008. Built of panels covered with transparent plastic foil, it looks as if it is made of bubbles. This type of 3D pattern appears in nature in cells and minerals. A steel frame within the skin gives earthquake resistance.

Tenerife Concert Hall
This wave-shaped concrete building sits on the waterfront of the island of Tenerife, in the Canary Islands. The outside walls follow the curves of the large performance hall inside, which is designed for its acoustics (sound quality). The building saves energy by allowing cool sea air into some areas as natural air-conditioning.

▶▶See also: Skywalk p190, Big ds p192, Shelters p234

Biodiversity

Forest cleared by fire

▲ People have cleared more than 80 per cent of the forests that once covered Earth's surface, and half the world's remaining forest is concentrated in the tropics. Tropical forests have very high biodiversity: they contain more than 90 per cent of the world's species. But people are still destroying them to grow crops.

EDEN PROJECT

▶▶ Humans have now transformed more than half of Earth's total land surface area, destroying in the process huge areas of the environment and driving many plants to the brink of extinction. Eden, a giant greenhouse complex in Cornwall, England, aims to conserve threatened plants for future generations. ▶▶

Eden's two giant "biomes" (plant houses) mimic the biomes (major ecosystems) in the natural world. At 240 m (780 ft) long, the humid tropics biome is the world's largest conservatory and s like the steamy, sweltering interior of a tropical forest.

Humid tropics biome is nearly five times longer than an Olympic swimming pool.

KEY FEATURES OF THE EDEN PROJECT

Biome structure
Eden's unusual greenhouses are reinforced steel covered with a transparent plastic material. This lets light pass through, but traps the heat and moisture inside. The interlocking hexagonal pattern distributes the weight of the roof evenly so no internal supports are needed.

Fertile soil
Eden was built on a desolate clay quarry and all the soil it needed – 85,000 tonnes of it – had to be specially made. Some was produced by recycling household kitchen and garden waste in a giant pit. Thousands of worms were added to digest the waste into rich compost.

Rarest of plants
With less than 120 specimens left, *Impatiens gordonii* is one of the world's rarest flowers. Using samples rescued from threatened habitats in the Seychelles, a new variety has now been bred at Eden. With the right habitat and the right soil, Eden is a perfect home for rare plants like this.

See also: Hydroponics p28, Building blocks p178, Skywalk p190

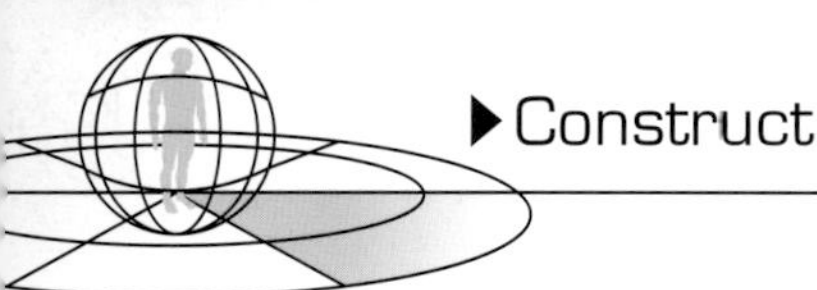

FALKIRK WHEEL

▶▶ The world's first rotating boat lift is like a giant ferris wheel weighing more than 1,000 family cars. Using the science of balance, it can swing huge barges into the sky in just four minutes. ▶▶

>> HOW THE WHEEL WORKS

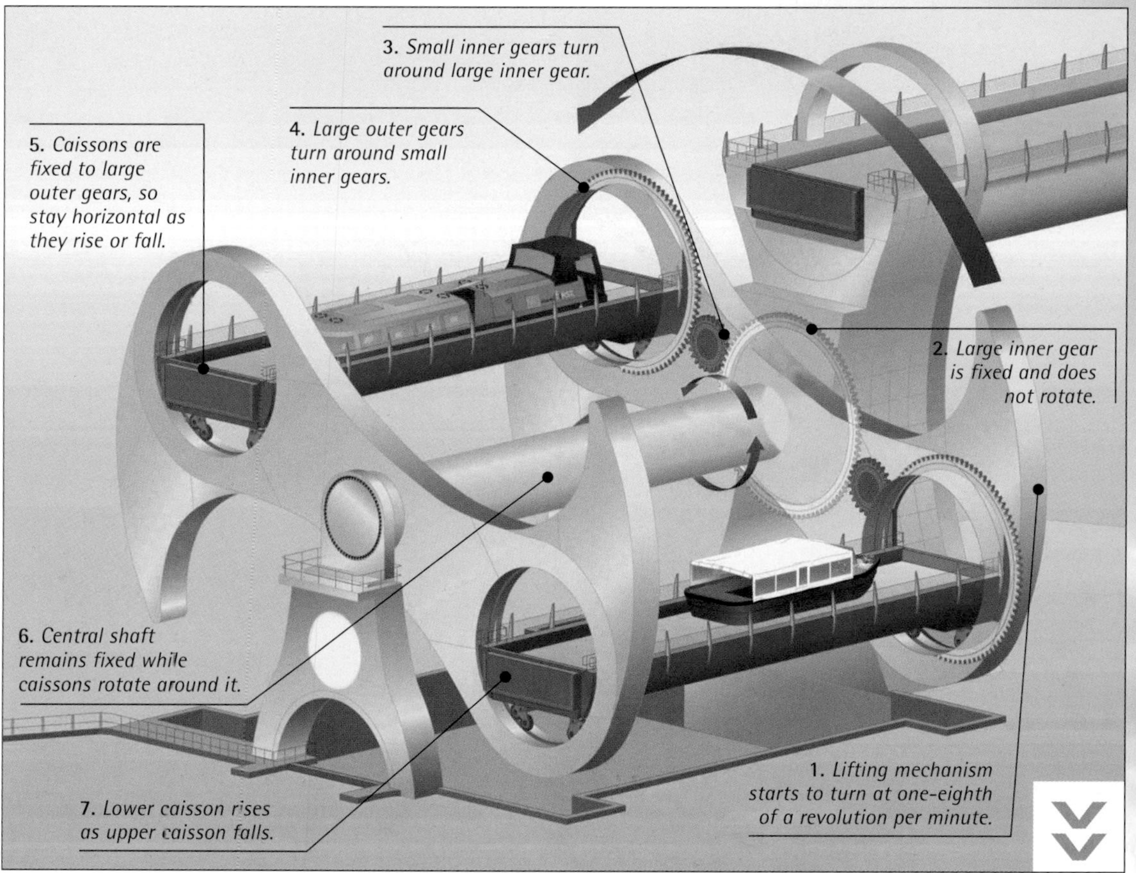

1. Lifting mechanism starts to turn at one-eighth of a revolution per minute.
2. Large inner gear is fixed and does not rotate.
3. Small inner gears turn around large inner gear.
4. Large outer gears turn around small inner gears.
5. Caissons are fixed to large outer gears, so stay horizontal as they rise or fall.
6. Central shaft remains fixed while caissons rotate around it.
7. Lower caisson rises as upper caisson falls.

It's hard to lift someone off the ground, but if you're both sitting on a seesaw you can lift them easily – even if they're heavier. That's because your weight, magnified by the seesaw lever, acts as a counterbalance that helps move the other person into the air. If you both weigh the same, the forces balance and lifting is effortless.

The Falkirk Wheel's two huge caissons (water tanks) balance like the seats on a seesaw. As one falls, the other rises. This means the lift's electric motors and hydraulic rams (water-filled pumps) can operate the lift with very little power. Gears (wheels with teeth) magnify the lifting force like the lever in a seesaw and keep the caissons level.

Both caisson compartments can hold four boats, each up to 20 m (65 ft) long.

▶▶ See also: Concrete p176, Millau Viaduct p182, Skywalk p190

Reinforced concrete aqueduct connects to canal at top.
Large inner gear is locked in place and does not rotate.
Small inner gear rotates around large locked inner gear.
Large outer gear rotates around small inner gear.
Water pressure seals boats safely behind tight-fitting doors.

▼ This giant concrete lift in Falkirk, Scotland, moves up to eight boats at a time between the Forth and Clyde Canal and the Union Canal approximately 30 m (100 ft) above it. Despite its size, its counterbalance system means it needs no more power than a small car engine.

▲ **Image:** Falkirk Wheel, Scotland

SKYWALK

▶▶ Rivers sculpt the landscape, and nowhere more spectacularly than in North America's Grand Canyon. This deep chasm was gouged through Arizona's dusty landscape by the Colorado River. What better way to see it than from a glass observation platform, balanced 1,200 m (4,000 ft) above the void? ▶▶

Footings under the Skywalk can support the weight of 75 jumbo jets.

Image: The Skywalk on opening day

>> KEY FEATURES

Cantilever platform
The Skywalk is a cantilever – a structure that stretches into space with no support beneath. This is possible because the two ends of the horseshoe are embedded 14 m (46 ft) into the rock with 94 steel rods. The super-tough platform can support the weight of 120 visitors at any time.

Glass floor
The deck is built from very strong, laminated glass. This is made by bonding multiple layers of glass and plastic to form a tough material that is around 5 cm (2 in) thick. Visitors have to put on cloth slippers over their shoes to avoid scratching the glass.

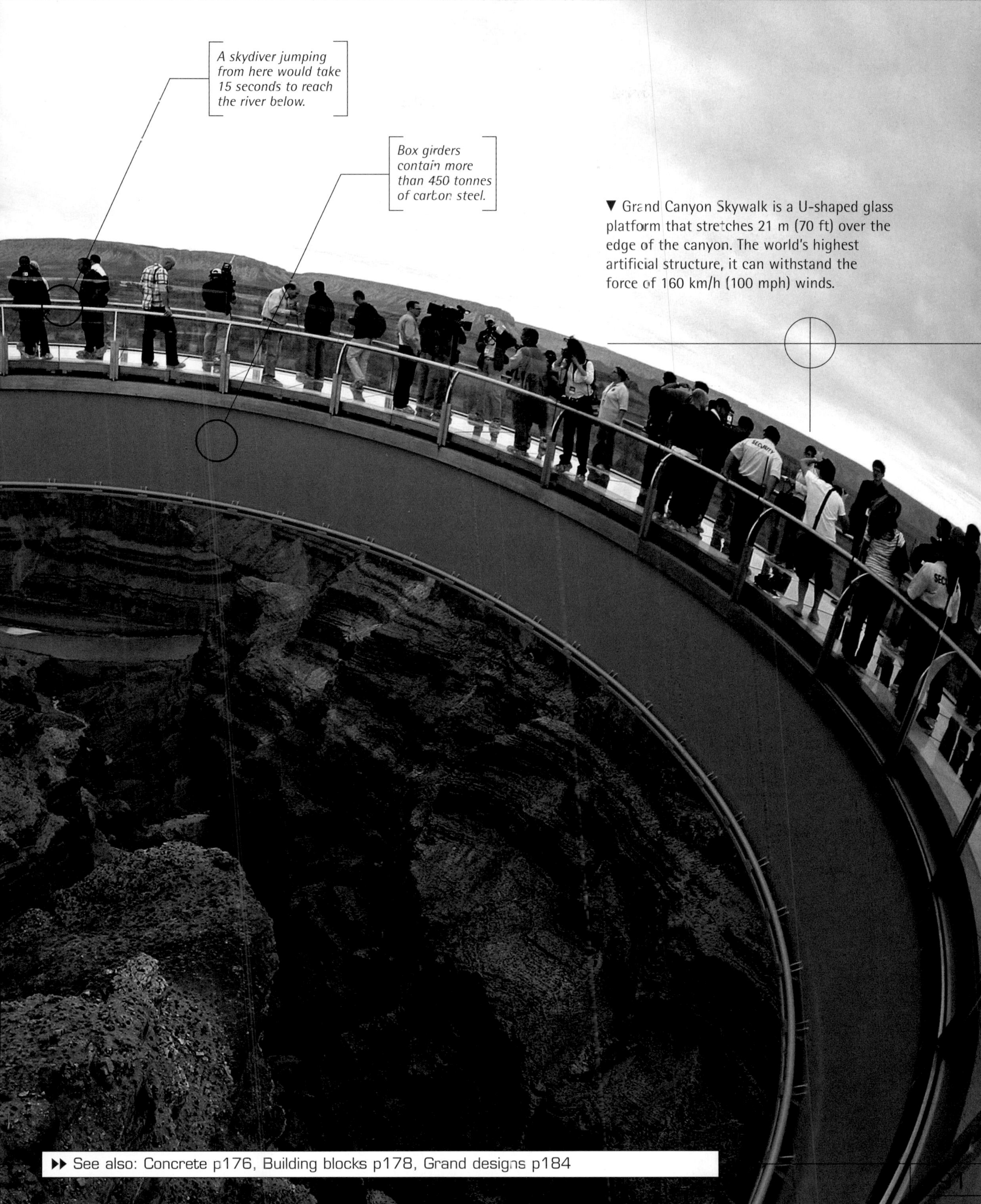

A skydiver jumping from here would take 15 seconds to reach the river below.
Box girders contain more than 450 tonnes of carbon steel.

▼ Grand Canyon Skywalk is a U-shaped glass platform that stretches 21 m (70 ft) over the edge of the canyon. The world's highest artificial structure, it can withstand the force of 160 km/h (100 mph) winds.

▶▶ See also: Concrete p176, Building blocks p178, Grand designs p184

Easy to shape yet strong enough to support immense loads, steel and concrete revolutionized engineering. These very versatile building materials have enabled architects and engineers to fashion bold and beautiful structures on a scale that would once have been unimaginable.

« Longest suspension bridge

The Akashi Kaikyo Bridge stretches 1.99 km (1.24 miles) between the Japanese mainland, Honshu, and the smaller island of Shikoku. The bridge is suspended from above by large cables and was designed to withstand devastating earthquakes.

^ Largest airport

^ Completed in 1983, the King Khalid International Airport in Riyadh, Saudi Arabia, covers an area that is bigger than 15,000 baseball fields. Its four large terminal buildings are able to handle more than 8.3 million passengers a year.

Widest street

The street called Avenida 9 de Julio in Buenos Aires, Argentina, is 130 m (425 ft) wide – twice the width of most streets in the country's capital. With 18 lanes of traffic and three areas of garden, this huge road can take 10 minutes to cross on foot. The street gets its name from 9 July, Argentina's Independence Day.

Largest stadium

The Indianapolis Motor Speedway Stadium in Indiana, USA, has room for more than 250,000 people in its stands. If the whole audience stood in line, they would stretch for a distance of about 80 km (50 miles).

Largest building

NASA's Vehicle Assembly Building (VAB) in Florida, USA, has more room inside it than any other building in the world. The gigantic doors are 139 m (456 ft) high to allow space rockets to be wheeled in and out.

See also: Building blocks p178, Grand designs p184, Shelters 234

Image: Tuned mass damper in Taipei 101 tower, Taiwan

MASS DAMPER

▶▶ Skyscrapers sway in the wind – if they didn't they might snap! In strong gusts, and with the wind blowing in a particular direction, these wobbles can become severe, causing motion sickness to those inside and damage to the building. A tuned mass damper reduces this swaying by using a large moving weight. ▶▶

▶ The moving weight of the Taipei 101 tower's mass damper is a massive ball that can swing about 1 m (3 ft) in any direction as the building sways. The damper reduces swaying by a third even though the tower is a thousand times heavier than the ball.

Weight was constructed inside the tower from 41 steel discs each 12.5 cm (5 in) thick.

Four sets of steel cables allow ball to swing as building sways.

1. Tower sways in the wind – as it moves left, the ball swings right.
2. Hydraulic dampers on the left resist being lengthened.
3. At the same time the dampers on the right are squeezed shorter and resist the swinging motion.
4. A few seconds later sway has reversed – the building moves right and the ball swings left.
5. Dampers on the left are squeezed shorter – their resistance removes energy from the swaying motion.
6. Dampers on the right resist being lengthened, and the swaying/damping sequence begins again.

Ball has diameter of 6 m (20 ft) and weighs 660 tonnes – more than two jumbo jets!

▶ The mass damper hangs between the 87th and 92nd floors of the 509-m (1,670-ft) Taipei 101 tower in Taiwan. Surrounded by restaurants, bars, and observation decks, the damper is a tourist attraction in its own right.

>> HOW A MASS DAMPER WORKS

A damper is a device designed to reduce unwanted movement, such as the swaying of a tower. Like a pendulum of a clock, the hanging ball in this damper takes a fixed time for each swing and can be tuned to match the swaying of the tower. As the building moves one way, the ball swings the opposite way. The ball is linked to the building with hydraulic (liquid-filled) dampers that are repeatedly squeezed or extended as the tower and ball move in opposite directions. Inside each one, a rod moves a disc through an oil-filled cylinder. Friction, as the disc resists being pushed and pulled through the cylinder, slows the swaying.

▶▶ See also: Concrete p176, Building blocks p178, Big builds p192

Image: Proposed Australian solar updraft tower
Tourists can take an amazing journey by lift to reach the viewing gallery at the top.
Warm air rises up concrete and steel tube 1,000 m (3,300 ft) tall.
Turbines at base of tower generate enough electricity for 200,000 homes.

All done with mirrors

Solar thermal power plant, California, USA

▲ Another type of solar power plant uses sun-tracking mirrors to reflect sunlight onto a central cylinder that is mounted on a tower. This cylinder becomes very hot, and heats oil or molten salt flowing through pipes inside. The hot liquid is used to boil water, making steam which in turn drives electricity generating turbines.

HOW POWER TOWERS WORK

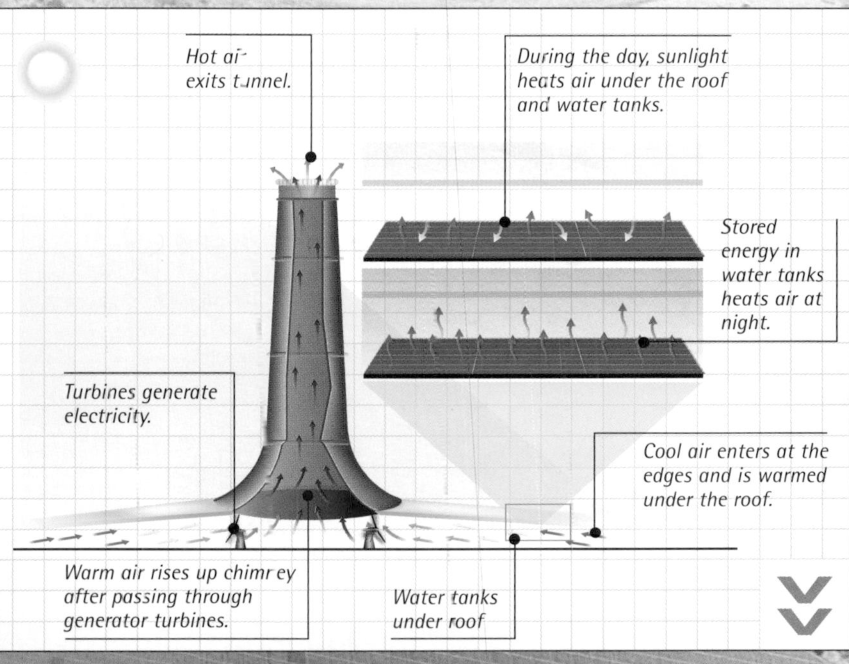
Hot air exits tunnel.
During the day, sunlight heats air under the roof and water tanks.
Stored energy in water tanks heats air at night.
Turbines generate electricity.
Cool air enters at the edges and is warmed under the roof.
Warm air rises up chimney after passing through generator turbines.
Water tanks under roof

In the glass-roofed area around the tower, sunlight shining through the glass warms the ground and air below. The warmest air, being least dense, rises up the tower. The moving air passes through turbines at the base of the tower and these drive electricity generators. The outer edge of the glass roof is open, which allows the cooler air outside to be sucked in to replace the warm air. Special water tanks under the roof warm up during the day and store the heat energy. At night the tanks heat the air around them, maintaining the airflow and keeping the turbines running.

◀ No smoke comes out of this chimney, only warm air. The glass-roofed area below collects energy from sunlight like a giant greenhouse. This trapped energy is used to generate electricity. No fuel is required, just a plentiful supply of sunshine, so sunny areas in southern Europe and Australia are proposed sites. A 200-m (660-ft) prototype solar updraft tower in Spain ran successfully for eight years.

Glass roof 4 km (2.5 miles) across traps air that is warmed by sunlight.

POWER TOWER

▶▶ Deep in the desert, a hollow tower almost three times as tall as the Empire State Building rises from the centre of a town-sized circle of glass. In the near future, structures like this could be generating pollution-free electricity without needing to be powered by any fuel. ▶▶

▶▶ See also: Wind turbine p22, Hydroponics p28, Eden Project p186

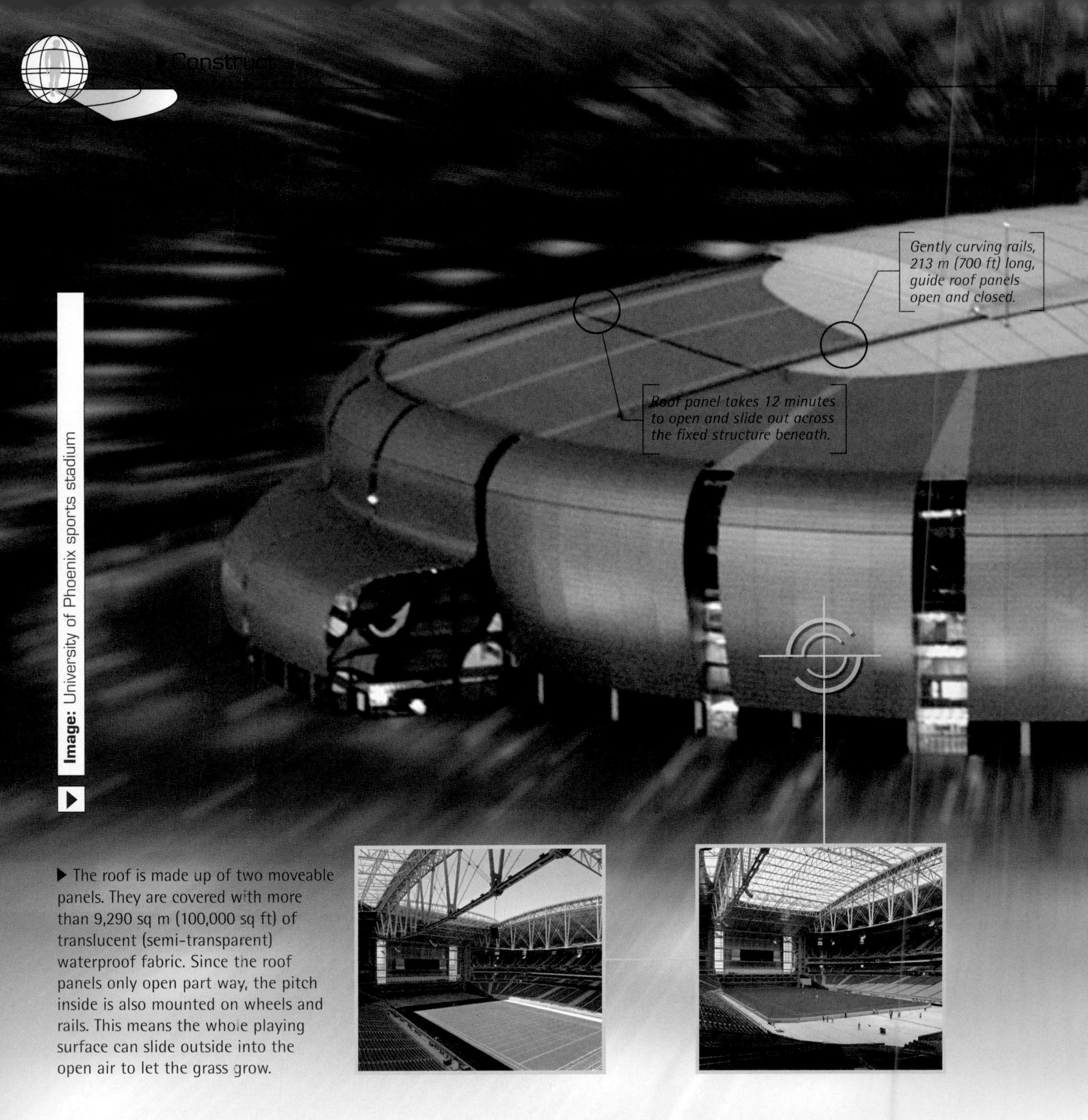

Gently curving rails, 213 m (700 ft) long, guide roof panels open and closed.
Roof panel takes 12 minutes to open and slide out across the fixed structure beneath.
Image: University of Phoenix sports stadium

▶ The roof is made up of two moveable panels. They are covered with more than 9,290 sq m (100,000 sq ft) of translucent (semi-transparent) waterproof fabric. Since the roof panels only open part way, the pitch inside is also mounted on wheels and rails. This means the whole playing surface can slide outside into the open air to let the grass grow.

STADIUM ROOF

▶▶ The University of Phoenix stadium in Arizona, USA, is a spectacular piece of engineering. The 63,400-seat arena has a computer-controlled retractable roof that can be shut to create an air-conditioned environment during the hot summer months. ▶▶

Two roof panels move apart, opening out from midpoint.

Most of the stadium roof area is permanently closed.

>> HOW THE ROOF OPENS AND CLOSES

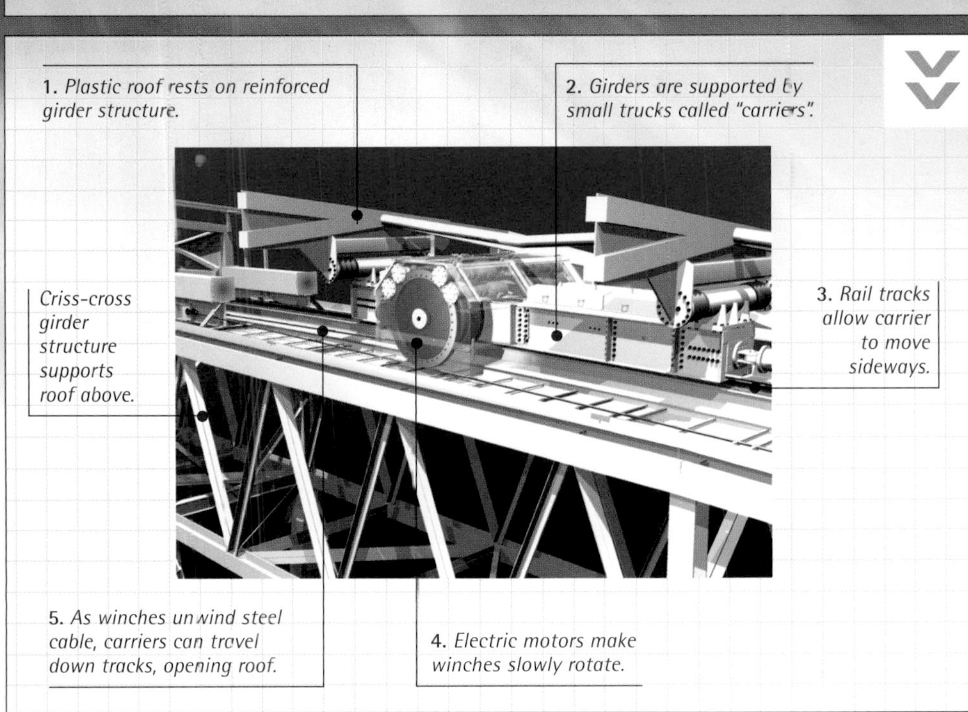

1. Plastic roof rests on reinforced girder structure.
2. Girders are supported by small trucks called "carriers".
Criss-cross girder structure supports roof above.
3. Rail tracks allow carrier to move sideways.
5. As winches unwind steel cable, carriers can travel down tracks, opening roof.
4. Electric motors make winches slowly rotate.

The roof is in two halves that can slide open or closed. Each half rests on wheels that run on rails stretching in a huge arc, lengthwise across the stadium. The roof panels are opened or closed by electric-powered winches underneath them. Strong cables run from the winches to the middle of the stadium structure. As the winches turn, they slowly reel out their cables. The weight of the roof panels lets them move down the rails and the roof opens. When the winches reel in the cables, they pull the entire roof closed again. A computer coordinates the movement.

▶▶ See also: Hawk-Eye p88, Grand designs p184, Skywalk p190

MICRO MACHINES

▶▶ Micro machines are mechanisms on a miniature scale. They can range in size from a micrometre (a millionth of a metre) to a millimetre (a thousandth of a metre) and are used in all sorts of technologies, from pressure sensors on car tyres to minute moving mirrors inside the latest cameras. ▶▶

▶ This fly's glasses were made to demonstrate what is possible with the latest micro-scale manufacturing processes. Pulses of laser light were used to cut them out of a thin sheet of tungsten metal.

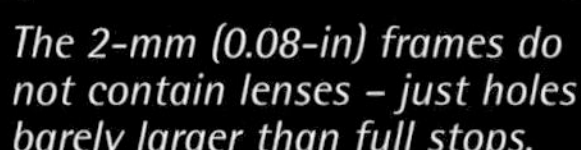

The 2-mm (0.08-in) frames do not contain lenses – just holes barely larger than full stops.

›› MAKING MICRO MACHINES

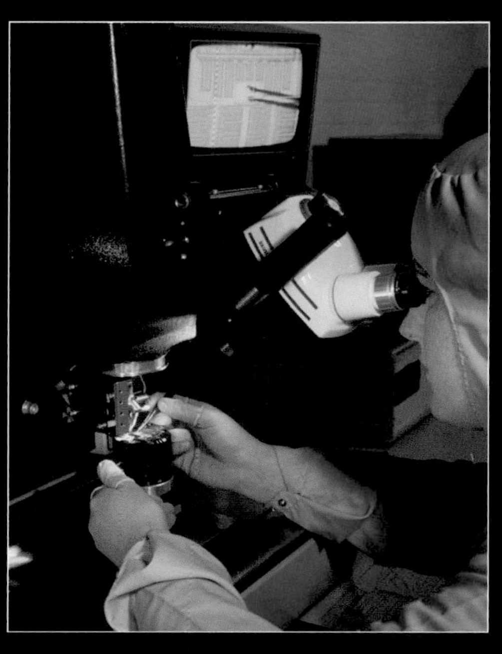

«Micro machines, or Microelectromechanical Systems (MEMS), can be cut out using lasers, but the most complex are made out of an element called silicon. To build up a micro machine's structure, layers of silicon are laid down one at a time. Most micro machines have about six silicon layers, each just a few micrometres thick. The correct shape for each layer is marked on the silicon's surface and the unwanted silicon is then dissolved chemically. A powerful microscope is required to connect tiny electrical wires to each micro machine.

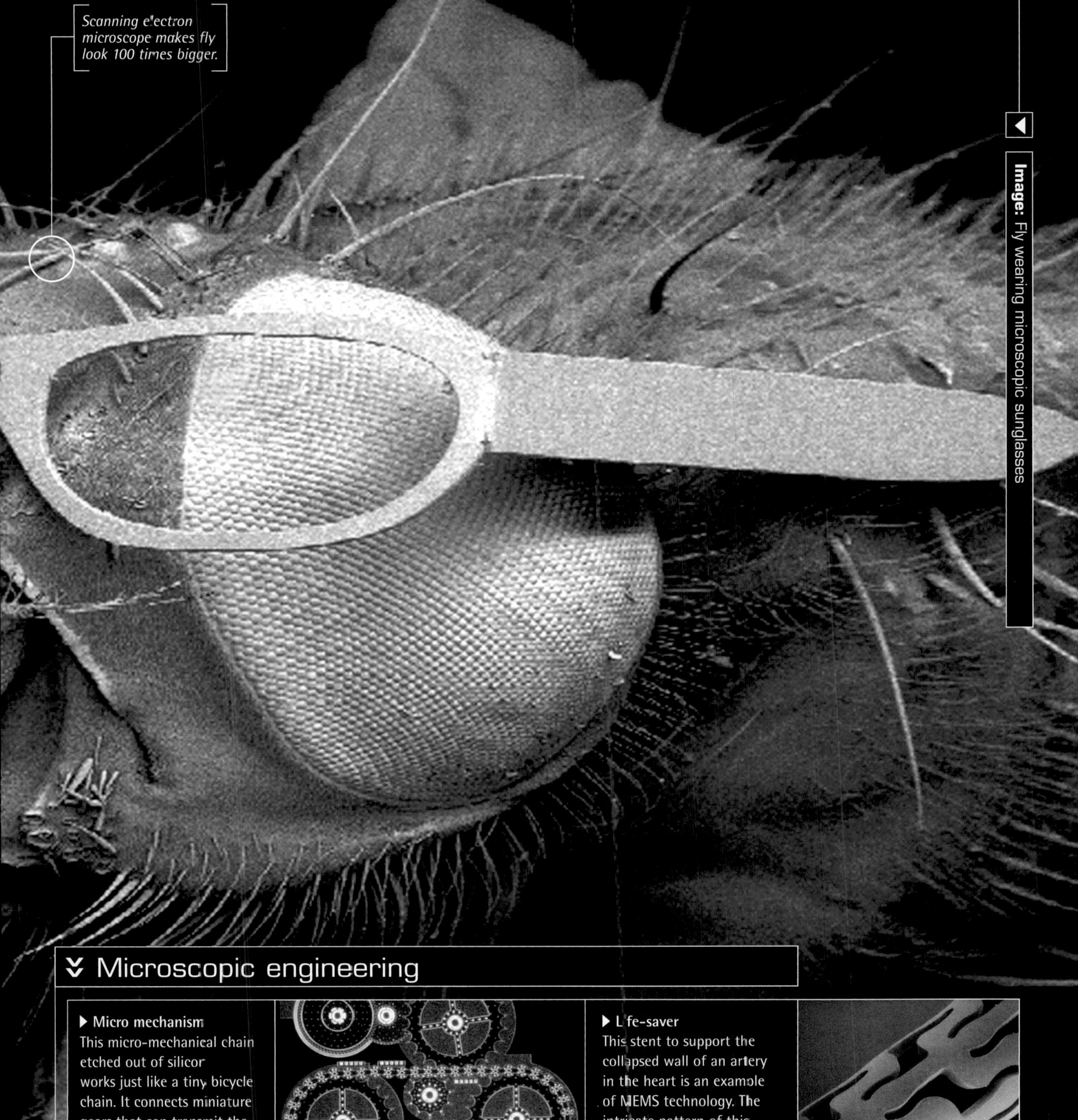

Scanning electron microscope makes fly look 100 times bigger.

Image: Fly wearing microscopic sunglasses

Microscopic engineering

▶ Micro mechanism
This micro-mechanical chain etched out of silicon works just like a tiny bicycle chain. It connects miniature gears that can transmit the power of a micro motor to where it is needed. Each chain link is shorter than the width of a human hair.

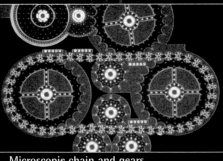

Microscopic chain and gears

▶ Life-saver
This stent to support the collapsed wall of an artery in the heart is an example of MEMS technology. The intricate pattern of this hollow tube, less than 2 mm (0.08 in) in diameter, was cut using a highly accurate laser.

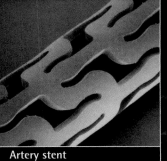

Artery stent

▶▶ See also: Artificial retina p34, Convergence p56, Microscope p162

▶▶ See also: Sup

Multiple beams are created when a single laser is pointed in different directions for short bursts.

Laser cutting

Laser cuts through super-strong Kevlar®

▶ A cutting laser can vaporize, melt, or burn its way through a variety of tough materials. The energy that is created by the laser is concentrated into a small area, and a computer controls the cutting with great accuracy. Gas is blown continuously through the nozzle to clear molten metals and other waste material from around the cutting zone.

LASER

▶▶ Once the stuff of science fiction, lasers are now part of everyday life – displayed at rock concerts, inside DVD players, and in the hands of surgeons. Lasers concentrate fine beams of intense light into a small area and have the power and precision to cut through metal and other materials. ▶▶

Image: Laser light show

>> HOW A RUBY LASER WORKS

2. Energy makes ruby atoms send out photons (energetic light particles).

5. Escaping photons all travel in step, making a powerful red laser beam.

3. Mirror bounces photons again and again through ruby rod, intensifying the light.

1. Flash tube pumps energy into ruby rod.

4. Partial mirror reflects some photons back into the rod and lets some escape.

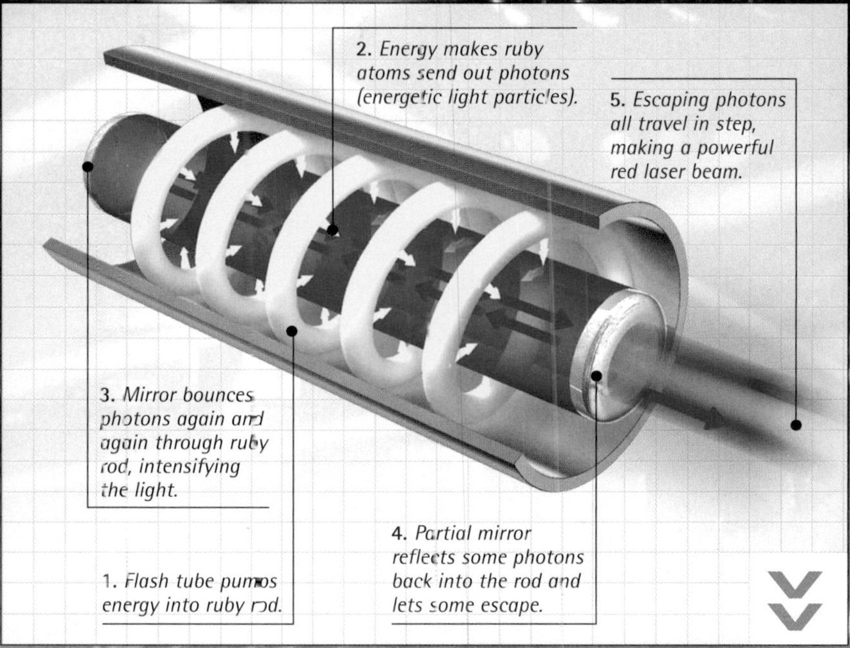

A laser makes powerful red light by pumping energy into a rod-shaped crystal of ruby. Energy is pumped in by a glass tube around the ruby, which flashes with light. The atoms in the ruby absorb this light energy, becoming unstable. They become stable again when they send out photons (particles of light). Mirrors at either end bounce the photons up and down, making the ruby give off even more photons, which emerge as a powerful laser beam.

Beams are constantly moving so they don't shine on one spot long enough to do any damage.

◀ Clubs and concerts entertain audiences with spectacular, multi-coloured laser shows. Each type of laser emits one particular colour of light. Additional colours can be made by mixing the light from two or three different lasers. Computers can control motor-driven mirrors, which change the direction of the beams in time to the music.

>>PROTECT

Money >> Biometric ID >> Airport security >> Spy >> DataDot >> Stealth >> Ejector seat >> Kevlar >> Hard wear >> Rebreather >> Fire extinguisher >> Eyewear >> LifeStraw >> Shelters >> Lighthouse >> Tsunami alert >> Flood barrier

Can you see what's right in front of you? p230

▸▸ For almost every danger we come up against, there is an invention to protect us. Our bodies are no match for fire, but aluminium suits can carry us safely through the flames. Supersonic planes can kill if they crash, but with luck ejector seats will fling the crew clear. New threats are always emerging from crime, terrorism, and natural disasters. But science and technology are keeping up. Clever gadgets are being invented to help us spot dangers – and keep out of harm's way. ▸▸

Why put stars in your pocket? p208

What does this hide? p218

Can you follow this? p214

Image: 50-Euro banknote in ultraviolet light

▲ This 50-Euro banknote contains fluorescent inks that show up only in ultraviolet light. Numerous other security features make this note impossible to fake by photocopying. You can check a note is genuine by looking at the patterns, feeling the paper, and tilting to check the hologram.

Defeating counterfeiters

▼ Counterfeiting
At a glance, the fake Euro notes shown on the right seem passable copies of the genuine ones on the left. Counterfeiting is a constant problem for banks, who regularly change the design of notes to stay one step ahead.

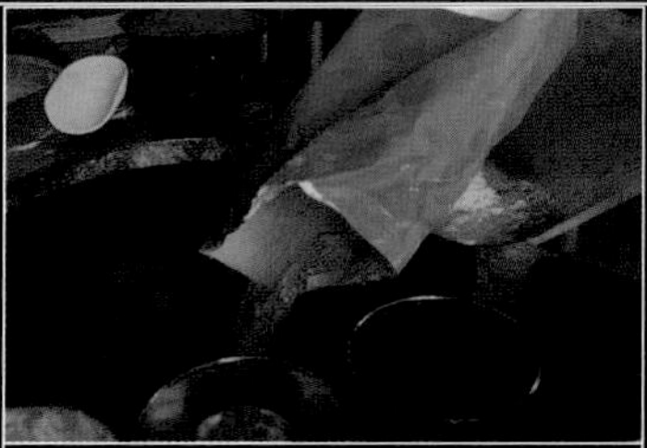

High-security inks

▼ Coins
Coins are relatively difficult and expensive to cast in metal, so they tend to be safer than notes. All coins are made to exact weights, which makes it harder for people to use fake coins in vending machines.

C...terfeit currency

▲ Special inks
Some banknotes are printed with optically variable inks (OVIs) that change colour in different light. On a 50-Euro banknote, the "50" printed on the back changes from purple to green when you tilt the not

Close-up of 100 yen coin

▶▶ See also: Supermarket p30, Biometric ID p210, DataDot p216

MONEY

▶▶ Much of the world's wealth is not locked in vaults, but circulating freely as paper banknotes. Some banknotes contain as many as 15 different high-security features to stop counterfeiters producing fake currency. ▶▶

›› SECURITY FEATURES

Banknotes are designed for maximum security. They are printed on cotton paper that feels crisp and smooth, not thin or waxy, with coloured threads or metal strips woven inside. Swirling patterns printed in special inks are combined with holograms and watermarks.

CHERRY BLOSSOM

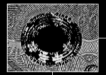

FACE VALUE

LOGO OF BANK

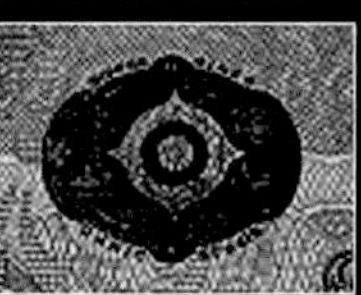

As you tilt a banknote, the metallic holographic image seems to rotate and change colour.

WATERMARK

The famous person on a banknote can also be seen in the watermark in the centre.

RAISED PRINTING

A raised printing technique means you can feel the ink on a banknote, unlike that on a photocopy.

MICROPRINTING

Swirling patterns and tiny writing are designed to blur if the note is photocopied.

Image: Comparing biometric passport data

BIOMETRIC ID

▸▸ To help in the fight against identity theft and forgery, many countries around the world now issue passports and ID cards with built-in chips that can be read electronically. The chips contain information about the document, but can also hold biometric data – information that can confirm a person's physical ID, such as eye and fingerprints scans. ▸▸

▶▶ See also: Airport security p212, Spy p214, DataDot p216

Basic data is read using an optical scanner.

▲ To check a person's printed passport details have not been altered they are compared with the data in the chip, which is read wirelessly by a computer. Unauthorized changes to information on the chip can also be detected.

>> BIOMETRIC DATA

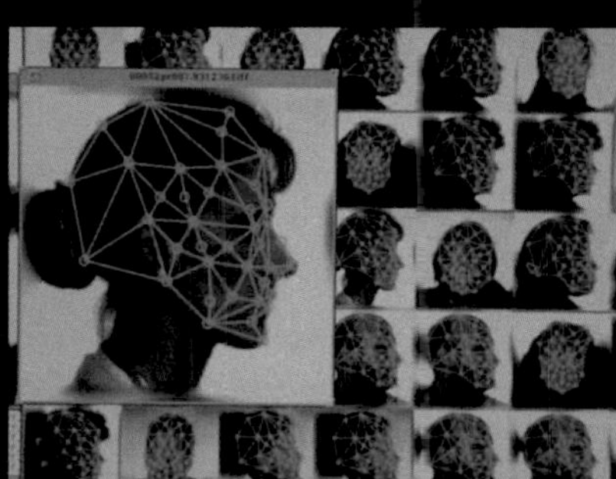

Facial recognition
Details of an individual's face can be taken from a photograph by a computer, which then maps the key features and calculates the distances between them. This data can be compared with the measurements from the photo on the chip or information stored on a central database.

Fingerprints
The pattern of ridges and troughs on the ends of your fingers are unique to you. This fingerprint pattern can be read using an optical or pressure sensitive scanner and matched to your identity using a database. In some places you can now pay for your shopping using your fingerprint.

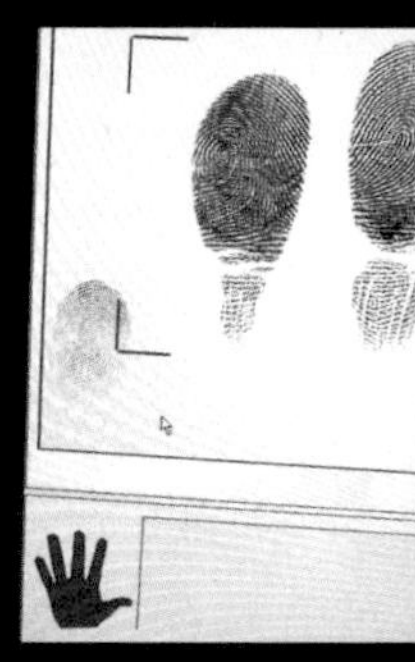

Iris scan
No two people have the same pattern of flecks and lines in their iris – the coloured part of their eyes. Even an individual's two eyes are different. This pattern can be captured by a camera and turned into a unique digital code that can be used to confirm your identity.

Passport chip

▶ Inside a biometric passport is a data chip, smaller than a fingernail, connected to an aerial made from a loop of fine copper wire. This is the same radio-frequency identification (RFID) technology as smart cards and wireless shop tags. The chip is scanned using radio signals. Some passports also have metal shielding to prevent unauthorized scanning

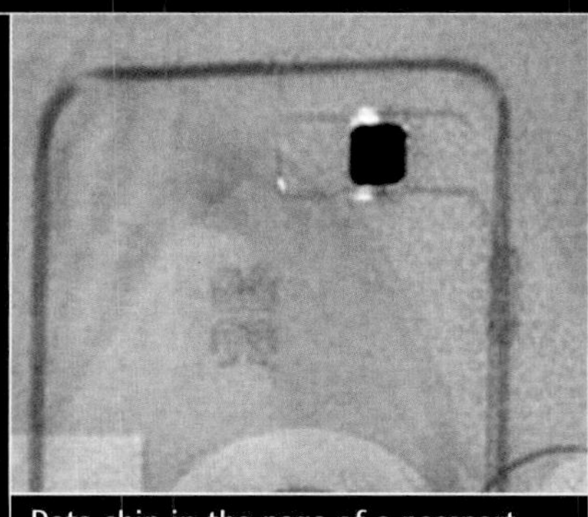

Data chip in the page of a passport

AIRPORT SECURITY

▶▶ What's in that case – a book or a bomb? More than 600 million passengers pass through the world's 10 busiest airports each year. It's just as well that new airport scanners can search 400 bags per minute. ▶▶

Image: Contents of hand luggage

◀ At most airports, every item of luggage has to pass through an X-ray scanning machine like this. A see-through image of the contents (like the one below) appears on a monitor in front of the security officer. Separate CT (computerized tomography) scanners can identify explosives.

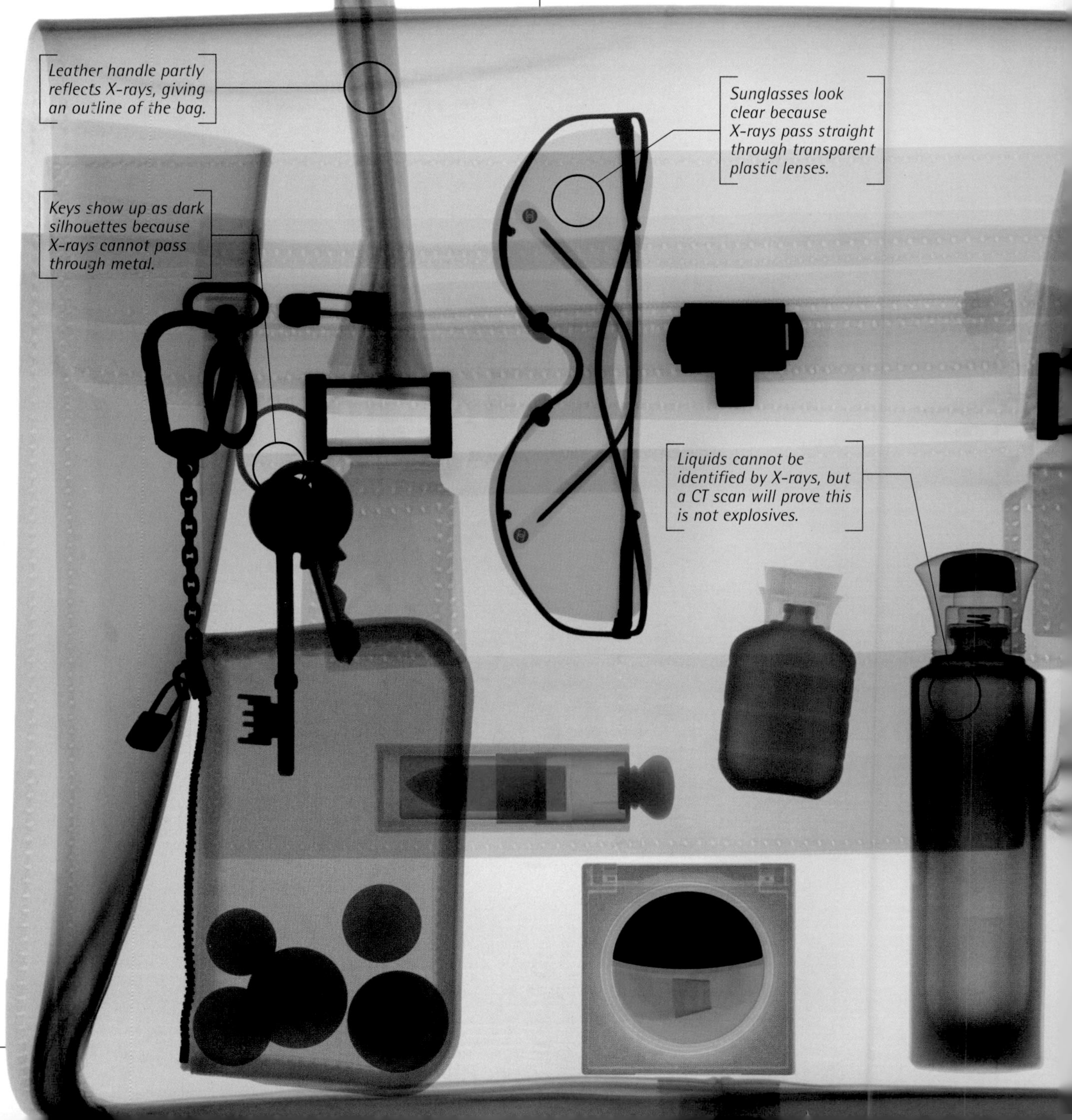

Leather handle partly reflects X-rays, giving an outline of the bag.

Sunglasses look clear because X-rays pass straight through transparent plastic lenses.

Keys show up as dark silhouettes because X-rays cannot pass through metal.

Liquids cannot be identified by X-rays, but a CT scan will prove this is not explosives.

>> HOW X-RAY SCANNERS WORK

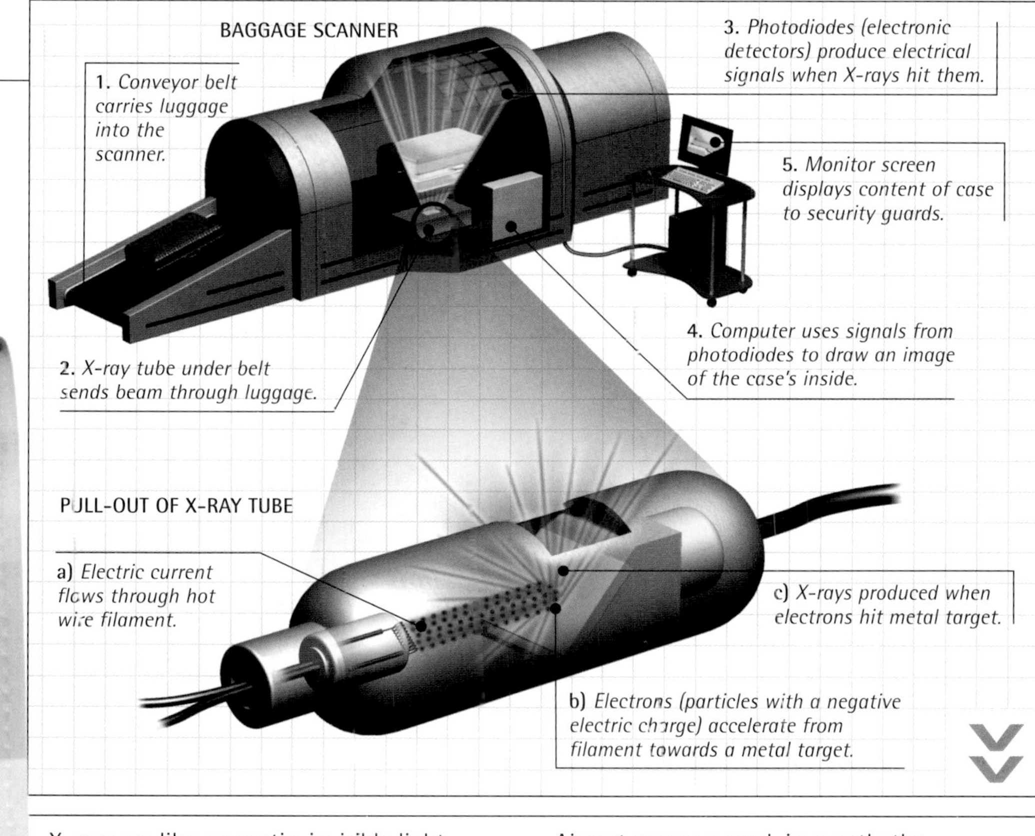
BAGGAGE SCANNER
1. Conveyor belt carries luggage into the scanner.
2. X-ray tube under belt sends beam through luggage.
3. Photodiodes (electronic detectors) produce electrical signals when X-rays hit them.
4. Computer uses signals from photodiodes to draw an image of the case's inside.
5. Monitor screen displays content of case to security guards.
PULL-OUT OF X-RAY TUBE
a) Electric current flows through hot wire filament.
b) Electrons (particles with a negative electric charge) accelerate from filament towards a metal target.
c) X-rays produced when electrons hit metal target.

Mobile phone components are clearly revealed because X-rays pass through plastic case.

X-rays are like energetic, invisible light carried by waves of electricity and magnetism. Light bounces off most objects, but X-rays are intense enough to pass through. If you shine X-rays at someone's body, they pass through soft tissues but not through hard bones or teeth. This is how a medical X-ray scanner can make an image of your body's inner structure.

Airport scanners work in exactly the same way. When X-rays shine on luggage, they pass straight through the plastic or leather case and any soft materials like clothing. But they cannot penetrate hard, metal items like keys or coins. This means an X-ray photo will show shadowy images of all the hard items you are carrying in your suitcase.

CT scanning

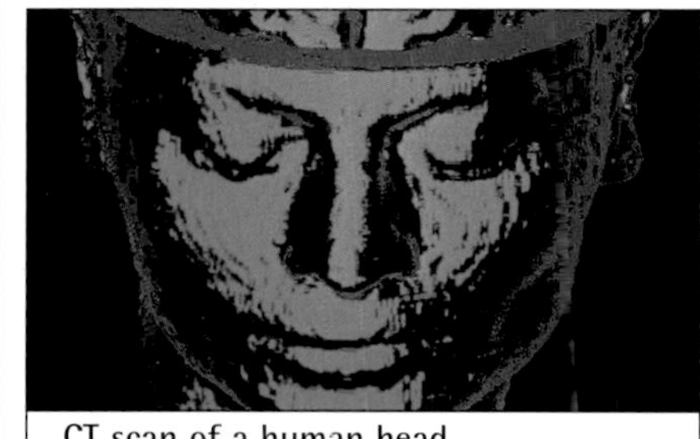
CT scan of a human head

◀ Although two-dimensional X-rays can locate suspicious objects, they cannot always identify their contents. New airport scanners use an advanced form of scanning called CT (computerized tomography), widely used in medical diagnosis. CT scans use rotating X-ray beams to make three-dimensional images and measure the exact density of objects.

▶▶ See also: Biometric ID p210, Spy p214

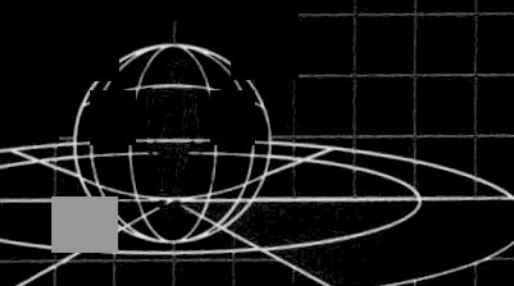

SPY

« Tracking device No bigger than a matchbox, this tiny tracker is easy to hide in a suspect's vehicle. Using GPS (Global Positioning System) satellites, it calculates its location every second, and sends it via wireless Bluetooth® to a computer. Trackers like this can automatically monitor a car's movements without someone needing to follow it on the road.

» Pinhole camera The size of a button, this digital camera has a pinhole aperture (hole through which the picture is taken) smaller than a pencil lead. It can be concealed anywhere – in rooms or even in a person's clothing – to make still photos or video images. A tiny, powerful microphone beneath the camera lens captures sound.

Thanks to ever-shrinking electronics, spying has never been easier. Modern microchips can squeeze more than 500 million transistors (electronic switches) into an area the size of a fingernail. That means cameras, trackers, and listening devices are smaller, more powerful, and easier to hide than ever before.

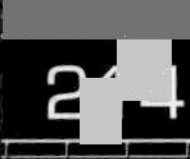

Listening device
This sensitive electronic ear uses a small curved dish to capture sounds more than 90 m (300 ft) away. Amplifier circuits built into the handle boost the sounds, play them through headphones, or store them in a built-in digital recorder.

Camera watch
Spies have always hidden cameras in ordinary objects, such as this innocent-looking digital watch. It can store up to 100 pictures and transmit them wirelessly to a computer.

Security cameras
There are more than 25 million CCTV (closed-circuit television) cameras worldwide, watching our every move. The latest cameras record digital images on computer hard drives or DVDs. Using the Internet, cameras can be monitored from anywhere in the world.

▶▶ See also: Bluetooth® p50, Night vision p160, Biometric ID p210

DATADOT

This magnified DataDot is the size of a grain of sand and very difficult to spot.

▶▶ Imagine attaching thousands of name tags to valuables to deter thieves. If the tags were almost invisible it would be impossible to remove them all. This is what DataDots do using tiny laser-etched discs. ▶▶

▲ **Image:** DataDotDNA under magnification

>> HOW DATADOT WORKS

This car is having thousands of DataDots mixed with glue sprayed onto key locations. Without special illumination, the DataDots look like spots of dirt or corrosion. With so many on the car some will always remain even if someone tries to clean them all off. Thieves often change the identities of stolen cars using false number plates and altered identification numbers, so they can be sold more easily. If police find even one DataDot on a vehicle, they can use it to uncover the car's original identity.

◀ Hundreds of DataDots on a motorcycle glow here under ultraviolet light. Under normal light they are difficult to spot. Each one is a disc with a unique number etched into it using a laser. Any object with DataDots on it can be traced back to its owner or manufacturer. The number from the disc is matched to the owner on a central database. Would-be thieves are unlikely to steal things that they know carry DataDots as the objects will be identifiable.

▶▶ See also: Microscope p162, Money p208, Biometric ID p210

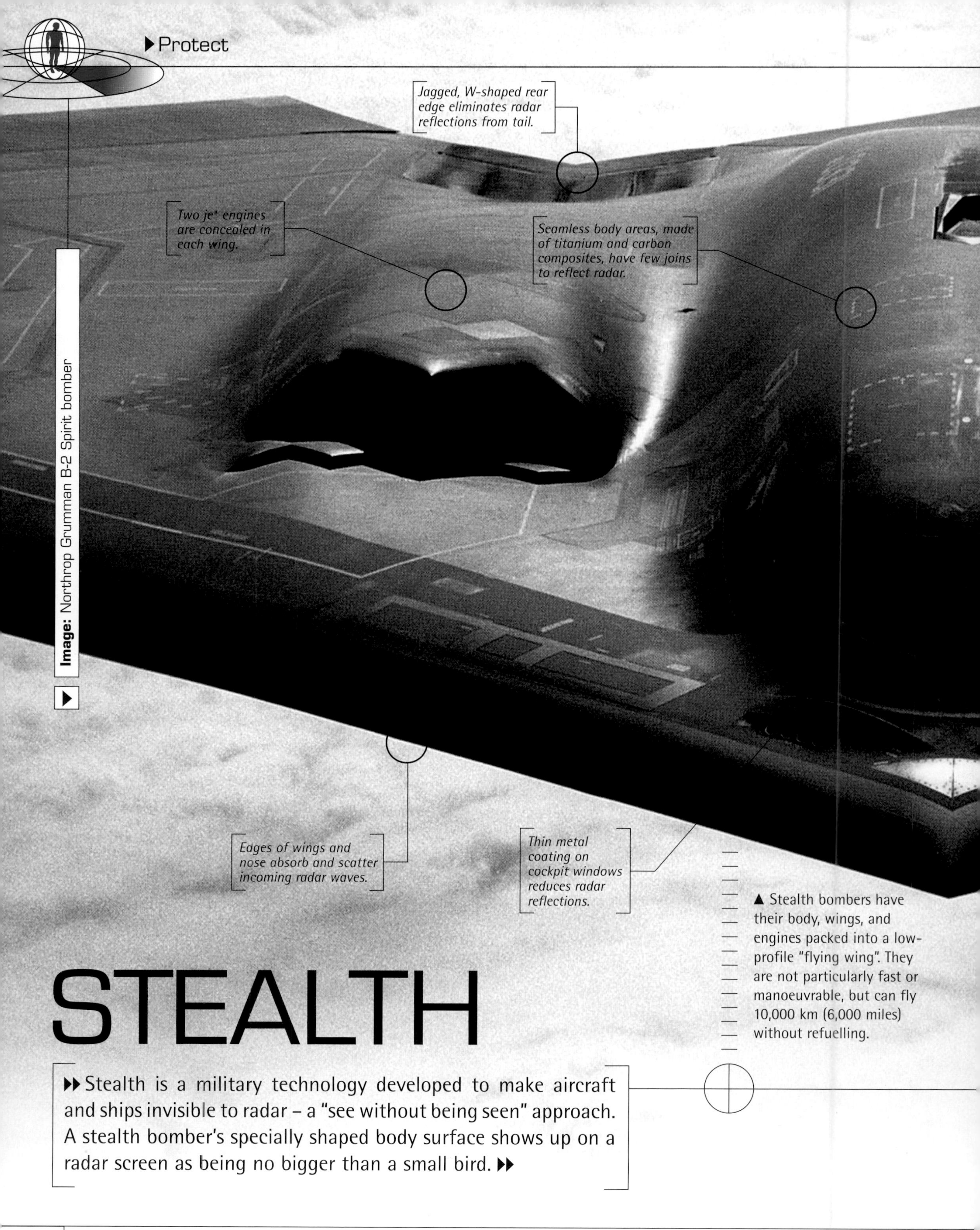

Jagged, W-shaped rear edge eliminates radar reflections from tail.
Two jet engines are concealed in each wing.
Seamless body areas, made of titanium and carbon composites, have few joins to reflect radar.
Edges of wings and nose absorb and scatter incoming radar waves.
Thin metal coating on cockpit windows reduces radar reflections.

Image: Northrop Grumman B-2 Spirit bomber

▲ Stealth bombers have their body, wings, and engines packed into a low-profile "flying wing". They are not particularly fast or manoeuvrable, but can fly 10,000 km (6,000 miles) without refuelling.

STEALTH

▶▶Stealth is a military technology developed to make aircraft and ships invisible to radar – a "see without being seen" approach. A stealth bomber's specially shaped body surface shows up on a radar screen as being no bigger than a small bird. ▶▶

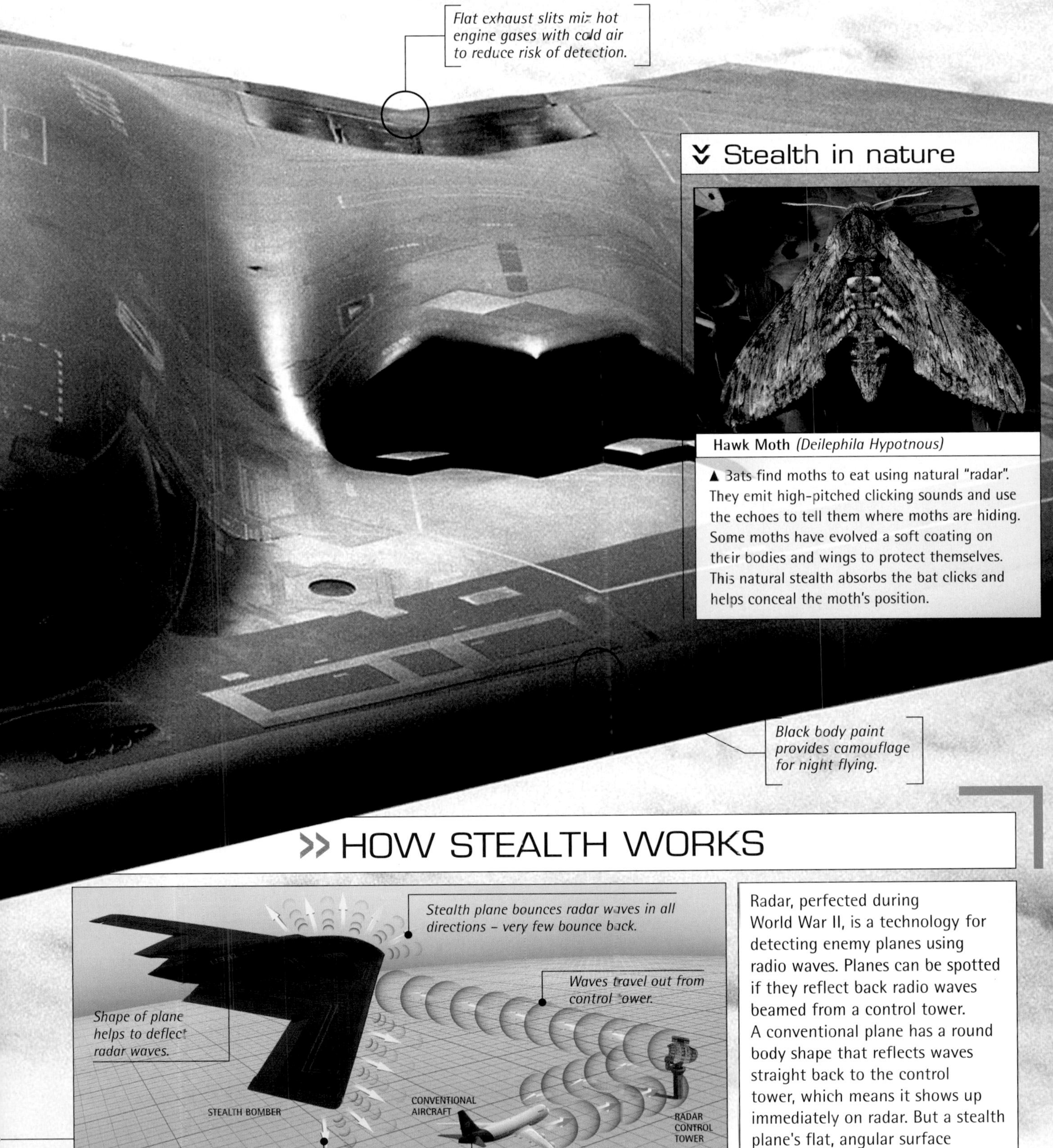

Flat exhaust slits mix hot engine gases with cold air to reduce risk of detection.
Black body paint provides camouflage for night flying.

Stealth in nature

Hawk Moth *(Deilephila Hypotnous)*

▲ Bats find moths to eat using natural "radar". They emit high-pitched clicking sounds and use the echoes to tell them where moths are hiding. Some moths have evolved a soft coating on their bodies and wings to protect themselves. This natural stealth absorbs the bat clicks and helps conceal the moth's position.

HOW STEALTH WORKS

Stealth plane bounces radar waves in all directions – very few bounce back.

Waves travel out from control tower.

Shape of plane helps to deflect radar waves.

STEALTH BOMBER

CONVENTIONAL AIRCRAFT

RADAR CONTROL TOWER

Radar waves do not reflect back to control tower.

Radar waves from conventional plane reflect directly back.

Radar, perfected during World War II, is a technology for detecting enemy planes using radio waves. Planes can be spotted if they reflect back radio waves beamed from a control tower. A conventional plane has a round body shape that reflects waves straight back to the control tower, which means it shows up immediately on radar. But a stealth plane's flat, angular surface scatters and absorbs radar waves, making it virtually invisible.

▶▶ See also: Simulators p70, Silent flight p126, SpaceShipOne p148

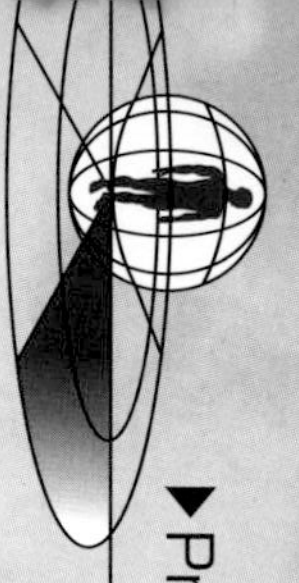

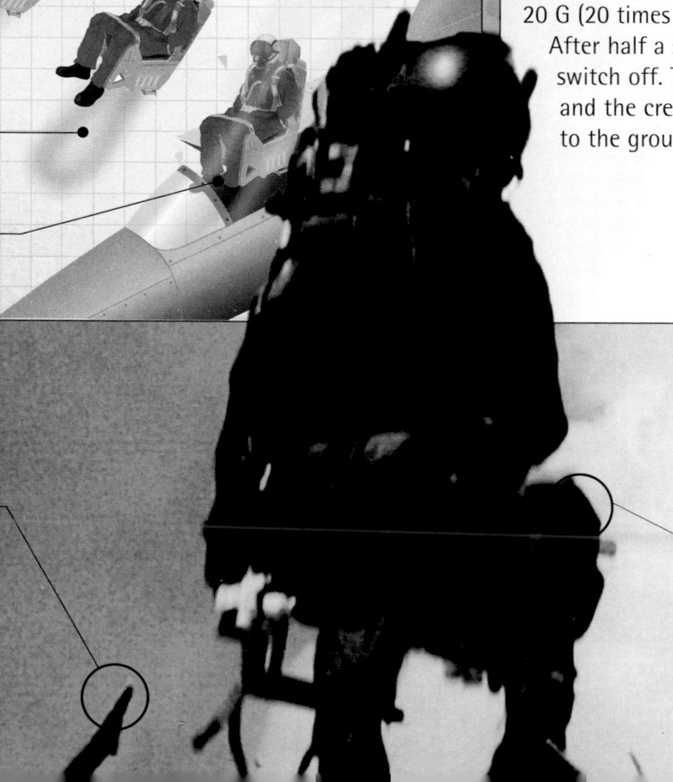

Image: Navigator being ejected from a plane

» HOW AN EJECTOR SEAT WORKS

1. Pilot pulls handle to begin escape and open canopy.
2. Rocket motor fires and seat rises.
3. Parachute opens when pilot is clear of the plane.
4. Safety restraint opens to release pilot from seat.
5. With parachute open fully, pilot descends slowly to the ground.

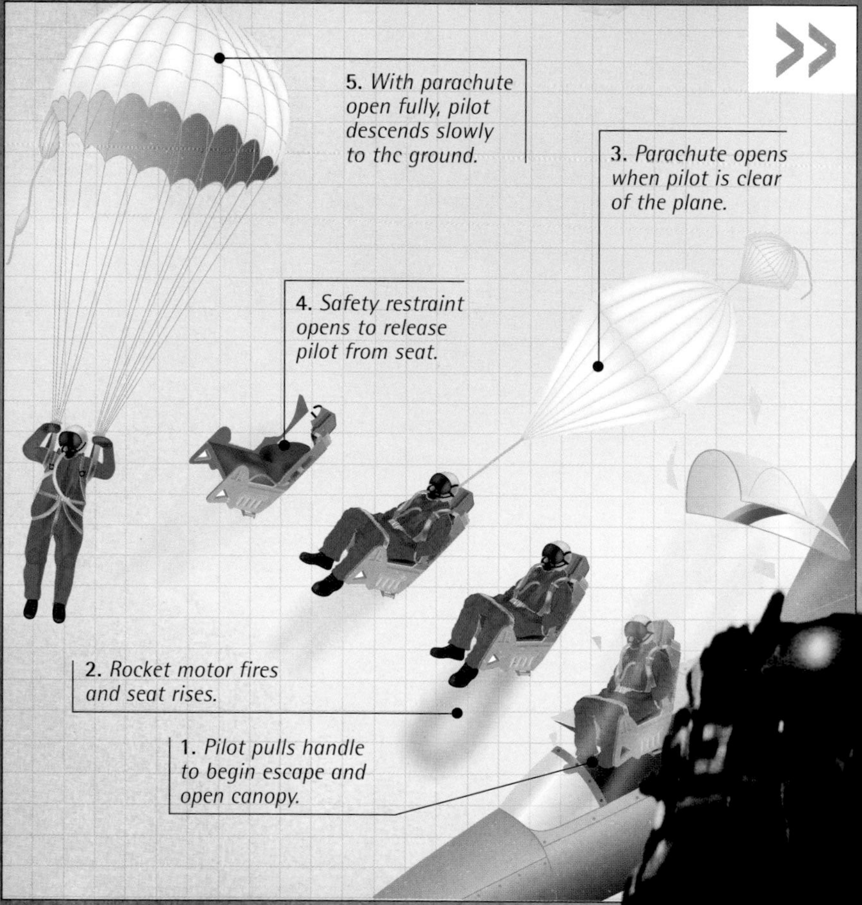

An ejector seat is a rocket-powered chair designed to help a pilot escape safely from a plane that is doomed to crash. When the crew decide to eject, they pull safety handles under their seats. Explosive charges immediately blow open escape hatches in the back of the plane's cockpit, clearing the area above the crew. Rockets ignite under the seats, firing out the navigator first and then the pilot a split-second later (to avoid them colliding in midair). The rockets are incredibly powerful. The crew accelerate from 0–260 km/h (0–162 mph) in just a quarter of a second (100 times faster than a sports car) and experience forces more than 20 G (20 times the force of gravity).

After half a second, the rockets switch off. The parachutes open and the crew glide safely to the ground.

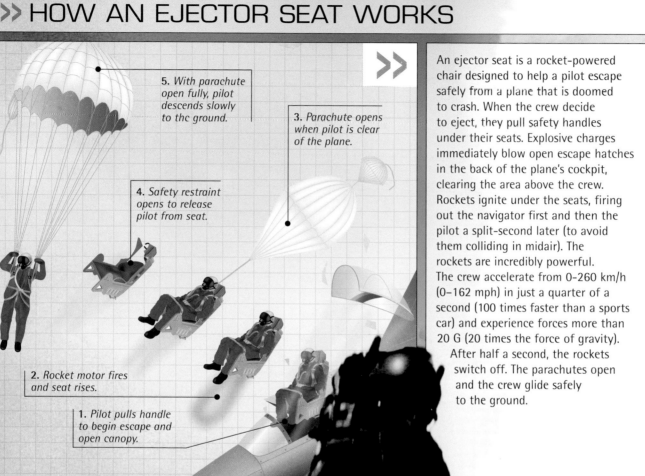

Canopy is blown into tiny pieces so escaping crew will not injure themselves if they collide with it.

Pressurized suit keeps blood pumping around the body to stop person blacking out during extreme acceleration.

EJECTOR SEAT

▶▶ Jet fighters scream through the sky at speeds of more than 2,000 km/h (1,243 mph) – six times faster than a Formula 1 car. When a jet has to crash land, rocket-propelled ejector seats can blast the crew out of the cockpit in under four seconds, so they can gently parachute to safety. ▶▶

◀ Rocket motors on ejector seats fire for only half a second. This is just enough time to blast the crew above the fast-moving plane and its jet engines.

Pilot remains in cockpit until navigator has safely ejected.

▶▶ See also: Bodyflight p86, Aerobatics p128, Vomit comet p140

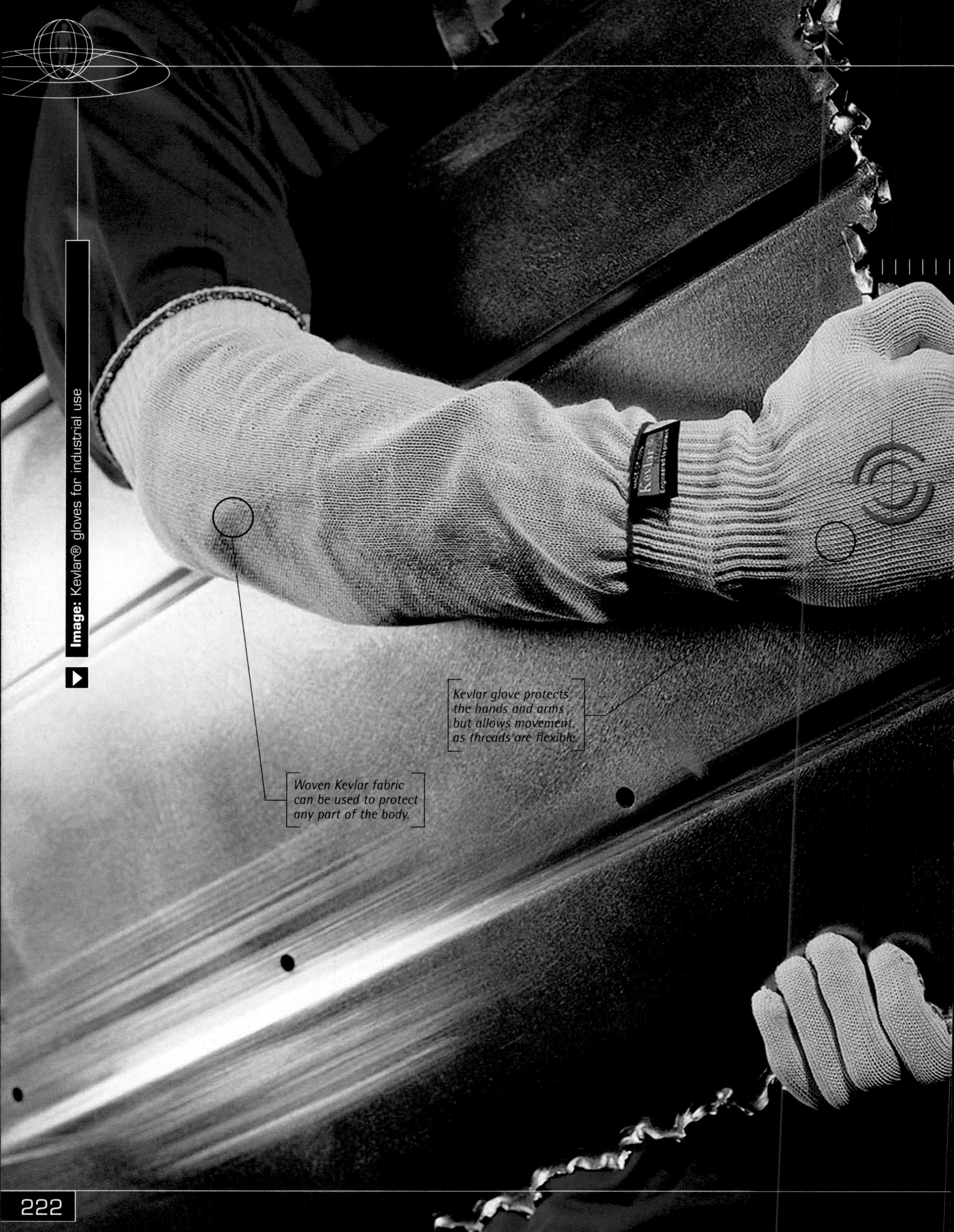

Kevlar glove protects the hands and arms but allows movement as threads are flexible.
Woven Kevlar fabric can be used to protect any part of the body.

Image: Kevlar® gloves for industrial use

▼ Kevlar gloves protect hands from all kinds of dangerous materials. Kevlar is hard to cut through, it is also resistant to chemicals and will not conduct electricity.

KEVLAR

▶▶ Kevlar® is an amazing artificial material. Lightweight and flexible, it is five times stronger than steel. It is used in super-tough equipment such as body armour, chainsaw-proof protective clothing, ropes for anchoring battleships, and puncture-proof bike tyres. ▶▶

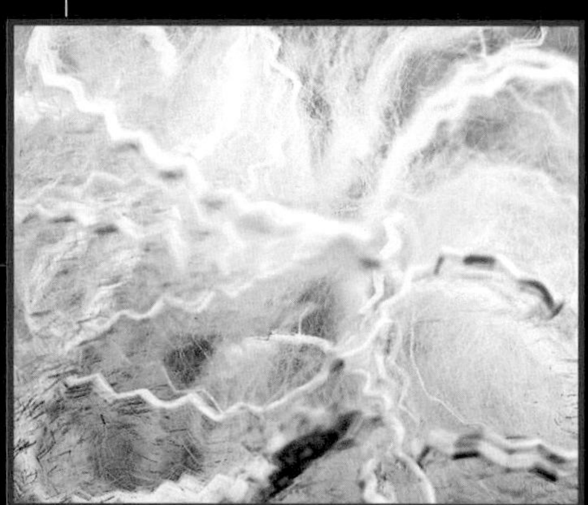

◀ The Kevlar fibres that these gloves are made from can be added to specialist paints and coatings to give a tough outer layer. Kevlar can also be combined with another material such as a plastic to give a composite material with the best properties of both.

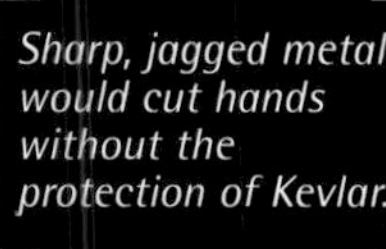

Sharp, jagged metal would cut hands without the protection of Kevlar.

>> HOW KEVLAR WORKS

<< Flexible thread
Kevlar is a polymer. This means that it consists of very strong, long molecules lined up together. As a result, it is possible to draw out Kevlar into a thread, which is flexible and can be woven.

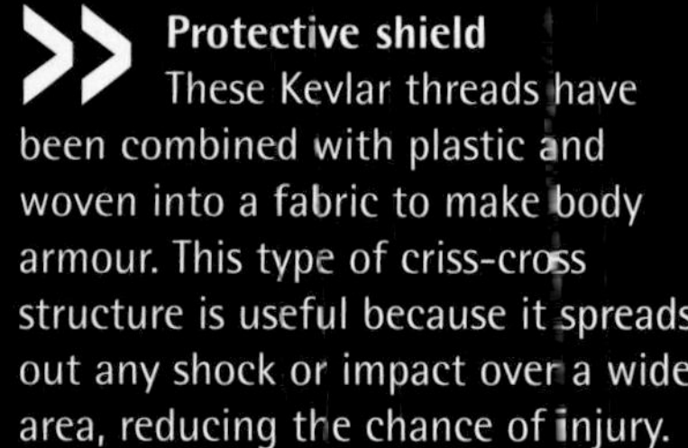

>> Protective shield
These Kevlar threads have been combined with plastic and woven into a fabric to make body armour. This type of criss-cross structure is useful because it spreads out any shock or impact over a wide area, reducing the chance of injury.

▶▶ See also: Bioplastic p26, Building blocks p178, Fire extinguisher p228

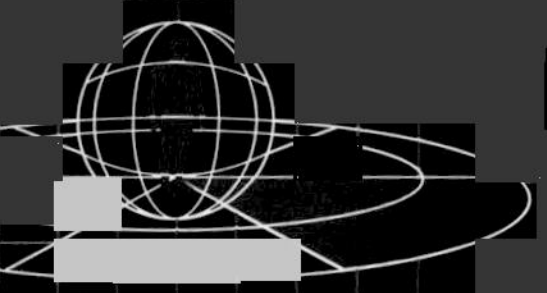

HARD WEAR

Smooth, flexible, long-lasting and self-repairing, human skin is an amazing material. But it is still no match for the threats we face in the modern world. Toughened clothing, made from specialized plastics, materials, and rubbers, gives us the protection we need to take on bullets, blows, chemicals, and fire – even the challenges of outer space.

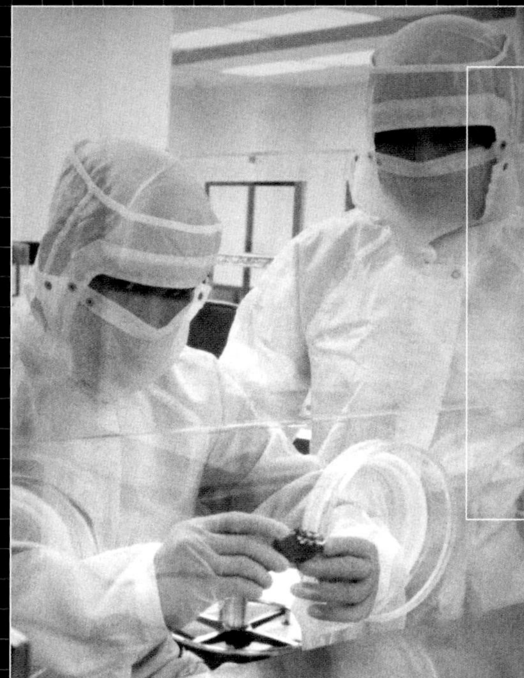

Cover up These forensic scientists are wearing disposable suits made from Tyvek®, a rip-proof polyethylene (a type of high-tech plastic) that is as light as paper and as strong as fabric. Worn with face masks and latex gloves, suits like this allow criminal investigators to examine evidence without any risk of contaminating it.

Space wardrobe These heavy-duty spacesuits are made for space shuttle astronauts to wear during space walks. More than just an outerspace overcoat, each suit contains a complete life-support system that includes oxygen packs and battery units. It gets so hot inside the suit that the astronaut has to wear special underwear with built-in refrigeration pipes.

Cool inside

Firefighters dress for one of the toughest jobs on Earth. Made from carbon fibre with an aluminium outer coating, this suit reflects heat, keeping the firefighter safe inside. It can withstand a blaze of up to 500°C (950°F) – hotter than the burning temperature of wood, oil, or coal.

Chemical-free

Made from two layers of butyl (a type of rubber) separated by carbon fibre, this chemical-protection suit is like an all-over rubber glove. Breathing apparatus housed inside allows emergency personnel to work in total safety, though toxic chemicals have to be hosed off before the suit can be removed.

Body guard

Five times stronger than steel, Kevlar® is a tough, knitted fibre that offers police officers protection against bullets and knives. Police helmets are also made from Kevlar, toughened with metal plates, and have special neck visors to protect against blows to the back.

See also: Trainers p50, Kevlar® p222, Fire extinguisher p228

REBREATHER

▶▶ The world record for holding breath underwater is 8 minutes and 58 seconds – but not breathing for so long is difficult and dangerous. Using an underwater breathing device called a scuba rebreather, divers can survive under the sea in perfect safety and without resurfacing, for hours at a time. ▶▶

◀ As well as needing air to breathe, scuba divers wear wetsuits to keep warm. Cold water rapidly chills the body and causes a life-threatening condition called hypothermia. These tight-fitting costumes made from neoprene (synthetic rubber) trap water inside, which quickly heats up and keeps the body warm.

Toughened face mask magnifies objects by more than 25 per cent.

Swim fins with large blades help propel the diver forwards.

Wristwatch monitors dive depth, time, and water temperature.

Torch needed because little light penetrates more than 30 m (100 ft) below the surface.

Image: A scuba diver explores a coral reef

» HOW REBREATHERS WORK

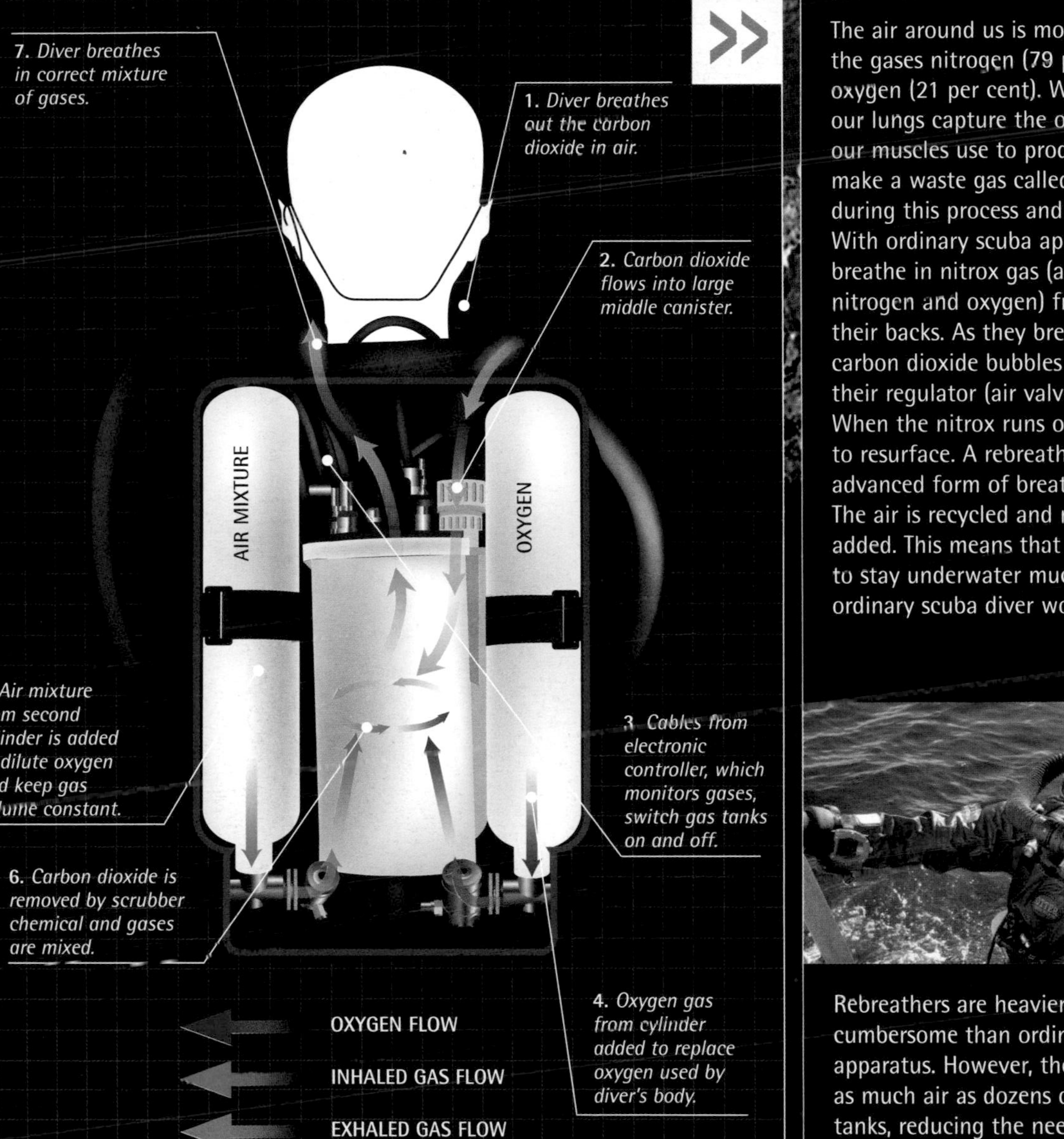
7. Diver breathes in correct mixture of gases.
1. Diver breathes out the carbon dioxide in air.
2. Carbon dioxide flows into large middle canister.
AIR MIXTURE
OXYGEN
5. Air mixture from second cylinder is added to dilute oxygen and keep gas volume constant.
3. Cables from electronic controller, which monitors gases, switch gas tanks on and off.
6. Carbon dioxide is removed by scrubber chemical and gases are mixed.
4. Oxygen gas from cylinder added to replace oxygen used by diver's body.
OXYGEN FLOW
INHALED GAS FLOW
EXHALED GAS FLOW

The air around us is mostly a mixture of the gases nitrogen (79 per cent) and oxygen (21 per cent). When we breathe, our lungs capture the oxygen, which our muscles use to produce energy. We make a waste gas called carbon dioxide during this process and breathe it out. With ordinary scuba apparatus, divers breathe in nitrox gas (a mixture of nitrogen and oxygen) from a tank on their backs. As they breathe out, the carbon dioxide bubbles out through their regulator (air valve) into the sea. When the nitrox runs out, the diver has to resurface. A rebreather is a more advanced form of breathing apparatus. The air is recycled and new oxygen is added. This means that the diver is able to stay underwater much longer than an ordinary scuba diver would be able to.

Rebreathers are heavier and more cumbersome than ordinary scuba apparatus. However, they can provide as much air as dozens of ordinary nitrox tanks, reducing the need to resurface.

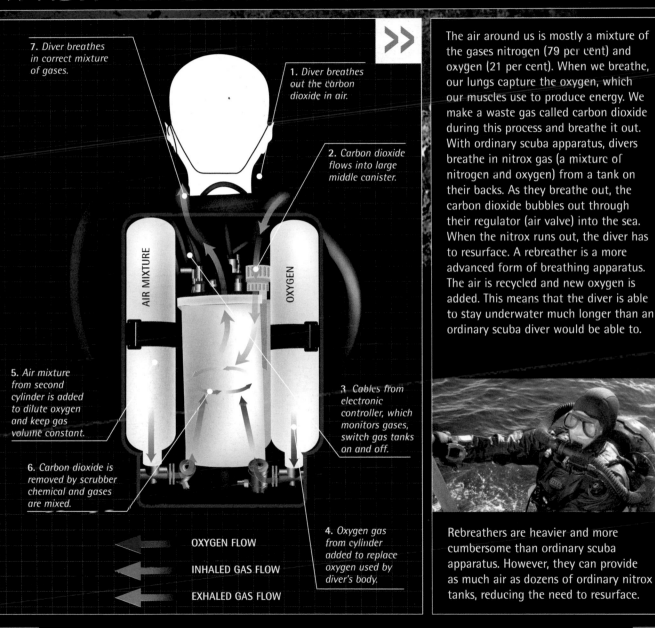

▶▶ See also: Explorers p154, Hard wear p224, Eyewear p230

FIRE EXTINGUISHER

▶▶ Left unchecked, fires can destroy homes and offices in minutes. Fire extinguishers, portable firefighting kits packed into handy metal containers, can tackle most blazes quickly and effectively. ▶▶

>> HOW FIRE EXTINGUISHERS WORK

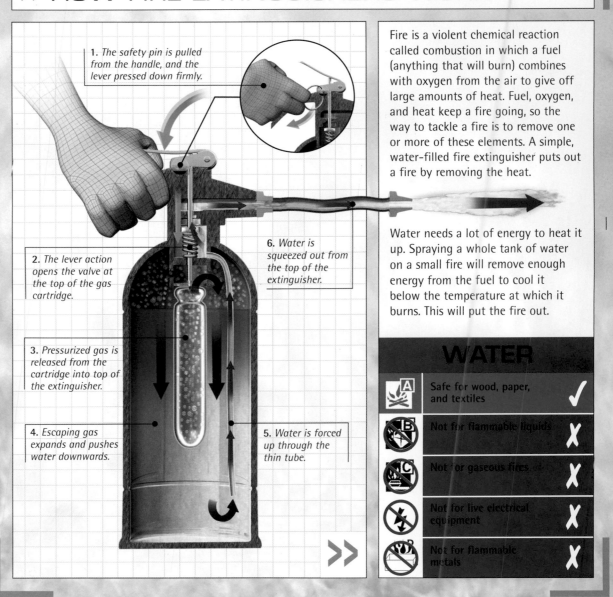

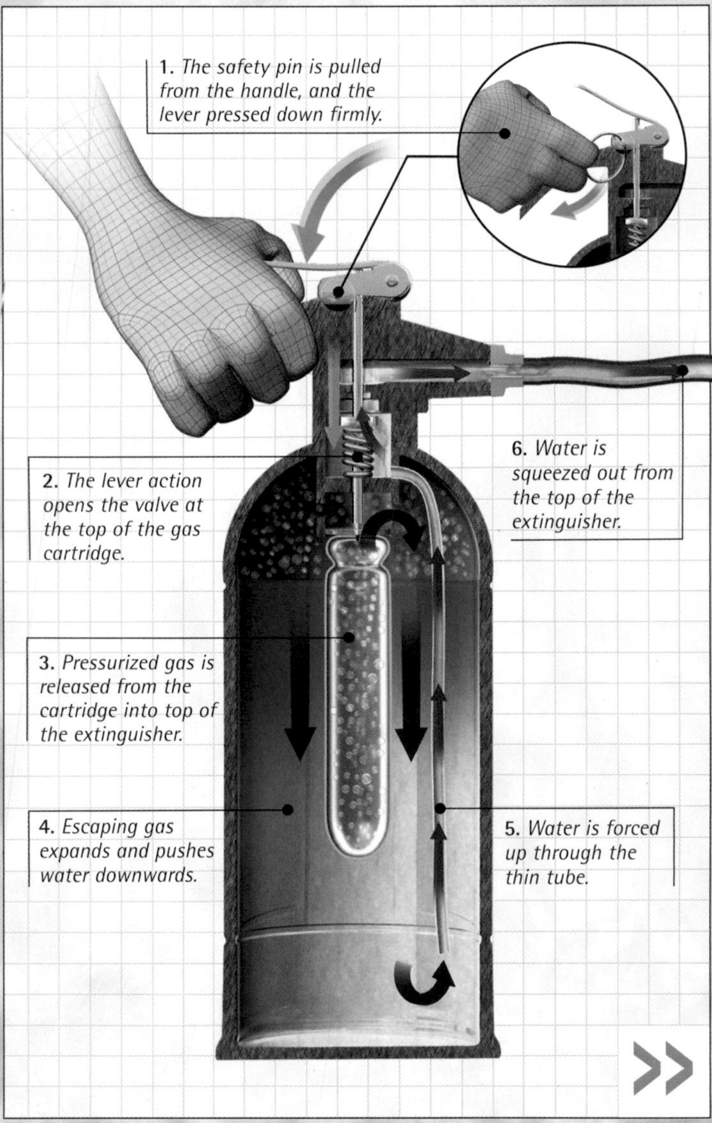

1. *The safety pin is pulled from the handle, and the lever pressed down firmly.*
2. *The lever action opens the valve at the top of the gas cartridge.*
3. *Pressurized gas is released from the cartridge into top of the extinguisher.*
4. *Escaping gas expands and pushes water downwards.*
5. *Water is forced up through the thin tube.*
6. *Water is squeezed out from the top of the extinguisher.*

Fire is a violent chemical reaction called combustion in which a fuel (anything that will burn) combines with oxygen from the air to give off large amounts of heat. Fuel, oxygen, and heat keep a fire going, so the way to tackle a fire is to remove one or more of these elements. A simple, water-filled fire extinguisher puts out a fire by removing the heat.

Water needs a lot of energy to heat it up. Spraying a whole tank of water on a small fire will remove enough energy from the fuel to cool it below the temperature at which it burns. This will put the fire out.

WATER		
A	Safe for wood, paper, and textiles	✓
B	Not for flammable liquids	✗
C	Not for gaseous fires	✗
	Not for live electrical equipment	✗
D	Not for flammable metals	✗

▶▶ See also: Smoke detector p12, Building blocks p178, Hard wear p224, Eyewear p230

Choosing the right extinguisher

▶ Carbon dioxide (CO_2) extinguishers contain pressurized CO_2 in liquid form. When you squeeze the handle, the CO_2 escapes and expands to make a freezing cold gas. CO_2 extinguishers work by smothering oxygen and removing heat.

CARBON DIOXIDE		
	Safe for flammable liquids	✓
	Safe for live electrical equipment	✓
	Not for gaseous fires	✗
	Not for wood, paper, and textiles	✗
	Not for flammable metals	✗

▶ ABC powder extinguishers are widely used in homes. They work by blasting a blanket of powder (made of baking soda or similar chemicals) across the fire. This cuts off the fuel's oxygen supply so the fire goes out.

ABC POWDER		
	Safe for flammable liquids	✓
	Safe for live electrical equipment	✓
	Safe for gaseous fires	✓
	Safe for wood, paper, and textiles	✓
	Not for flammable metals	✗

▶ Foam spray extinguishers also work by cutting off the oxygen supply. They are very effective for use on burning liquids. The trick is to layer the foam over the liquid so that a barrier forms between the fuel and the air above.

FOAM SPRAY		
	Safe for flammable liquids	✓
	Safe for wood, paper, and textiles	✓
	Not for gaseous fires	✗
 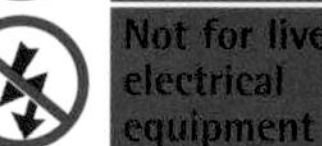	Not for live electrical equipment	✗
 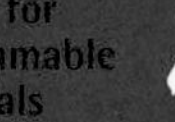	Not for flammable metals	✗

▶ This carbon dioxide fire extinguisher can put out a medium-sized oil fire in less than a minute. Standing at a safe distance, the firefighter aims the cold gas spray at the base of the fire and sweeps the nozzle back and forth, pushing the flames gradually back until the fire is completely extinguished.

Helmet made from fibreglass composite does not melt at ordinary fire temperatures.

Gloves protect from heat of fire and cold of carbon dioxide jet.

Narrow hose enables extinguisher to be directed very precisely.

Flames rise upwards because burning fuel vapour is less dense (lighter) than air.

[illegible] air [illegible] from [illegible]urized extinguisher.

Image: Firefighter using carbon dioxide fire extinguisher

EYEWEAR

Our eyes are incredibly versatile. They can look up into the sky like a telescope to see stars beyond the Sun or zoom in like a microscope on objects as thin as a hair. Like a camera, they can capture images in the blink of an eye that we remember all our lives. A quarter of our brain is devoted to processing things we can see. But our vision is imperfect. Often we need gadgets to improve our eyesight or protect it.

Surgical head-mount Surgeons use head-mounted cameras like this to see inside a patient's body. The head-mount is wired to a flexible, fibre-optic tube called an endoscope, which pipes light deep into the patient's body and carries an image back out again. It enables surgeons to carry out difficult manoeuvres with precision.

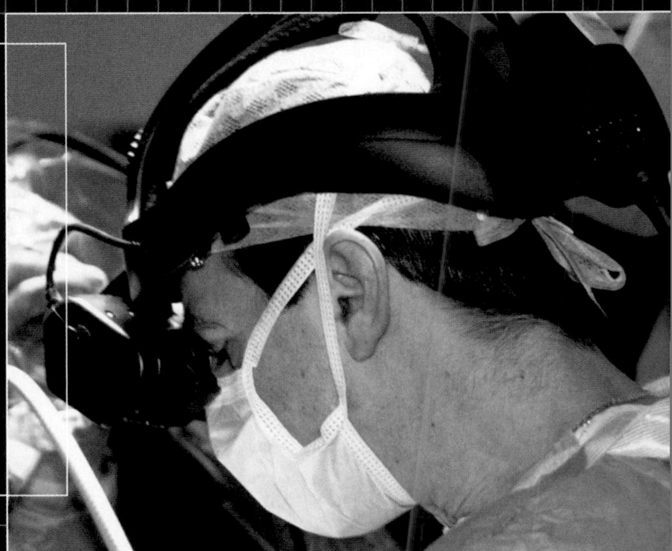

Contact lenses

Available in many colours, contact lenses correct the curvature on the surface of the eye to achieve a sharp image. Made from plastic or glass, a contact lens refracts (bends) incoming light rays so that they focus precisely on the sensitive retina at the back of the eyeball.

Eclipse glasses

Never stare directly at the Sun: its intense rays could burn your retina and blind you. These people are watching a solar eclipse (when the Moon blocks the Sun) using safety goggles that block out 99.999 per cent of visible light.

Industrial goggles

This welding torch produces an intense flash of light, as well as damaging ultraviolet (UV) and infrared radiation. Together, these can cause a painful "flash burn", which damages the eye's cornea (front coating). Welding goggles block all but a fraction of the visible light and wrap around to give total protection.

Snow goggles

Bright white snow and polished ice can reflect back up to 90 per cent of the light that falls on it. Skiers on mountain slopes, and people who live or work in the polar regions wear protective snow goggles to avoid dazzling and painful "snow blindness".

See also: Simulators p70, Trainers p132, Hard wear p224

>> HOW LIFESTRAW WORKS

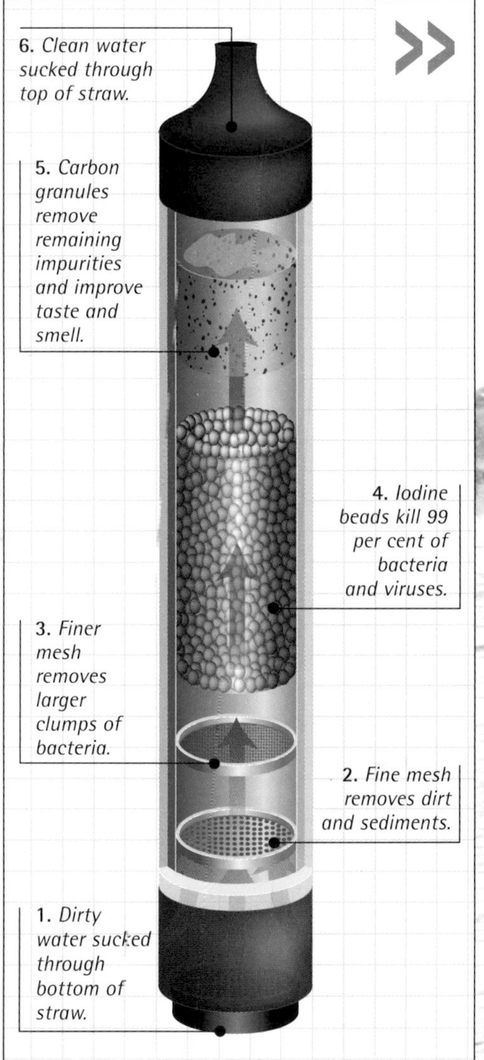
6. Clean water sucked through top of straw.
5. Carbon granules remove remaining impurities and improve taste and smell.
4. Iodine beads kill 99 per cent of bacteria and viruses.
3. Finer mesh removes larger clumps of bacteria.
2. Fine mesh removes dirt and sediments.
1. Dirty water sucked through bottom of straw.

Water in rivers and ponds is unsafe to drink because it contains a mixture of impurities. LifeStraw removes these in stages. At the bottom, a pair of textile filters remove soil and dirt and the larger clumps of bacteria. Filtering alone is not enough to make the water safe, because viruses and bacteria are small enough to pass through. So the next stage of the process uses a chemical called iodine to disinfect the water by killing the bacteria and viruses. At the top of the filter, there are millions of active carbon granules. Each of these acts like a tiny chemical laboratory, and the water is purified on its surface through a process called catalysis. The carbon also helps to remove any unpleasant iodine taste.

Carbon granules (here magnified around 4,000 times) from a filter attract the contaminants like a magnet as the water flows through.

LIFESTRAW

▶▶ Just imagine if the only place to drink from is a dirty river, or having to walk an hour each day to collect water. More than 1.1 billion people (one-sixth of the world's population) still do not have access to clean water. The portable LifeStraw® drinking straw could help to improve their lives. ▶▶

Image: Two boys drink water through LifeStraws®

▼ Water, the essence of life, covers more than 70 per cent of Earth's surface, but less than 1 per cent of that is usable freshwater. If all the world's water could fit in a bucket, the amount people could drink would barely fill a teaspoon.

Risk of disease

▶ Every day, more than 5,000 children in developing countries die of diseases such as cholera and typhoid because they lack clean water. Typhoid is transmitted when the bacteria from human faeces contaminates water.

Micrograph of typhoid bacteria

▶▶ See also: Hydroponics p28, Converter p102, Rebreather p226

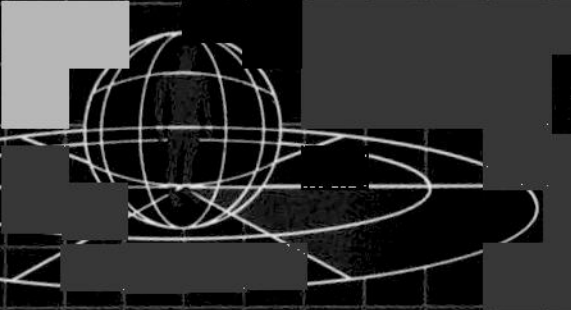

SHELTERS

Finding shelter is a basic human need. Humans have been living in fixed settlements for more than 10,000 years, but historians think people have been making temporary shelters for almost 400,000 years. Today, imaginative shelter designs meet a variety of needs, from emergency housing in disaster zones to portable units for leisure pursuits.

<< paraSITE
This paraSITE shelter is designed to improve the quality of life for homeless people, forced to sleep on the streets. Designed by American artist Michael Rakowitz, it hooks up to air conditioner outlets on office buildings. Waste heat from the building flows between a double plastic skin, inflating the shelter and keeping it warm.

>> Creative crates
Japanese architect Shigeru Ban is famous for making emergency refugee shelters out of cardboard tubes. He also built the vast Nomadic Museum art gallery in California, USA, in 2005. The walls are stacks of shipping containers and the roof is made of steel. Cardboard tube pillars support the roof with a strong triangular framework, creating a vast exhibition space inside.

Pod-House

In cities where building land is scarce, floating homes like this glass pod could house people on rivers or in unused docks. This three-storey glass sphere naturally captures the light and heat from the Sun and was designed by the Polish-born architect Marcin Panpuch.

BoKlok homes

Many people buy flat-pack furniture and assemble it themselves; the Swedish IKEA company is trying the same idea with homes. These timber-framed houses come as kits and can be erected in as little as a day. Thousands have already been built in countries like Sweden, where more than 70 per cent of new homes are prefabricated.

Surf tent

A surfer's life is devoted to catching the perfect wave, but that can be tricky if you live far from a beach. This portable surf tent was inspired by a whale's gaping mouth and can be pitched on sand. It has an inflatable sleeping pod and an adjustable canopy.

See also: Recycling p24, B[illegible]ding blocks p178, Grand designs p184, Big [illegible]cs p192

▶▶ See also: Water craft p116, Binoculars p158, Night vision p160

LIGHTHOUSE

>> HOW THE LAMP WORKS

Light rays shine out of the lamp parallel, making a powerful beam.

Lamp at centre sends out rays of light in all directions.

"Bullseye" lens concentrates light at the centre.

Further away from the centre, light rays are refracted (bent) by steps in the lens.

Prisms at the top and bottom of lamp refract and reflect light through very steep angles.

To make a powerful beam bright enough to be seen far away, a lighthouse needs a large lamp and lens (curved piece of glass). It is difficult to make an ordinary lens big enough, because glass is heavy. So lighthouses use a Fresnel lens with a stepped outer surface. The steps of glass bend the light by increasing amounts as they get further from the centre, so that all the light rays shine out of the lens in the same direction. At the top and bottom, light has to be bent at greater angles, so prisms (glass wedges) are used.

Xenon gas lamp inside typical lens can produce as much light as 450,000 candles.

Lens wraps completely around lamp, sending light in every direction.

▶ A typical lighthouse lamp is about 40 m (130 ft) above sea le This means that the lamp can be seen five times further away tha if it were positioned at a height just 2 m (6 ft). Most lighthouses have a rotating lamp – as it turn the light flashes. This lighthouse, however, has a fixed lamp.

▶▶ Even in this age of satellite navigation and radar, the friendly glow from a lighthouse still reassures ships' crews that they are on the right course or steering clear of danger. On a clear night, a powerful lighthouse beam is visible at

Image: Mukilteo lighthouse, Washington, USA

Spectrum of light is visible because glass splits white light into colours.
At base and top of lens, prisms (wedges of glass) bend light rays at steepest angles.

TSUNAMI ALERT

▶▶ When a tsunami wave hits a coast the immense force of the water rips up trees, demolishes buildings, and puts the population in grave danger. A warning network is being developed to raise the alarm in time for those at risk to evacuate. This will save thousands of lives. ▶▶

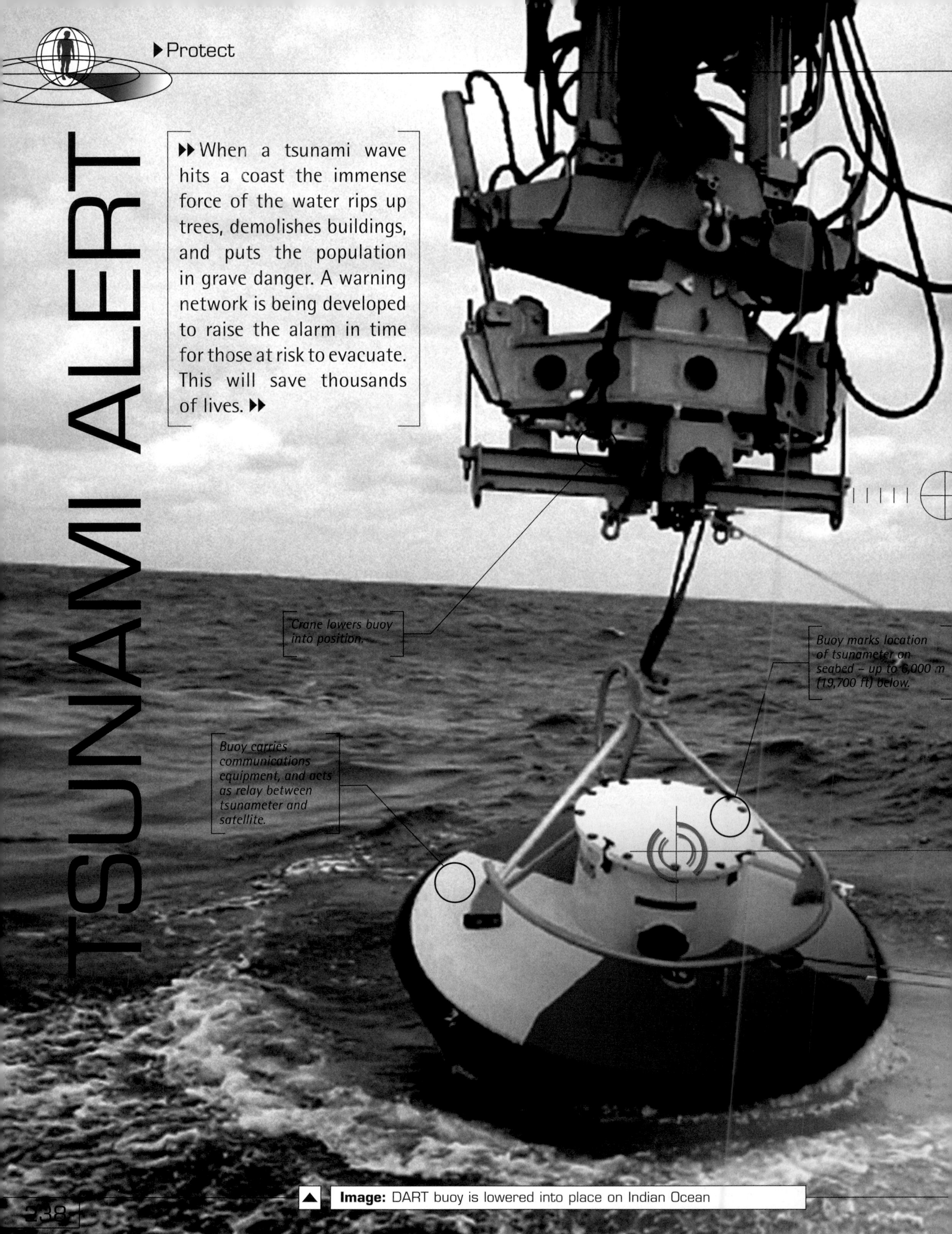

Crane lowers buoy into position.
Buoy marks location of tsunameter on seabed – up to 6,000 m (19,700 ft) below.
Buoy carries communications equipment, and acts as relay between tsunameter and satellite.

▲ **Image:** DART buoy is lowered into place on Indian Ocean

▶▶ See also: Lighthouse p236, Flood barrier p240

» HOW TSUNAMI ALERTS WORK

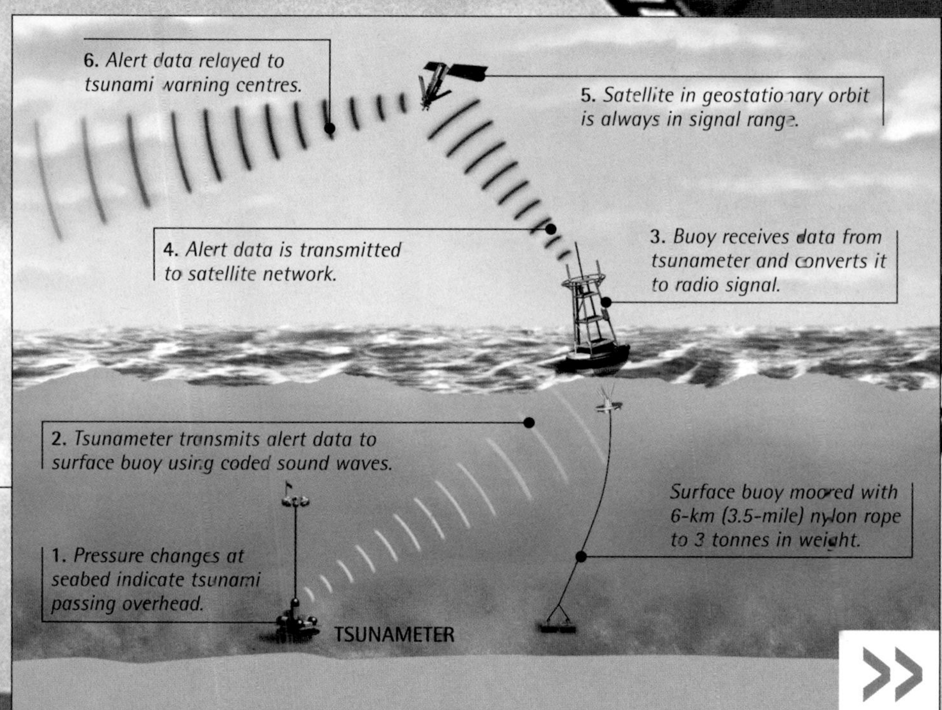

6. Alert data relayed to tsunami warning centres.
5. Satellite in geostationary orbit is always in signal range.
4. Alert data is transmitted to satellite network.
3. Buoy receives data from tsunameter and converts it to radio signal.
2. Tsunameter transmits alert data to surface buoy using coded sound waves.
Surface buoy moored with 6-km (3.5-mile) nylon rope to 3 tonnes in weight.
1. Pressure changes at seabed indicate tsunami passing overhead.
TSUNAMETER

Tsunamis can be predicted when an underwater earthquake is felt by seismic detectors, but this is not very accurate. To improve warning times, tsunamis need to be observed out at sea. On the seafloor below each surface buoy is a pressure monitoring device (tsunameter) sensitive enough to detect a passing tsunami only 1 cm (0.5 in) high. This detector looks for a special pattern of changes in pressure due to the extra weight of water caused by a tsunami wave moving overhead. If a wave is detected, the information is relayed to a tsunami warning centre, which analyzes the details to identify and alert coasts at risk. The warning is spread locally by sirens, blown whistles, or automatic texts to mobile phones.

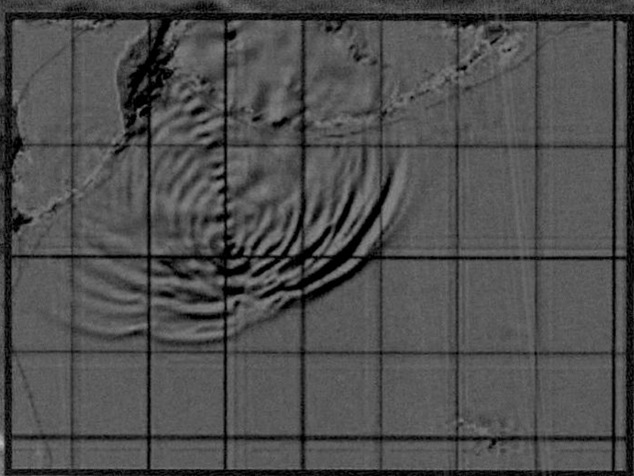

◀ A Deep Ocean Assessment and Reporting of Tsunamis (DART) buoy (left) floats in the open ocean. It is part of the new worldwide monitoring network. A DART buoy was placed off the west coast of Thailand in December 2006 to give early warning of tsunamis in the Indian Ocean, such as the one shown in the computer simulation (above).

Location of DART tsunami buoys

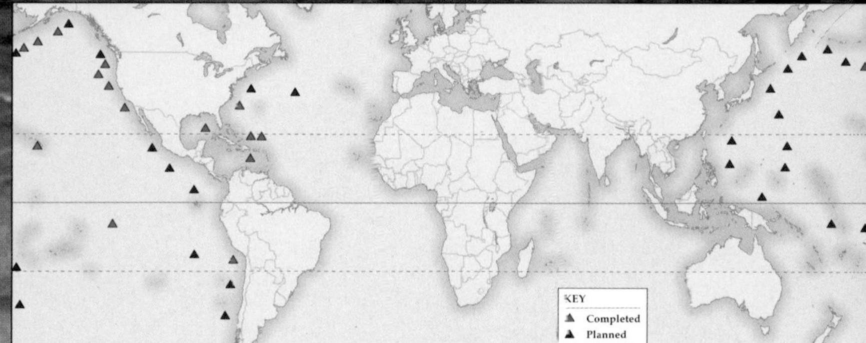

World map showing the planned location of DART buoys

▲ The planned worldwide network of detection buoys will cover all coasts that are vulnerable to tsunamis. A tsunami can travel across the ocean at hundreds of kilometres per hour, so the buoys must be located a long way from shore in order to give sufficient warning for people to evacuate to higher ground. The network is expensive to maintain. Buoys must be replaced every year and seafloor tsunameters every two years. Until recently only rich countries had warning systems in place, but this is changing.

FLOOD BARRIER

▶▶ Much of the Netherlands is below sea level and therefore vulnerable to flooding. The mighty Oosterscheldekering barrier, stretching 9 km (5.6 miles), keeps the country safe. ▶▶

Sixty-five concrete piers, each 53 m (174 ft) high.

>> HOW THE BARRIER WORKS

Cylinders use hydraulics (fluid pressure) to move rams up and down inside them.

Hydraulic rams raise and lower steel gates weighing up to 535 tonnes.

Gates normally below sea level move up to block sea during high tides.

Roadway runs behind dam on sturdy concrete box girder.

Rough gravel base stops currents washing away sand that supports barrier.

The estuaries of the Oosterschelde region contain brackish water (mixed seawater and freshwater). Local fishing industries would suffer if the barrier prevented seawater from entering the estuaries, so the Oosterscheldekering (Oosterschelde flood barrier) was built using gates that normally allow as much saltwater to flow through as possible. The massive gates are completely closed only during storms, when tides are higher and the flood risk is considered to be far greater.

Overhead view of the flood barrier

Sixty-two steel gates, each 43 m (141 ft) long, 5.4 m (18 ft) thick, and weighing up to 535 tonnes, hold back waves.
Hydraulic rams raise steel gates by up to 6 m (20 ft) to hold back the sea.
A road (Rijksweg 57) runs along the back of the barrier on a spine of concrete girders.

▼ The Oosterscheldekering was built to protect the Netherlands after stormy high tides in February 1953 flooded 200,000 hectares (500,000 acres) of land, damaging 47,000 homes and killing 1,835 people. With the barrier in place, a major flood should only happen once every 4,000 years.

◀ **Image:** The Oosterscheldekering, the Netherlands

⌄ Devastation in New Orleans, USA

Flooded New Orleans levees (flood barriers)

◀ Catastrophic floods, like those that followed Hurricane Katrina in 2005, could be a bigger problem in the future. Global warming is melting polar glaciers and so adding more water to the seas. It is also heating the oceans, causing them to expand. These effects could make sea levels rise as much as 1 m (3.3 ft) by 2100.

▶▶ See also: Falkirk Wheel p188, Stadium roof p198, Tsunami alert p238

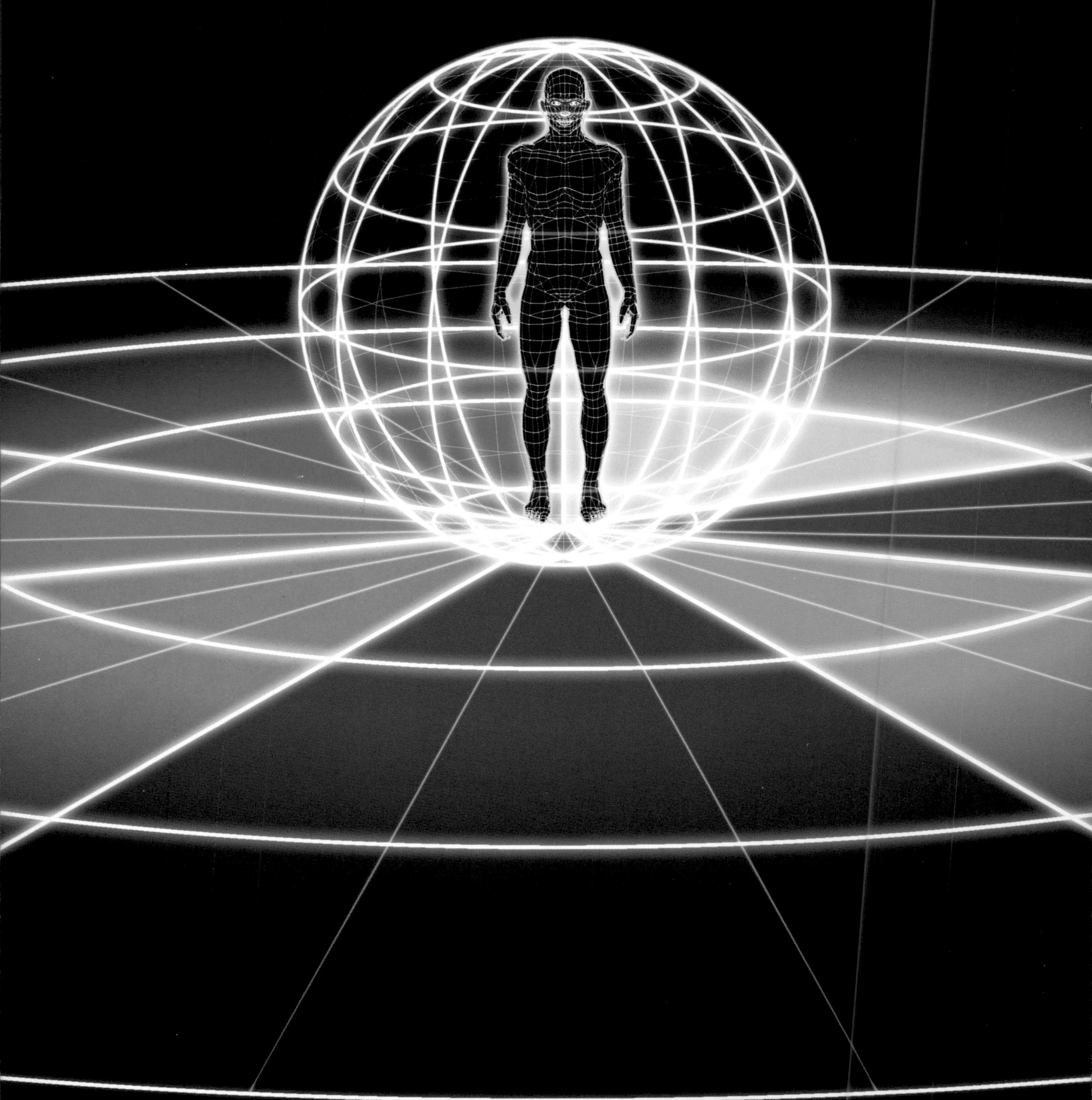

>>REFERENCE

What's next? >> Glossary >>
Index >> Acknowledgements >>

COMPUTERS & COMMUNICATIONS

Faster computers will tackle ever more complex problems. Along with advances in wireless communications, they will provide new services we can only guess at today.

- Full immersion virtual reality – for example a head-mounted device that takes the user into a simulated 3D environment.
- Chips embedded in everything will use wireless technology to communicate freely with other devices.
- Home schooling and home working via the Internet will become more common.
- A computer capable of simulating the human brain will be developed.

NANOTECHNOLOGY

A nanometre is a thousand-millionth of a metre – a single human hair is around 80,000 nanometres in width. Nanotechnology involves working with things on an ultra-small scale. It will be applied to many areas in the future.

- Materials created by nanotechnology will be stronger and lighter – up to 100 times stronger than steel and only one-sixth of the weight – making it possible to build lighter aircraft, cars, and spacecraft.
- Nano-scale computer chips will shrink computers and electronics to a fraction of their current size.
- Nanobots injected into the human body will be able to repair cell damage, kill tumours, and carry out other medical procedures at the cellular level.

MILITARY

The leading military powers will continue their race to develop smarter, more powerful and accurate weapons and more effective intelligence-gathering systems than their enemies.

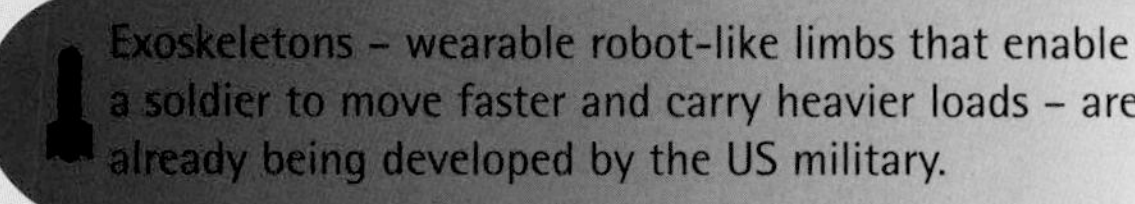

- Exoskeletons – wearable robot-like limbs that enable a soldier to move faster and carry heavier loads – are already being developed by the US military.
- E-bombs are also under development. These leave people and property undamaged, but fry electronics, computers, and power grids.

ENERGY

The demand for energy all over the world is growing faster than ever. New, more efficient, and less environmentally damaging ways of supplying energy must be found.

- Fusion reactors will generate electricity.
- Bacteria will make hydrogen fuel from waste sludge.
- Need for reduced dependence on fossil fuels will see increased take-up of biofuels, micro-power generation in homes, hydrogen power, and renewable energy sources.

BIOTECHNOLOGY

The use of living cells or organisms, such as bacteria, in industry is known as biotechnology.

- Adhesives will be developed based on lizard foot-pads.
- Synthetic bacteria and viruses will be developed to fight pests and diseases.
- Bacteria in toothpaste will be able to attack plaque on teeth.
- Extinct species may be brought back to life by recreating their DNA.
- Super-strong materials based on spider web silk will be available.

- Chameleon-like uniforms will be able to automatically change their camouflage patterns to match their surroundings.
- Armed combat robots will increasingly replace soldiers on the battlefield and robots will also do the dangerous work of evacuating casualties.

HEALTH AND MEDICINE

Medical science and technology are advancing rapidly. Future treatments will increasingly be targeted at individual cells, especially cancer cells. A better understanding of our DNA will lead to treatments that turn individual genes on or off to treat illnesses and inherited conditions. It may even be possible to extend the human lifespan.

- An individual's genome (complete DNA set) will be stored on a personal ID card.
- Artificial skin and blood will be available. The first few products are already coming onto the market and more are being developed.
- Advances in spinal-cord repairs will enable people with back injuries to walk again.
- Humans may have a 150-year lifespan, later even increasing to 200 years, made possible by the ability to reverse ageing damage to organs at the cellular level.

SPACE

Astronauts will return to the Moon and manned space missions will explore other parts of the Solar System.

- A permanent base will be established on the Moon.
- A manned mission will be sent to Mars.
- Life will be discovered elsewhere in the Solar System. The most likely places are Mars, Europa (a moon of Jupiter), or Titan (a moon of Saturn).
- Contact will be made with alien intelligent life.

EVERYDAY LIFE

In the past 50 years, our everyday lives have changed dramatically, because of a multitude of advances in many areas of science. This has led to social changes, too. The next 50 years will see equally dramatic changes.

- Paper money and coins will be replaced by electronic cash.
- Mile-high buildings will be constructed creating vertical cities.
- Weather forecasts will become so accurate that street-by-street forecasts will be possible.
- We will be watching programmes on 3D television. This is already being trialled in laboratories.

ROBOTICS

In the future smarter robots will be able to do more of the most dangerous, dirty, and boring jobs done by people today.

- Domestic robots will take over routine cleaning tasks in homes and offices.
- Rat-like and snake-like robots will be used to search rubble for survivors after an earthquake. Experimental search-and-rescue robots like this have already been built.
- Tasks like road-gritting, snow clearance, and lawn-mowing will be taken over by robots.
- Robots will develop social skills, and will be able to express emotions and recognize emotions in other people.
- Robots will be able to provide in-home care for the disabled and elderly.

TRANSPORT

Until now, transport has relied on fossil fuels, but future transport technology will have to be cleaner and kinder to the environment.

- Smart cars capable of self-driving will take control on specially equipped roads.
- Hypersonic planes will reach speeds of more than Mach 5 – five times faster than the speed of sound.
- Cargo planes and airliners will adopt the "flying wing" design of the Stealth bomber, which blends the wing and body.
- Flying cars will take to the skies. Prototypes have already flown.

A

acceleration
The way something speeds up when a force acts on it.

aerial
A device used for transmitting or receiving radio waves.

aerodynamics
The science of how air moves around something, especially a fast-moving vehicle like a racing car.

air resistance
The force that tends to slow down objects when they move through the air. Commonly known as drag.

aluminium
A strong, lightweight, rust-proof metal often used in the structures of aeroplanes and spacecraft.

asphalt
A sticky, black, tar-like substance used to surface roads and pavements.

atom
The smallest possible amount of a chemical element. Atoms are the basic building blocks of matter and join to make larger units called molecules. An atom is itself made up of even smaller subatomic particles. The nucleus in the centre contains protons and neutrons, and particles called electrons whizz around the nucleus.

B

bacteria
A micro-organism made of one cell. Although some bacteria carry disease and are harmful, others, such as those used in making food, are not.

battery
A collection of chemicals that generate a steady supply of electricity through two electrodes when connected into a closed path called a circuit.

Bluetooth®
A way of linking computer equipment over short distances using wireless (radio) connections.

C

carbon dioxide
A colourless gas, present in air, that is made from carbon and oxygen atoms. Carbon dioxide is produced when things burn in air and when we breathe out.

catalyst
A chemical that speeds up the rate of a chemical reaction, but does not itself change in the process.

cell
The smallest unit of a living organism. Cells are the building blocks from which plants and animals are made.

chip
A computer component, about the size of a fingernail, containing thousands of separate switches called transistors. Memory chips store information. More advanced chips called microprocessors work like miniaturized computers.

circuit
An unbroken path that allows electricity to flow around it.

composite
A material made from two or more different materials. A composite is often stronger, more durable, or more heat resistant than the materials from which it is made.

computer
An electronic machine that can process information according to a set of instructions called a program. Computers need a way of receiving information (input), somewhere to record information (memory), something to process the information (processor), and a way of displaying their results (output).

concrete
A durable building material made by mixing cement with sand and gravel.

control surface
A flap or rudder on an aircraft that changes the airflow to control steering.

crystal structure
The inner structure of a solid material. The atoms in a crystal are typically arranged in an invisible framework that repeats itself every so often.

D

database
A collection of information filed on a computer in a very orderly form.

density
The concentration of mass in an object. The density of something is measured by dividing its mass by its volume. A dense object has a great deal of mass per unit of its volume.

deuterium
An isotope of hydrogen in which atoms have one proton and one neutron, instead of just one proton.

digital
A way of representing information in binary form (with only the numbers zero and one). Computers and electronic gadgets like mobile phones store, process, and transmit information in digital form.

drag
An informal name for air resistance.

E

efficiency
The amount of energy something uses well. An efficient machine, like a bicycle, uses most of the energy supplied to move the rider forwards.

elastic
A material that stretches when a force pushes or pulls it. Usually, an elastic material returns to its original shape when the force is removed.

electric current
The movement of electricity around a circuit. An electric current is a steady flow of charged particles – usually either negatively charged electrons or positively charged ions (atoms missing electrons).

electric motor
A device that uses electricity to drive a machine. When an electric current flows into a motor, it generates magnetism, making its inner axle spin around at high speed.

electrode
The electrical terminal at the end of an open electric circuit. An electrode is usually a piece of metal or carbon that captures or releases electrons or ions.

electron
A tiny negatively charged particle, much smaller than an atom. Electrons move in paths called orbits around the nucleus (central part) of atoms.

emission
A polluting gas made by an engine or an industrial process.

energy
A source of power (such as a fuel) or the ability to do something (such as climb stairs). In science, energy means the ability to work against a force.

F

fibre
A thin piece of material similar to a thread. Natural fibres are made from plants such as cotton, while artificial (synthetic) fibres, such as nylon, are made by a chemical process.

fibreglass
A composite material made by embedding strong glass fibres in a plastic base to produce a tougher, more durable material.

filament
A piece of wire designed to get very hot when electricity flows through it. Filaments make the light in traditional (incandescent) light bulbs.

flash memory
A type of computer memory chip, widely used in digital cameras and other devices, that stores information even when the power is off.

fluorescence
The way a material gives off visible light when invisible (often ultraviolet) light strikes it.

focus
A way of concentrating light or radio waves in one place with a lens or mirror.

force
A push or pull that makes something move, changes the way it is already moving, or changes its shape.

frequency
The number of times something happens in one second. The frequency of a sound is related to its pitch (how high or low it sounds).

friction
A force between two things that are in contact, which tends to stop them sliding past each other.

fuselage
The main body of an aircraft (usually the central compartment and not including the wings).

G

G-force
The amount of force on something that accelerates or decelerates compared to the force of gravity. A force of 3G is three times the force of gravity.

gear
A wheel with notches cut into its edge that meshes with a similar wheel, which is larger or smaller, to increase the speed or force of a moving machine.

generator
A device made from magnets and coiled wire that produces an electric current when it rotates.

GPS
Global Positioning System. Network of space satellites that transmit signals to Earth so electronic navigation devices can locate their positions.

gravity
The force of attraction between any two masses in the Universe. On Earth, gravity is a force that pulls things down towards the planet's surface.

gyroscope
A wheel rotating rapidly inside a pivoting framework. When spun rapidly, a gyroscope will point in the same direction, no matter which way the wheel is turned.

H

heat
A type of energy stored inside hot objects by invisible movements of their atoms or molecules.

hydraulic
A type of machine that uses water pressure to transmit or magnify forces. For example, hydraulic jacks are used to lift cars in garages.

I

inertia
The way an object that is still tends to remain still, or a moving object tends to keep moving, unless a force acts on it.

isotope
A type of a chemical element in which the atoms have the same number of protons but have a different number of neutrons.

J

jet engine
A type of engine that burns fuel continuously in a huge cylinder. A jet engine makes a fast-moving, backwards jet of hot gas that pushes an aircraft forwards.

K

kinetic energy
The energy something has because it is moving.

L

laser
A concentrated beam of light.

LCD
Liquid crystal display. LCDs use electric currents to make crystals appear either light or dark, so forming letters and numbers on a screen.

LED
Light-emitting diode. A small electronic component that glows when electricity flows through it.

lens
A curved piece of glass that refracts (bends) light rays, usually to make objects some distance away appear bigger.

lever
A long bar that increases the size of a force, so reducing the effort needed to do something.

lift
An upward force on an aircraft wing caused by the movement of air around it.

light
A type of energy that moves at high speed in vibrating electrical and magnetic waves.

liquid
A state of matter in which atoms or molecules are loosely linked but not joined rigidly together.

M

magnetic field
The invisible area of activity that stretches around a magnet and affects magnetic materials.

mass
The amount of matter something contains.

micro-organism
A tiny living thing too small to be seen with the naked eye. They include bacteria.

microphone
An electromagnetic device that turns sound energy into electricity.

microscope
Optical microscopes use lenses to make objects seem bigger by bending light. Electron microscopes, used to see things even smaller than the wavelength of light, use magnetic coils to bend electron beams.

molecule
The smallest possible amount of a chemical element made from two or more atoms joined together.

momentum
The way a moving object tends to keep moving unless a force acts on it.

MP3
A type of digital computer file used to store music. MP3 files are relatively small, so they are quick to download.

N

network
A collection of computers and computer equipment linked together by cables or wireless connections.

neutrino
A fast-moving particle with almost no mass and no electric charge.

neutron
An uncharged particle in the nucleus of an atom.

nucleus
The central part of an atom, consisting of protons and neutrons.

nylon
A plastic made from synthetic fibres, themselves made from very long carbon-based molecules.

optics
The study of how light behaves.

P

particle
A small quantity of matter. Particles found in atoms are called subatomic.

phosphor
A chemical that glows when bombarded with energetic particles such as electrons.

photon
A particle that carries a "packet" of light or another type of electromagnetic radiation.

piezoelectricity
The way in which some materials produce a pulse of electricity when they are squeezed, or vibrate when electricity passes through them.

pixel
A tiny coloured dot that makes up part of the picture in a television, computer, or other electronic display.

plasma
A kind of very hot gas in which the electrons break free from their atoms.

plastic
A synthetic, carbon-based substance that can be moulded into shape only when it is soft.

pneumatic
A type of machine that uses compressed (high-pressure) air to transmit or magnify forces.

polymer
A very long carbon-based molecule made from a chain of individual units called monomers.

positron
A particle identical to an electron only with a positive electric charge.

potential energy
The energy stored by an object that can be converted into other forms, such as kinetic energy.

pressure
A force exerted by a liquid or gas over a relatively wide area.

processor
The main chip inside a computer or electronic gadget.

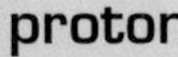

proton
A positively charged particle found in the nucleus of an atom.

R

radar
A navigation system that uses radio waves to locate ships or other objects.

radio wave
A type of invisible electromagnetic wave that travels at the speed of light and can be used to carry sounds, TV pictures, or other information.

radioactivity
The process by which unstable atoms naturally tend to disintegrate into smaller atoms, giving off particles or energy known as radiation.

recycling
A way of reusing materials instead of throwing them away.

refraction
The way in which light bends when it passes from one material to another material of different density.

retina
The light-detecting part of the eye. The retina contains two types of light-sensitive cells – rods and cones.

robot
A self- or computer-controlled machine designed to do repetitive jobs automatically.

rocket
A type of engine similar to a jet engine but with its own self-contained oxygen supply.

S

satellite
An object that orbits a planet. Artificial satellites are unmanned spacecraft that travel around Earth in a fixed orbit. The Moon is a natural satellite of Earth.

SEM
Scanning Electron Microscope. A type of microscope that uses a beam of electrons to make images of extremely small things.

silicon
A chemical element found in sand from which solar panels and electronic components are made.

simulation
A representation of something in the real world, usually shown on computer.

solar panel
A flat rectangle of silicon that generates electricity or captures heat energy when sunlight shines on it.

solid
A state of matter in which atoms or molecules are rigidly joined together.

steel
An alloy (mixture) made mostly of iron and carbon that is stronger and more versatile than iron alone.

subatomic particle
A particle found inside an atom, such as a proton, neutron, or electron.

suspension
The system of supports that connect a car's wheels to its body. Suspension is designed to absorb bumps, both to protect the car itself and to make the ride comfortable for people inside.

synthetic
An artificially made material, such as nylon or Kevlar®.

T

tritium
An isotope of hydrogen in which atoms have one proton and two neutrons, instead of just one proton, used in nuclear fusion.

turbine
A windmill-like device that rotates when a liquid or gas flows past it.

turbulence
A disrupted flow of air or water around (or following behind) a moving object, such as an aeroplane.

U

ultraviolet
A type of electromagnetic radiation that is similar to light, but invisible. Ultraviolet (UV) light has a higher frequency than visible light as well as a shorter wavelength.

V

virus
A microscopic non-living particle than invades living cells and causes diseases.

W

wave
A back-and-forth or up-and-down motion that travels through or over a material and carries energy.

wavelength
The distance between the crest of a wave and the crest of the wave that follows it.

weight
The force that pulls an object towards Earth, caused by gravity. Weight is not the same as mass, but the more mass something has, the more that object weighs.

Wi-Fi
A type of network in which computers (and other electronic equipment) connect wirelessly instead of using cables.

wireless
A way of sending information or signals between two places using radio waves instead of wires.

X

X-ray
High-energy electromagnetic radiation that travels at the speed of light.

Index

Bold page numbers refer to main entries; *italic* numbers indicate the glossary section

Acknowledgements

DK would like to thank:

Shaila Brown, Steven Carton, and Fran Jones for editorial assistance. Ed Merritt for cartography. Jackie Brind for the index.

The publisher would like to thank the following for their kind permission to reproduce their photographs:

Key:
a-above; b-below/bottom; c-centre; f-far; l-left; r-right; t-top

1 Gustoimages Ltd: (r). **2** Courtesy Nabaztag (bl). Courtesy Siemens VDO: (bc). Samui Moon by Time Technology (br). **2-3** Gustoimages Ltd: (t). **3** Courtesy LiveScienceStore.com: (br). **3** Mattel: (br). NASA: JPL-Caltech (bl). Science Photo Library: Peter Menzel (bc). **8** Corbis: Darrell Gulin (br). Gusto/Refocus-now.com: (bl). Courtesy Neorest: (bc). **9** Doheny Eye Institute: (br). Courtesy Ecoist: (bl). Science Photo Library: Dr Tony Brain (bc). **10** Corbis: Darrell Gulin (l). Gusto/Refocus-now.com: (r). **10-11** Science Photo Library: Gustoimages. **11** Science Photo Library: (t); Dr Tony Brain (b). **12-13** Gusto/Refocus-now.com. **13** Science Photo Library: Volker Steger/Siemens AG (br). **14-15** Courtesy Neorest: (bl) (bc) (br). **16** Alamy Images: Kevin Foy (bl). **16-17** Universe Architecture, Netherlands. **18** Corbis: Darrell Gulin (tl). **18-19** Corbis: Darrell Gulin. **19** Corbis: Darrell Gulin (tr). **20-21** Science Photo Library: Gustoimages. **22-23** Getty Images: Getty Images News. **24** Courtesy Ecoist: (t). Courtesy The Spiral Foundation: (b). **25** Courtesy Bike Furniture Design: (r). Courtesy materious: Brian Sorg (t). Courtesy Mio: (b). **26** Corbis: Christian Schmidt/zefa (c). Science Photo Library: Dr Jeremy Burgess (tl) (tr). **27** Alamy Images: Paul Glendell (bl). Science Photo Library: (br). **28-29** Alamy Images: Visions of America, LLC. **29** Courtesy AeroGrow International, Inc.: (l). **30** Alamy Images: David Williams (r). Corbis: Touhig Sion/Corbis Sygma (tl). **31** Corbis: Rick Friedman (r). Getty Images: Jean Louis Batt (l). PunchStock: Photodisc Green/Andre Kudyusov (cb). **32-33** Science Photo Library: Dr Tony Brain. **33** Science Photo Library: Dr Jeremy Burgess (cb); Photo Insolite Realite (tr). **34** Science Photo Library: Dr Jeremy Burgess (br). **34-35** Doheny Eye Institute. **35** Science Photo Library: Sam Ogden (cb). **36** Alamy Images: Emmanuel Lattes (br). Samui Moon by Time Technology (t). **37** Swatch Ag: (bl). Courtesy www.thinkgeek.com: (br) (t). **38** fuseproject: (bl). Iseepet, AOS Technologies: (br). Courtesy Polymer Vision: (bc). **39** Courtesy Garmin Ltd.: (bl). Lawrence Livermore National Laboratory: (br). Reuters: You Sung-Ho (bc). **40-41** Courtesy Nabaztag (t). Science Photo Library: Volker Steger. **41** Alamy Images: Michael Booth (b). Corbis: Reuters (cr). **42** fuseproject: (tl). **42-43** fuseproject. **43** Images provided by Freeplay Energy: (br). **44** 3Dconnexion : (t). Courtesy Dicota.: (b). **45** Alamy Images: Michael Booth (r). Courtesy Dr ir. Tiene Nobels: (b). Courtesy Perific: (tl). **46** Courtesy Nabaztag. **47** Courtesy of Apple Computer, Inc.: (b). **48-49** Courtesy Polymer Vision. **50** Corbis: Reuters (t). Reuters: Eriko Sugita (b). **51** Corbis: Gene Blevins/LA Daily News (c). Courtesy of Motorola: (br). Seiko Instruments Inc.: (t). **52** Iseepet, AOS Technologies. **53** Getty Images: Getty Images News (br). Iseepet, AOS Technologies: (bl). **54** Courtesy Siemens VDO. **55** Antony Loveless www.black-rat.net: (br). **56** Photo courtesy of designer for the Microsoft Next-Gen PC Design Contest, Pussycat Submission #461: (tl). Science Photo Library: Volker Steger (b). **57** Finis, Inc - Livermore, CA USA- www.finisinc.com: (cr). Courtesy Garmin Ltd.: (tl). © 2007 High Tech Computer Corp. All rights reserved.: (bl). **58-59** Reuters: You Sung-Ho. **59** Corbis: Reuters (cra). PA Photos: AP (cla). **60-61** Lawrence Livermore National Laboratory. **61** Lawrence Livermore National Laboratory: (br). NASA: (bl). **62** Corbis: Roger Ressmeyer. **63** Corbis: Stephanie Maze (t). Courtesy of Seti (b). **64** Courtesy Rafael Lozano-Hemmer: Commissioned by the East Midlands Development Agency (emda) www.emda.org.uk with Project Direction from ArtReach www.artreach.biz (bc). Courtesy Second Life: (bl). Zorb South UK Ltd and Zorb Ltd New Zealand: (br). **65** Courtesy Gekkomat: (bl). Mattel: (br). Simon Ward: (bc). **66** Courtesy of Mass MoCA: Tim Hawkinson (bl). Science Photo Library: Peter Menzel (br). **66-67** Gustoimages Ltd. **67** Bandai: (br). PA Photos: (t). **68** Corbis: Michael S. Yamashita (b). **68-69** Gustoimages Ltd: (t). **69** Courtesy IBM: (br). Sony Computer Entertainment Europe: PlayStation and PSP are trademarks of Sony Computer Entertainment Inc. [Images appear by kind permission of Sony Computer Entertainment Europe]. (cr). Sony Computer Entertainment Europe: LocoRoco™ ©2006 Sony Computer Entertainment Inc. Published by Sony Computer Entertainment Europe. (cr). **70** © 2007 Electronic Arts Inc. All Rights Reserved: (b). Getty Images: Greg Pease (t). **71** AP/PA Photos: (c). PunchStock: Image Source/Cybernaut (br). University of Michigan Virtual Reality Laboratory: (tr). **72-73** Courtesy Second Life. **74** Courtesy Rafael Lozano-Hemmer: Commissioned by the East Midlands Development Agency (emda) www.emda.org.uk with Project Direction from ArtReach www.artreach.biz (t). **74-75** Courtesy Rafael Lozano-Hemmer: Commissioned by the East Midlands Development Agency (emda) www.emda.org.uk with Project Direction from ArtReach www.artreach.biz. **75** Kit Monkman/KMA Creative Technology: (b). **76** Courtesy of Mass MoCA: Tim Hawkinson (t). Reuters: Tim Shaffer (b). **77** Garry Greenwood, Joanne Cannon & Stuart Favilla, Bent Leather Band: (br). Corbis: Patrick Robert/Sygma (c). Courtesy www.thisfabtrek.com: (t). **78-79** Alamy Images: Gunter Marx. **79** Alamy Images: Wesley Hitt (br). PA Photos: (bc). Courtesy Six Flags Great Adventure: (bl). **80** Corbis: Kevin Muggleton (r). Courtesy of Simeon Dignam-Crotty - www.RiserRaptors.com: (l). **80-81** Courtesy Gekkomat: (r). **81** Alamy Images: Buzz Pictures (t). Corbis: Hein van den Heuvel/zefa (r). Zorb South UK Ltd and Zorb Ltd New Zealand: (b). **82-83** Courtesy Flybar, SBI Enterprises. **83** Masterfile: (b). **84** Corbis: Wolfgang Kaehler (tl). Science Photo Library: Steve Gschmeissner (clb); Claude Nuridsany & Marie Perennou (cl). **86-87** Simon Ward. **87** www.bodyflight.co.uk: (bl). Paige Rudolph: (br). **88-89** Courtesy Hawk-Eye Innovations. **89** Courtesy Hawk-Eye Innovations: (b). **90** PA Photos: AP (l) (r). **91** PA Photos: AP (t) (b). Science Photo Library: Peter Menzel (cl) (cr). **92-93** © 2004 The Lego Group: (c) 2004 Lego Group **94** Mattel. **95** Bandai: (b). Mattel: (t). **96** Courtesy of Advanced Transport Systems Ltd: (br). Science Photo Library: Astrid & Hanns-Frieder Michler (bl); Robin Scagell (bc). **97** AirTeamImages.com: (bc). Courtesy Sailrocket: Mark Lloyd Images (bl). The Silent Aircraft Initiative: Cambridge University/MIT (br). **98** Courtesy MTB: (r). Segway Inc. : (l). **98-99** Courtesy BMW Sauber F1 Team. **99** Science Photo Library: Jim Amos (r). **100** Courtesy BMW Sauber F1 Team: (tl). **100-101** Courtesy BMW Sauber F1 Team. **101** Corbis: Schlegelmilch (tl) (tc). **102** Science Photo Library: Astrid & Hanns-Frieder Michler. **103** Still Pictures: AC/ (br). **104** Camera Press: Frederic Neema (bl). **104-105** Carnegie Mellon University. **105** Alamy Images: Cameron Davidson (ca). **106** Science Photo Library: David Nunuk (tl). **106-107** Getty Images: Nicklas Blom. **108** Science Photo Library: Ken Biggs (t). **108-109** Science Photo Library: Robin Scagell. **110-111** Venture Vehicles, Inc.. **111** PA Photos: (br). Venture Vehicles, Inc.: (tl) (tr). **112-113** Segway Inc. **114-115** Courtesy of Advanced Transport Systems Ltd. **116** 2006-2007 Marine Advanced Research, Inc.: (b). Jim Burkett: (t). **117** Exomos: (bl). Innespace Productions: (t). M Ship Co/Bobby Grieser: (br). **118-119** Science Photo Library: Jim Amos. **119** Scripps Oceanography: (b). **120** Kawasaki (UK) : (bc) (br). naturepl.com: Jeff Rotman (bl). **120-121** Kawasaki (UK). **122-123** Courtesy Sailrocket: Mark Lloyd Images. **123** Courtesy Sailrocket: (t). **124** Perlan Project. Weather Extreme Ltd: (r). **124-125** AirTeamImages.com. **126** AirTeamImages.com: (b). **126-127** The Silent Aircraft Initiative: Cambridge University/MIT. **127** Department of Mechanical Engineering, University of Sheffield: (b). **128-129** Alamy Images: Transtock Inc.. **130-131** AirTeamImages.com. **131** Courtesy AgustaWestland: (tr). AirTeamImages.com: (tl) (c). Courtesy Carter Aviation Technologies: EAA Photography (br). **132** Courtesy Inchworm Shoes: (b). Courtesy MTB: (tl) (c). **133** Courtesy Heelys: (t) (ca). Courtesy Worn Again: (r). Zanic Design, Alberto Villarreal. www.zanicdesign.com: (b). **134-136** Alamy Images: Ulana Switucha. **136** NASA: (bl); JPL-Caltech (bc). Rick Sternbach/The Planetary Society: (br). **137** Nightvision Fox Image supplied by J J Vickers & Sons Ltd, sole UK distributors of Bushnell: (bc). Science Photo Library: Christian Darkin (bl); Thomas Deerinck, Ncmir (br). **138** Getty Images: AFP (br). Max Planck Institute for Plasma Physics : (tr). Science Photo Library: David Parker (l). **139** NASA: (b). **140-141** Reuters: Stringer Russia. **141** NASA: (b). **142-143** NASA: JPL-Caltech **144** NASA: (t) (b). **145** ESA: (c). NASA: (b); JPL-Caltech (t). **146-147** Rick Sternbach / The Planetary Society. **147** NASA: (t). **148** © 2004 Mojave Aerospace Ventures LLC. Photograph by Scaled Composites. SpaceShipOne is a Paul G Allen Project: (br) (t). Science Photo Library: Detlev Van Ravenswaay (cb). **148-149** Science Photo Library: Christian Darkin. **149** Courtesy Virgin Galactic: (b). **150** Corbis: Roger Ressmeyer (b). Science Photo Library: California Association For Research In Astronomy (tl). **150-151** Alamy Images: Richard Wainscoat. **152-143** NASA. **154** Intersection Media Ltd: (c). Still Pictures: Christopher Swann (tr). **155** Alamy Images: sharky (bl). Getty Images: AFP (tr). iD Solaire/Energy Limited: (cr). **156-157** Alamy Images: Stock Connection Blue. **158-159** Science Photo Library: Gustoimages. **159** Courtesy US Navy: Airman Ricardo J. Reyes (b). **160** Science Photo Library: Omikron (br). **161** Nightvision Fox Image supplied by J J Vickers & Sons Ltd, sole UK distributors of Bushnell. **162** Science Photo Library: Thomas Deerinck, Ncmir (ca). **162-163** Science Photo Library: Thomas Deerinck, Ncmir. **163** Science Photo Library: Steve Allen (br). **164** Alamy Images: Utah Images/NASA (c). **164-165** Reuters: Adeel Halim. **165** GRAW Radiosondes GmbH & Co. KG Germany (www.graw.de) : (c). **166** CERN. **166-167** Science Photo Library: David Parker. **167** Science Photo Library: Cern (b); David Parker (c); Bruce Roberts (cb). **168** Kamioka Observatory, ICRR (Institute for Cosmic Ray Research) , The University of Tokyo : (b). **168-169** Kamioka Observatory, ICRR (Institute for Cosmic Ray Research) , The University of Tokyo. **169** Science Photo Library: NASA/ESA/STSCI/C Burrows (b). **170** Max Planck Institute for Plasma Physics . Science Photo Library: Seymour (t). **171** EFDA-JET: (b). **172** Alamy Images: Mark Zylber (bc). Courtesy Michael Jantzen. www.humanshelter.org: (br). Science Photo Library: Pascal Goetgheluck (bl). **173** Corbis: Gerry Penny/epa (bl). Stephen A Edwards: (bc). Hunt Construction Group Inc.: HOK Sport (br). **174** Alamy Images: Mark Zylber (t). Stephen A Edwards: (b). **174-175** Courtesy Micreon GmbH. **175** Science Photo Library: Manfred Kage (r). **176** Science Photo Library: Alex Bartel (l). **176-177** Science Photo Library: Pascal Goetgheluck. **177** Science Photo Library: Calvin Larsen (r). **178** Science Photo Library: (t); Dr Jeremy Burgess (b). **179** Science Photo Library: Manfred Kage (tl); Astrid & Hanns-Frieder Michler (tr); Sheila Terry (br). **180-181** Alamy Images: Richard Levine. **182-183** Alamy Images: Mark Zylber. **183** François Célié and Eva Tissot.: (t). **184** Courtesy of Michael Jantzen. www.humanshelter.org: (l). Christian Richters: Living Tomorrow Pavilion, UNStudio (b). **185** Alamy Images: VIEW Pictures Ltd (c). Arup: PTW/CCDI (b). spacelab Cook-Fournier/Kunsthaus Graz. Photo by Nicolas Lackner, LMJ: (t). **186** Corbis: Gustavo Gilabert/SABA (cl). **186-187** Corbis: Gerry Penny/epa. **187** Alamy Images: Adrian Davies (br). DK Images: © Rough Guides (bl). **188** Courtesy Wave PR: Image courtesy of British Waterways (l). **188-189** Sean McLean. **190** Corbis: David Kadlubowski (br). Grand Canyon West. **190-191** Corbis: Jeff Topping. **192** Alamy Images: Aflo Foto Agency (t); Trip (b). **193** Alamy Images: Chad Ehlers (t). Corbis: Reuters (bl). NASA: (cr). **194-195** Stephen A Edwards. **195** Corbis: Louie Psihoyos (r). **196** Science Photo Library: Peter Menzel (b). **196-197** © Schlaich Bergermann Solar. **198** Hunt Construction Group Inc.: HOK Sport (b). **198-199** Hunt Construction Group Inc.: HOK Sport. **199** Uni-Systems, LLC: (br). **200** Science Photo Library: David Parker/Seagate Microelectronics Ltd (l). **200-201** Courtesy Micreon GmbH. **201** Courtesy Micreon GmbH: (bc). Science Photo Library: Sandia National Laboratories (bl). **202** Science Photo Library: Bruce Frisch (t). **202-203** Alamy Images: Stephen Shepherd. **204** Getty Images: Stuart Paton (bl). **205** Alamy Images: Barry Lewis (bl). Science Photo Library: Philippe Psaila (bc); Bruce Roberts (br). USAF: photo by Staff Sgt. Mark Olsen (br). **206** Alamy Images: Oleksiy Maksymenko (r). **206-207** Science Photo Library: Philippe Psaila. **207** Courtesy Holux Technology Inc.: (br). USAF: (bl). **208** Robert Harding Picture Library: PhotoTake (br). Science Photo Library: Bill Bachman (bc); Philippe Psaila (bl). **208-209** Science Photo Library: Mauro Fermariello. **209** Alamy Images: Malcolm Fairman (c). The Bank Of Japan: (ftl) (bl) (br) (tc) (tl) (tr). **210-212** Corbis: Yoshiko Kusano/Epa. **211** Corbis: Peter MacDiarmid/Reuters (r). Getty Images: Ian Waldie (cb). Science Photo Library: Volker Steger/Peter Arnold Inc. (t). **212** Corbis: Peter Vrom/epa (t). **212-213** Science Photo Library: Gustoimages. **213** Science Photo Library: GJLP (br). **214** Courtesy EyeTek Surveillance: (b). Courtesy Holux Technology Inc.: (t). **215** Casio Electronics Co. Ltd.: (cr). Getty Images: Stuart Paton (br). Courtesy LiveScienceStore.com: (t). **218-219** USAF: photo by Staff Sgt. Mark Olsen. **219** Alamy Images: Andrew Palmer (r). **220-221** Courtesy Martin-Baker Aircraft Company Limited. **222** Courtesy Kevlar/Dupont. **223** Courtesy of Kevlar/Dupont: (t). Science Photo Library: Rosenfeld Images Ltd (c); Sinclair Stammers (br). **224** Alamy Images: Phototake Inc. (t). Science Photo Library: (b). **225** Alamy Images: Colin Edwards (b); Barry Lewis (t); ni press photos (cr). **226** FLPA: R Dirscherl. **228-229** Science Photo Library: Philippe Psaila. **230** Getty Images: Riser (b). Science Photo Library: Antonia Reeve (c). **231** Alamy Images: Oleksiy Maksymenko (t). Corbis: (br); Reuters (c). **232** Science Photo Library: Andrew Syred (c). **232-233** Vestergaard Frandsen. **233** Science Photo Library: Professor E S Anderson (br). **234** Corbis: Art on File (b). Courtesy Michael Rakowitz and Lombard-Freid Projects: (t). **235** Courtesy Home Architects: (c). Courtesy LIFESTYLEDESIGN, Inc.: (b). Courtesy Marcin Panpuch: (t). **236-237** Science Photo Library: Bruce Roberts. **238-239** PA Photos: AP. **239** NOAA: (cl). **240** Courtesy studio van droffelaar (bl). RWS MD; afd. Multimedia. Deltapark Neeltje Jans: (br). **240-241** Courtesy Colorstone Beeldmakers BC. **241** Corbis: Vincent Laforet/epa (b)

Jacket images: Front: Gustoimages Ltd: cb (lenticular); Sony Computer Entertainment Europe: PlayStation and PSP are trademarks of Sony Computer Entertainment Inc. [Images appear by kind permission of Sony Computer Entertainment Europe]. cb; LocoRoco™ ©2006 Sony Computer Entertainment Inc. Published by Sony Computer Entertainment Europe. cb (screen shot); **Front Endpapers:** Gustoimages Ltd; **Back Endpapers:** Gustoimages Ltd

All other images © Dorling Kindersley
For further information see: www.dkimages.com

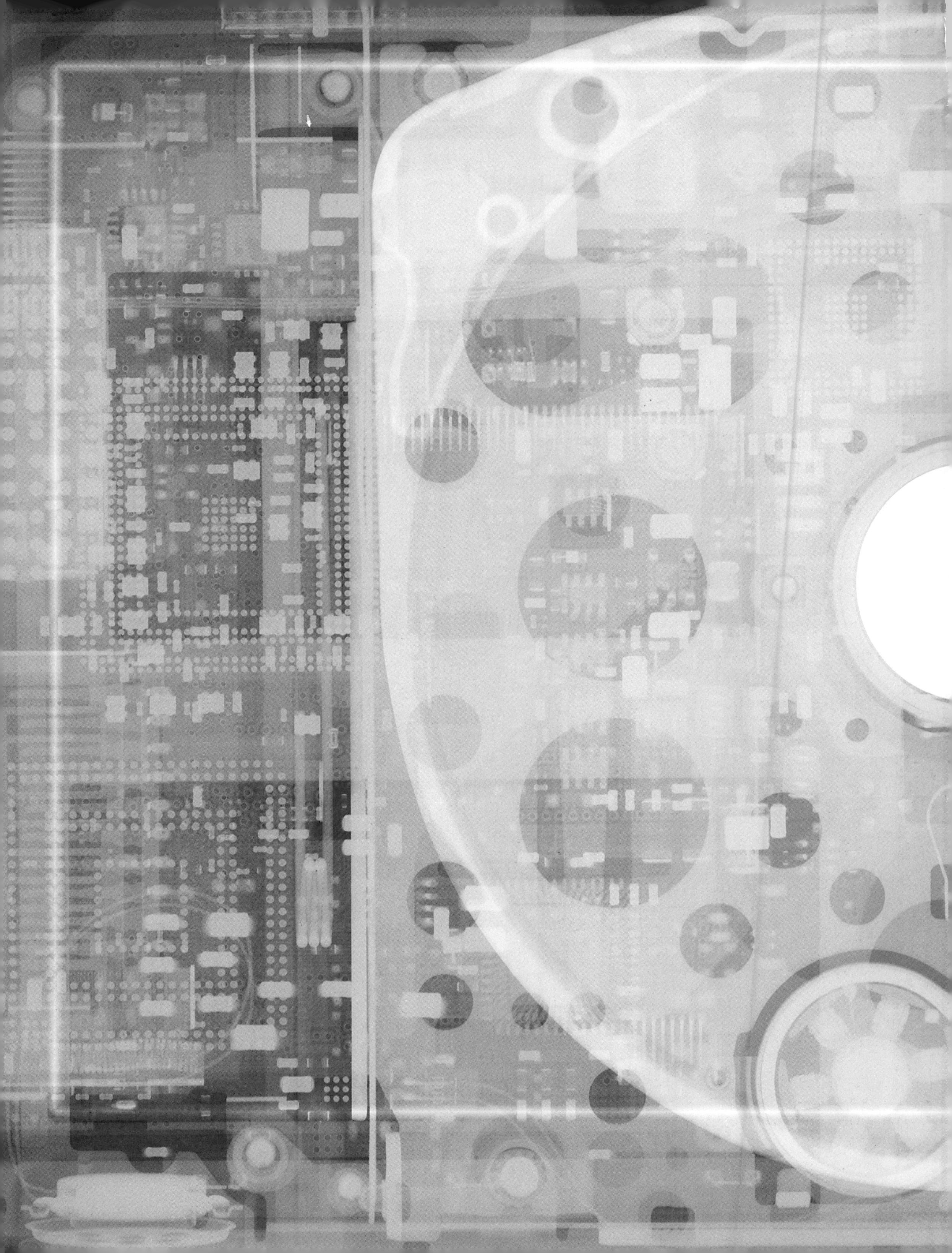